HAMMER FROM ABOVE

HAMMER FROM ABOVE

Marine Air Combat Over Iraq

JAY A. STOUT

PRESIDIO
PRESS

BALLANTINE BOOKS • NEW YORK

Published in the United States by Presidio Press, an imprint of The Random House
Publishing Group, a division of Random House, Inc., New York.

PRESIDIO PRESS and colophon are trademarks of Random House, Inc.

ISBN 0-89141-865-2

Printed in the United States of America

Designed by Joseph Rutt

For all the wives and all the mothers.
All of them.
The warrior's burden is nothing compared to the terrors they bear.
And for my dear childhood friend and fellow dreamer,
Dale Douglass.

Contents

═══

Foreword

≡≡≡

A common perspective outside the military has the Army, the Navy, the Air Force, and the Marine Corps in constant competition — quarreling with each other over a wide range of issues. While I would be the last to pretend that there is no rivalry among the different services, I would also be among the first to highlight the fact that dramatic changes have occurred during the past couple of decades. Rather than squabbling siblings, the various branches are now unabashed teammates. This transition has been driven not only by legislative and doctrinal pressures, but also by a variety of contemporary combat realities — the nation simply cannot afford a military that fails to leverage the advantages created when its different services cooperate in battle.

This closer collaboration among our soldiers, sailors, airmen, and marines has filtered down through the ranks; today's warfighters work far more closely with their brothers-in-arms from the other services than ever before. This exposure has in turn led to the creation of cross-service friendships between individuals on one level, and a broader professional awareness on another, higher level. Combined, they have helped produce the successes that have been the hallmark of recent joint American military actions.

I am a fortunate beneficiary of the interservice collaboration that has burgeoned since I was commissioned into the Air Force in 1971 out of Texas A&M's Corps of Cadets. I, too, have been blessed with close personal and professional relationships with members of all the armed services, including the Marine Corps—the service that is featured in this book. The Marine Corps has always maintained a unique place in my estimation of the world's military forces. To me—as a young officer during the years immediately following the war in Vietnam—the Marines seemed to perfectly match their stereotype as a tough, tight-knit group of loudmouths who always seemed to get their mission accomplished—although not always by the book, and certainly not always without stepping on some toes. They were a hardworking and hard-playing crowd, not unlike Air Force fighter pilots known for their swagger and their swashbuckling attitude.

My perspective broadened as I advanced through the ranks, and I began to understand and appreciate the Marine Corps for what it is beyond its clichéd "streetfighter" image. It was, and is, a superbly trained naval infantry organization with its own air arm that has typically had to make do with very limited resources. It is this paucity of resources, this institutional burden of having to "do more with less," that has been at least partly responsible for creating the brash, in-your-face men and women who make up the Marine Corps. The service demands the sort of self-possessed, get-the-mission-accomplished people who can make things happen with the assets at hand. A most admirable trait . . .

Aside from their reputation for toughness, the Marines are also known for their distrust of anyone outside their society. Some observers have gone so far as to characterize their fiercely guarded nature as a mild organizational paranoia.

I knew and understood all of this when I assumed command of the Coalition Forces Air Component for the United States Central Command late in 2001 (on the floor of the Combined Air Operations Center at Prince Sultan Air Base in the Kingdom of Saudi Arabia while conducting combat operations in Afghanistan). While holding this post I was responsible for—in fact commanded—all air activities of all the participants in Operation Enduring Freedom, the operations in the Horn of Africa, the operations within the Southern No

Fly Zone (Operation Southern Watch), and what was later named
Operation Iraqi Freedom. I was excited and honored at this prospect
and looked forward to working with all the services and a variety of
Host Nation and Coalition partners. Nevertheless, I was aware that
there would be sensitivities associated with an Air Force general commanding Navy, Army, and Marine Corps units—as well as the air
components of several other countries. And I knew that the Marine
Corps—with its unique history and pedigree—would potentially be
the most prickly of all.

The rank-and-file Marines didn't know me like I believed I understood them. With five joint assignments behind me and after com-
manding the F-15 Squadron of the Air Force's Fighter Weapons
School and later commanding the 57th Wing at Nellis with what
seemed like a thousand weapons school classes, joint exercises, Red
Flags, Maple Flags, and Cope Thunders under my G-suit . . . I believed there was a better way to work together. And the rank-and-file
Marines didn't know that I consider folks like Jim "Red Dog" Collins,
Earl "Titan" Hailston, Mike Hagee, Jim Mattis, Bill "Spider" Nyland,
Jim "Tamer" Amos, Martin "Wiley" Post, and Jim Conway as not
only close personal friends—but true comrades in arms and part of a
contemporary "joint Band of Brothers." Or said another way . . . my
desire to work more closely with them was more than just a planning
and execution drill—it was personal.

At one of my first meetings at Miramar with a panel of the service's
senior aviation leadership, I sensed some resistance and a notion of
posturing to maintain control of their units for the coming fight in
Iraq. To make my point, I stopped their briefings and declared that I
was aware of their role and their "traditional" mission. But, I allowed
this wasn't going to be a traditional fight. I stressed our task was to be
very light and very fast and very lethal, and that everything depended
on getting control of the Iraq airspace and hitting them hard everywhere at once. I stressed that this couldn't be done piecemeal or without a central focus for planning and execution. I allowed that these
are attributes the Air Force and the Marines understand very well and
with the right command/control construct, the right joint planning,

and having the right weapon in the right place, the end-state results would be better than any of us had ever seen.

I told the assembled Marine leadership that afternoon at Miramar that I truly didn't care what was painted on the side of the aircraft that would deliver decisive blows to the Iraqi forces—USAF, RAF, RAAF, USMC, USN, et cetera—and that I didn't care which squadron got which target set . . . only that we get at and destroy the Iraqis as a joint/coalition team better than any Air Component has ever conducted an air campaign. At the same time I reiterated my command obligations to the overall theater commander General Tommy Franks as well as to our joint and coalition warriors and to the nation—which expect a great deal from us. In order to meet the tasks and responsibilities that I had been given by General Franks, I needed the Marines in that room as teammates—not as rivals. I was in charge of all the planning and execution of all air activities within Central Command and I pledged to them that while I was in charge I would ensure that the Marine Corps ground forces would have access to every bit of the Air Component's tool kit. My pledge to them was that when the first Marine lieutenant steps off across the line of departure, he's *my* lieutenant. As the senior Airman, I would buy his task as well as mine. And, I stressed, there would be no Marine infantryman wanting for air support while I was in command.

They believed me, but more important . . . they trusted me. Everyone pulled together and rallied from that point on—as a joint team. The beddown of Marine Air Wing assets on established Air Force expeditionary bases was a "no-brainer." Likewise the sharing of billeting facilities, force protection capabilities, maintenance facilities, fuel, and munitions was also a "no-brainer." Cooperation early on developed into support that was eagerly given and enthusiastically received. Marine crews joined players from the Air Force, the Royal Air Force, the Royal Australian Air Force, the Army, and the Navy to help form the most effective combatant and truly joint staff any air commander has had the good fortune to lead. The Combined Air Operations Center at PSAB was a sight to behold . . . all joint and all focused. As the fight began, planning work and execution responsibility was taken and shared so effectively that lines between the services faded over the battlefield. Again, it doesn't matter what's painted on the side of the aircraft! What matters is having the right weapon at the right place at the right time.

While my leadership perspective was more theater-focused, I still received daily reports that described the skill and professionalism of all our nation's fighters. That the Marines who fought from the air performed superbly was no surprise to anyone. Their stories, set in the context of the fight on the ground, are told here in detail and cover all aspects of their operations. Chronologically organized, these accounts impart a greater understanding of the significant role that Marine Corps aircrew played in the success of General Franks's brilliant campaign. These Marines added yet another wonderful chapter to the service's outstanding and rich legacy, and were everything that the nation has come to expect. Marine Corps aviation's contributions to the fight helped to ensure a triumph like no other, and I personally am glad to have had the opportunity to serve with the brash, get-it-done men and women who make it what it is. I am, and will always be, an ardent admirer of these fellow warriors.

T. Michael "Buzz" Moseley
General, United States Air Force

Introduction

═══════

I felt like an old, worn-out gundog—left behind and scratching at the kennel door on the opening day of hunting season while all the young pups headed to the field.

I couldn't believe that they actually went to war without me. Of course, there was the small matter of my retirement, an event that had taken place two years earlier during 2001. That same year, shortly after my exit from Marine Corps service, my budding airline career was squashed when I was furloughed after the horror that was September 11. Subsequent to being tossed into the unemployment line I fell back on what I knew best and went to the Middle East to fly F/A-18s with the Kuwait Air Force. A year of that was enough, and by the time that Operation Iraqi Freedom began, I was back in the States working for a defense industry giant.

During the Coalition's run up to Baghdad I did a couple of stints as a talking head for the Fox News Channel. At Al Jaber one of my old squadron buddies was startled when he looked up from his mission planning charts. He had to do a double take when he saw me puffed up in a suit and tie on the television screen: "You looked . . . like, responsible!" It was a stinging backhanded compliment. I really was a fighter pilot no longer.

As much as I wanted to be overseas with my Marine Corps brothers, that was the closest I got.

When they returned I was eager to talk with them, and after doing so I realized that they had done quite a bit more than the media had relayed home to the rest of us. I don't believe that the news professionals intended this as any sort of snub or slight; rather, it happened because there was so much else to cover—to include the fight on the ground and the worldwide reaction to the war. There just wasn't enough airtime or print space to give the aviators the coverage they had enjoyed during Desert Storm. What the fliers had done wasn't captured very well, and there was a risk that the record would survive only as barroom stories, or perhaps in forgotten, drily written squadron histories.

So I decided to write this book. It is an exciting description of the role of Marine Corps aviation that uses firsthand accounts to give the reader a real feel for how that part of the war was actually fought. My intent is to show the war through a fairly broad cross section of Marine fliers. That being said, it is hardly a scientific survey; instead it is a description that follows the fighting chronologically through the recollections of those who were throwing the punches.

The reader will note that although the book includes all the tactical aircraft that the Marine Corps used, there is a focus on those platforms that did the majority of the shooting and killing. I believe that most people understand the reasons for this. A transport helicopter pilot told me: "I really don't know what I can tell you that would be worth putting into a book. I hauled trash [supplies] around. Sometimes we got shot at, but most of the time we didn't. It was hot and dirty—okay, it was *really* dirty—but for me it wasn't that exciting."

But for others it was absolutely terrifying. Bullets smashing through a thin Plexiglas canopy can be real attention getters. Skidding across the dirt of an enemy airfield, upside down, in a helicopter gunship will likewise elevate the blood pressure somewhat. In that same category is the act of racing over the Mesopotamian Plain at more than five hundred knots at only a couple of hundred feet, at night, in order to drop napalm on an unsuspecting enemy. Stories like these are what make up this book.

It is a collection of anecdotes reasonably leavened with strategy, tactics, and the how, who, why, what, where, and when of day-to-day operations. But it is not an all-inclusive, analytical, unit-by-unit, hour-by-hour drudgery of written tedium. That very necessary type of historical record will remain the work of someone else.

The reader will be reminded, perhaps too many times, that Marine Corps aviation exists to support the infantryman. That being the case, it was necessary to depict the aviation side of the story in the context of the fight on the ground. I believe there is just enough information about the land campaign included here to accomplish that objective without taking away from what aviation enthusiasts enjoy most— accounts of fighting from the air. Nevertheless there were many opportunities to stray from the core purpose of the book in order to discuss interesting aspects that were only remotely related to the fighting. I endeavored to resist those temptations while still including the sorts of fascinating bits that can make a book readable.

One of the strengths of the manuscript, to me, is that the participants were interviewed shortly after they returned from Iraq. This was important because it ensured that the events described were relatively fresh in each interviewee's mind. He could recall the story, warts and all, and with some detail. Additionally, time hadn't worn away the details about what had gone wrong and why—the negative aspects that time has a tendency to wear away. It was interesting that these retellings were often haltingly delivered as the participants struggled to accurately recall each and every detail. This was in marked contrast with my previous experiences interviewing World War II veterans for other projects. Usually the older gentlemen delivered smooth, carefully crafted stories. This was because their more dated tales had in large part been honed and refined after more than fifty years of telling. They were neatly wrapped packages that were undone from time to time in order to be recounted. As the years pass the stories from Operation Iraqi Freedom will become just as smoothly polished.

Another strength of the book is the collection of photographs. In many instances there are photos from the very missions that are described. James Isaacs describes how his flight of UH-INs exploded a set of Iraqi artillery pieces; a photo of that equipment as it goes up in flames is included here. Likewise, there are photographs that record part of the battle for Saddam's presidential palace on the banks of the Tigris. Technology being what it is, many of the crews carried digital cameras, which provided pictures of quite acceptable resolution. We are the beneficiaries of that technology.

As well as Marine aviation performed its role, it would be a sham to portray an operation where everything was executed perfectly. That was not the case; mistakes were made all up and down the chain of command. This should be obvious, as the participants were human. Some of the interviewees were reluctant to speak about the frictions, and some were not; it depended to some degree on where they were in their careers or what amount of semiofficial criticism or scrutiny they thought they could bear. Nevertheless, I believe that the real strength of the Marine Corps is showcased as we see Marines on the battlefield making decisions in the heat of combat and taking responsibility for those decisions. This is not something seen in many of the world's militaries.

I liked writing this book. One of the primary reasons I enjoyed it so much was that I was only a short time removed from doing the same sort of work as the men I interviewed. I understood the tactics they flew, the problems they encountered, and the workarounds they developed. I had been a Marine for twenty years, and it was a pleasure to reconnect with old friends.

While reading this collection of accounts, it might be easy to forget that the Army was conducting its own campaign just to the south and west of the Marines. That would be a mistake; the Army also fought well, and there is no doubt that the nation's soldiers executed their mission with brilliance and bravery. I hope that someone records that brilliance and bravery. Likewise, the Air Force and Navy made inestimable contributions to the fight.

While I enjoy writing about aerial campaigns, I always bear in mind that what they are about is killing from the sky. And I also try to remember that who gets killed is usually someone's baby boy; someone's baby boy who was brought proudly home soon after his birth —

often to great celebration; someone's baby boy who was loved, cared for, and coddled; someone's baby boy whose picture sat at someone's bedside during all the years it took for him to grow up to perhaps become someone's husband or father. We must always remember that someone's baby boy was the one who got splattered in pieces all across the battlefield.

The fighting in Iraq is still going on at this writing. It can hardly be said that what is taking place there now is the solution that was hoped for when the war was started. I was an advocate of the war before it took place, and although it has become more protracted and bloody than I would have thought, I still believe—for a variety of reasons— that the decision that was taken was correct. It is silly to state the obvious—that I hope I am not wrong. But I do. I have no predictive gob of goat guts and will have to wait with the rest of the world until the endgame is recorded by history. In the meantime many of the men who told their stories here have returned for a second or third stint in Iraq. I wish them all the luck and success that they enjoyed the first time.

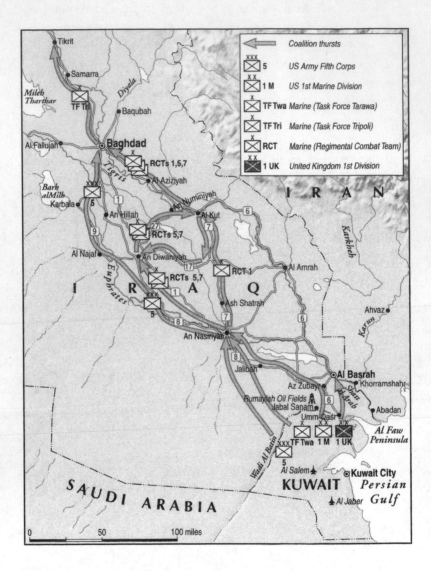

Coalition thursts

XXX 5	US Army Fifth Corps
XXX 1 M	US 1st Marine Division
X TF Twa	Marine (Task Force Tarawa)
X TF Tri	Marine (Task Force Tripoli)
X RCT	Marine (Regimental Combat Team)
XX 1 UK	United Kingdom 1st Division

Tikrit

Samarra

Mileh Tharthar

TF Tri

Diyala

Baqubah

Al Fallujah

Baghdad

Tigris

RCTs 1,5,7

Al Aziziyah

Barh alMilh

Karbala

5

1

An Hillah

An Numiniyah

Al Kut

6

9

27 RCTs 5,7

7

Al Najaf

An Diwaniyah

17

RCT 1

Al Amrah

RCTs 5,7

1

Ash Shatrah

Karkheh

Ahvaz

I R A Q

5

8

7

6

An Nasiriyah

8

Jalibah

Al Basrah

Karun

Khorramshahr

Az Zubayr

Rumayleh Oil Fields

Jabal Sanam

6

Abadan

Umm Qasr

Shatt al Arab

I R A N

I R A Q

Wadi Al Batin

XXX TF Twa 1 M 1 UK

Al Faw Peninsula

5

Al Salem

Kuwait City

KUWAIT

Persian

Al Jaber

Gulf

SAUDI ARABIA

0   50   100 miles

HAMMER
FROM
ABOVE

———

1

Marine Aviation Primer

The Marine Corps sent many brave men into the skies over Iraq during the spring campaign of 2003. This book will describe their actions and perhaps bring more awareness to a public that for the most part is barely aware the air arm of the Marine Corps even exists. That this is so is remarkable considering the many legends who have flown in our country's service while wearing a Marine uniform.

Ted Williams twice interrupted one of the most fantastic careers in baseball to fly and fight in both World War II and Korea. Likewise, Marine Corps pilot John Glenn flew in the same two wars and went on to become the first American to orbit the planet. Ed McMahon started adulthood as a pilot with the Marines during World War II and years later sat beside *Tonight Show* host Johnny Carson and entertained millions. Joe Foss, the great sportsman, governor of South Dakota, and chairman of the NRA, won the Medal of Honor while flying in World War II as a Marine Corps fighter pilot. And Gregory "Pappy" Boyington fought and drank himself into one of aviation's most colorful and enduring legends.

Regardless of public awareness, Marine Corps aviation has been producing these types of men since 1912. It was in May of that year that First Lieutenant Alfred A. Cunningham was directed to report to the Naval Aviation Camp in Annapolis, Maryland. A few months later, on August 20, he soloed after two hours and forty minutes of flight time and became Marine Aviator Number 1.

Aviation in the Marine Corps grew slowly until the United States entered World War I in April 1917. At the time the entire aviation complement of the Marine Corps numbered only fifty-two officers and enlisted men. Just more than a year later, 758 men staffing three squadrons arrived in France on July 30, 1918. They came without their own flying machines; it wasn't until the end of September that they received their first aircraft. Still, during the short time before the war ended in mid-November, the Marines managed to make their mark by shooting down several German aircraft. Indeed, their ferocity was such that Second Lieutenant Ralph Talbot and Gunnery Sergeant Robert Guy Robinson each earned the Medal of Honor while flying together for actions that are described in part by the following excerpt from Robinson's citation:

> . . . on October 14th, 1918, while on a raid over Pittman, Belgium, his plane and one other became detached from the formation on account of motor trouble, and were attacked by twelve enemy scouts. In the fight which ensued he behaved with conspicuous gallantry and intrepidity. After shooting down one of the enemy planes he was struck by a bullet which carried away much of his elbow and his gun jammed at the same time. He cleared the jam with one hand while his pilot maneuvered for position. With the gun cleared, he returned to the fight though his left arm was useless, and fought off the enemy scouts until he collapsed after receiving two more bullet wounds, one in the stomach and one in the thigh.

Robinson survived despite suffering multiple bullet wounds and having his arm very nearly shot off. Talbot received his medal posthumously; he was killed only a few days later in a plane crash.

Immediately following the war Marine aviation underwent a period of massive reductions, as did the air branches of all the services. By 1921 the Corps carried only forty-three pilots on its rolls. Despite the huge cutbacks that most of the world's militaries underwent, the interwar years were a time of rapid technological development in aeronautics that saw a gradual buildup of capabilities within the Corps's air arm. During this time the Marine Corps was the only U.S. service to put its fliers into combat. Flying and fighting throughout various Caribbean and Central American insurrections, Marine aviators experimented with tactics and techniques that would be refined and used years later. Some of these were exceedingly dangerous. During fighting in Nicaragua from January 6 to January 8, 1928, First Lieutenant Christian Schilt made ten separate sorties under enemy fire into a makeshift landing strip in Quilali to evacuate eighteen Marines who had been seriously wounded in an ambush. For his efforts, Schilt was rewarded with the Medal of Honor.

Schilt's extraordinary mission marked the unbreakable relationship between the infantryman and the aviator that has become a pillar of the Marine Corps ethos. Simply put, the primary reason the service keeps aircraft and the men and women to fly and maintain them is to support the Marine on the ground. This is an indissoluble tenet that every Marine aviator learns from the first day he puts on a uniform. Parallel to this is the dictum that every flier is a rifleman first; he receives basic infantry skills and training before he ever approaches an aircraft. This fosters empathy and understanding between the ground and air communities and also serves a more practical purpose: It enables the aviator to more readily understand the ground commander's intentions and requirements.

Through the 1930s the Marine air arm continued to develop and grow. It was during this time that a close relationship with the Navy became even more so. Marine squadrons saw service on aircraft carriers, and the Marine Corps became wholly and fully committed to developing a navalized air arm in terms of operations and equipment. And as doctrines and strategies were matured to address Japanese aspirations in the Pacific and Asia, more emphasis was placed on joint operations with the Navy; these joint operations were oriented toward the seizure of advance bases in the event of war. The execution of this strategy would be the centerpiece of naval operations during World War II.

By the late 1930s the U.S. military still lagged behind the other great nations in preparing for the coming cataclysm that was World War II. The situation was so abysmal that second-tier countries such as Portugal fielded larger armies than America. The Marine Corps was a reflection of this lack of readiness, particularly where its air arm was concerned. In June 1940, while France was being overrun by the Nazis, Marine aviation numbered less than nineteen hundred personnel. More than a year later the Japanese attack on Pearl Harbor caught the Corps as much by surprise as anyone else: Every airplane at the Marine airfield at Ewa was destroyed.

Farther out in the Pacific, Marine fliers made the Japanese pay more dearly for the tiny speck that was Wake Island. Although seven of its twelve aircraft were destroyed on the ground at nearly the same time as the attack on Pearl Harbor, VMF-211 continued to fight for the next several weeks. The squadron's pilots sent the destroyer *Kirasagi* to the bottom and shot down seven enemy aircraft. When their last F4F Wildcat was destroyed, the twenty pilots and mechanics from the unit who hadn't been killed or wounded climbed out of their flight gear and dropped their wrenches to fight as infantry. Those who survived the final Japanese assault spent the rest of the war as POWs.

But it was at Guadalcanal where the Marine Corps's fliers and "wrench turners" earned a permanent place in history. When the Navy's aircraft carriers were forced to retreat under the threat of superior Japanese forces, the aerial defense of the beleaguered Marines on the ground was left to the handful of their brothers who piloted a pitifully small and hard-worn collection of F4Fs against a seemingly unceasing stream of Japanese fighters and bombers. Living in the rot and wet and filth of the jungle, they fought alongside a hodgepodge collection of airplanes from both the Navy and the Army for several months until the island was declared secure. It was here that the Marine Corps showed the world that the Japanese Zero was far from invincible. And it was at Guadalcanal where Joe Foss equaled the twenty-six aerial victories scored by America's greatest ace of World War I, Captain Eddie Rickenbacker.

By the end of the war the Marine Corps counted more than 125,000 men in its air arm alone—more than a sixtyfold increase in five years. These officers and enlisted men had slugged their way across the Pacific and had seen action over such legendary battlefields as Bougainville, Rabaul, Iwo Jima, Okinawa, and even Japan itself. In doing so they shot down more than twenty-three hundred enemy aircraft and produced 121 aces. Aside from killing other aircraft, perhaps their most important contribution to the war was the hard-hitting support they provided to the infantrymen on the ground. As airborne "artillery" they provided such a volume, range, and flexibility of fire that no Marine commander would ever again seriously consider a major operation without Marine airpower overhead.

Less than five years after the end of the greatest conflict in history, the Corps's fliers were at war again. Korea saw more refinement of cooperative operations between the "ground pounder" and the pilot. When Red China surprised the world by launching a million men over the border and into the fight during October 1950, Marine aircrews surprised those same Chinese by chopping them down by the thousands. It was this sort of closely coordinated support that enabled the First Marine Division to "attack in the opposite direction" and execute an orderly withdrawal in the face of overwhelming numbers. Had these men not been supported from the air, the outcome of the conflict may very well have been different.

Korea also marked the first really large-scale use of helicopters in a major conflict, and the Marines were at the forefront. Having recognized the obvious utility of the relatively new machines, the Corps had invested heavily in equipment and training between the wars. When the opportunity came they were ready, and on September 13, 1951, HMR-161 executed the first ever mass combat resupply. Later operations included lifting combat troops into the thick of the fighting. The helicopter added a vertical dimension to the Corps's playbook and remains a cornerstone of Marine assault capabilities today. But perhaps the chief advantage the rotary-wing aircraft gave in Korea was its ability to replenish units in rough terrain while bringing back the dead and the wounded. There were ten thousand casualties evacuated by Marine helicopters during the Korean conflict. Many of the injured would have died were they not speedily delivered to field hospitals by the novel aircraft.

Marine Corps aviation operations will likely never again be as broad or extensive as they were during Vietnam. Flying several different types of jets, Marine fliers punished enemy forces throughout Southeast Asia. Along with CAS (Close Air Support), their operations ran the gamut from electronic warfare to all-weather attack. Marine pilots even claimed three air-to-air kills against an enemy that fielded very few aircraft.

But it was the helicopters that did most of the flying. During one year alone—1968—the Marine Corps flew nearly 750,000 sorties in Vietnam. The bulk of them were rotary-wing missions—the war was, at least on the American side, largely a helicopter conflict. There was only one good highway in the country, and the rugged nature of the terrain was such that surface transport was difficult. Most Marines got to where they were going via the venerable CH-34s that were replaced in the war's later years by newer UH-1s, CH-46s, and CH-53s. As we shall see, these more modern aircraft evolved through time to become the aged warriors that eventually served in Iraq and still fly with today's Marine units.

The ferocity of the Marines in combat was one aspect of the Vietnam conflict that did not differ from earlier wars. Major Stephen Pless was escorting a MEDEVAC (Medical Evacuation) mission on August 19, 1967, when he learned of four American soldiers who had been stranded on a beach near the My Lai village area. The men were part of an Army helicopter crew that had been left behind when their ship came under fire and the pilots fled. Pless raced his UH-1E Huey gunship toward where the soldiers were engaged in a life-or-death, close-quarters firefight. The following excerpt from his Medal of Honor citation describes his heroism:

Maj. Pless flew to the scene and found 30 to 50 enemy soldiers in the open. Some of the enemy were bayoneting and beating the downed Americans.

Maj. Pless displayed exceptional airmanship as he launched a devastating attack against the enemy force, killing or wounding many of the enemy and driving the remainder back into a tree line. His rocket and machine-gun attacks were made at such low levels that the aircraft flew through debris created by explosions from its rockets.

Seeing 1 of the wounded soldiers gesture for assistance, he maneuvered his helicopter into a position between the wounded men and the enemy, providing a shield which permitted his crew to retrieve the wounded. During the rescue the enemy directed intense fire at the helicopter and rushed the aircraft again and again, closing to within a few feet before being beaten back.

When the wounded men were aboard, Maj. Pless maneuvered the helicopter out to sea. Before it became safely airborne, the overloaded aircraft settled 4 times into the water. Displaying superb airmanship, he finally got the helicopter aloft.

The other three members of the crew received the Navy Cross for their bravery. In total Pless flew 780 *combat sorties* before leaving Vietnam.

Following the exit from Vietnam during 1973, Marine aviation elements did not see major combat operations again until the Gulf War of 1991. Whereas Marine aircraft had cooperated side by side with the other services in other conflicts, this was the first time that the service's aviation elements were fully integrated under a Joint Forces Air Component Commander (JFACC)—in this instance a U.S. Air Force general. This fact caused a great deal of consternation among Corps traditionalists, who were fearful that the infantryman on the ground would not get the support he needed when he needed it.

Ultimately, however, the nation's military professionals were just that; they worked to ensure that the JFACC had the assets—including Marine aircraft—he needed to fight the deep strategic fight, as well as the wherewithal to shape and prepare the battlefield. In layman's terms, this meant killing as many Iraqi tanks, artillery guns, and soldiers as possible before committing men to the fight on the ground. Marine F/A-18s and A-6s flew a gamut of missions supported by KC-130 tankers and EA-6B electronic warfare jets; these strikes ranged deep into Iraq, even as far as Baghdad. The shorter-legged AV-8B Harriers and slow-flying OV-10 Broncos concentrated on targets in Kuwait.

As the date of the ground attack into Kuwait neared, most Marine aircraft were shifted away from the deep fight and dedicated almost entirely to obliterating everything within the Marine Corps's projected ground scheme of maneuver. Elsewhere the Air Force, Navy, and other Coalition forces also blasted away at the entrenched Iraqis. The efficacy of their efforts was such that the ground campaign lasted only one hundred hours. The support the Marine infantryman received from his winged brothers had never been better. The numbers bore this out. Aside from the United States Air Force, a service that exists solely to project the nation's airpower, no other service or nation flew more combat sorties than the Marine Corps.

The twelve years between Desert Storm and Operation Iraqi Freedom (OIF) saw real changes within Marine Corps aviation. Most important was a significant downsizing that saw the size of the F/A-18 community drop from twelve single-seat fighter squadrons to eight. The A-6 was retired and replaced by a lesser number of two-seat F/A-18D squadrons, and the OV-10 was pastured completely. The Harriers and the helicopter communities saw their ranks thinned as well. The Navy—also hit hard by force reductions—was forced to augment its aircraft carrier complements with Marine F/A-18 squadrons; this was a move that had a palpably negative impact on the service's readiness and training. Too, the Corps lost a good deal of control over its EA-6Bs, now considered a national asset, particularly in light of the USAF's retirement of its EF-111s.

On the other hand, changes were made to improve the quality of the fewer aircraft remaining. The AV-8Bs went through a rebuild program that gave them an air-to-air radar, a more powerful engine, major avionics and airframe upgrades, as well as enhancements to improve their survivability. Likewise the F/A-18s saw improvements, as did the KC-130s and EA-6Bs. Changes to the helicopter fleet—particularly to the CH-46E—were more modest, as it was expected that the arrival of the MV-22 Osprey would obviate the need to spend too much money in modifications. Unfortunately, hopes pinned to the failure-plagued Osprey have not yet been realized.

Improvements in weapons also increased the efficacy of the Corps's fleet of attack aircraft. Precision Guided Munitions (PGMs) such as Laser Guided Bombs (LGBs) became more readily available and more fully matured. And the advent of Global Positioning System (GPS) munitions meant that rather than putting his aircraft at a precise point in space, at an exact airspeed, altitude, attitude, and heading, a pilot could simply fly to the vicinity of a known set of target coordinates, release a bomb, and reliably expect that the bomb would guide directly to the target. He could do this without ever seeing what he was attacking—day, night, or in poor weather.

Improvements in sensors further contributed to the capabilities of the Marine fliers. Night Vision Devices (NVDs), also known as "goggles," enabled the aircrews to literally see in the dark. Particularly for helicopter pilots, the NVDs were a tremendous aid in maintaining formation and navigating low over enemy terrain. Taking off and landing were easier, too. These attributes were not lost on the KC-130 community. And depending on the illumination provided by the stars and the moon, or man-made lighting, targets could be struck by AH-1W Cobra and fixed-wing pilots without relying on more expensive and heavier devices such as FLIR (Forward Looking Infra Red) pods.

More expensive and heavier they may have been, but the improvements made in FLIR pods since Desert Storm included greater magnification, laser-designating capabilities, and better reliability. These pods could make all the difference between success and failure on nighttime interdiction missions. In fact, it was mostly due to the features and characteristics of the Litening pod that the AV-8B Harrier was able to be a contributor of any merit at all. Although it carried a relatively small bomb load, that load could be delivered very precisely.

Although it was a smaller force than at any time since the beginning of World War II, the Marine air component that existed on the eve of Operation Iraqi Freedom was therefore still a potent force—roughly equivalent in size and capabilities to the United Kingdom's Royal Air Force (RAF). And its men and women were well trained and ready to add to the service's legacy.

2

The MEF

The First Marine Expeditionary Force, or I MEF, was the chief Marine Corps combat component during Operation Iraqi Freedom. In the vernacular, it was known as a MAGTF—a Marine Air Ground Task Force. This is a purpose-built fighting force that can range in size from just a couple of thousand men to the size of the one that was now poised to support and execute the vault into Iraq—more than sixty thousand.

There are three pieces that make up a MAGTF: a Ground Combat Element (GCE), an Air Combat Element (ACE), and a Combat Service Support Element (CSSE). Once assembled, this force is essentially a self-contained armed service in its own right. Embarked aboard Navy warships, the MAGTF will have its own infantry and—depending on its size—its own armor and artillery. Augmented by a contingent of Marine aircraft and supported by its own logistics train, the MAGTF provides the president with a versatile force capable of meeting myriad needs. These requirements span the spectrum of military operations from quick, hard-hitting strikes on one end to more peaceful activities such as humanitarian relief on the other. Tailor-made for specific contingencies, the MAGTF is designed to be a potent, rapidly deployable expeditionary force that is capable of taking and holding an objective until the mission is accomplished, or until the Army can arrive with its heavier, more powerful formations. Or, as in more recent operations, the Marine Corps can fight alongside Army units while taking on roles that capitalize on the faster, more maneuver-oriented fighting the MAGTF was designed for.

The commander of I MEF during Operation Iraqi Freedom was Lieutenant General James Conway. A big, brusque, but well-read man, Conway had held a number of commands, including the First Marine Division, and was at ease both in the field and in garrison. In the Central Command (CENTCOM) region Conway reported to the CFLCC (Coalition Forces Land Component Commander), Army Lieutenant General David McKiernan, who in turn was accountable to General Tommy Franks—the commander of CENTCOM and of all Coalition forces in the region.

The largest component in Conway's GCE was the First Marine Division, heavily augmented by units and personnel from all across the Marine Corps. The "Blue Diamond," as the division was nicknamed, was made up of three Regimental Combat Teams (RCTs): RCT-1, "Inchon," RCT-5, "Grizzly," and RCT-7, "Ripper." A fourth regiment, Eleventh Marines, was an artillery unit that augmented and supported the RCTs. The division was commanded by Major General James Mattis, another well-educated and savvy Marine who took his art so seriously that he was known as the "warrior monk." After the campaign it was Mattis who downplayed his own generalship by declaring: "I'm not a great general. I was just up against other generals that don't know shit."

Aside from Mattis's First Marine Division, Conway also owned Task Force Tarawa (RCT-2), an ad hoc collection of more than seven thousand Marines—largely from the Second Marine Expeditionary Brigade—that was commanded by Brigadier General Rich Natonski. Rounding out Conway's ground combat formations was the 1st UK Armoured Division commanded by Major General Robin Brimms; its twenty-five thousand men made up the three brigades that would ultimately take and hold Iraq's "second city," the strategic Iraqi port of Al Basrah. This contribution by America's closest ally was crucial to the campaign and underscored the deep and abiding friendship between the two nations.

Providing the logistical support that would enable Conway to march to Baghdad was Brigadier General Edward Usher's First Force Service Support Group (1st FSSG) and its Combat Service Support Companies (CSSCs). The CSSCs—using new concepts especially developed for the campaign—would make certain that the Marine "trigger pullers" had the food, fuel, ammunition, and medical attention they needed to meet their mission. Although the units technically served in a support role, the fact was that all their Marines were trained marksmen and brought considerable field experience to the fight. This would be important in the coming confrontation, as the FSSG's many and varied elements would see plenty of action.

Conway also had at his command something that—outside of the Marine Corps—few infantry generals in history have ever possessed: his very own air wing. Although the Army could count on its considerable helicopter formations as well as on support from the Air Force, Conway had at his disposal an entire air force in the form of the Third Marine Aircraft Wing—3rd MAW. The wing was made up of Marines who maintained and flew helicopters, tactical jets, and aerial refuelers. Two small squadrons of Unmanned Aerial Vehicles (UAVs) further enhanced the mix. The wing was no paper tiger, either; it was made up of modernized aircraft maintained and flown by top-notch professionals. On its own it was more potent than the entire air forces of most nations.

But, as is often the case when something is too good to be true, there was a rub. Major General James "Tamer" Amos, the commander of 3rd MAW, had to dance to the tunes of two different masters. He was responsible to Conway to support the Marines and British soldiers of I MEF, but during this campaign his aircraft were technically "owned" and parceled out by the Coalition Forces Air Component Commander (CFACC). The CFACC, Air Force Lieutenant General Michael Moseley, worked directly for Tommy Franks and commanded all the Coalition air assets in theater—Army, Air Force, Navy, and Marine Corps, as well as the foreign air forces. Acting as the sole authority responsible for meeting Franks's aviation requirements, Moseley and his staff would control every fixed-wing sortie that got airborne as well as a sizable percentage of the helicopter missions. In turn, it would be up to the other air component commanders—again, the Army, Air Force, Navy, and Marine Corps—to meet his demands. This centralized command combined with decentralized execution had proved effective during Desert Storm and had been successfully practiced since then, most recently during the campaign in Afghanistan.

That didn't mean that it was easy. Or popular. To say that the Marine Corps has historically been reluctant to relinquish control of its own air component would be among the grossest of understatements. When directed to cooperate with the Air Force to develop a plan for the coming campaign, the Marines looked forward to the initial meetings as if they were scheduled for root canal surgery. For their part, the officers who made up Moseley's staff were likely not very keen to the upcoming conferences with their ofttimes prickly Marine Corps "in-laws."

One of the first significant meetings took place at 3rd MAW headquarters in San Diego during the fall of 2002. Moseley brought a contingent of staffers to visit with Amos and his own planners. Amos's deputy, Brigadier General Terry "Guts" Robling, remembered the meeting: "We started out with some briefs that essentially reiterated how Marine aviation existed to support the Marine on the ground." The Marines in the room thought that all was well until Moseley stopped the proceedings midway. "He essentially," recounted Robling, "reminded us—very pointedly—that he would own all the aviation assets in the plan. They were his. Period."

The Marines in the room girded for the worst. Moseley surprised them when, after a brief silence, he cited a bit of history to let his hosts know that he was familiar with Marine Corps doctrine, particularly as it applied to its air components. He then went on to say that although he would retain ultimate authority over the allocation of Marine avia-

tion assets, he planned on using them to support Marine Corps operations, and he further intended to give the Marines whatever other
help they needed from the Air Force and the Navy. "In other words,"
Robling said, "he was pretty much going to let us have full access to
our own aircraft, and was promising us more if we needed it."

Still, actions speak louder than words, and it took awhile to build a
mutual trust between the CFACC and the Marines who were assigned
to work with him and his staff. "We sent a lot of fine officers and enlisted men to interface with the CFACC," Robling recounted. "One of
the keys to our success was Colonel Ron McFarland. He spearheaded
our efforts inside the CFACC staff by educating them as to what our
requirements were, and at the same time letting them know what we
were able to contribute to the overall campaign." Ultimately McFarland and the host of other Marines assigned to work with the CFACC
developed a relationship that was noteworthy for its effectiveness. "We
really hit a home run with that one," Robling recalled.

Planning for the invasion of Iraq had been ongoing in one fashion or
another for more than a decade. Always, during the twelve-year period between the conclusion of Desert Storm at the end of February
1991 and the start of Iraqi Freedom during the latter half of March
2003, there had been a scheme to topple Saddam and destroy his
armed forces. "We had actually gotten very serious about it during
early 2002, the year prior," recalled Robling. "But politically things
slowed down and the weather heated up and it looked less likely that
we would deploy." But then, during the summer of 2002, Saddam's
intransigence and rhetoric seemed to make an American deployment
more likely despite the brutal summertime heat that would make operations on the battlefield a torture. Again, though, diplomatic efforts
checked the start of any major military mobilization. These sorts of
on-again, off-again episodes characterized much of the year that pre-
ceded the actual commencement of hostilities.

Robling recalled: "We finally started sending small advance parties
out to Kuwait during late 2002." In fact, the wing commander, Major

General James Amos, spent November of that year in Kuwait, anticipating that his units would follow him shortly thereafter. When the
expected deployment did not transpire, he returned to his command
in the States. Even so, by the end of 2002 there was little doubt in
anyone's mind that the United States was set to invade Iraq. Preparations to do just that proceeded apace.

Those preparations for the Marine Corps revolved around I MEF,
and more specifically Mattis's First Marine Division. Although the
focus of this volume is directed at Marine Corps aviation, the reader
will be reminded several times that the air effort was wholly dedicated
to supporting the ground scheme of maneuver. In that context a brief
overview of the plan is warranted in order to understand the descriptions of the air operations that make up the lion's share of this book.

The broad scheme devised by the CFLCC and his staff was a two-
pronged assault that had the Army's V Corps driving northwest from
Kuwait through the deserts of southern Iraq, and then north through
the Karbala Gap straight into Baghdad. The Marine Corps's I MEF
was to support the Army with an attack that ran north and west from
Kuwait and then through the territory between the Tigris and Euphrates—the area known to archaeologists and historians as the
Mesopotamian Plain. If all went as intended, the Marines would link
up with the Army at Baghdad.

The day after I MEF received its assigned battlespace from the
CFLCC it was handed a study that described most of the terrain in its
area of operations as untrafficable. In other words, the ground would
not support the movement of a mechanized force. This was not a factor that the planners at the First Marine Division had been unaware
of. They had studied the World War I battle during which a British division had been trapped in the same marshy terrain and was defeated
by the Turks. That battle had taken place near Al Kut, and Al Kut sat
smack in the middle of the planned Marine advance. Granted, since
that time Saddam had drained most of the marshes in an effort to isolate and punish the Shia Muslim "Marsh Arabs" who made up the re-

gion's population and who had traditionally been enemies of his government. But the sodden ground that was left behind was crisscrossed by canals and was distinctly unsuitable for the type of mechanized warfare the Marines were planning.

This meant that the First Marine Division's advance would be tied to the limited road and highway network that serviced the region. It was a challenge that vexed the division's planners at every turn—both before and during the campaign. Nearly every move the division would make revolved around the availability of roads and bridges that were capable of handling the type of weapons and machinery the Marines would be moving. Much of the equipment that would be hauled was bridging material. As heavy and cumbersome as it was, the planners recognized the need; if the Marines lacked the ability to span a river from scratch, the Iraqis would only have to destroy a few key spans to slow them considerably. It was paradoxical that the staff was frustrated by canals, rivers, and waterlogged terrain in a part of the world that most of the world envisioned as dry desert.

In fact, a very serious danger that never materialized was inundation warfare, or war by water. There was real concern that the Iraqi regime might stall the attack by diverting water from canals and rivers into the path of the Marines. It was a possibility that had potential; the entire region had gone underwater during a flood in 1954. And during Iraq's war with Iran in the early 1980s, Saddam's forces successfully rerouted water to deny avenues of approach to the Iranians. If such a strategy was effectively executed, the Marine Corps could be stalled long enough for the Iraqis to shift more resources against the Army's drive.

The Marine planners rightly recognized that having their advance confined to existing roadways not only limited their maneuver options but also channeled their forces and made them predictable. They feared that the Iraqis would develop a coordinated catalog of firesacks or ambush locations that would enable them to employ their long-range artillery and rocket launchers against preregistered points on the highways. Done properly, these ambushes could trap the Marines on the hard surfaces and decimate them on the spot.

Just more than a month before the campaign would start CFLCC presented I MEF with a gift that would dramatically lower the risk to the Marine Corps's planned scheme of maneuver. Highway 1, an unfinished roadway that was intended as a newer, more modern link between Al Basrah and Baghdad, had originally been within the Army's AOR (Area of Responsibility). A change in the Army's plan meant that they no longer needed or wanted it. The Marine Corps has long been accustomed to receiving castoffs from the other services, and this one was accepted gladly.

Although Highway 1 wasn't entirely finished, significant portions of it were paved, and there was a reasonably robust roadbed along its entire length. A thorough analysis by Marine intelligence experts showed that the entire route promised to be able to handle what the Marines wanted to put on it. It joined Highway 8 from the north, just west of An Nasiriyah, and it gave Conway another avenue of approach to relieve pressure from the other highways. The road also gave him the ability to flank and envelop his adversaries if the situation demanded it. Best of all, it was likely that the Iraqis gave no serious consideration to the idea that the Americans would use it. Almost giddy with the new option, the MEF staff made significant changes to their plans to take full advantage of the windfall.

Although the chief highways—sensibly enough—ran through major cities, there was never any intent on the Marine Corps's part to take these urban areas in protracted battles. The costs in lives and time would be too high. Rather, the scheme called for the ground elements to either punch their way through or bypass those cities that straddled the route of advance. While this strategy would leave pockets of enemy units all along their lines of communication, it was a risk that the MEF commander was willing to take.

Truth be told, many risks were accepted by all of the commanders in order to support the primary tenet around which everything else revolved: speed. Mattis summed it up for his division in three words, "Speed equals success." It was the factor on which the commanders were prepared to risk everything; a swift offensive would allow them to take an enormous territory with far fewer resources than would have traditionally been required in a more conventional campaign. Such an assault would cut communications, cause confusion, and isolate enemy units; all of this would make it difficult for the Iraqis to maneuver their divisions and coordinate an effective defense. Speed would also make the Coalition units difficult to track, and that in turn would make them tricky artillery and WMD targets. Speed would, if all went well, reduce casualties. Finally, a swift attack into the heart of Iraq would make it difficult—if not impossible—for Saddam's government to make entreaties for intervention by the UN or other nations sympathetic to his government.

This call for speed impacted every aspect of the MEF's planning and preparations. Units were directed to lighten their loads. Afterward they were inspected and ordered to trim more. The emphasis was on mobility and hitting power. Over and over the process took place until the commanders were assured that the units that made up I MEF were the leanest, most potent fighting forces the nation had ever fielded.

One commander neatly summarized the way most of the Marines understood the importance of speed to the campaign:

"It was hey-diddle diddle, straight-up-the-middle, and the last one to Baghdad eats shit!"

Marine aviation's role in the coming campaign was crucial. So critical was the support of 3rd MAW to the ground scheme of maneuver that Mattis had declared that the First Marine Division would be the most "air-centric" division in history. He was able to make this declaration because of the confidence he had in the MEF's aviation Marines. He commented to the wing staff prior to the deployment into theater: "The boys [First Marine Division] are looking forward to the brawl, and have a level of trust in you that I think would surprise you . . . this is why we're willing to accept the risk of a fight with odds of less than three-to-one."

Mattis considered the Iraqi indirect fire weapons—artillery, multiple rocket launchers, and surface-to-surface rockets—to be his biggest threat and the enemy's tactical center of gravity. It was these systems he wanted destroyed above all others, and his desire to have them killed in the deep air war were considered early in the construction of the overall plan. Nevertheless, recognizing that there was no guarantee that the execution of the deep air war would be perfect, his staff worked with 3rd MAW to develop "quickfire" tactics that would rapidly detect, target, and obliterate those enemy indirect fire systems that escaped early destruction. On the other hand, tanks and armored vehicles, while worthwhile targets, were dangers that Mattis felt his Marines could handle toe-to-toe. If air could kill them, fine. If not, the division would take care of them itself.

Mattis and his staff appreciated the importance of air strikes carried out by tactical jets well in front of the division, but the air support that they would touch and see more than any other would be that provided by the wing's rotary-wing components. The helicopters would provide his air assault capability and would support him with CASE-VAC (Casualty Evacuation) aircraft, resupply missions, transport assets, and more. Too, the Hueys and Cobras would become the platforms that his RCT commanders would come to depend on most; they provided CAS and command and control capabilities, without which the campaign may have been very different. Finally, Mattis's staff recognized the airlift that the wing's KC-130s could provide; ultimately, during the middle of the advance, these big ships would bring his Marines the supplies they would need to maintain their momentum into Baghdad.

Because the ground assault would be so tied to the main highways, the wing would be counted on to sweep a constantly moving cordon of destruction in front of the RCTs that would travel the routes. The plan called for the neutralization of the Iraqi units that possessed weapons capable of ranging the highways; they were to be killed before they could engage the division.

Of course the tasking and coordination were much more expansive and complex than the brief description above, and the combined staffs of the division, the wing, and the various support components spent a great deal of time together. They planned, planned again, and then planned some more. Although none of the schemes that were written was executed in its entirety, the staffs spent so much time together that when the fighting actually started it was easy to make changes when operational requirements demanded them. Conway knew this before the conflict ever began and explained that he would not be crippled by the lack of a detailed plan, ". . . because plans always change crossing the line of departure." He went on to explain that even though the MEF would be facing eight Iraqi divisions, the airpower that 3rd MAW would provide would help to ensure success. In the end he gave a two-word plan that every Marine would be able grasp and execute. "I MEF's guidance is simple," he said. "Attack north!"

It was simple enough in theory, but putting it into practice when confined to the limited highway infrastructure available was going to be considerably more complex. This was emphasized in a very basic fashion during what became known as the "LEGO Drills." Lieutenant Colonels Rob Whitters and Steve Santa Ana purchased more than six thousand of the plastic toy blocks. These were then carefully placed on a scaled outdoor terrain model of the regions of Kuwait and Iraq where the initial attack was to take place. *Every single vehicle* in the division was represented—one per block. The long lines of colored plastic toys, and the logistical and operational challenges they signified, were sobering. Nevertheless the exercises were useful in illustrating just how large the fully fielded division would be and how much space it would take up. They further helped to devise schemes of movement and timetables, identify potential bottlenecks, and delineate reasonable unit boundaries.

The Marines—air, ground, and support alike—approached the coming war the way they always had: as one big team. The plans and adjustments that they made were nothing more than the fine-tuning of an enduring operational legacy that has made the Marine Corps unique in the history of warfare.

3

Staging for War

He had assembled bikes at JCPenney during the few months be-tween his graduation from Central Washington University and his call to active duty. That was during the summer of 1976, just after he'd gotten married. Now Brigadier General Terry "Guts" Robling was second-in-command of the largest air wing in the United States Marine Corps.

Not that it was obvious to the casual observer. He was dressed in civilian clothes, and his military haircut was only one of several others that he could see as he deplaned and stepped into the terminal at Kuwait City International Airport. Military haircuts—particularly American military haircuts—had been a regular feature in Kuwait since the end of Desert Storm in 1991. Now, in January 2003, the United States was putting together a force that would finally bring an end to Saddam Hussein's government in neighboring Iraq—a regime that actively murdered its own citizens and brutally repressed those it left alive. The in-your-face intransigence that Hussein had been dish-ing out in reply to United Nations sanctions was going to become a thing of the past.

Robling brushed past a gaggle of giggling Arab girls. Their Western dress—designer jeans, tight shirts, and high heels—caught him by surprise. So did their affinity for makeup; it was applied in quantity, and with a gusto that back home in San Diego would only have been appropriate on the opera stage—or under a lamppost. The girls represented one end of the spectrum of dress and demeanor that made up the crowd inside the airport. At the other extreme were women dressed in the full, head-to-toe black robes traditional in that part of the Arab world. The jet-black abayas covered their faces and cloaked every feminine bump and curve; their purpose was to make the women as uninteresting as possible. Many years before, American servicemen had nicknamed these darkly clad women BMOs—Black Moving Objects. The Arab men who weren't dressed in Western attire were more conservatively garbed in flowing dishdashas, and generous headdresses or gutras, held in place by black circular bands called ogals.

Through everyone weaved swarms of men from the belt of poorer southern Asian countries. These included Pakistanis, Bangladeshis, Indians, and Filipinos, among others. They were the hired laborers who did the difficult, demeaning, and dirty jobs in the Emirate of Kuwait.

After collecting his suitcases, Robling approached the customs area where uniformed Kuwaiti officers were pawing through the bags and boxes of incoming laborers. Responding to the beckoning wave of another officer, Robling made his way over to a counter and showed his military identification card.

The Kuwaiti gave it only the barest of glances. "Do you bring the liquor?" Alcohol was illegal in Kuwait.

"What?" Robling answered.

"Whiskey," the Kuwaiti tried to clarify.

Robling was still confused. "No, thank you."

Exasperated, the Arab gave up and waved him on without looking through his baggage.

Once through customs, Robling stepped into the throngs of families and friends who were waiting for their loved ones. Other than the

Marine Corps, he had no family in Kuwait. It took only a moment for him to spot his driver. After introducing himself, the young Marine led Robling past the terminal's Starbucks and KFC franchises and into the parking garage. He wouldn't see the airport again for several more months.

He had an air war to help plan and execute.

Robling set up shop in 3rd MAW's forward headquarters at Ahmed Al Jaber—the Kuwait Air Force base that was scraped out of the desert and located very near the center of the tiny nation. From there he would help lead the effort to get the wing's Marines into the country and prepared for the coming fight. A small cadre was already in place and more would soon be on their way, including Major General Amos, the wing commander.

It was the morning of January 17 when Captain James "Pinky" Finnegan left San Diego Bay aboard LPD-8, the *Dubuque*. He was an AH-1W Cobra pilot assigned to HMLA-267. Standing out in the breeze with his fellow fliers that day, he remembered the start of the journey that would ultimately take him into the heart of Iraq:

> . . . out on the flight deck, drinking coffee, talking a little and watching the spectacular San Diego skyline pass by. Although the weeks leading up to the departure were shrouded in secrecy, we all knew where we were going and what we would ultimately be doing, which made our slow sail out of the harbor and past the thousands of cheering, waving, and crying families an emotional event.

Finnegan had no way of knowing that two of the men he was sharing those sentiments with would not be returning home with him.

Marines on both coasts were saying good-bye to loved ones. It was never easy regardless of whether it was a master gunnery sergeant with two-plus decades of service and a dozen overseas deployments under his belt, or a nineteen-year-old lance corporal with a new wife and baby. Across the Corps families endured tempests of emotion. One Marine remembered looking down at his sleeping daughter—his cheeks wet with tears:

> . . . and her face, so peaceful and innocent. I find myself thinking the unthinkable—that I might not be around this time next year. I might never get to scare off her first boyfriend . . . all because of some sadistic, neurotic, wildly unstable dictator in a crap-ass third-world country.

When the Marine Corps goes to war it is the Navy that traditionally gets them to where the fighting is. Finnegan and HMLA-267 and the *Dubuque* were part of Amphibious Task Force (ATF) West, a group of warships that also included two Landing Helicopter Docks (LHDs), the *Boxer* and the *Bonhomme Richard*, as well as another LPD, the *Cleveland*. Between the four ships they embarked twenty-four AV-8B Harriers, sixteen CH-53Es, eighteen AH-1Ws, nine UH-1Ns, twelve CH-46s, and a substantial complement of Marines and equipment. Their counterpart, ATF East, would sail from the eastern seaboard and meet them in the Persian Gulf. ATF East was made up of two LHDs, the *Kearsarge* and the *Bataan*, as well as an LHA, the *Saipan*. Those three ships carried the exact same catalog of aircraft as ATF West—plus an additional AV-8B.

And there were more. The Fifteenth Marine Expeditionary Unit (MEU)—led by the *Tarawa*—was on station more than a month prior to the fight, while the 24th MEU with the *Nassau* would arrive at the end of March after having already been at sea on other duties for eight months. These two MEUs combined put a total of sixty-two more aircraft on 3rd MAW's roster.

And there were still more. The KC-130s—a total of twenty-four—came into theater in ones and twos, while sixty F/A-18s, ten EA-6Bs, and another sixteen AV-8Bs were nursed across the globe and into

Kuwait and Saudi Arabia by Air Force KC-10 and KC-135 aerial re-fuelers. The Air Force contributed more to the effort by airlifting in additional helicopters (sixty-three for MAG-39), equipment, and Marines. Nevertheless, the bulk of the air wing's Marines arrived courtesy of the CRAF—the Civil Reserve Air Fleet. The CRAF is made up of commercial aircraft provided by major domestic air-lines—the same ones that take us to Grandma's house for Christmas each year. A national treasure, this system was one of the primary rea-sons that the Army, Marine Corps, and Air Force were ready for war as early as they were.

All of this was augmented by equipment and supplies from Mar-itime Prepositioning Ships (MPS)—combat-loaded ships staged for-ward at different ports around the world. The concept had been a huge success during Desert Storm and had been refined since then. Always crewed and ready to go on short notice, eleven of these huge vessels supported the MEF. The Navy further supplemented the force with men and gear off-loaded from twenty different amphibious ships, while three more transports were dedicated wholly toward the delivery of ammunition.

By the time it was all in place 3rd MAW had fifteen thousand per-sonnel and 408 aircraft in theater. But it didn't have many places to put them. During Desert Storm the United States had stationed its forces all over the region—especially Saudi Arabia and Turkey. This time Turkey wasn't going to play at all, and the Saudi participation was much more limited; the kingdom forbade the stationing of any "shooters" on its soil. This is where the Corps's normally unarmed EA-6B electronic warfare aircraft went. All but sixteen of the AV-8Bs were kept aboard two LHDs, the *Bonhomme Richard* and the *Bataan*. These two ships were dubbed "Harrier Carriers" and would serve their unorthodox complement of jump jets unfailingly through the entire campaign.

The F/A-18 Hornets were scheduled to be land-based in Kuwait. Nevertheless, there were few good options available to them. In the end they went to Ahmed Al Jaber, where Robling was working at 3rd MAW's forward headquarters. Still, it was a tight fit as they joined several Air Force units as well as the forty-two F/A-18s that made up the Kuwait Air Force. As if that wasn't enough, a squadron of sixteen AV-8Bs was thrown into the mix.

The Marines outnumbered their host Kuwaitis at Al Jaber many times over; nevertheless the Kuwaitis maintained ownership of their base. Although, as might be expected, there were cultural differences and minor misunderstandings between the Kuwait Air Force and the Marines, a shared purpose and past friendships carried the day. One of Marine Air Group (MAG) Eleven's majors had left the Marine Corps during the late 1990s and taken a job as an F/A-18 instructor with the Kuwait Air Force. There he built up a great camaraderie and friendship with the host of Kuwaitis he instructed and worked with. Following the events of September 11, 2001, he returned to the States, much to the disappointment of his Arab friends, and was recommissioned into the Marine Corps. When he reappeared at Al Jaber as part of 3rd MAW, his happy and surprised former students exclaimed: "See, we always say that you cannot stay away—that you will miss Kuwait and be back to visit us!"

Actually the Marine units were relative newcomers, as the U.S. Air Force had been rotating units through Al Jaber for a decade in support of Operation Southern Watch. The men in blue lost no time in rolling out the welcome mat for their Marine brethren. Robling remembered: "They couldn't have been more gracious—everything was open and available to us. There was a little bit of grumbling down at the lower levels—they accused our young Marines of stealing their girls. Of course that was true, but by and large everyone got along great.

"There was some pain early on without a doubt," continued Robling. "But it wasn't long before we started getting our gear in and our tents up and our Marines out of the dirt. And we operated our jets pretty much from day one." Notwithstanding the get-to-it attitude of the wing's men and women, conditions were certainly challenging early on and were the subject of considerable grousing.

Some of their pain, though, was of their own making. Since before the time of the Roman legions military men have marched off to war

with a required list of gear or equipment mandated by their commanders. The Marines who deployed to Kuwait during late 2002 and
early 2003 were no different. Nevertheless, Captain Anthony "Curly"
Bolden didn't pack the sleeping bag prescribed by the yard-long list
that had been disseminated prior to the deployment. He opted instead to save room and weight by just bringing a poncho liner and a
roll-up mat. "I thought that I would be a badass," he recalled. "I
wouldn't need all that sissy gear—after all, Kuwait was the desert,
right?" As it turned out, his unit spent the first few nights in the open,
under the stars. February can be quite cool in Kuwait; this was a fact
that wasn't lost on Bolden after the first night. "Rather than a badass,
I felt like a dumb ass when I woke up in the middle of the night freez-
ing my backside off."

When I myself had deployed for the 1991 Gulf War more than a
decade earlier, one of the chief complaints upon arriving in theater
centered on the dearth of toilet paper. Evidently this was a lesson
learned and then forgotten. For this campaign, although the Marine
Corps had managed to arrange for the transport of more than twenty-
five thousand *tons* of ammunition, they had failed to bring enough
toilet paper. One squadron officer remembered, "Because I was the
Executive Officer I was more or less responsible to the Commanding
Officer for everything. I guess that included shit paper because one
night he came into my tent and kicked the hell out of me while I was
asleep in my cot. He had just finished 'taking care of business' and
now had to take a shower because he couldn't find anything to wipe
with."

Regardless, things gradually improved at Al Jaber as Marine Wing
Support Group Thirty-seven (MWSG-37) continued to receive the
Marines and equipment it needed to get the air wing functional and
make things more comfortable. The work of the MWSG was augmented by the efforts of the Navy's Construction Battalions—units
better known as Seabees. These rough-and-ready sailors poured their
biggest concrete project since Vietnam, a twenty-five-acre, three-foot-
thick ramp that provided space for scores of aircraft. This project and
others made the base a better place from which to fight a war.

Approximately twenty-five miles to the north of Al Jaber was the other Kuwait Air Force base, Ali Al Salem. Closer to Iraq, it was where the air wing would base more than a third of its helicopters. Those helicopters shared the field with thirty-five British rotary-wing aircraft and fourteen Army UH-60 air ambulance helicopters. At its peak the base supported more than three hundred aircraft and five thousand personnel from several different nations. Like the Marines at Al Jaber, the men and women at Al Salem suffered through their share of hardships.

The majority of the rotary-wing outfits operated from the various LHAs, LHDs, and LPDs that the Navy deployed to the region. The shipboard amenities those units enjoyed were paid for by their fliers in the currency of longer transit times to and from the battlefield. Still, operations afloat are always a challenge, and even more so during war.

The big but essential KC-130s were more problematic when it came to finding a location from which to operate. With a wingspan greater than 130 feet they were real estate hogs, and it was difficult to find a place to put them all. The solution was provided by Bahrain. Even more diminutive than Kuwait, Bahrain is a small island nation linked to Saudi Arabia by a long causeway. The ruler there offered up Shaikh Isa Air Base, the same base where the Marine Corps had staged its F/A 18s during Desert Storm.

Still, Shaikh Isa was nearly 250 miles from the center of Kuwait. This translated into nearly an hour of flight time for a KC-130, and the command wanted to keep at least a small contingent of the big ships closer to Iraq. Another element that came into play was the fact that the Bahrainis would permit the Marines to base no more than twenty aircraft at Shaikh Isa. The problem was that there simply wasn't any space available at either of the two military airfields in Kuwait.

So, 3rd MAW built another.

Amos gave the go-ahead while negotiations to scour it out of the desert were still under way with the Kuwaiti government. "Tamer was back in theater by now and he fell in love with the idea," remembered

Robling. The men and women of MWSG-37 set their heavy graders and rollers and trucks to work leveling and filling a stretch of desert in the north-central region of Kuwait only about thirty miles or so from the Iraqi border. Two parallel runways, each six thousand feet long, were scraped out of the earth with the intention of operating from one while repairing and maintaining the other. The end result was a dirt-and-sand airfield that would remain so because the time and the resources weren't available to make it more permanent. There was also the fact that the Kuwaitis still had not granted permission for it to be constructed.

The airfield was completed on the same day that the Marines received approval from the Kuwaitis to commence building it. Part of the Camp Coyote TAA (Tactical Assembly Area), the two strips were collectively named the Joe Foss Expeditionary Air Field in honor of the great Marine ace who had passed away only months earlier. It was a dusty, dirty, noisy place. Situated adjacent to the main north–south highway that bisected that portion of the country, the base served as a staging point for equipment and supplies that were trucked in from the port at Kuwait City.

Operating off a dirt strip is one thing for a small aircraft, but quite another for an eighty-ton, four-engine transport. Getting a fully loaded KC-130 plowing through the loose sand fast enough to get airborne was always an exercise in patience and nerves. Captain Rick Fee of VMGR-352 was one of the pilots qualified to operate out of the primitive setup. "Taking off could be interesting, depending on when the runway had been repaired last," he remembered. "Often, after we added power the aircraft picked up speed and then hit a soft spot in the sand. We'd pitch forward in our seats as we decelerated and then we'd slowly build up momentum again. Then we'd hit another dip and slow down again. We'd lurch along through the dirt like that until we finally got up enough speed to get away."

Landing back at Joe Foss provided its own set of challenges. "The biggest problem we had," recalled Fee, "was just spotting the place during the daytime. It was a pair of sand strips in a sandy desert. Throw in a little windblown dust or some haze and the runways

would almost vanish." Landing at night was easier for the "Herk" pilots because the infrared covert lighting made the strips stand out
from the surrounding blackness of the Kuwaiti desert. Once the aircraft was safely on the ground, the aircrews had little trouble getting
stopped. The same sand traps that made getting airborne so difficult
were quite effective at slowing the heavy airplanes down.

Despite the added capabilities and options that Joe Foss Field gave
the Marines, there was no denying that it was hard on the KC-130s.
Powdery sand got into everything, and the propellers and tires zinged
rocks hard into the airframe. A year after the campaign Fee stated:
"We're still suffering from the effects of that dirt. Even today we're
finding sand in the aircraft." How much service life was beaten out of
the KC-130s by these operations is still being guessed at. Even so,
there is no arguing the fact that the supplies the big ships lifted out of
Joe Foss Field to the Marines fighting in Iraq were crucial to the conduct of the war.

War is often about waiting, but the Marines who fought this campaign generally spent less than two months in Kuwait before being
sent into combat. Nevertheless, two months was plenty of time to
get hurt. Because most Marines fall into the exact demographic
that makes insurance executives lie awake at night, there were a lot
of incidents. Training accidents, or lacerations and broken bones
from sports were common, while vehicle crashes also caused injuries. And predictably, because they were young men with guns,
there were mishaps involving firearms. Then there were those incidents created by spectacular lapses of common sense. One young
Marine was refueling a truck in the dark and, unable to see well,
drew his lighter from his pocket for additional illumination. The results were as you'd expect, and the badly burned young man was
sent home.

The aviators of 3rd MAW did their best to use the time they had to
hone the skills that were so critical to their missions. This wasn't
much of a problem for the helicopter pilots, as there were plenty of

Marines in the field and training opportunities abounded. It was a different story for the fixed-wing fliers, though; Kuwait's diminutive territory was overlaid by an equally small airspace, and there simply wasn't much room for the jet crews to train. The flying they managed to do over the tiny emirate was only barely adequate to maintain their proficiency.

4

Operation Southern Watch

Most sources declare March 20, 2003, as the start of the Second Gulf War, whereas in reality, in the air at least, the war had been going on for years. The conclusion of Desert Storm in 1991 marked the start of an air campaign against Iraq that did not end until Coalition forces ejected Saddam Hussein's government in 2003. UN resolutions following the 1991 conflict prohibited, among other actions, the Iraqi military from operating aircraft south of the 32nd parallel (and, from 1996, the 33rd) and north of the 36th parallel. These resolutions were intended to protect Shiite populations in the southern part of the nation and Kurdish peoples to the north. The operations that enforced these resolutions were known as Southern Watch (OSW), supported primarily from bases in Saudi Arabia and Kuwait, and Northern Watch (ONW), executed around sorties flown mainly from Incirlik Air Base in Turkey. Combined, the two efforts denied Iraq two-thirds of its own airspace. U.S. and British forces flew more than three hundred thousand combat and support flights to police these two so-called no-fly zones.

The enforcement of the no-fly zones had several major effects.

First, as intended, it did prevent the Iraqis from attacking the Shiites and Kurds from the air. In part because of the protection they were afforded from above, the Kurds were able to establish an autonomous political region in northern Iraq.

Second, it provided a real-world training ground for virtually all of the USAF's tactical airmen during the nearly twelve years from the end of Desert Storm to the start of Iraqi Freedom. Almost every Air Force aviator had done a stint "in the sandbox" in support of one or the other of the operations. There is no better training than the "real thing," and the low-grade tempo of combat missions over Iraq provided just that. Several Iraqi jets were shot down as they violated the no-fly zones, and the list of Iraqi radar sites and antiaircraft systems that were attacked and destroyed was very extensive. The experience gained was invaluable.

Finally, in concert with weapons embargoes, the operations had the effect of degrading the Iraqi air defense system to a significant degree. It is remarkable that during more than a decade not a single Coalition aircraft was lost over Iraq for any reason. This is all the more astonishing when it is considered that the normal accident rate for an effort this size—even in peacetime—would have seen the loss of perhaps a dozen or more aircraft.

The USAF carried the bulk of the burden for enforcing the two no-fly zones, particularly at the beginning. As time passed and the effort became more of a grind, units from other services—including the Marine Corps—rotated through the duty. And as mentioned earlier the British maintained a smaller but steady effort through the duration.

During most of the period the level of effort was steady and the intensity was low—with occasional spikes in activity, such as during Desert Fox in 1998. Mostly the operations were little more than an exercise of tit for tat. An Iraqi antiaircraft unit would illuminate a Coalition aircraft with its radar, or fire antiaircraft artillery, and the Coalition would respond with a limited air strike. On rare occasions the Iraqis would actually fire a missile, but always without effect. Iraqi fighters occasionally played games of cat-and-mouse but nearly always stayed well out of missile range of U.S. aircraft. When they didn't they were often blown out of the sky.

Nevertheless, during 2002 the level of effort increased significantly from a tempo that had already been gradually increasing since the late 1990s. This was due in part to more aggressive Iraqi activities in the two zones; as incentive, Hussein had offered substantial rewards for downing a Coalition aircraft. And the Coalition undoubtedly ratcheted operations up not only in response to the Iraqis but also with the goal of grinding down Iraqi antiaircraft capabilities in preparation for the impending conflict. Coalition actions also included reconnaissance flights that contributed greatly to the construction of a portfolio of targets and coordinates.

No-fly zone operations reached their peak just before the official start of Iraqi Freedom. During the period from March 1 to March 20, 2003, there were four thousand sorties flown. Targets included fiber-optic nodes, SAM (Surface to Air Missile) sites, antiaircraft artillery batteries, and command and control installations.

Marine Corps Hornet and Harrier squadrons took part in OSW flights soon after arriving in theater in mid-February. Just as had been the case with the Air Force, these missions served as familiarization flights by getting the aircrews used to the established operating procedures, and by getting them acquainted with the lay of the land in southern Iraq.

It wasn't a simple task—even from the standpoint of just getting bombs onto the target. For a variety of reasons most of the air-dropped weapons during this stage of OSW (and the coming campaign) were precision-guided—either Global Positioning System bombs that depended on satellites for their steering, or Laser Guided Bombs that were directed to the target by a beam of laser energy from an aircraft or a ground unit. While extremely accurate, both of these weapons types required much more planning and attention to detail to employ effectively than did the free-fall, or "dumb," bombs of the past. This was particularly true of the GPS munitions; encrypted codes had to be coordinated and loaded into the aircraft and the bombs themselves, and these codes had to jibe with the data that the satellites provided. Also, the weapons had to be able to receive the satellite information while loaded on the aircraft and while in flight. The vagaries of radio frequencies being what they are, this wasn't always guaranteed.

In short, there were plenty of opportunities for mistakes or shortcomings, and all of these could cause the weapons to fail. Successful employment of these bombs depended on a chain of people—from the nineteen-year-old ordnance loader to the forty-year-old pilot—doing everything exactly right. This was something that didn't always happen. Still, when compared with the average miss distance of a hundred feet or more for a conventional dumb bomb, the average miss distance of a GPS weapon of perhaps less than a dozen feet made the satellite weapons very attractive.

Additionally, the command and control procedures and routing processes that the USAF had developed over more than a decade seemed overly complex to many of the Marines. And everything depended on encrypted communications—something that they weren't used to using day to day. All of these factors combined resulted in a good bit of eye rolling during what the Marine aircrews considered the exceedingly tedious briefs that their Air Force brothers provided.

Soon after landing their first jets at Al Jaber, the F/A-18D crews of VMFA(AW)-533 started attending the Air Force–conducted briefings and classes that qualified them to fly inside the southern no-fly zone. At the same time, they flew training missions in the limited airspace above Kuwait. There were OSW missions scheduled as well, but until February 22—for a variety of reasons—the missions that included the squadron had all been called back or even scrubbed before the crews got to their jets. These cancellations were extremely frustrating.

The mission scheduled for the night of February 22 would break the streak. Lieutenant Colonel L. Ross "Migs" Roberts was the Commanding Officer (CO) of VMFA(AW)-533 and was scheduled to lead the four jets that his squadron was contributing to the strike. The mission was part of a Response Option, or RO. An RO was intended to punish Iraqi intransigence in the no-fly zone.

The four crews that Roberts put together for the mission were a cross section of his squadron. Rightly, he put himself in the lead of his squadron's first combat mission. His operations officer, Major John "JP" Farnam, would man the WSO (Weapons System Officer) cockpit behind him. The rest of the division was a leavened mixture of combat veterans and relatively new "cherry boys"—young crews who had never been shot at. Their assigned target was relatively unexciting: a set of four fiber-optic cable repeaters. The weapons load for each aircraft was two GPS-dependent, GBU-32, thousand-pound Joint Direct Attack Munitions, or JDAMs.

On this night Roberts had the flight start their jets earlier than normal in order to work through some of the weapons and communications glitches that were bound to occur during this, the first of what would ultimately be a long series of combat missions. This decision to start early was a good one because, just as expected, there were problems with the cryptographic interfaces between the JDAMs and the aircraft. Nevertheless the maintenance Marines and aircrews worked together to fix the problems.

But the flight's difficulties weren't over. "We found ourselves five minutes from our takeoff time without being able to talk to the AWACS via HAVEQUICK," Roberts recalled. AWACS (Airborne Warning and Control System) was the Air Force aircraft that was controlling the overall strike, while HAVEQUICK allowed frequency-agile, jam-resistant communications. Roberts continued: "The official policy was that if you couldn't talk on HAVEQUICK, then you couldn't launch. I was starting to contemplate the embarrassment of having to cancel the mission. Luckily, Captain 'Mumbles' Simmons, the WSO in the dash-four aircraft, figured out the problem and we were able to manually load the required frequencies." After a short taxi, the four aircraft were ready for takeoff.

On the runway, Roberts pushed the throttles of his aircraft all the way forward and released the brakes. The afterburners lit with a roar; purple-white plumes of brilliantly hot exhaust shot from the rear of the jet, and within seconds he was airborne, followed in short order by the other three aircraft of his formation.

Turning toward Iraq, Roberts looked over his shoulder through his night-vision goggles as each of his wingmen closed the distance and settled into formation. From the cockpit behind him, Farnam checked in the other crews over the radio and brought them through the maze of command and control frequencies that OSW operations necessitated. At the same time, the pilots and WSOs checked the status of their aircraft and completed their combat checklists. Roberts listened with satisfaction as each aircraft reported in with good weapons systems.

It wasn't long before the four-ship of Hornets—callsign Marauder 11—was inbound toward the target. Closer in, the crews checked and rechecked the status of their weapons. The JDAMs were new to them. Because they were new and because they were also expensive, this was the first time that any of the eight Marines in the flight had ever used them.

One of the chief advantages of JDAM weapons is that, unlike a conventional dumb bomb, the aircrew doesn't have to drop it from an exact point, at an exact airspeed, altitude, attitude, and angle, in order to hit the target. Instead the pilot can the release the bomb once his aircraft enters a pie-shaped envelope that is calculated by the onboard mission computer and depicted on the navigation display. Once the bomb leaves the airplane, its tailfins adjust its trajectory and guide it to the preprogrammed coordinates. In essence the JDAM is a launch-and-leave bomb that guides itself to the target.

The formation was less than a minute from the release point when Roberts's bomb indicated a degraded status. This was not what he needed as the flight lead of his squadron's first mission—a high-visibility sortie that he wanted to go well in order to set a tone for the squadron for the combat that was likely only a short time away. "We started to troubleshoot the problem, and after a short discussion and review of the checklist I decided that it was working well enough to release." The formation was fast approaching the JDAM minimum launch range, and only seconds later he mashed down on the red bomb release button on his control stick and felt a thump as the weapon cleared the aircraft. Taking his cue, the other three crews dropped their own bombs in quick succession.

Angling away from the targets, the four crews watched their FLIR displays intently, at the same time doing their best to keep from running into each other and watching for enemy missile fire. The FLIR pods were slaved to the target coordinates and remained fixed there regardless of which way the aircraft were pointed. When all four JDAMs smashed into their targets almost simultaneously, there was an eruption of cheering from each cockpit. VMFA(AW)-533's first mission was a resounding success.

Upon returning to Al Jaber, the crews rolled the mission videotapes over and over again. High fives were exchanged, and cigars were lit. Roberts remembered: "The boost to morale in the ready room and all across the squadron was contagious. Because I hadn't loaded the flight with the heavy hitters, every one of my aviators knew that I had confidence in them and that they would be trusted to execute the mission they were assigned." Although the Iraqis hadn't defended against the formation in any meaningful way, it was still a validation of what his Marines were capable of—on the flight line and in the air.

With combat just around the corner, Roberts was glad that his crews were getting some preparatory combat under their belts.

By the middle of March it was becoming obvious that there was going to be no diplomatic arrangement that would satisfy both the United States and Saddam Hussein. The UN weapons inspectors who had been allowed back into the country during December had made no significant WMD finds. Yet the same lack of cooperation that earlier teams had encountered prevented them from being able to certify that the rogue government did not possess them. UN inspector Hans Blix reported his frustration to that world body in early March. The response to Blix's report was mixed; some nations wanted to give diplomacy more time. Others did not. Despite fervent opposition from France, Germany, China, and Russia—as well as the UN Security Council—the United States and Britain made final preparations to lead their much smaller Coalition partners into Iraq.

The world watched on March 17 as U.S. President George W.

Bush demanded that Saddam Hussein leave Iraq within forty-eight hours. Tired of the diplomatic wrangling that had gone on for too long, the United States was going to see to it that Iraq's president was removed from power one way or another. His murderous legacy of terror and torture, and the potential threat he posed to peace in the future, was going to end.

When they weren't training or flying OSW missions, the men who were about to go to war had time to meditate on what the approaching conflict would demand of them. Stereotypes aside, the majority of these Marines weren't hard-bitten killing machines, ready and eager to visit death on the enemy. More typical was the attitude of Major Michael Rodriguez:

> . . . some [of us] don't give it too much thought, maybe as a defensive mechanism, but most feel the same way I do, I think. When we look north and see the soldiers who are going to die for Saddam, we are saddened. None of us wants to kill them, but every one of us will do what we have to do to defend the Marines who may be called upon to move north on the ground. It's a sad plight. I've seen stories on the news of defectors that report that if the Iraqis surrender, they'll be executed, as will their families. How would you like to be in that position? You surrender, your own army kills you. You don't surrender and the Marines roll over you.

Contemplative they may have been, but as the third week in March came to an end the Marines who made up 3rd MAW were also ready for war.

5

Harrier Carrier Teamwork

During OSW it wasn't the Iraqi air defenses that posed the biggest threat to the Coalition's fliers. Rather, it was the region's unpredictable weather. Sandstorms had the potential to sweep entire formations out of the sky in a figurative instant. That there weren't more accidents or deaths was a tribute to the skill and experience of the aviators. These attributes in turn were a result of the considerable investment that the nation had made in the training of its servicemen and -women. A particularly vicious squall caught up with three AV-8B Harrier pilots from VMA-223 on the night of March 13.

Captain Tom "Shine" Gore was the flight lead of a three-ship of AV-8Bs that was scheduled to patrol southern Iraq that evening. Flying off one side of his aircraft was Captain Mike "Trout" Hunting; on the other side was Major John "Seabass" Hicks. The named areas of interest for the mission and the execution had been meticulously briefed hours earlier, and each pilot knew his role. Shortly after crossing into enemy territory, however, the controlling AWACS aircraft passed word that the sortie had been scrubbed. Disappointed, Gore double-checked that this was indeed the case and then swung the formation around and pointed the three aircraft southeast. If all went well, the three pilots would be back aboard the *Bataan* in half an hour or less. They had had no idea that a furious sandstorm had spun itself up out of nowhere and was currently racing east from over central Kuwait.

Regardless, the pilots who only moments before had been mentally prepared for imminent combat now had to ready themselves and their aircraft for getting back aboard the ship. At night, this was no small feat. All of them went through their individual checklists, backing their aircraft out of a combat-ready status and making them ready for the recovery. At the same time—almost automatically after years of training—their hands and feet moved their flight controls and maintained the aircraft in their respective places in the formation.

Only twenty minutes later the flight was within sight of the ship. "We could easily see the coast of Kuwait," remembered Gore. "But mother [*Bataan*] reported the visibility as six miles and wanted us to land immediately as there was a dust storm rapidly approaching." The Harriers, having been airborne only a short time, were too heavy to come aboard the ship, and Gore directed the flight to dump fuel in order to get to an acceptable landing weight. The three pilots had no idea how bad the weather was about to become as they each reached down in the dark and, without looking, threw the appropriate switches. Three streams of jet fuel trailed the formation as it descended toward the water.

Inside the ship's darkened HDC (Helicopter Direction Center) Chief James Wood looked up at the radar screen hanging over his crew station. Two civilian freighters had strayed into the *Bataan*'s operating area, a twelve-by-twelve-mile box just off the Kuwaiti coast. With wind gusts now approaching gale force, the OOD (Officer of the Day) on the ship's bridge had two options. The first was to turn to center the winds straight down the deck so that the Harrier pilots could land without fighting a crosswind. But doing so would require the ship to "thread the needle" between the two freighters that were now only two thousand yards apart. The OOD's second option was to run with the wind; this would force the pilots to land at night with a tailwind that was blowing at speeds beyond anything they had ever dealt with before. It would also require the *Bataan* to steam out of her operating area and toward the shoal waters to the south. Neither option was good.

Wood heard the first change of BRC (Base Recovery Course) and immediately realized that the OOD intended to drive the ship between the two freighters. It would probably take the OOD several attempts to get the final bearing correct, and each intermediate correction would require changing the Harriers' final approach heading to the ship. Adding to the problem was the fact that the *Bataan*'s precision approach radar system was out of service. This meant that the pilots would receive heading information only and would have to gauge their descents without any help from the ship. Technically, executing an approach to the ship with the existing combination of equipment malfunctions and weather was forbidden. Practically, there was no other choice—the airfields in Kuwait were also socked in and the aircraft didn't have enough fuel to go elsewhere.

Chief Wood checked the latest weather observation. The ceiling extended all the way down to the water, and visibility was barely a quarter mile. He looked through the dimly lit space to where his two most junior controllers were watching their radar screens. He called for them to step back and replaced them with his two most experienced men. A moment later he stood up and placed himself directly behind the three men who would be responsible for getting the Harrier pilots down.

Gore remembered what happened next: "We finished dumping and headed for the initial only to be told to go to 'max conserve' while mother turned into the wind." Through his night-vision goggles he caught sight of the approaching storm. "It was like nothing I'd ever seen—a moving wall of sand. As long as I live I will never forget that sight, or the sense of helplessness that came with realizing that we were below bingo [minimum fuel] and committed to landing on the ship—there was nowhere else to go and nothing else to do." To the horror of the three fliers, the *Bataan* turned directly into the storm. It was right about then that the three Marines started to miss the fuel they had just jettisoned overboard. Now it was nothing more than useless vapor slowly settling toward the Persian Gulf.

Things began to happen fast. The approach controllers split Gore's division up for individual instrument approaches. The low man on fuel, Hunting, was given vectors to come down first. As Gore followed his own vectors to follow Hunting, he knew things were going to get ugly. In the *Bataan*'s Strike Operations Center, just outside of HDC, Major Don Sterling, the Strike Duty Officer, also knew that the situation was becoming critical. "Go get the CO, and send him up to the tower," Sterling ordered his assistant.

In the meantime the three jets arced through the night sky, each pilot following his individual vectors while the aircraft burned twelve to fifteen gallons of fuel per minute. Inside their cockpits the fliers anxiously watched their fuel gauges drop toward empty while they waited for their turn to land aboard the ship's pitching deck. HDC adjusted the vectors six different times as the OOD changed BRC while trying to correct for winds and avoid colliding with the two freighters.

All of this was maddening to the pilots. Darkness and blowing sand combined to bring visibility to nearly nothing, and there was no option but to focus their entire attention on flying by instruments. Trying to do otherwise would crash them into the water in less than a minute. The unfamiliar sound of sand blasting against their aircraft added to their apprehension.

Hunting was the first one down the chute. He was the most junior night-qualified pilot in the squadron and had fewer than 250 flight hours in the Harrier. This was his first deployment, and his first night approach to a ship in bad weather. Even though the ship's precision approach radar was inoperative, Chief Wood and his sailors were able to guide Hunting down toward the ship until he reached the minimum authorized descent altitude of four hundred feet. It was no good; he wasn't able to see the *Bataan*. "I was a mile and a half behind mother," recollected Gore, "when HDC asked me if I could slow down—Trout had waved off. About five seconds later I heard him come up on approach frequency and declare that he was turning downwind with emergency fuel." Gore had no way of knowing that Hunting's mouth had gone completely dry—his body's physiological preparation for an imminent ejection had left him unable to swallow.

Chief Wood studied the radar screen and realized that the situation was slipping out of control. If he didn't get those pilots aboard the ship, they were very well going to die. Below them, although they couldn't see it, the surface of the Persian Gulf was being churned into angry whitecaps. Wind gusts approaching gale force tore across the water. If the pilots ran out of fuel and had to eject, the wind would drag them across the water in their parachutes until they were beaten to death or drowned. If they managed to shuck their parachutes after hitting the water, there was little hope that an SAR helicopter would be able to find them in the furiously blowing storm. In fact, it was doubtful that the helicopter would even be able to launch. Wood grabbed the shoulder of Hunting's controller and signaled that he would personally take control of the pilot's approach.

"At that instant," Gore recalled, "I decided that I was going to use every last bit of my gas to get aboard on that pass. I knew that if I didn't . . . there would be zero fuel left for another chance." He thought of Hunting—somewhere in the wind-torn sky around him—and wished there was something he could do to help. It was difficult to focus on the task at hand knowing that his friend might not survive. Gore followed Wood's vectors toward the ship. Flying by instruments alone, he fought the urge to look out into the distance, knowing that it would be useless until he was nearly on top of the 850-foot-long ship. Over the radio Gore heard Wood direct Hicks to circle once. The chief was working to vector Hunting, who was critically low on fuel, in between Gore and Hicks.

Approaching one mile from behind the *Bataan*, Gore was already down to only 250 feet above the water. The ship was nowhere in sight, and he positioned his engine exhaust nozzles to "hover stop." This redirected the jet exhaust from almost fully aft to straight down, and rapidly decelerated the aircraft. Through the luminescent green symbology of his HUD (Heads Up Display) he could see nothing but the black-brown opaqueness that the windblown sand had made the night.

Now in the flight control tower of the *Bataan*, Lieutenant Colonel Pete Woodmansee, the CO of VMA-223, looked desperately behind the ship for the approaching Harrier. He saw nothing and briefly considered taking over the duties as the Landing Signals Officer (LSO). He rejected the notion: "I had to trust my subordinates." Like Woodmansee, Captain Mike Perez, the controlling LSO, was unable to make out Gore's aircraft through the storm that swirled overhead. After hearing Hunting wave off and disappear into the night, he pulled his night-vision goggles away from his face in frustration. They were useless in the storm. Then he was struck by an idea that was nowhere in the manual. Perez lifted the goggles back to his eyes and called for Gore to turn his landing light on. Seconds later he spotted a light well left of course and closing rapidly. It was Gore.

"At less than a half mile from the ship—while in a full braking stop—I saw a light," Gore remembered. Now only two hundred feet above the water, he heard Perez call, "Contact, you are well left of course." Taking advantage of the Harrier's unique vertical landing capabilities, Gore continued to slow and pedal-turned the nose of his aircraft thirty degrees to the right toward the faint light that was the ship. One minute later he crossed over the edge of the flight deck with only about ninety gallons of fuel remaining—enough to have kept his aircraft aloft for only a few more minutes.

Just as Gore was touching down, Hunting turned to intercept the final approach course, in front of Hicks's aircraft. He had just less than a hundred gallons of fuel remaining and was three miles from the ship. He knew he wouldn't make it if he flew a normal approach, but he also knew that Gore had landed and that there was a problem with the ship's surveillance radar. Once he got in close, he would have to look well to the right to find the *Bataan*. Hunting followed Chief Wood's heading corrections and kept his nozzles aft. By one mile he was down to 250 feet, and much faster than he normally should have been. In the control tower Mike Perez was stunned to discover from HDC that Hunting was on short radar final to the ship. He had assumed that Hicks would be next, as Hunting had to be only moments away from ejecting. Anxious to get Hunting aboard he shouted over the radio: "Turn your landing light on!" Peering through the swirling sand, Perez saw the Harrier's landing light half a mile away, well left of course, and moving too fast. "Slow down now!" Perez directed. Hunting glanced one last time at his fuel gauge and selected full braking stop, pointing his nozzles sixteen degrees forward of his wing line. The effect was similar to jumping on the brakes at high speed in a sports car; Hunting slammed forward hard against his harness and for an instant fought to maintain control of his aircraft. Illuminated by just a very few NVD-compatible lights, the deck of the ship was barely visible through the clouds of dust that ripped down its length; Hunting struggled to judge his aspect and closure to the *Bataan.* Perez shouted at Hunting two more times to slow down before the pilot finally managed to get his airspeed under control. A moment later he was aboard the ship with only fifty gallons of fuel remaining. Had he crashed, the jet wouldn't even have burned.

Major John Hicks was still out there somewhere in the sand-blown night. Having served as an instructor in the Harrier training squadron at Cherry Point, he was a very experienced pilot and as qualified as any to handle the extremes that the storm had dealt the flight. Like Gore and Hunting, Hicks came off his approach well left of course. By now, however, Perez knew where to look and what to expect. For Hicks, though, the skewed approach was a surprise; he had been on a separate frequency from Gore and Hunting and expected to spot the *Bataan* directly in front of him at any instant.

As anticipated, Perez caught sight of Hicks's landing light behind and to the left of the ship at about half a mile. He quickly directed Hicks to slow down and tried to talk the pilot's eyes onto the ship. For his part, Hicks was dumbfounded to hear Perez yelling at him when as far as he could tell he was nowhere near the ship. Still, he responded reflexively to the LSO's commands and did his best to decelerate while being careful to keep from settling into the water.

On the flight deck of the *Bataan* the SAR helicopter's rotor blades were spinning. The helicopter pilots and the rescue swimmer had listened with elation as Gore and Hunting completed their landings. They knew that launching to find one of these pilots in the water might easily turn into a one-way trip for them as well. Nevertheless, while listening to Hicks's approach the mood turned grim. If Hicks ejected, the Navy pilots were going to launch. They all knew the risks but would never let a man die while they remained safe aboard the ship.

Under Perez's direct control, Hicks slowed to a hover from a quarter mile abeam the ship. It was a position completely out of normal parameters and one that would never have been accepted during normal conditions. These conditions were hardly normal. Still not realizing that the ship was ninety degrees to his right, Hicks struggled to maintain his spatial awareness. With no visual reference points, no horizon, and no ability to see the water beneath him, he was in big trouble and he knew it. It was while he was struggling to find the ship that his jet began drifting backward and started to fall toward the water. "Power! Power! Power!" Perez shouted into the radio. Woodmansee, directly behind him, could hardly bear to watch. Jolted by the LSO's calls, the SAR helicopter's commander called to his rescue swimmer over the intercom. "Get ready," he said, expecting Hicks to eject at any second. Looking over his shoulder, the pilot saw that the swimmer already had his mask down and snorkel in.

Then Hicks caught sight of the ship. With less than 110 gallons of fuel left, and burning almost forty gallons per minute, he didn't know if he could close the distance to the ship in time. In exasperation he radioed: "I see you, but I can't get there from here." At only one hundred feet above the waves, the transition from instrument flight to visual flight had nearly paralyzed him. Still, he overcame his vertigo and air-taxied his jet sideways to the flight deck.

With the last jet on deck Mike Perez slumped back into his chair. He was soaked through in sweat—absolutely exhausted. Down in the HDC, Chief Wood also collapsed into his seat. *I'm too old for this shit*, he thought.

Operating at the very edge of their limitations the pilots of the three Harriers, the *Bataan*'s Chief Wood and his controllers, and LSO Mike Perez saved three jets valued at more than a hundred million dollars. Less than a month later Chief Wood and his two controllers were awarded the Navy Achievement Medal for their role in saving the Harrier pilots. In May 2004 Captain Hunting was awarded an Air Medal for the composure he maintained, under extreme duress, in saving his jet. It was nothing that would make the news. It was nothing the public would ever learn.

The recovery of the three aircraft was indeed a remarkable effort. Nevertheless, accidents did occur. Three weeks later, on April 1, an AV-8B went into the water while trying to land aboard the *Nassau*. Fortunately the pilot survived the ejection and was rescued with only minor injuries. This made the news.

6

Cobras in the Attack

President Bush's deadline passed. Early on the morning of March 20—the evening of March 19 in Washington, D.C.—a series of missiles and bombs struck Iraq. It was an attempt by U.S. forces to personally target Saddam Hussein. It failed to kill the Iraqi president, but it was the start of the campaign that would topple him from power. The strike began a sequence of events that forced the campaign's timetable forward; commanders all over the theater frantically hurried to adjust their plans.

A series of chest-rattling booms roared across Ali Al Salem Air Base on the morning of March 20 as Patriot missiles exploded out of their launchers and streaked off to intercept targets hurtling down from the northwest. The Patriots were successful; none of the enemy rockets found its mark. Lieutenant Colonel Steve "Woodman" Heywood and his flight of four AH-1W Cobra gunships, already circling to the east, were sent to investigate the point where one of the Iraqi SCUDs had exploded in the desert only a few miles away. Even before he got the flight pointed toward the crater his orders changed and he was instructed to divert his helicopters to Ahmed Al Jaber Air Base; the threat of more inbound rockets made it too dangerous to operate around Al Salem. With just barely enough fuel to reach the other airfield Heywood wheeled the flight around and headed south. It was fifteen minutes later when, closely followed by the three other helicopters, he finally set down at Al Jaber in a whirling shroud of dust. The landing marked the end of one of the most frustrating sorties of his career. As the commanding officer of HMLA-267 he would see many more during the next few weeks.

Heywood recalled how the mission had begun: "We were getting trained on a new survival radio late that same morning when the call came that the MEF headquarters was under terrorist attack and that they wanted Cobras overhead ASAP." The order seemed a bit bizarre to the squadron commander, but nevertheless he collected his copilot, Captain "Vinny" Burton, and three other crews and put together a quick brief. Within minutes they had a game plan. Heywood grabbed the new survival radio and his M4 carbine and led his crews to the flight line.

"My plane captains," recounted Heywood, "beat us out to the birds and had us turning and ready to go in record time." After getting airborne the flight joined quickly, despite the worsening weather, and headed northeast to Camp Coyote to provide the cover that the MEF had requested. Heywood was stymied in his efforts to establish communications with any controlling agency—there appeared to be no one minding the store. Once overhead the MEF headquarters there didn't seem to be anything out of the ordinary going on—and he still couldn't contact anyone. He remembered: "Finally we saw that the Kuwaiti Defense Forces and the Marines had several prisoners rounded up near the main entrance. Other than that, everything appeared normal." A few minutes later the flight made contact with the Tactical Air Operations Center (TAOC) and were sent on a series of goose chases that saw them ultimately landing at Al Jaber.

Shortly after setting down at the other base, Heywood was out of his aircraft and debriefing with his crews. A veteran of operations in northern Iraq immediately after Desert Storm, and Somalia a couple of years later, he cautioned the younger pilots in the flight. "I told them to get used to it. Confusion and the inability to communicate were the norm rather than the exception." Across the runway more than two hundred fighter and attack jets were crowded together, ready for war. Heywood felt a bit self-conscious; his light, spidery helicopters seemed oddly out of place. Regardless, one fuel truck and one SCUD alert later, he led his flight airborne again and arrived back at Ali Al Salem late in the afternoon. Frustrated by the day's events, he still expected to lead his squadron into combat that very evening, shortly before midnight.

Heywood hadn't been back at Ali Al Salem very long when he had the squadron assembled for a quick briefing and pep talk. Most of them had spent the day in and out of gas masks, as the SCUD alerts had been nearly continuous. Now it was time to give his Marines an overview of how their Cobras would be put into the battle. "I explained the plan in broad terms, outlining how our Marines would attack from east to west; I told them that our squadron's pilots would be the first to cross the border in order to take out the enemy's OPs [Observation Posts]."

The elimination of these OPs was crucial to the success of the initial push into Iraq. Unmolested, the Iraqi soldiers who manned them would be able to call deadly accurate artillery fire onto the masses of men and equipment that were queued up that very moment, ready to charge through the cuts in the high earthen berms that separated Kuwait from Iraq. A concentrated bombardment would kill hundreds—or even thousands—of Marines.

"I reminded them to listen to their leaders and to understand that this wasn't a game or training any longer. I also told them to be careful—that getting hurt in a senseless accident would do no one any good. Finally, I told them that if I—or any of the others—did not make it back that they were to keep working hard to accomplish their mission." After dismissing his people Heywood couldn't help but feeling some pride as his unit's noncommissioned officers—the backbone of the squadron—set about getting the younger Marines organized and hard at work.

Eager to get a quick meal and a situation brief from the MAG's operations shop, he couldn't help but feel bothered when his cell phone rang. "It was Woody Lowe," he remembered—Lieutenant Colonel Brad Lowe, the MAG operations officer. "He said, 'Just go, man, just go!' I asked him what he was talking about and he said that the First Marine Division was going to shoot the breach early and that the OPs needed to be taken out immediately."

The ensuing scramble was almost a mirror image of the morning's chaotic rush. But because the mission called for sixteen aircraft rather than four, it was a much more frenzied event. "This was it—the real thing," Heywood recalled. "As I walked to my aircraft I came across my dear friend Jim Braden, the CO of HMLA-169. I had known Jim and his wife for twenty-one years—we had started in the Marine Corps together. After we shook hands and wished each other luck I said a little prayer, hoping that he would make it through the first night."

Heywood drew comfort from the fact that his own mission was one that the squadron had briefed and practiced several times already. Because the OPs were so close to the border, the practice flights had been exact replicas of the planned attack—except that the crews hadn't actually shot their weapons. "After we got our engines online everyone checked in on cue," Heywood recalled. "That didn't happen without a lot of backbreaking work—my maintenance Marines had done an outstanding job." Still, the commander couldn't help but wonder if some of his crews were taking aircraft that were less than perfect. His pilots were hard chargers, and the temptation to launch with a sick airplane would be difficult to resist.

In short order Heywood was airborne and at the head of the most powerful column of aircraft he had ever led. The flight was divided into four smaller flights of three aircraft each—two Cobras and one Huey. A fifth flight was made up of three Cobras and a spare Huey. Each of the flights was charged with destroying a single OP. The Cobras were armed with precision-guided TOW (Tube-Launched Opti-cally-Tracked Wire-Guided) and Hellfire missiles, as well as 2.75-inch rockets and a 20-millimeter cannon. The Hueys also carried rockets, as well as a .50-caliber heavy machine gun and a GAU-17 minigun. The minigun was capable of spewing out more than four thousand 7.62-millimeter rounds per minute and so was particularly effective at keeping enemy troops pinned down. The Hueys also had the potential to act as rescue ships; this provided some small measure of comfort to the crewmen as they pressed ahead on their first mission of the war.

"As powerful a feeling as it was to lead that much firepower into combat," Heywood said, "I still knew that the mission had the poten-tial to go bad quickly." An entire career in tactical aviation and the fresh memory of the morning's abortive flight led him to that in-evitable conclusion. Too, he knew that if he and his own Marines were scrambling to catch up to the hastily adjusted timeline, then ev-eryone else in Kuwait was flailing as well. Rushed as the situation was, there was no way that all the pieces were going to come together perfectly.

The visibility had deteriorated badly, to less than a mile in haze. Heywood recalled: "The weather was so bad that if there hadn't been so many Marines at risk, I would have scrubbed the entire thing—it was that dangerous to fly." Still, clattering along just a hundred feet above the desert, the train of gunships charged ahead at a hundred knots. From the front cockpit of his aircraft Heywood cycled through multiple frequencies trying to raise the DASC (Direct Air Support Center) in order to get an intelligence update, and perhaps to coor-dinate his strike with the F/A-18s that were originally scheduled as part of the overall mission. His calls were answered by nothing but static. On his tactical frequency he heard the individual flights from his column calling out that they were peeling off to prosecute their individual objectives. "Still unable to get any direction from the DASC," he recalled, "I told them to press on and kill their targets."

Heywood's copilot, Burton, would do most of the flying from the rear cockpit while his commander concentrated on leading the mission. The second Cobra was commanded by Captain Aaron "Jimmy" Marx, while the Huey's crew was led by Captain Lonnie "Cheevo" Camacho. Nearing the border, the flight flew over the endless rows of vehicles that were lined up to smash into Iraq. "Marines were standing on top of their tanks and AAVs [Assault Amphibian Vehicles], and LAVs [Light Armored Vehicles]. We could see them yelling and waving and cheering us on. It was a sight that I'll never forget. They knew what we were there to do for them. For our part, we knew that from that very moment they wouldn't be stopping until they reached Baghdad. Behind me I heard Vinny say 'Good luck, boys.' " Seconds later, like airborne cavalry, the crews of the two Cobras and the single Huey disappeared beyond the view of their earthbound brothers.

For their part, the men and women of the First Marine Division were ready to move. They had by now received Major General Mattis's message—the one that would see them off to battle. One portion called out their need to have trust and conviction in the Marines who were overhead at that very moment, and who would continue to protect them through the fight:

> You are part of the world's most feared and trusted force. Engage your brain before you engage your weapon. Share your courage with each other as we enter the uncertain terrain north of the Line of Departure. Keep faith in your comrades on your left and right and Marine Air overhead. Fight with a happy heart and a strong spirit.

Before the war, one of the chief fears of the Coalition's planners had been that the Iraqis would set fire to the immense petroleum infrastructure that laced much of the southern part of the country. One reason for that trepidation was the massive ecological damage that the torched wells and lines and processing stations would cause. More than a decade after the event, Kuwait and the northern reaches of the

Persian Gulf had still not recovered from the environmental holo-
caust the Iraqis had created during Desert Storm in 1991. Another
factor that concerned the Coalition was the expense that would be in-
curred in rebuilding a sabotaged petroleum producing, processing,
and transportation network. Reconstruction costs aside, the loss of
revenues would be staggering to the Iraqi people. But regardless of
the environmental and financial considerations, the factor that was
troubling Heywood and his gunships most on this night was the fire
and smoke that limited their visibility to near nothing.

"It was incredibly smoky," the commander remembered. "And the
huge fires from torched wells and burning lines created blanking
lines across my FLIR video screen." Through the roiling smoke, he
led the flight to the IP, or Initial Point; it was an oil-producing complex on the Kuwaiti side of the border. Whereas during their practices
they had been able to pick up their target at long range, now they
could not. There was no choice but to make a slow run toward the target and hope to pick it out of the murk—despite the risk to the flight.
"I simply trusted that the enemy was having as much trouble seeing
as we were," recounted Heywood.

Picking up a heading of fifty degrees, the three ships felt their way
through the black smog that shrouded their route. Heywood squinted
into his sensors, desperate to pick out a target that defied detection.
Burton called from the rear seat, "Sir, we're in Iraq now." Heywood
responded, "I know," and punctuated the statement with a nod and a
thumbs-up.

Finally Heywood located a blob on his Forward Looking Infra Red
that appeared to be the target. He hit it with a burst of laser energy
from the sensor's built-in range finder, but the effort was wasted. The
smoke and dust rendered the laser useless, and Heywood couldn't
confirm that what he was looking at was actually the target. In frustration, and no longer sure of where the target should be, Heywood
signaled the rest of the flight to reset back across the border into
Kuwait.

The squadron commander rechecked his chart against his surroundings, no longer willing to put all of his trust in the Cobra's state-

of-the-art GPS navigation system. At the same time, he fought the vertigo and disorientation brought on by looking from the green-black glow of his sensors, through his night-vision goggles to the fires burning in the dark outside, and back to his map. Nevertheless he confirmed that the formation was in the correct position and set up for another run at the target.

The three gunships closed to less than two miles from the OP when Marx, in the other Cobra, called out that he had the target in sight. Heywood immediately cleared him to fire and an instant later a forty-thousand-dollar Hellfire missile arced away from the gunship in a brilliant trail of fire, and then just as violently slammed itself into the ground, thrown off course by the laser scatter caused by the dust and smoke. "So much for shock and awe," Heywood recalled. Ever the optimist, Marx sent another Hellfire into the air; this one guided to a direct hit on one of the buildings in the OP complex.

Simultaneously Heywood caught sight of a large flash to the north of their position; the Iraqis were firing artillery at them. Burton wrapped the helicopter around in a hard left turn away from the target while also firing flares to decoy any shoulder-launched SAMs that might have been targeting them. With the OP marked by the Hellfire that Marx had fired into the compound, the three ships separated for individual firing runs, coordinating their efforts over the radio.

Frustrated at having made two separate runs without having fired a shot, Heywood selected a wire-guided missile. The TOW was an older weapon but not dependent on laser energy for guidance. Again, Heywood's attempt was botched when the missile failed to fire. Despite all the closely choreographed training that he and his squadron had put themselves through, the fog of war was proving their match.

Burton swung the aircraft around for their fourth attempt. Choosing the easternmost building in the compound, and flying in from the south, Heywood sent the TOW rocketing through the dark. He had to hold the missile-guiding crosshairs on the building for only a very short time. The TOW smashed into it with a terrific blast. "Chunks of bricks and other material went flying several hundred meters into the desert," he remembered.

For the next five minutes the three helicopters savaged the OP like airborne sharks after blooded prey. "I looked up over my shoulder," said Heywood, "and there was Jimmy just pummeling the target with 2.75-inch rockets. And as we spun around for another run Cheevo brought his Huey in. His crew chiefs were hammering the area with their minigun at four thousand rounds per minute as well as with the heavy .50-caliber machine gun."

Heywood cleared Burton to attack the compound with the 2.75-inch fléchette rockets that were nestled in the pods slung underneath their helicopter's stub wings. These were nasty weapons; they were designed so that—just before impact—they would explode and send twenty-two hundred individual metal darts flying at bullet-like speed. For obvious reasons they were particularly deadly against troops in the open. Burton rippled seven of the rockets into the complex at close range. The scene was like something from the apocalypse. Everything was ablaze—even the ground burned in places. Streaks of tracer rounds lashed out from the helicopters, and oil fires punctuated the black, shadowy gloom of the surrounding landscape. The shroud of dust and smoke in combination with the flames that burned in every direction made it all take on a hellish, orange-red cast.

Then, incredibly, Heywood's ship began to take fire from within the OP; someone inside was still alive. White tracers raced down the left side of his aircraft. Not only was someone in the compound still alive and well enough to fire a heavy gun, but he also had the guts to do it! Burton reacted instantaneously and racked the Cobra into a hard right turn. At the same time, still more surprised than anything else, Heywood sprayed the area with the aircraft's three-barreled 20-millimeter cannon. Camacho's crew in the Huey followed up the cannon fire with machine-gun rounds. The stream of enemy tracers ceased.

With the enemy gunner killed—or at least suppressed—the greatest risk was the danger of a midair collision, or perhaps the threat of shooting one another down. In for another run, Heywood and Burton had to hold their fire, because Camacho's crew in the Huey was in their way. Unable to shoot, they pulled away from the target. "I looked up," recalled Heywood, "just in time to see us fly right through a burning forest of natural gas blow-off pipes. Fortunately Vinny missed them and we didn't catch fire."

Now scarcely more than forty minutes since Heywood had led his squadron airborne, there was only one building left standing in the target area. From less than a mile away he sent another TOW missile hurtling after it. Behind him he heard a half-whispered chant. "Oh, come on, baby . . . come on." It was Burton, urging the missile downrange. The TOW smashed into the structure and detonated with a ferocity that blew the building into smithereens. A cloud of fire reached five hundred or more feet into the sky. "Clearly, that place was being used as an ammunition storage point," Heywood deadpanned.

There was little left of the OP that merited any more attention. Almost desultorily, the three gunships blasted the rest of their ammunition into the fire and debris that marked what was left of the compound. Finally Heywood called off the attack and rejoined his three-ship formation across the border in Kuwait. Together again, they flew past the wreckage one more time in order to extract BDA (Battle Damage Assessment) for the intelligence debrief. With that pass complete, Heywood turned the formation toward its assigned FARP (Forward Arming and Refueling Point) and started to check in the rest of his squadron over the radio.

The campaign had just begun. It had been a very long day.

7

Hornets Get into the Fight

The campaign's kickoff had been a frenzied reaction to a muddled mess for Heywood's Cobra squadron. Farther south, the war wasn't getting off to a clean start at Al Jaber, either. Ross "Migs" Roberts was the Commanding Officer of VMFA(AW)-533, a two-seat F/A-18D squadron. He and the squadron operations officer—Major John "JP" Farnam—were supposed to be airborne as part of the scheduled kickoff at 0300 on March 21. "I was in the rack [sleeping] when the first SCUD alert sounded at around 1130 on March 20," he recalled. Roberts leapt out of his cot and tore open the packaging that held his bulky NBC (Nuclear Biological Chemical) suit. The rest of his squadron, spread across the air base, was doing the same. This was a standing procedure; U.S. forces were not going to be caught unprepared in the event that the Iraqis opted to use chemical weapons.

After what seemed an eternity but was actually only a minute or so Roberts had struggled into his NBC suit, mask, gloves, and boots and clomped over to a bunker accompanied by Farnam. Through it all, a female voice droned into the basewide loudspeaker: "This is not a drill, this is not a drill." Crammed into the bunker, Roberts and Farnam hunkered down with a dozen or more other Marines. It was an odd feeling; he probably knew every one of the other men in the bunker with him, but encased as all of them were in the black rubber masks and the rest of the awkward ensemble that made up their protective NBC gear, he couldn't have named a single one.

"We were all huddled in there, kind of staring at each other, when the all-clear sounded about an hour later." Immediately Roberts and the rest of the Marines reached up and pulled off their masks. After breathing through the masks, even the dusty air in the sandbagged shelter seemed refreshing. Roberts didn't delay long in the bunker. "I grabbed JP and we ran over to the MAG headquarters to see what was going on."

Like all of the leadership—up and down the chain—the command at the MAG was trying to react to various issues that often were at odds. Not least of them was the question of what to do with the aircraft and troops when a SCUD alert was sounded. For some, it made sense to get the aircraft airborne and out of harm's way. On the other hand, the short warning time that usually accompanied a SCUD launch meant that the jets could hardly get aloft before the enemy missile hit—unless the aircraft were manned full-time at the end of the runway. There was also the considerable risk to the Marines on the flight line in the event that the Patriot anti-missile defenses were penetrated and the base was actually hit.

Roberts and Farnam left the MAG with no clear direction and headed to the ramp where the squadron's aircraft were parked. "On my own initiative I took JP to the flight line—we were going to man a bird in case the order to launch was given. The MAG had four aircraft per squadron loaded with live weapons for this contingency. We had no sooner gotten into our flight gear when the alarm was sounded again." It was another SCUD alert. Everyone in the air group was getting frustrated as simply the threat of an enemy missile attack had essentially brought operations aboard the base to a halt.

The two fliers spent another hour in another bunker, this one on the flight line. Saddam had yet to hit Ahmed Al Jaber Air Base, and already the situation bordered on chaos. "I was getting exasperated,"

Roberts recollected. "JP and I went back to the MAG and found the CO, Colonel [Randy] 'Tex' Alles, and his operations officer, Lieutenant Colonel [Kevin] 'Wolfie' Iiams. I suggested that, in this situation, fighters airborne were better than fighters on the deck." Alles disagreed with Roberts. He believed that shotgunning his jets into the air every time there was an alert was counterproductive and dangerous. He informed Roberts that during the confusion of the morning's SCUD alert several of the jets that had been airborne had landed dangerously low on fuel. They had circled overhead waiting for a clearance to land that almost didn't come; the Marines who manned the tower were in a bunker.

It was while this discussion was going on that the MAG received a call from the First Marine Division's Air Officer (AO), Lieutenant Colonel Bruce "Iron" Shank. There was information that seventy to eighty Iraqi T-72 tanks were moving into position just beyond the earthen berm that demarcated the northern boundary between Kuwait and Iraq. The enemy tanks were supposedly digging in exactly opposite of where RCT-7 was scheduled to breach the border. If the report was true and the division was caught in a trap, the entire plan ran the risk of coming apart before it even began.

Roberts recounted: "I already had one crew on standby alert with their engines turning. Captains Jason "Flamer" Pratt and Lance "Puny" Muniz were ready to go. I recommended that we get them airborne to verify the report and Tex agreed. We gave them a quick brief over the radio and launched them. Then Tex turned to me and said, 'Well, what are *you* waiting for?' "

It was all the prompting Roberts needed. Less than a minute later he and Farnam were racing toward the flight line. "Once we got our engines up and running we realized that in all the confusion we didn't have a callsign or an IFF squawk assigned," recalled Roberts. Both were important from a command and control standpoint in order to let everyone know who they were and what their mission was. Not to be stymied by a technicality, Farnam dug up a bogus callsign and Identification Friend or Foe (IFF) squawk from the previous day's schedule, and the two fliers roared airborne. It was the tactical aviation equivalent of bullying past the maître d' at a fine restaurant.

Loaded with four Mk-20 cluster bomb munitions and eight 5-inch rockets, the F/A-18D's crew checked in with the DASC. It was the DASC's mission to track and direct air traffic to the ground units that needed supporting. On this day the DASC was just as confused as the rest of the air wing. Not sure of what Roberts and Farnam were doing, the DASC directed the two fliers to proceed to a CAS "stack" and await further instructions. It seemed that the center had not been informed of the Iraqi tank division that was reported to be on the other side of the berm.

Roberts wasn't having any of it: "The entire ground scheme of maneuver called for us to be out in front of the division looking for the enemy—not holding inside of Kuwait." In the two-seat F/A-18D, the backseater—or WSO—runs the radios. Roberts remembered: "I told JP to do what we always did when the DASC turned itself a speed bump. We just 'rogered' their instructions and pressed on with what needed to be done." The crew started a descent and contacted Bruce Shank, the division's Air Officer. It had been Shank whom they had been talking with in the MAG headquarters only a short time earlier.

"Iron asked us to search Highways 6 and 8 directly to his front, and then to look to the north along the highway that connects Umm Qasr and Basrah," Roberts said. It was getting late in the afternoon, and haze and smoke from the oil fires that were burning to the north made visibility poor. "We searched the roads twice and saw nothing—not even a car." Pratt and Muniz—who had launched before Roberts and Farnam—had also come up empty-handed. To their west the two airmen could make out the brilliant smoke trails that marked the paths of multiple volleys of U.S. Army ATACMS (Army Tactical Missile System) missiles. Flying through their trajectory could have resulted in disaster, but the Marines were well to the east of where the missiles were ripping through the sky. Roberts and Farnam pressed on, intent on finding the Iraqi armored unit.

Just as the sun was about to drop below the horizon they spotted a column of sixteen armored vehicles stopped on an overpass on RCT-7's route of advance. "JP," remembered Roberts, "did his magic radio stuff and got in touch with the division and the various RCTs to ensure that none of our guys had crossed into Iraq. We talked personally to Bruce Shank again and he was confident that none of the grunts had pushed past the LOD [Line of Departure]. JP then contacted RCT-7's FSC [Fire Support Center] and asked them to confirm that there were no friendly units at the coordinates where we had found the armored column." The situation was still unclear, and the DASC declared the vehicles friendly. Not confident that anyone knew exactly what was going on, Roberts and Farnam headed toward the Iraqi city of Al Basrah to scout for enemy artillery units. Minutes later RCT-7 came back on the net and pronounced that the armored vehicles were positively hostile. Farnam responded: "You better be damn sure because we're going to kill them all." RCT-7 reiterated the declaration.

"All along," Roberts continued, "we were complying with the altitude restrictions that the wing had developed and we were having no luck identifying the vehicle types from where we were at ten thousand feet." Farnam, in the rear cockpit, captured the lead portion of the column on the FLIR pod. Following the cueing that the FLIR displayed on his Heads Up Display, Roberts winged over to the west and dived toward the armored vehicles. There was no sign of enemy fire.

Only seconds earlier he had programmed the aircraft's weapons system to select two of the Mk-20 Rockeye cluster bombs that were slung under the jet's wings. The Rockeye canister is designed to separate into two halves prior to hitting the ground. When Roberts's Rockeyes came apart, they would each spread a wide-ranging, deadly shower of more than two hundred small, armor-piercing bomblets. Checking for the last time that his master armament switch was on, Roberts mashed down on the control stick's red bomb release button with his right thumb. Only a second or two later as he guided the aircraft into the proper parameters the jet automatically released the two bombs.

Roberts remembered: "We pulled off target, rolled left, and watched for the hits as we climbed back up above ten thousand feet." Instead of the football-field-sized pattern of sparkling explosions he expected, there were two sharp flashes approximately a hundred feet south of his aim point. The Rockeye canisters had failed to open.

It was vexing in the extreme.

"JP backed me up," Roberts said, "and we rechecked our system and delivery parameters to make sure that we hadn't screwed anything up." They hadn't. Farnam found the targets with the FLIR again—it was almost dark now—and Roberts dropped the nose of the Hornet down for another run at the enemy armor. "This time one of the canisters opened and we had effects on one of the vehicles. The other missed."

The only weapons that Roberts and Farnam had remaining were 5-inch rockets and the 20-millimeter cannon. These are primarily daytime weapons—unguided—and require that the pilot visually aim them in order to have any effect. Still, with no other option in the smoky dusk, the two Marines decided to make their attacks using the FLIR. Once more Farnam put the targeting diamond of the FLIR over a set of enemy vehicles. Roberts made two runs and shot all eight rockets; their motors burned a brilliant violet-white in the dim light. Each time the rockets went wide. It was later discovered that the FLIR was not properly "boresighted" to the aircraft. It was akin to trying to shoot straight with a rifle that had a bent gun sight. Nevertheless, Roberts and Farnam didn't give up easily. They made two more runs and sprayed the area with the aircraft's 20-millimeter cannon.

The confusion and bad fortune that had been their figurative wing men all day were still in tight formation. Although they were out of weapons, they could still serve as an airborne Forward Air Controller, or FAC(A), and bring other aircraft in to hit the target. "But we were getting low on gas," Roberts said, "and there were no tankers airborne. The DASC was still in reaction mode like everyone else and evidently there weren't any aircraft available that could continue to prosecute these targets anyway." The pair had no good options. They passed the position of the enemy armor column to the DASC and returned to Ahmed Al Jaber.

After landing uneventfully and parking their jet Roberts and Farnam climbed down onto the ramp to be greeted by many of the squadron's Marines, who were eager to hear how the mission had gone. "The first Marine to meet us was Sergeant Anderson, our plane captain," remembered Roberts. "He was anxious to find out what we had hit. I wished that I could have given him a more positive report."

The crew found out that the Marines working the flight line had been in and out of the bunkers three separate times while they were airborne. Now that they were out again they were excited and angry and wanted to know if Roberts and Farnam "had kicked some Iraqi ass." The crowd of Marines continued to press the two fliers for more information. Roberts reached inside his "nav bag" and pulled out his chart of southern Iraq. He dropped to a knee as he spread it out on the concrete. With Farnam shining his flashlight on the map, Roberts gave his Marines an impromptu debrief of the entire mission—warts and all. He was obviously displeased with the way the sortie had gone, and he could see the disappointment in the faces of the young men gathered around him. He recalled: "I could see that they were unhappy. They worked their hearts out every day so that I could do my job. Morale in a squadron moves up and down based upon the success of the aircrews." As the squadron commander—or "the Old Man"—Roberts was especially aware of their frustration. It stuck in him like a wooden knife.

Following the recap, Roberts and Farnam made their way to the MAG headquarters tent. Finding Tex, Roberts and Farnam recounted what they had found, and Tex directed them to report their mission to the Tactical Air Command Center (TACC) a few yards away. Roberts and Farnam found the atmosphere inside the command center calm but tense. Roberts recounted: "Major General Amos was there and waiting, as were Colonels Miclot, Sawyers, and Fox—all key players in the wing's operations. They were stern-faced—apprehensive about the prospect of our Marines running into the mysterious Republican Guard tank division." Amos, the wing commander, was working his chewing gum hard as Roberts and Farnam laid out a chart and reviewed the mission they had just flown. They pointed out that the steadily worsening visibility caused by the burning oil fires would make locating the tank division even more difficult. As to whether or not the Iraqi tanks even existed, Amos said that Mattis had emphasized that the original report came from a credible source.

The small group continued their discussions as they pored over the map. Areas where the Iraqis might be hiding, either in locations that Roberts and Farnam hadn't overflown, or in areas that were obscured by smoke, were given particular scrutiny. "There was some concern as to what effect the smoke might have on our laser-guided ordnance—Mavericks, Hellfires, and LGBs," Roberts recollected. If it was too thick, it would keep the precision weapons from guiding to their targets. On the other hand, it would also be difficult to use the more traditional free-fall or dumb bombs if the aircrews couldn't even see the enemy. A decision was made to arm most of the aircraft with unguided ordnance. A few aircraft would stay loaded with thousand-pound GBU-16s; they would stay on alert to drop a bridge to the north of the division's advance in the event that the Iraqis attempted to attack or reinforce from that direction.

As the consultation wound down, Amos reported that the wing had already recorded its first "blue on blue" (friendly-fire incident). An AH-1W Cobra from HMLA-169 had hit a Marine M1A1 tank just inside the northern Kuwaiti border. Roberts and Farnam collected their notes and exited. This was hardly the decisive, hard-hitting start to the aerial campaign that had been hoped for. But it was already in the past. And although the carefully plotted script was in disarray, the Marines on the ground were still being protected and supported from above. It could have been worse.

After his mission against the border OPs, Lieutenant Colonel Steve Heywood led his flight to the Astrodome FARP in north-central Kuwait. (All the FARPs were named for major-league baseball stadiums—one of the planners was a baseball nut.) The horrendous visibility made him feel fortunate that all the crews had been able to land without incident. Now, only hours after the start of the war, the newly adjusted plan called for his squadron to continue the fight through the night in support of the Regimental Combat Teams. However, smoke and worsening weather made that course of action seem un-likely.

"The wind was blowing out of the west-northwest," Heywood re-membered. "The stuff that was rolling over our heads—oily smoke and dust and fog—was like black cotton. If I could have reached high enough, I think I could have torn pieces off of it." After checking on the status of his crews and their aircraft, he used his Iridium satellite telephone to make contact with Major Woody Lowe at the MAG-39 operations center. Lowe was busy trying to gather information about the friendly-fire incident; it wasn't clear yet what had happened. Hey-wood reassured Lowe that his flight hadn't fired on any tanks.

"Aside from finding out who had shot up the tank," Heywood said, "Woody was anxious to get us airborne again to help out the grunts." Requests from the RCTs were coming in, and Cobra support was at the top of the list. Heywood was torn. He would never have launched in similar weather during peacetime, and he questioned if it was truly worth the risk at that moment. Because the Iridium wasn't encrypted, Heywood and Lowe couldn't talk about what was going on at the bor-der except in generalities, but Heywood made the decision to stay on the ground until the weather improved.

Two more calls came in over the Iridium: The grunts needed help. Despite the atrocious flying conditions, Heywood reluctantly changed his mind and grabbed a copilot and two more Cobra crews. After a quick brief they manned up, started their engines, and checked in over the radio. Heywood looked up at the oily scum that was passing only about a hundred feet over their heads and second-guessed his judgment one more time. He had thousands of hours of flight time, and the conditions were well beyond bad enough to give him pause; he could only imagine what the younger pilots he was about to lead into that goop were thinking.

"I had Jon Livingston on the controls in the front cockpit for this sortie," Heywood said. "I wanted him to fly because I wanted to keep an eye on the rest of the flight and coordinate our communications with the grunts." Heywood gave the command to lift off; at 2220 Liv-ingston got the aircraft airborne and transitioned to forward flight.

They had hardly gone half a mile when Livingston became badly disoriented in the swirling black smog.

"I've got vertigo—really bad," Livingston called over the intercom.

"Okay," Heywood answered. "Get on the instruments and just try to fly yourself out of it."

"No, I mean . . . I can't even fly the aircraft."

"I've got the controls." Heywood grabbed his set of flight controls.

"Roger, you've got the controls."

They had handled the situation by the book. Nevertheless, as soon as he began to fly the aircraft Heywood started to wrestle with the same vertigo that had nearly overwhelmed Livingston. It took every bit of his training and experience to set up an inside–outside scan that double-checked what little he could see through his night-vision goggles against what the instrumentation in his cockpit was telling him. Once, twice, three times the warning from his radar altimeter sounded, alerting him that he was too close to the ground. Each time he lifted the aircraft away from the desert floor only to settle back toward it again. On each side of the gunship his two wingmen stayed tucked into formation as best they could.

Heywood turned the flight north along the east side of the main highway toward the RCTs, clustered along the border. "We were basically doing the Helen Keller thing," he recalled, "only making about fifty or sixty knots and hoping not to run into anything while we felt our way along." A thin sliver of moon reflected against the airborne sludge and made visibility through their night-vision goggles worse rather than better. After a short time the crews were able to make out flashes to their front where Eleventh Marines was putting preparatory fires downrange in front of the RCTs.

The bright flashes from the guns illuminated what looked to be a solid wall at the border. Heywood didn't believe it was possible, but the choking black miasma they were chopping their way through was getting thicker. "By this time," he remembered, "I was totally task-saturated. I couldn't raise anyone on the radios and it was all I could do to keep from flying the aircraft into the dirt." Just prior to the border he eased his helicopter into a gentle left-hand turn.

Heywood weighed the risks of continuing against what little help his flight may have been able to provide the Marines on the ground. The Marines would have to do without his Cobras. "I made one of the hard decisions that I get paid for," Heywood said. "I was taking the flight back." As the flight leader he was responsible for completing the mission, but not at the expense of four aircraft and eight crewmen. And certainly not when it was doubtful that he would have been able to see well enough to help anyway.

Heywood felt twice blessed when the last aircraft in his formation landed safely back at Astrodome.

It was just past 0130 on March 21 when the Commanding Officer of MAG-39, Colonel Rich Spencer, received the latest intelligence update: Enemy resistance on the Al Faw Peninsula was expected to be fierce. The report indicated that the Air Force AC-130 gunship assigned to prep the Landing Zone (LZ) had stayed on station longer than scheduled, as the defending Iraqis were more firmly entrenched than predicted. Despite the pounding the gunship had dealt the enemy positions, there was concern that they hadn't been hit hard enough. Spencer would have to discover the truth for himself when he got there. Around him he could see Marines making final preparations as the helicopters—sourced from several different air groups—were readied for the mission. In a very short time he would be leading a flight of more than forty aircraft on the largest Marine Corps combat lift since Vietnam.

However, the troops that the Marine Corps was taking into battle that very early morning were not U.S. Marines. Rather, they were Royal Marines from the United Kingdom led by Lieutenant Colonel Buster Howe. Marines from both services had been planning and rehearsing the mission for several weeks. What had started as a company-sized insertion to capture a few key oil pumping stations had evolved into the operation that was about to unfold: When the helicopters touched down and the Royal Marines leapt out onto the desert, they would be charged with sweeping across the Al Faw Peninsula to the edge of Al Basrah. Now, despite the worsening weather, they were anxious to get airborne and start their part of the war.

Spencer was a Cobra pilot by training and would be leading the mission from the command and control ship—an HMLA-169 Huey piloted by Lieutenant Colonel Jim Braden, the commander of that unit. Spencer was in the main cabin, from which he could best monitor the mission's progress with the specially configured communications suite that had been installed just for this effort. At Spencer's side was the Royal Marine commander, Lieutenant Colonel Howe. The formation was made up of every helicopter type in the Marine Corps inventory: There were sixteen CH-46Es, ten CH-53Es, twelve AH-1Ws, and four UH-1s. Many of the ships—particularly the beloved CH-46E "Frogs"—were veterans of the war in Southeast Asia. Now the aged birds squatted in the dirt, their rotor blades drooping languidly in the dark. The aluminum skin that was riveted to their aluminum frames was patched and seemed to sag in places. The venerable aircraft looked every bit their age.

A few minutes before 0200 the last of the Royal Marines were aboard and the helicopters whirled to life. Their once floppy blades spun themselves into shadowy discs, and a cloud of dust whipped overhead the massive formation. Inside each cockpit the pilots completed their checklists while the gunners and crew chiefs readied their weapons and gave the aircraft their final inspections. For their part, the Royal Marines double-checked and rechecked that their personal gear was strapped into place and that they would be ready for combat the instant they bounded from the helicopters.

It would be a short flight from where they were staged in northeast Kuwait to the Al Faw Peninsula. Over the radio Braden checked the status of each division of aircraft. After he confirmed that the formation was ready, Spencer gave the order to lift off. Braden quickly checked that the area around him was clear then coaxed the heavily burdened ship airborne amid a cloud of swirling dust. "Just as we climbed into the air," Spencer recounted, "Jim noticed a severe torque split—we had to land immediately." Braden quickly put the Huey back on the ground, and the rest of the ships pressed on without them.

Scrambling in the dust and the dark, the crew of the command and control ship hustled their gear and equipment to the backup aircraft. Minutes felt like hours, but before too much time passed Braden and Spencer and the rest of the crew were airborne again. Braden wasted little time; instead of following the turns in the preplanned route he raced directly toward a point where he hoped to intercept the formation.

No one will know exactly what happened in the cockpit of the CH-46E where Major Jay Aubin and Captain Ryan Beaupre sat at the controls. Nevertheless, it is almost a certainty that they both fought against an enervating vertigo brought on by the blanket of smoke and sand and fog that the formation was flying through. But in the rear of the aircraft it is likely that neither Staff Sergeant Kendall Watersbey nor Corporal Brian Kennedy knew that things were going bad. Neither is it likely that any of the eight Royal Marines—mentally and physically keen for combat—had any idea that disaster was imminent.

Once he had the Huey on course, Braden called out over the radio for a communications check. It was then that Lieutenant Colonel Jerry Driscoll called out—very calmly—that his third aircraft was "down." Driscoll's remarkable composure led Spencer to believe that the aircraft in question had simply been left behind with mechanical problems. In fact, the helicopter had crashed.

At just this moment Braden and Spencer flew into the shroud of black dust that the rest of the formation had been clawing through for the last several minutes. Spencer remembered: "I noticed that my goggles started to sparkle and that I could no longer see objects that had been clear only a few seconds before." Realizing that he was likely going to lose more aircraft and men if he continued to press the mission, Spencer called for an abort. The radio crackled as Braden made the transmission and got the rumbling mass of aircraft turned south. A short time later Lieutenant Colonel Ron Radich called that he had the flames from the downed helicopter in sight. Spencer cleared him to detach from the rest of the flight to assume duties as the on-scene commander.

The remainder of the aircraft returned to the start point without further incident. Once he was safely back on the ground, Spencer made his way to the Royal Marine command post and offered his apologies and condolences. It was a dreadful moment—he had lost four Marine crewmen, and the British had lost eight of their rock-hard Royal Marines. Regardless, there was still a war to be fought, and he and the Command Post (CP) staff conferred on the merits of continuing the operation. It was decided that, weather permitting, another attempt would be made at first light.

As it developed, the weather at dawn was not permitting and the joint effort was scrubbed. The Royal Marines planned to make another attempt later in the day with their own much smaller helicopter forces, and Spencer released his crews to support ongoing First Marine Division operations. In the meantime Spencer was still anxious about the crew he had lost. He and Braden got airborne and carefully felt their way through the morning fog toward the crash site.

After having flown much of the route at only fifty feet, Braden set the Huey down close to Radich's aircraft and he and Spencer climbed out to talk to the other officer. "Ron met us and briefly tried to prepare us for what we were about to see." It was a hopeless effort—there was nothing to say to adequately prepare anyone for viewing the carnage that was still smoldering only a short distance away. "Simply put," Spencer said, "it was the most horrendous scene I had ever encountered—and that included two previous wars and twenty-seven years of service." There in the smoldering wreckage was the pride and love and hope of twelve different families. All were sons; some were husbands and fathers and brothers. All of them were gone. The sight shook Spencer and the other men to their cores.

Aside from the human tragedy, a very here-and-now concern was the ammunition that had been aboard the helicopter; it was cooking off sporadically and posed a real danger to the Marines from the other two ships. Spencer realized that there was little that they could do. Dealing with the site would be "the grim task of the mortuary affairs and aircraft mishap teams." When Spencer and the other Marines left the crash site later that morning, it was with a sad sense of loss and helplessness. There was nothing they could do that would make right what had gone so badly wrong.

By afternoon they were supporting other operations.

8

Harrier Strike

Through his night-vision goggles Lieutenant Colonel Mike "Zieg" Hile could make out the silhouette of the USS *Bonhomme Richard* only a couple of miles in front of him. "Mother in sight," he reported to the controller. "Contact tower," came the response. Hile adjusted his heading slightly, knowing that his wingman, Captain Jason "Bearclaw" Duncan, was tucked tightly into position just under his right wingtip. A moment later the two AV-8Bs were over the top of the *Bonhomme Richard* at 350 knots. Hile quickly checked that Duncan was in position then twisted back around to the left to make certain that there were no other aircraft in the traffic pattern. An instant later he snapped his Harrier into a hard left turn and brought the throttle back toward idle as he pulled on the jet's control stick.

After 180 degrees of turn, Hile rolled his wings level and swiveled the nozzles on his jet down nearly vertical at sixty degrees. Duncan timed his turn to arrive a mile and a half in trail of his leader to ensure thirty seconds of spacing between the two aircraft for their separate landings on the deck of the Landing Helicopter Dock. From about a mile and a half abeam the ship's port side and headed in the opposite direction, Hile extended the aircraft's landing gear and set the flaps for landing before starting his descent out of eight hundred feet.

Landing aboard the ship at night was busy and dangerous; doing it safely and successfully demanded the most of every aviator's skill and attention. He scanned his jet's instruments and then looked back into the dark, then back inside again, and then back out . . . Descending now, he timed his turn to arrive directly behind the ship at about a mile. He could see it through his goggles, gray-green with points of bright light that aided his approach. The wake that the big LHD generated glowed brighter than the undisturbed water around it.

Hile continued to slow as he drew near the ship, transitioning to a creeping hover as he sidled up the left side of the deck. Adjusting his speed to only a few knots faster than that of the *Bonhomme Richard*, he eyed his landing spot and adjusted his flight path to approach it from a forty-five-degree angle; compared with a true sidestep, this allowed him to keep more of the deck in view and to maintain a better sense of depth perception. Cleared to cross over the deck by the Landing Signals Officer, Hile eased his jet over the assigned spot and slowly let the aircraft down, reaching for steel with the rubber tires of his landing gear. On making contact he snapped the throttle to idle in response to the LSO's call, felt the jet settle to the deck, and watched the signals from the enlisted crewman who directed him to taxi to the refueling point at the front of the ship, referred to as the "forward bone," where he would take on gas for his next mission.

He needed the fuel, but there was no need to take on more ordnance. A veteran of Desert Storm and, as an exchange pilot with the RAF, Deliberate Force, Hile had just finished his first mission of Iraqi Freedom without dropping his bombs. Like many of the craft airborne that first night, Hile had experienced a great deal of trouble getting in contact with the DASC before he had finally been handed off to a ground FAC. "We were assigned to support one of the RCTs as it crossed through the breach on the northern border of Kuwait.

There had been reports of Iraqi units in front of them. As it turned out the visibility was poor, but despite the weather we really looked their route of advance over pretty well. To be honest there just wasn't anything to attack—nothing threatening them at that time." After reconnoitering the area in front of the RCT, Hile and Duncan recovered back to the *Bonhomme Richard.*

With his Harrier taking on fuel, and with Duncan also safely back aboard the ship, Hile reviewed his notes for their subsequent mission. The next sortie was an assignment to bomb the Alamo bridge, a span that crossed the main canal approximately twenty miles northwest of Al Basrah. Part of 3rd MAW's mission was to act as a blocking force against the Iraqi units along the border with Iran. Rather than guarding that flank with Marines on the ground—a resource already in short supply—the plan relied on the air wing to protect the main effort. Taking out the bridge would make it more difficult for the Iraqi units to mobilize and threaten the Marines.

At the same time he reviewed his notes, Hile double-checked his aircraft's weapons systems while one of his squadron's enlisted men looked over the jet's exterior. This was part of the teamwork that made his squadron efficient. Hile was the commander, the pilot, but he knew that nothing happened without the hard work and loyalty of the young men and women who made up the greater part of his squadron. During a career that had spanned nearly twenty years he had entrusted his life to Marines like them every time he strapped on a jet.

His AV-8B was loaded with a single, thousand-pound GBU-16 LGB, or Laser Guided Bomb. Slung underneath his jet on the innermost station of the right wing was an AN/AAQ-28 Litening II navigation and targeting pod. This device enabled him to guide not only the GBU-16 on his own jet to a direct hit, but also the two five-hundred-pound GBU-12s on Duncan's. Because the AV-8B couldn't carry a great deal of bomb tonnage while operating from a ship, it was important for the weapons it did carry to be accurate. The Litening pod's capabilities turned the ordnance-limited Harrier into a sharpshooter.

"The Litening pod had better resolution and magnification than anything in the Marine Corps," Hile recalled. "During the planning phase of the campaign the goal for the Harrier was for each section of two aircraft to kill two targets on each sortie. At first we thought this was a little bit too aggressive, but once things got in sync it became more the norm than the exception."

The pod was useful for more than just steering weapons. With its high resolution it was a boon for Marine commanders who needed an accurate picture of what was deep in front of them—deeper than where the Cobras and Hueys could range. And it was useful for spotting and guiding targets for other aircraft as well. Just as Hile could steer the Laser Guided Bombs of his own wingman, he could guide them for other aircraft as well. The pod also had an Infra Red (IR) pointer; through goggles at night this powerful beam could finger targets to other fighters or bombers from miles away. The aviators often called it "the Finger of God." And because it was slaved to the aircraft's navigation system, the pod could use grid or latitude/longitude coordinates to stare at a precise geographic point; conversely, the exact location of anything it found could also be accurately extrapolated.

The pod also provided remarkable value in delivering accurate, undeniable BHAs, or Bomb Hit Assessments. Combat can be confusing, and pilots can sometimes misinterpret the effectiveness of their weapons. The videotaped evidence provided by the Litening pod provided irrefutable proof. This capability was particularly important to the commanders, who could reallocate sorties to hit a target that had been missed or reapportion aircraft against secondary targets in the event that a given target had been neutralized or destroyed earlier than planned. In short, this one device increased the effectiveness of the AV-8B—and the air wing—by a significant degree.

"These pods were great," Hile confirmed. "They were easy to use, easy to maintain, and reliable. And after dropping your own bombs you could guide weapons for other aircraft. The biggest problem we had was that we only had enough pods for one of about every two jets."

The thump of the fuel hose being broken away from his aircraft took Hile's attention away from his notes. In short order he was taxiing away from the forward bone and toward the back end of the ship. Unlike conventional aircraft carriers, the amphibious assault ships that operated the Harriers had no catapults or arresting gear. Instead the little jump jets had to accelerate down the ship's deck as quickly as possible before vectoring their thrust downward and pushing themselves airborne.

Hile followed several sets of waving light wands to the stern of the ship and then pivoted his aircraft around until it was pointed toward the bow. He could see that Duncan was positioned not far from where he sat, ready to launch. He followed the deck officer's signals as both of them—the deck officer on the outside, Hile on the inside—made certain that the Harrier was ready. The nozzles and flaps were checked, then positioned for takeoff. At the same time, his enlisted Marines gave the aircraft one last inspection before giving him a thumbs-up indicating that all was in order.

Finally cleared for takeoff, Hile confirmed that the nozzles were pointed directly aft and shoved the Harrier's throttle all the way forward. He checked his engine and flight controls one more time then dropped his feet off the aircraft's brakes. In an instant he was hurtling toward the front of the ship, and only a few seconds and 750 feet later he reached for the knobbed lever that controlled the nozzles. He pulled it aft, rotating the nozzles fifty-five degrees toward the deck, and felt the jet lift into the sky.

Safely airborne, Hile raised the landing gear and flaps and continued to climb while waiting for Duncan to clear the *Bonhomme Richard*'s deck and join on his wing. Within a few minutes Duncan had done just that, and the two jets winged their way toward southern Iraq. "We checked in with AWACS—callsign Karma—and they cleared us to hit the bridge without any delay at all," remembered Hile. "This surprised me a little bit because the MEF had flip-flopped for several days about whether or not they wanted this bridge hit." The command's indecision can perhaps be understood to a certain degree. If the enemy couldn't use a destroyed bridge, neither could friendly forces. And of course there was the desire to achieve the objectives of the campaign while destroying as little of the country's infrastructure as possible.

The mechanics of bombing the bridge presented several problems to the two Harrier pilots. At altitude, the winds were excessively strong out of the west at sixty-five to seventy-five knots, thus dictating an east-to-west run on the bridge. Hile didn't like the fact that they would be attacking the bridge at a perpendicular angle; the span ran north and south. "If our bombs hit just a little long or short, we'd miss it completely," he remembered. And because the bridge was located not far from the Iranian border, the formation would be forced to make a turn to the left to stay clear of Iran.

Whereas other Coalition aircrews that night were fighting the Iraqis, poor communications, and limited visibility, Hile and Duncan found themselves already cleared to drop their bombs, and with time, fuel, and weather for a practice run. Hile's radar warning receiver displayed only the occasional spurious signal; there was no indication that they were being targeted by enemy SAMs. In all likelihood the Iraqis were completely unaware of the two small jets racing overhead. Hile recalled: "We had plenty of gas, and no one was shooting at us, so I didn't see any reason why we shouldn't make a dry run at the bridge. This was a mission we had been planning for a while and there was no real reason to rush it."

The mock attack went well, and Hile spun the flight around for the real thing. "One nice aspect about making the attack during this time of the night was the fact that no one was up and around," he recalled. It was just short of 0530 and there wasn't a car or truck—or for that matter any sort of traffic—in sight.

From twenty miles away Hile rolled out of a left-hand turn and put the bridge dead ahead of the two AV-8Bs. Even at this range the Litening pod showed the bridge as a dark, elongated, easily recognizable form. Rushing toward the target at five hundred knots, he had only about two minutes to complete his final checks before he would send the flight's bombs earthward. For perhaps the fifth time that night he confirmed that his single GBU-16 was ready to go. Fifteen or so feet away in a right echelon formation, Duncan was readying his two GBU-12s.

At less than ten miles the bridge was clearly visible on the Litening pod's display. Hile was relieved to see that there was still no traffic. He carefully slaved the pod's targeting pointer over the center of the southernmost span. As the two jets raced toward the release point, he continued to refine the pointer's placement over the desired point of impact. Finally he followed the steering on his HUD and mashed down on the control stick's "pickle" button. He felt a sharp thump, and the aircraft seemed to leap as the heavy bomb fell away. Duncan, hearing the bomb release tone transmitted from Hile's jet, released his own two weapons.

The flight leader's attention went right back to the targeting pod as he started a left-hand turn, away from the target. This was the most crucial part of the mission. Even if everything else went perfectly, the entire effort would be a bust if the bombs failed to hit their target. Keeping the targeting pointer steady on the bridge, Hile waited until the bombs had fallen nearly half the distance, then squeezed the trigger that fired the pod's laser.

The laser detection devices on all three bombs—tuned to the same frequency as the Litening pod—captured the energy reflecting from the bridge and immediately began snaking through the sky toward where Hile held the targeting diamond on the southernmost span. He didn't see the bombs before they hit, but the sudden explosion of light that momentarily blanked out the pod's display told him that the bombs had found their mark. He called out "splash" to Duncan to let him know that they had hit the bridge.

Despite the perfect delivery, when the smoke drifted away Hile could see that the span was still more or less intact. The three bombs had hit in the center of the easternmost lane and much of the roadway was chewed up, but it would likely take more strikes before the bridge would be unusable. Still, this wasn't overly surprising to the combat veteran; successfully weaponeering an attack to destroy a modern, well-constructed bridge is perhaps one of the most difficult tasks that a combat aviator can face.

Only a couple of minutes after dropping their bombs the two aviators were back over the northern Persian Gulf and heading back toward the cluttered deck of the *Bonhomme Richard*. For Hile the night
had been almost a nonevent; he had been on training flights that had
been more demanding. Still, he knew that the coming campaign
would challenge him and his squadron much more than this first
night had.

9

Rockets and Bombs and Guns, Part I

It had been impossible to get anything that merited being called sleep. Stuffed into their NBC suits, they had flopped around in their cots for most of the night. The physical discomfort of tossing and turning in the stifling tent while wearing full MOPP (Mission Oriented Protection Posture) gear was bad enough, but the combination of repetitive SCUD alerts and the continuous howl of jet engines in full afterburner was a double guarantee against the notion of rest. The icing on the cake was the fact that they had finished an adrenaline-stoked mission only a few hours earlier and on this day, March 21, they were scheduled for a full day of flying that would begin just after first light. Both of them knew that they would be drawing on the rest they had gotten during previous nights rather than the rest they should have been getting on this particular evening.

Majors Jay "Chewy" Frey and Scott "Weeds" Wedemeyer of VMFA(AW)-533 were too excited to be exhausted when they walked into the TACC at Al Jaber. In a very short time they would be strapped into their F/A-18D supporting RCT-7's plunge across the border of Kuwait into Iraq. They were scheduled for a Forward Air Controller (Airborne) mission; this called for them to conduct reconnaissance ahead of the regiment while directing other aircraft and supporting fires onto enemy targets. It would be their job to find and kill the Iraqis before the Iraqis had an opportunity to engage the RCT. Frey recalled: "I'm certain that we were as prepared to support RCT-7 as anyone has ever been to support any ground unit." During the previous several weeks Frey and Wedemeyer had had daily contact with the two regimental Air Officers, Majors Ken "Kid" Maney and Jim "Mighty" Quinn. "At least one of them would come down to Al Jaber daily and brief us on the latest pieces of the plan. We also made several trips up to their area to meet with the regimental staff."

The RCT commander, Colonel Steven Hummer, had taken time to visit Al Jaber in order to coordinate with his counterpart commanders and to "fly" the TOPSCENE training system. TOPSCENE assimilates satellite imagery, ATARS (Advanced Tactical Airborne Reconnaissance System) photos, and other data to create a multidimensional representation of any battlespace for which data exist. In essence the TOPSCENE unit at Al Jaber allowed Hummer to take a virtual flight over the exact territory he would be fighting his unit through. It was a capability that commanders in previous conflicts could only have dreamed of.

Now with the RCT just pushing through the breach, the two aviators gathered as much information as they could about what was going on across the border. "We talked to the watch officers as well as the crews that had just come back," recollected Frey. "This, in combination with briefs from our intelligence sections, real-time information coming in over the radio, and map studies of the current tactical situation, made up a continuous flow of information that kept us pretty much on top of the game." As the campaign progressed VMFA(AW)-533's aircrews would be some of the best informed; their twenty-four-hour support of operations as FAC(A)s gave them an unmatched battlefield presence.

*   *   *

One of the issues still being reacted to was the supposed brigade-sized force of Iraqi T-72s that was conjectured to be waiting to ambush RCT-7 as it crossed into Iraq. By now Mattis and his staff had generated a plan that involved shifting boundaries between the RCTs and bringing the British units farther west than they had originally been tasked. With the support of 3rd MAW they were looking to find and fix the Iraqi tanks—and then reverse the trap. They would crush the enemy force in an overwhelming envelopment.

Wedemeyer and Frey climbed into the bed of the squadron's pickup truck for the short ride to the flight line. The route was the same, the buildings and tents were the same, even the people were the same, but somehow, in the context of what was happening only a few miles away, everything was different. Already the smoke from Saddam's burning trenches and oil wells was mixing with the natural airborne dust to create a brown-black haze that cast everything and everyone in a faint sepia hue. Screened from the normally brutal sun, eyes that usually squinted during the day were wide open and saw more detail and with greater sharpness. But regardless of the environmentals, the Marines and airmen on the base were stepping and moving with more purpose. There was a war on. What they did or didn't do directly affected who might live and who might die. People weren't running from place to place, but it didn't take a practiced eye to see that they were doing their best to restrain themselves to a fast walk.

When the truck stopped, the two Marines walked into the squadron's maintenance area and checked their assigned aircraft's "book." This was a log that delineated what type of maintenance had recently been done and what minor gripes remained to be fixed, as well as how the aircraft was configured, armed, and fueled. "On this day," Frey said, "our jet was set up in what we called the 'goofy gas' configuration. We had an external fuel tank on the right wing and another on the centerline station under the fuselage. It was an uneven-looking arrangement but it gave the FLIR a better overall field of view, and it freed up another precision weapons station. And as ugly as it was, it really didn't affect the flying qualities of the jet that much." The rest of the weapons consisted of two 1,000-pound Mk-83 bombs, two CBU-99 Rockeye Cluster Bomb Units (at 509 pounds each), eight 5-inch White Phosphorous (WP) rockets, and five hundred rounds of 20-millimeter ammunition for the cannon. After a quick review of the book, Frey and Wedemeyer stepped out to the jet.

The preflight, start, and post-start sequence went quickly. The SCUD alerts hadn't abated, and the young enlisted mechanics made short, snappy work of their procedures. Frey, the WSO, readied the navigation system and radios from where he sat in the rear cockpit while Wedemeyer checked and rechecked the aircraft's flight controls, engines, and weapons systems from the front cockpit. After taxiing to the south end of the base and receiving clearance to take off, Wedemeyer positioned the aircraft on the runway and shoved the two throttles forward. An instant later the crew felt a kick in their backsides as the two engines shot out a combined thirty-six thousand pounds of violet-hot thrust that slammed the aircraft from a standing start to more than 150 knots in just a few seconds. Less than a third of the way down the runway the jet broke ground. It was 0714 local time.

"The visibility was horrible," remembered Frey. There was a single layer of smoke that hung at about two thousand feet with only occasional breaks. Even through the openings, depending on the angle of the sun, it was still very difficult to see through the haze to the ground below. This would make their job extraordinarily difficult. Nevertheless, Wedemeyer climbed up to twenty-two thousand feet and winged the sixty miles or so to where RCT-7 was trying to cram itself across the border at the northernmost point of Kuwait. It took only a few minutes to cover the distance.

"After we checked in through the TACC and the DASC and everyone else in the world we made contact with Kid; he and Mighty had been up all night while Colonel Hummer was working to get everyone through the cut in the berm," Frey recounted. Mattis had known that his RCTs would take time to pass through the elevated lines of earth that demarcated the border but he wanted it to take as little time as possible. He was only too aware that the largest of the Iraqi artillery guns, the Austrian-made GHN-45, 155-millimeter cannon, could outrange his own artillery and had the ability to drop rounds into the masses of Marines who were staged on the Kuwaiti side of the border. Those guns were also the most likely to be used for firing chemical shells. "It was a fact," Frey said, "that Mattis fully expected to take casualties in the staging areas." For that reason Iraqi artillery was at the top of the general's target list.

Maney directed Wedemeyer and Frey—callsign Nail 33—to push north along the Main Surface Routes (MSRs) that the RCT would advance along later that morning. The two fliers were about four miles south of Division Objective 2, the Rumaylah oil field pumping stations, when they spotted a trio of tan-colored tanks oriented east-to-west behind a set of hastily scraped revetments. Wedemeyer dropped the jet low enough to make a positive ID; it was a pair of older T-55s along with a newer T-72. Their guns were pointed south. "I got hold of Kid on the radio and he told us to go ahead and kill them—that there were no other targets being reported," Frey remembered. With clearance to engage, Wedemeyer dropped the Hornet's nose down toward the enemy armor and pickled off one of the two Rockeyes that were slung underneath the jet's left wing. The weapon worked just as advertised; an instant before striking the ground it separated into two halves and showered 247 small, anti-armor bomblets over the center of the three tanks. This was exactly what the Rockeye was designed for; the shaped-charge warheads of the bomblets drove a stream of molten metal into the tanks with a force of 250,000 pounds per square inch. Frey recounted: "That tank was totally destroyed, and if there were any crewmen inside they were dead, too."

Wedemeyer pulled back on the control stick and got the aircraft moving skyward again while he set up for another attack. As their eyes adjusted to the dim light and became better acquainted with the flat desert terrain, Frey and Wedemeyer were able to make out more and more targets. "Every time that Weeds jinked or banked we spotted something new," Frey said. "Not far from the tanks were several Armored Personnel Carriers as well as other equipment that was covered in camouflage netting." They rocketed earthward once more as Wedemeyer targeted the westernmost tank and dropped the remaining Rockeye canister.

Wedemeyer pulled the nose up hard again and started a left-hand turn. Both of them looked back over the left side of the aircraft and watched for the familiar sparkling pattern of explosions that should have covered the second tank. Instead, there was a single bright flash to the west of the target. The Rockeye had failed to open and had hit the ground and exploded—or gone "high order." This was a problem that had plagued the weapon since its introduction. And because most of them were now twenty or more years old, the failure rate was significant.

"Just after we came off target we spotted a pair of GHN-45 artillery tubes to the southwest," remembered Frey. Although their aircraft was armed and they were cleared to engage targets as opportunities were presented, the FAC(A) crew's real job was to coordinate attacks by other aircraft on the targets that they found. "We kind of viewed the aircraft we controlled as 'bomb trucks,'" Frey said. "They were just flying tools we used to kill the stuff we found."

Frey had kept one of his two radios tuned to the DASC frequency and knew that there were several MAG-11 F/A-18s airborne and available. Knowing that the controlling agency had its hands full, he more or less hijacked a pair of the jets to work the two artillery tubes. "I told the DASC what I had and then directed one of the sections of Hornets to contact me on the TAD [Tactical Air Direction] frequency we were working on the other radio. The DASC didn't put up a fuss."

As Frey was briefing the two single-seat F/A-18C pilots, Wedemeyer rolled over into a steep dive from the north and designated the artillery position through his Heads Up Display. At the same time he armed the FLIR's laser designator; this enabled Frey to derive an accurate ten-digit grid coordinate, which he subsequently passed to the other two jets. For good measure, Wedemeyer sent down a wake-up call in the form of three 5-inch rockets.

The rockets were designed as marking rounds. The nature of the White Phosphorous or "Willy Pete" warheads was such that they burned brilliantly hot and produced exceptionally dense, white smoke. They were intended to help other pilots more easily "get their eyes on the target." Frey recalled: "In this instance the smoke from Weeds's rockets mixed with Saddam's smoke and made it difficult for the other two pilots to get a fix on the individual guns—they were flying a lot higher than we were." Nevertheless, the ten-digit grid that Frey had captured and passed to them was good enough. After he finished his brief and was certain that they had the general target area in sight, he cleared the two F/A-18 pilots to attack. They set up a wagon-wheel-type pattern and made swooping runs using just the steering cues on their HUDs.

"It worked out really well," Frey said. "Both of the guns were demolished within a matter of minutes." Frey gave the two jets routing back to Al Jaber and passed the BDA, or Battle Damage Assessment, back to the DASC: two GHN-45s destroyed. By now they had been airborne almost an hour—it was time to get more gas. Frey checked off station with Maney and the DASC and established contact with "Raider," a Marine KC-130 that was orbiting just a few miles to their south.

The Marine Corps would be a less effective fighting force were it not for the KC-130. It is an old, high-wing, four-engine design that is neither fast nor pretty. On the other hand, it is the most versatile and efficient transport aircraft ever put into operation. More than fifty nations have used the transport in one capacity or another. The Marine Corps introduced its first KC-130F during 1962; there are approximately seventy-five KC-130s of various types still in service. Odds were that most of the aircraft airborne that morning had seen service during both Vietnam and Desert Storm. Odds were also good that the machines were older than most of the men and women who made up the Marine Corps.

Aside from possessing the ruggedness and power to bring large numbers of troops and supplies into relatively small and unforgiving airfields, the aircraft's refueling capabilities essentially multiply the effectiveness of the Marine Corps's tactical jet force. In the words of one KC-130 pilot: "By giving them gas and keeping them airborne, we turn one jet into two or three or more."

It was certainly true in this case. Rather than returning all the way south to Al Jaber, landing, taxiing, taking on more fuel, and then taxiing and taking off again, the FAC(A) crew would only need to take a short, airborne timeout. Once southbound, Wedemeyer made radar contact with the tanker while Frey ran the radio drill. Almost as soon as he established a radar lock on the big ship, Wedemeyer was able to pick it up visually and adjusted his intercept point and airspeed to arrive at a position just a couple of hundred feet above and offset to the right. Streaming back from the two refueling pods mounted on the KC-130's wingtips were thick black hoses that ended in dirty white refueling baskets.

A quick light signal from the observer's window located at the tanker's midsection signaled Wedemeyer that he was cleared to refuel. Without looking he reached down to his cockpit's left console, flicked a switch, and felt and heard the airflow over the jet change ever so slightly as the refueling probe unfolded itself from the right forward fuselage. At the same time, he nudged his control stick to the left and adjusted his power while he slid the jet into a position just a few feet behind the gently oscillating basket on the left-hand hose. On the rear of the refueling pod he could see that an amber light was illuminated—confirmation that the KC-130 was prepared to pass the fuel that would keep him and Frey in the fight. For perhaps the thousandth time in his career he added just a small bit of power and nudged the jet forward until the refueling probe slid into the basket and seated itself into the refueling receptacle. Once stabilized, a quick look down at his fuel gauge confirmed that the jet was taking fuel.

During the few minutes that Wedemeyer held the aircraft in the refueling basket, Frey continued to work the radios. "Before we had even gotten to our jet that morning, we had heard about a supposedly huge force of Iraqi tanks that was set to ambush our RCTs as they came across the border—but no one had found anything really significant yet. Now, listening on the radios, it was becoming clear that our guys were still anxious to find and kill this threat."

Once Wedemeyer had taken on a full load of gas he backed out of the refueling basket, edged away from the tanker, then made a hard turn back toward RCT-7. "Kid came up on the radio and confirmed what we had been hearing," Frey recollected. "He told us that the whole division was staying put until the mystery with the Iraqi tanks was solved. They hadn't even crossed the Line of Departure—General Mattis wanted to know where those tanks were."

Frey and Wedemeyer took on the assignment to do just that. Adhering to the Rules of Engagement (ROE) that the wing had assigned them, they pushed east from overhead the RCT toward the Persian Gulf. The mix of clouds and smoke was too thick; they could see nothing. Approaching Umm Qasr—almost at the water's edge—they still weren't able to see through the clouds. Knowing that nothing was going to happen until they got low enough to see what was actually taking place on the ground, Wedemeyer and Frey descended through the clouds in a left-hand turn. Leveling off only a thousand feet or so above the desert, Wedemeyer shoved the throttles forward until the jet was making more than five hundred knots. Here and there along the border they could see spots where strikes from the night before had left ugly black pockmarks that used to be Iraqi border posts.

Just east of the RCT they spied a large formation of tanks. But these were British and were on the Kuwaiti side of the border. There still was no enormous mass of hostile armor. Having cleared the area just ahead of the RCT from the east, Wedemeyer swung the jet deeper into Iraq and then turned east again until he reached the gulf. Once more there was no huge formation of tanks to be seen. The crew turned north, still farther into enemy territory, then paralleled the border back to the west. The result was the same: no tanks.

"After four passes up and down that border Weeds and I knew that there was no gigantic Iraqi tank formation," Frey said. "We told Kid that their information was bad—that there was nothing out there." Soon after, the Marines on the ground began to push north with vigor. Satisfied that the RCT had the information it needed, the two Marines sprinted back to the tanker for another top-off.

It was only a few minutes after they reported back on station in front of the RCT that Maney contacted Wedemeyer and Frey with news that the Marines on the ground had been taking fire and that counterbattery radar had plotted the position of a suspected Iraqi artillery emplacement. He passed the data to the F/A-18D crew and asked them to investigate. "Sure enough," Frey remembered, "we found a battery of six GHN-45s northwest of Division Objective 2 aligned in what we called a Crazy-W formation; it was similar to the layout of the rings on the Olympic flag." The guns were oriented from east to west with their tubes pointed south. This was exactly the threat that most concerned Mattis.

Frey recalled: "Weeds overflew the emplacements from the south and got the jet set up to drop a Mk-83. A fog of grayish white smoke was hanging low in and among the guns—an indicator that they had just finished firing." Wedemeyer pulled the aircraft around in a left-hand, 270-degree turn and dived on the enemy position from the west. Starting down from ten thousand feet in a thirty-degree dive, he designated the center tube through the HUD, quickly adjusted the designation, followed the steering line, and mashed down on the bomb release button. There was a gentle jolt as the thousand-pound bomb fell away from the jet. Behind him Frey pulled up the ten-digit grid that marked the position of the emplacement to an accuracy of several feet.

With the bomb on its way Wedemeyer simultaneously hauled back on the control stick and rolled right. With seven g's of gravity pulling down at them, both fliers strained to look behind the aircraft for the bomb to hit. Only about eight seconds after the Mk-83 had been released, the targeted gun disappeared in a concussive flash. The combination of smoke and humidity was such that the spreading shock wave from the explosion was clearly visible.

"With the ten-digit grid coordinate we had pulled from the bombing run I worked with Kid to get an artillery mission run against the Iraqi guns," Frey said. "I passed the grid and the spacing and orientation of the emplacements as well as the other details that our own artillery guys would need. When the brief was passed, Weeds set us up in an orbit to the northwest of the target." Now there was little for the FAC(A) crew to do but wait.

Miles to the south, artillery Marines from the Eleventh Marines prepared to run the mission. Into their M198, 155-millimeter howitzers were loaded DPICM (Dual Purpose Improved Conventional Munition) shells. These are the artillery equivalent of the air-delivered Rockeye; each shell carries seventy-two anti-personnel/anti-matériel grenades that detonate on impact. DPICM is one of the most devastating weapons on the battlefield.

Although DPICM is essentially an area weapon—each shell covers an area of approximately two hundred square yards—the state of the artilleryman's science has advanced to the point that accuracy is no longer an issue. As one Marine put it: "Given an accurate coordinate, our artillery will put steel directly on steel every single time." Indeed, factors as minute as relative humidity and the rotation of the earth are taken into account when computing a fire mission.

"We waited approximately a minute after the 'shot over' call was made," Frey said. The shells were on their way, and Wedemeyer maneuvered as best he could to keep the enemy emplacements in sight and on the FLIR while still staying clear of the incoming artillery shells. Frey remembered the astonishing accuracy of the first volley of DPICM: "It was incredible—as if six perfectly shaped, giant explosive doughnuts had been overlaid on top of each gun." While the two aviators watched the Iraqi positions burn, a call came over the radio asking if another mission was required. "It really wasn't," Frey said, "but we figured that in a case like this too much was probably better than not enough." Frey made the call and moments later another perfectly placed barrage of DPICM stirred up the burning wreckage that the first had created. Wedemeyer dropped the jet's last Mk-83 onto a nearby transport truck and fired his remaining rockets into a formation of Armored Personnel Carriers (APCs) before heading south again to top off the Hornet's fuel tanks.

After another quick trip to the tanker the FAC(A) crew was back in

Iraq, reconnoitering in front of RCT-7. Frey recalled: "We were scouting along Highway 8 when we came across five tanks parked behind newly shoveled berms in the vicinity of an intersection that we had dubbed 'the Paperclip.' Looking down from the air that's exactly what it looked like—it was unmistakable." The T-55s were oriented east-to-west across the highway, and their guns were pointed south; they were obviously intended to act as a blocking force. Frey made contact with the DASC, hoping to get aircraft to attack the Iraqi armor, but he came up empty—there was nothing available. "Weeds and I talked it over and made contact with Major George 'Sack' Rowell and Captain Douglas 'Oedi' Glover—callsign Nail 67—who were also working a FAC(A) mission close to our area. Neither crew had any ordnance remaining except 20-millimeter cannon, but it was better than nothing."

The books say that 20-millimeter cannon fire can't destroy heavy armor, but practical experience has shown otherwise. An attack from above and behind that puts shells into the engine compartment will set Soviet-era tanks afire. Wedemeyer coordinated with Maney to execute strafing runs against the T-55s. They would make shallow attacks from the north so that they could fire into the rear of the vehicles. Their ad hoc deconfliction plan put Rowell and Glover on the west side of the road and Wedemeyer and Frey on the east; colliding over the heads of the people they were killing would be a bad thing.

Rolling in from the north and just under the layer of smoke at about two thousand feet, Wedemeyer pushed the Hornet's nose down into a fifteen-degree dive and let the aiming reticle rest just atop the engine access doors on the easternmost tank. He didn't have the throttles fully forward—he wanted more time to aim and fire. In his HUD he could see the range bar on the clock-like aiming reticle compress back on itself. Passing through about twelve hundred feet above the ground, the words IN RANGE appeared in the HUD. Still he held his fire. Then just as he reached what the HUD showed him was minimum range, he squeezed a one-second burst into the tan-colored tank: *grrrrrrrriiiiip!* The fast-moving rounds looked like a column of angry bees racing down at the enemy vehicle.

The instant he let off the trigger Wedemeyer snapped the stick back hard and yanked the jet over to the left in a climbing turn. Bottoming out at five hundred feet, he knew that the wrong combination of ricochets and bad luck could result in shooting himself down. But not this time. Both fliers saw flashes as the API (Armor Piercing Incendiary) rounds smashed into the tank and surrounding desert. Dust mixed with smoke from the burning engine compartment. Under the hail of the deep booming crackle of cannon fire, Iraqi troops scurried from one hiding spot to another.

Both aircraft hurtled toward the ground several more times until their ammunition was exhausted. "Weeds and Sack killed every one of those tanks," Frey said. When the rest of the RCT passed through the intersection twelve hours later, Maney reported that the tanks were still burning.

With no more ordnance and after having been airborne for more than three hours, Wedemeyer and Frey headed back to Al Jaber. They needed to rearm for another sortie.

10

Rockets and Bombs and Guns,
Part II

Wedemeyer followed the plane captain's hand signals as he swung
the jet into its parking place on the flight line at Al Jaber. He
stepped on the brakes one last time as the young Marine raised his
hands over his head and clenched them into fists; another mechanic
threw a pair of chocks under the aircraft's wheels. Double-checking
that the aircraft was safely parked, the plane captain made a slashing
motion across his throat and Wedemeyer shut down one engine; a
moment later he secured the second.

The two fliers quickly unstrapped from their ejection seats,
climbed down from the jet, and stretched their stiff limbs. It was the
middle of the first full day of the war and they were one of dozens of
crews across the base who had either just returned from a mission or
were getting ready to go. All across the parking ramp Marines moved
with purpose; systems were checked or repaired, trailers of bombs
were trundled from aircraft to aircraft, and big green refueling trucks
snorted and roared as they shot thousands of gallons of jet propellant

into big bladders that in turn hot-refueled the jets before they returned to the flight line. The SCUD alerts continued, but rather than sending the Marines wholesale into nearby bunkers, they now caused little more than an anxious look skyward or perhaps an unconscious reach to check that a gas mask carrier was still strapped in place.

"Weeds and I split up while the squadron's young Marines hustled to get the jet ready to go again," said Frey. He stepped out of his flight gear and made the quick three-minute walk to the FLIC (Flight Line Intelligence Center) that had been set up before the shooting started. There a collection of intelligence experts from various units had been merged into a larger, albeit ad hoc, organization that was more responsive in gathering and disseminating information than a smattering of smaller squadron intelligence cells would have been. At the FLIC mission debriefs were collected and disseminated immediately. The information was vital not only to higher headquarters but also to the crews who were about to go into the fight. Along with manpower and expertise, scarce communications and video equipment was also pooled for better efficiency. Frey remembered: "They had all the connectivity they needed to reach just about anybody at any time." The equipment included SIPRnet (Secret Internet Protocol Router Network), NIPRnet (Non-secure Internet Protocol Router Network), STU III (Secure Telephone Unit) telephones, satellite communications, and other more typical telephone and radio gear. The center was also equipped with a broad spectrum of analytical equipment that better enabled the experts to determine what was actually taking place on the battlefield. In particular, mission videos were reviewed, evaluated, and forwarded to higher headquarters for more detailed scrutiny when required. At times some of the most spectacular of the footage was rerouted early, delivered into the public domain, and then broadcast on worldwide television only hours after it had arrived in the FLIC.

"Once I got to the FLIC," Frey said, "I gave them a quick debrief. The mystery Iraqi tank brigade had pretty much been discounted by this point, and our RCTs were moving forward fairly quickly." In fact, the leading elements of the division were already reaching their objectives in the Rumaylah oil fields. Although a few wellheads had been torched, the horrific environmental disaster that could have occurred had been headed off. Present-day hindsight frequently glosses over this early success, but had it failed the natural and political fallout would have been a disastrous and enduring legacy.

Because he had just come off the battlefield, there wasn't much that the FLIC could tell Frey about what was going on directly in front of the RCTs that he didn't already know. Still, the information he passed to the FLIC was useful, and after a short time he left and made his way to where Wedemeyer was waiting at the maintenance section. There a video machine had been set up, and the two fliers shared their successes from that morning with the men and women who were responsible for keeping the jets in combat-ready condition. After having spent years keeping the aircraft operational so that the aircrews could train, it was extremely gratifying to see what the fruits of their labor had wrought on the enemy.

The maintenance Marines were good at their job. An hour after Wedemeyer had shut the engines down, both he and Frey were walking back to the same jet. The aircraft had been checked, refueled, and rearmed with four Rockeyes, eight 5-inch WP rockets, and a full load of 20-millimeter cannon ammunition. It was ready to go.

Airborne again, the crew of Nail 33 checked in with the DASC and was subsequently directed to contact RCT-7 again. Frey recalled: "Kid passed us off to a FAC, callsign Pita, who was assigned to Second Tanks. They were stopped at the southern edge of the Rumaylah oil fields, east of Route 8 at Mahattat a Tubah, and were taking sporadic mortar fire." The Marines in their M1A1 tanks and HMMWVs were more concerned about Iraqi tanks than the harassing mortar fire they were taking, but it was still a threat that had to be suppressed. From where they were halted at an elevated intersection they could occasionally spot a pair of white pickup trucks to their north and east that would move, fire, then move again. They couldn't get a clear shot and wanted Nail 33 to kill the two vehicles.

"I got lucky and spotted the trucks immediately," Frey said. "But Weeds was having a hell of a time finding them; that was unusual for him, as he generally had great eyesight." The Iraqi vehicles stayed on the move and headed south across an east–west road before stopping in a prepared position not far from where a locomotive sat on the area's only rail line. But even after repeated attempts Frey couldn't get Wedemeyer's eyes on the enemy trucks. The still-degraded visibility and vagaries of trying to spot a small target while racing over a battlefield at hundreds of miles per hour were working against the crew.

It was then that a pair of HMLA-167 AH-1W Cobras came up on the radio net and called the targets in sight. "I asked them if they had anything that they could mark the target with," Frey said, "and they answered that they had 2.75-inch fléchette rockets." Frey knew that this could work. "These rockets typically fly a certain distance out in front of the Cobra and then burst with a characteristic reddish smudge. I knew if they could get close enough that Weeds would be able to pick up the trucks."

The mobile Iraqi mortars had started to move again and the pair of Cobras, led by Captain "Bull" Budrejko, pushed out from overhead the friendly tanks. A moment later several rockets streaked out from the helicopters' stub wings and burst just short of the trucks. The Cobras wheeled back around and headed back toward the friendly position. Budrejko had taken two small-arms rounds into his canopy, and his wingman had take one. They had missed being hit in the head by only inches.

"Weeds caught sight of the trucks as soon as Bull put the rockets downrange," recollected Frey. "He took us down low and fast just overhead the top of them and they both stopped." The two fliers tried to get clearance from Pita to attack the trucks with Rockeyes but were denied. One shortcoming of the cluster munition is that there is always a small percentage of bomblets that don't explode upon impacting the ground. Nevertheless, these "duds" are as likely as not to detonate upon making contact with a passing vehicle or infantryman's boot. They had killed and maimed several Coalition soldiers during and after Desert Storm. Pita was concerned that the two trucks were too close to the main MSRs—routes that would see very heavy traffic in the subsequent campaign.

Instead, Wedemeyer was cleared to engage the trucks with rockets.

"The problem with that," explained Frey, "was that the only rockets we had were White Phosphorous rounds—Weeds would have to hit the trucks dead-on in order to destroy them." With no other good option Wedemeyer rolled in on the trucks from the west, almost overhead Pita and Second Tanks. In a fifteen-degree dive and with no substantial anti-aircraft threat observed he set the jet up for a "training-wheels" delivery. At only 350 knots he carefully placed the reticle illuminated on his HUD just between the two trucks and held it there as the range counted down. Finally, passing down through 1,650 feet and at the absolute minimum range, he quickly mashed the red button atop his control stick once, twice, three times. Three rockets flashed out from the pods slung underneath his wings.

"The hits were unbelievable," said Frey. "Aside from the fact that Weeds is one of the most experienced Hornet pilots in the Marine Corps, there was a big dose of luck involved in where those rockets hit." Incredibly, each truck was struck by one rocket apiece while the third hit just between them. As close to the ground as he was, Wedemeyer heaved the stick back and to the left. "We turned so hard that I could feel us skidding sideways before we actually started going where we were pointed," Frey said. "Still, we came pretty close to the ground. I can remember looking back and thinking, *Holy shit, we're really low!*" As they climbed back to altitude the pair could see the molten heat of the WP warheads transforming the trucks into ashes.

It was while making their attack that Frey had spotted an MTLB multipurpose armored vehicle approximately two hundred yards south of where the trucks had stopped. Nearby there was other equipment screened by camouflage netting. The MTLB was farther away from the road than the trucks had been, and Frey prevailed on Pita to allow them to attack the armored vehicle with Rockeye.

Careful not to lose sight of the MTLB, Wedemeyer swung around to the west overhead Second Tanks again before diving east and dropping two Rockeyes. The canisters performed perfectly; a large pattern of sparkling explosions enveloped not only the MTLB, but also a good part of the area that was covered by the netting. The MTLB was destroyed, and fire started to consume much of the camouflage cover.

For good measure Wedemeyer dived on the area twice more, dropping another Rockeye and then spraying the netting with his 20-
millimeter cannon.

Frey recollected: "At the time we weren't exactly sure what we had
hit so the only thing we claimed was the single MTLB." The crew
later learned that the camouflage netting hid an entire Iraqi mechanized infantry company—six MTLBs, five BMPs, three Zil trucks,
and numerous soldiers. "And later on Bull told me that he had taped
the whole thing with his FLIR—his squadron actually included it in
their *Greatest Hits* video after the war."

The goal of the battlefield preparation had been to pummel the
enemy so thoroughly that the RCTs would have to do nothing more
strenuous than "wade through a sea of body parts." Wedemeyer and
Frey were doing their part to meet 3rd MAW's obligations.

After a quick trip to the tanker Frey and Wedemeyer were tasked
with reconnoitering the route toward Al Basrah. "From map and
ATARS photo studies, and because we had flown a sortie up there the
night before, we knew the area pretty well," Frey recalled. It was only
a few minutes before they came across an Iraqi tank column about
five miles east of where they had left Second Tanks. The line of tanks
was made up of about five T-55s. The aircraft had just one Rockeye
and five rockets remaining, and the two Marines thought better of
using up their remaining ordnance when other aircraft might do the
job better.

Instead Wedemeyer made a low, fast pass over the lead tank. "They
stopped immediately and ran from their tanks," recounted Frey. "No
doubt they had an idea of what we were capable of doing to them."
But it was here that the pair encountered the friction that so often
jams up the execution of a fast-moving war. "Aside from getting the
DASC to assign aircraft to work with us, we ran into a bigger problem
because the column we found was located right on the boundary between RCT-7's area of responsibility and RCT-5's. RCT-5 wasn't sure
that RCT-7 didn't have anyone close to those tanks, and it was the
same with RCT-7 relative to the whereabouts of RCT-5's forces. It
took almost a half hour to sort it all out."

In the meantime the Iraqi tank crews had gotten restive. When death didn't come immediately after Wedemeyer's initial pass, they climbed back into their T-55s and started toward Second Tanks again. A second pass stopped them again, and again they cleared their vehicles. When, after a few minutes, there still were no American bombs falling on their heads, the Iraqis started moving once more.

While trying to keep this first line of tanks distracted, Frey and Wedemeyer discovered a second column of five T-72 tanks moving in the same direction only a couple of miles or so to the east. The two fliers had their hands full—it was a "cat herding" situation. Wedemeyer pointed down at the lead tank of the second column and stopped it with a 5-inch WP rocket that hit the road just in front of it. In the meantime the initial column had started moving again. "Finally," Frey said, "we got a pair of Hornets overhead. They were very low on gas and had time for only one pass." Just as the two single-seat F/A-18Cs began their attack a civilian vehicle appeared out of nowhere and started down the line of tanks. Adhering to the extremely restrictive ROE that characterized this phase of the war, the F/A-18Cs aborted their run and, dangerously low on fuel, left the area.

Not long after, a pair of AV-8Bs arrived and Frey gave them a quick brief that included a ten-digit grid coordinate while Wedemeyer marked the area with several rockets. "I don't know if it was the weather or what," Frey recalled, "but for whatever reason they dropped their GBU-12s about five hundred meters south of the target and left. They were out of bombs and gas."

This was hardly Marine Corps aviation's shining moment. Low on fuel themselves, Frey and Wedemeyer decided to drop their last Rockeye on the lead tank of the first column they had discovered. "Weeds outdid himself on this run," Frey said. "The weather was garbage and we were fairly low to begin with. When he finally dropped that last Rockeye and we pulled clear it was probably the lowest I'd ever been on a bombing run—that tank filled more than half of the FLIR display."

The Rockeye canister didn't open. Instead it tumbled into the tank at the point just between the engine compartment doors and the turret. "A Rockeye canister isn't designed for that sort of attack," said Frey, "but in this instance it worked. A 509-pound bomb traveling at five hundred knots . . . well, simple physics says it's going to do a lot of damage." The tank caught fire and burned.

Before the crew of Nail 33 departed, they made one more sweep of the area. They discovered more targets including a SCUD under tow that was accompanied by other vehicles. They passed the data to the DASC. The targets would have to be prosecuted by someone else.

After having spent nearly seven hours airborne that day, Frey and Wedemeyer made their way back to the tent that served as their squadron's ready room. "We showed our videotape to several of the guys, and when word got out a lot of other aircrews stopped by to watch," remembered Frey. "Not to beat our own drum, but it was some pretty good footage."

Eventually word got back to the MAG's commanding officer, Colonel Randolph "Tex" Alles. "Tex called us over to the MAG headquarters and got into us pretty good," Frey recalled. The two were questioned as to why they had broken the altitude restrictions that the wing had laid out. Frey and Wedemeyer answered that there was no way to get any work done above the clouds and that in some instances—particularly with Second Tanks—there were Marines under fire. Alles answered that clearance directly from the TACC was required to deviate from the restrictions, and, absent that, deviations were approved only if the Marines on the ground were being overrun.

Everyone hated the Iraqi SCUDs. It wasn't because the SCUD was such a fearsome weapon; rather, it was because it was just barely capable enough to force the Marines to take precautions. Every time that a SCUD launch was detected, or whenever a launch appeared imminent, sirens would sound. Everyone was required to stop their work, climb into their protective gear, and get inside a protective bunker.

The odds of any of the Iraqi missiles actually hitting what it was aimed at were very poor. The design was a Soviet one that dated to the 1950s; it had an accuracy that—at the very best—was measured in football fields; it was launched by Iraqis with circumspect training. That the missiles got airborne at all was a small miracle. Still, the system had a small record of successes. Only by sheer luck did one of the weapons hit a barracks housing American soldiers in the middle of Dhahran, Saudi Arabia, during Desert Storm on February 25, 1991. The twenty-eight deaths it caused marked the only success the SCUD had ever enjoyed against U.S. forces.

And truth be told, many of the surface-to-surface missiles that the Iraqis threw at the Coalition during Operation Iraqi Freedom were indigenous derivations of the older Soviet weapons. The Al Hussein was one of these. Supposedly longer-ranged than the SCUD-B, it was intended to be an example of Iraq's emerging prowess as an arms manufacturer. Of questionable design, dubious manufacture, and poor employment, these weapons were even less successful than the SCUDs used a decade earlier during Desert Storm. Still, on paper they were a threat, and they were taken seriously.

Because the missiles had a remote but real chance of hitting Coalition installations, then, U.S. forces were required to react. Part of that reaction—a big part—was donning protective Nuclear Biological Chemical suits. These suits were uncomfortable and bulky. Fully kitted out, most Marines couldn't effectively carry out their duties. They dripped with sweat on the inside, and condensation made it difficult to see out of their gas masks. Too, the gloves absolutely precluded any precision work, and the boots were difficult not only to pull on and off, but even to move around in. Salt in the wound was the realization by most of the Marines that the SCUD systems were only *postulated* to be able to carry a chemical or biological warhead.

As primitive and inaccurate as the system was, just the threat of a SCUD attack still had an effect on the Coalition forces. Even though the defensive shield that the Patriots provided had proven almost perfect, overly prudent U.S. leaders required their troops to take cover with every alert. But after a time it became a case of crying wolf.

One Marine remembered the first SCUD alert that sounded at his installation. "It was like a bunch of old women at a yard sale. Clothes and NBC gear were flying everywhere. By the time most of us got our shit on, the alarm was over. But then there was another. And another. I think we had at least twenty-five alarms during the first ten days or so."

With each false alarm the Marines became more and more inured to the threat. The same Marine quoted above remembered his reaction later in the campaign. "After not getting any sleep for about the fourth night in a row, I finally said 'fuck it' and just rolled over. I figured my sleeping bag would be a good enough filter and so did most of the other guys."

As much trouble as the threat of the SCUDs caused, there ultimately were no U.S. casualties caused by the aged system.

11

Rules of Engagement and Command and Control

As well as the air campaign was going, there was still some friction between the leadership at 3rd MAW and the crews who were executing the missions. For the fast movers—the F/A-18 Hornet and the AV-8B pilots—nothing was more frustrating than the altitude restrictions that the wing had mandated. The crews were limited to a floor—a "don't-go-below" altitude—of ten thousand feet above the ground. The reasoning behind this line of thought was that the chances of the Iraqis hitting anything above this altitude were very, very small. And if the altitude restriction limited the efficiency of the attack jets somewhat, well, that was acceptable. The war was going to be won regardless, and the wing—quite understandably—didn't want to lose any aircraft needlessly.

The altitude restrictions were eased somewhat if an aircraft was operating under the control of a Forward Air Controller (Airborne). In this situation the floor was lowered to five thousand feet. The logic was that the airborne FAC crew, with two sets of eyeballs and a pair of binoculars, could make reasonably certain that there were no sophisticated anti-aircraft threats in the area.

The pilots hated the restrictions. The Rules of Engagement drafted by the theater commander required that every target—regardless of its location—be positively identified, or PID'd. This was driven by an extreme sensitivity to the political implications of the civilian casualties that might result from a misidentification. In fact, not only was a PID required, a Collateral Damage Estimate, or a CDE, was also necessary. If a valid and PID'd target was discovered, but was too close to civilian or cultural structures, then it was off limits.

From ten thousand feet with the naked eye it was difficult to make a positive identification or a Collateral Damage Evaluation except with the largest of targets. And it was simply impossible to PID small targets such as tanks or armored vehicles. Even equipped with FLIR pods that provided some level of magnification, it was not possible to distinguish enemy armor from friendly at an altitude of ten thousand feet.

This drove some aircrews to question the soundness of the restrictions. A PID could generally be made from three to four thousand feet, depending on the sensor and the atmospheric conditions. Still, it sometimes took more than one pass over the target. One squadron commander recalled: "To make the PID while complying with the restrictions, my guys were racing around over the top of the bad guys two and three and four times. However, if they had been allowed to make just one pass that was low enough to make the PID the Iraqis would have had little chance to take a shot. On the other hand, when they complied with the rules they normally weren't able to make a PID on the initial flyover. They usually didn't get shot at the first time, but they sure did on the subsequent runs. The first pass was like giving a wake-up call to the bad guys. By the time that bombs actually started to fall, my guys had wasted a bunch of gas, exposed themselves to enemy fire, and given the Iraqis a chance to run or dig in."

This was particularly frustrating from a leadership standpoint. "I was charged with leading these fellas," one commander remembered. "It was my job to make sure that we played by the boss's rules. On the other hand, I didn't want to leave enemy forces alive on the battle-field just because I couldn't go low enough to make a bulletproof PID. Those same enemy forces would be in the fight the next day—trying to kill Marines." Another flight leader recalled, "No matter what I did, I felt that I was being forced to set a bad example for my subordinates."

Restrictions aside, there was a loophole. If Marines on the ground were in extremis, all altitude limitations were lifted and the crews were expected to do everything possible to assist their comrades on the ground. This meant everything short of raising the canopy and opening fire with their 9mm pistols.

As might be expected, there were different interpretations of *in extremis*. Sometimes just the fact that the aircrews were in radio contact with Marines who were engaged in a fight was enough to bring them down. And for their part, the troops loved to see the fast jets streaking overhead; bombs and bullets aside, the sight was a tremendous morale booster for the friendlies, and terrifying for the enemy. Regardless of nuances, this caveat allowing the lifting of the altitude restriction worked; in numerous instances the fast movers blasted away dug-in fighters to clear the way for their ground-bound brothers. Indeed, at times there were Marine Hornets racing around at a thousand feet or less strafing all manner of targets, to include black-suited Fedayeen on foot.

But it wasn't just the jet jocks who chafed at their restrictions; the ROE was considered impractical at the tactical level by helicopter gunship pilots as well. Lieutenant Colonel Steve "Woodman" Heywood was the commander of HMLA-267, a composite squadron made up of AH-1W Cobras and UH-1N Hueys. Nearly all of his ships—twenty-three of twenty-six—sustained battle damage during the fighting.

Heywood believed the ROE was responsible for a significant portion of this damage—particularly that portion of the ROE that treated the engagement of enemy troops who may or may not have been surrendering. "The first group of my birds that was shot up, a flight of three engaging a GNH-45 artillery battery, exposed themselves to the enemy by adhering strictly to the ROE that was imposed. In this instance they pulled off without engaging because the enemy at the position was waving the white flag."

Heywood believed that the higher command's goal to spare those who did not wish to fight was a laudable one, and one that may have worked elsewhere. But attacks on his crews by Iraqis under white flags continued, and he and the other commanders became increasingly vexed. "You can imagine that it did not take long to alter our posture and engagement decisions vis-à-vis 'surrendering troops.'

"The problem with the ROE," the commander went on, "was that it was a single, all-encompassing set of rules. It was written for the lance corporal infantryman, the guy pulling the trigger in the Abrams tank, the fixed-wing pilots — everyone. It just didn't translate well across all the different weapons systems in the heat of battle when you had to decide very quickly what you were going to do."

Neither did he agree with those critics who claimed that the high percentage of battle damage his unit sustained stemmed from ranging too far afield — cowboys looking for a fight in Indian Country. "We went deeper forward when we felt that the particular aspects of a given situation warranted it. That's what we're trained to do. For instance," he continued, "there was an episode during the first week or so when a unit of Brits was taking casualties from an Iraqi artillery battery. The fixed-wing boys couldn't help, and one of my captains made the decision on the spot to take his four-ship — a division of Cobras — up to help.

"He made the judgment call to take the risk and go fourteen kilometers out in front of the friendlies. When it was all over, he and the other three crews killed that arty battery and destroyed a tank platoon, some anti-aircraft pieces, and a whole bunch of Iraqis. And he saved Coalition lives by doing it. This is what my guys get paid to do."

Heywood didn't argue the need for a good, effective ROE. Rather, he lamented the fact that little was done to modify or change it once it became apparent that the original set was not only ineffective, but also dangerous. Bottom line, he believed that realistic and effective training, combined with good personal leadership, were what made the difference in the face of doctrinal shortcomings. "There is a fine line between stupidity and good tactics, flight leadership and courage. Sometimes this is measured in results: If you killed the target, you did things right."

Heywood qualified his comment, "Of course that's a bit too simplistic. What is true is that positive results come from realistic and demanding training of the highest standards. What I think happened most of the time during the fighting was that the flight leaders made reasonable decisions based on the threat, the ground commander's desires, and the prevailing tactical situation. These decisions were devastating to the enemy."

It is the accounts of individual Marine fliers that make up the bulk of this book. While these narratives are interesting on their own, it is important to understand them in the context of the Marine command and control structure. As indicated earlier, 3rd MAW was commanded by Major General James "Tamer" Amos, while Brigadier General Terry "Guts" Robling served as Amos's deputy or assistant wing commander. Between the two they split the oversight of the wing's operations. Although Amos was always in charge, he delegated the "night page" to Robling while he led operations himself during the day. "This worked out reasonably well," Robling recalled. "Tamer was a pretty easy guy to work with, and it helped that he had a great relationship with the other generals throughout the Marine Corps and the rest of the theater." While the theory of daytime and nighttime shifts made perfect sense, the reality was that neither one of the two generals could stand to be away from the center of the action for more than a few hours during the day. "Truth be told," Robling said, "I think that we both averaged about twenty hours a day in the TACC."

The Tactical Air Command Center, callsign Icepack, was located at Al Jaber, and it was where Amos and Robling hung their hats—at least when they were awake. The Marine portion of the air war was directed from this center, equipped with wall-sized displays, banks of computers, extensive communications suites, and the staff to man it all. The action in the TACC revolved around the ATO, or Air Tasking Order.

The ATO was simply the flight schedule for the day. But it was far from simple. It was built in pieces by the staffs of all the various services using inputs from hundreds or more sources. These sections were then forwarded to the CFACC in Saudi Arabia. There it was assembled, reviewed, adjusted, approved, and disseminated. It was huge—hundreds and hundreds of pages per day. Not only did it list all the individual flights, but it also delineated units, types and numbers of aircraft, callsigns, targets, times, weapons, procedures, coordinating directions, special instructions, and more. It took a thousand or more people to build. This single paragraph can hardly do justice to the complexity of effort that goes into building the ATO; it is a science that people spend careers to learn.

"One of the keys to our success," said Robling, "was a system that we put into place especially for this fight." Amos and Robling tagged four experts to monitor the details of the battle around the clock. Each of them was an aviator, each of them was a colonel, and each of them understood the wing commander's intent and had the experience and expertise to execute it. "They would participate in building a given day's ATO," said Robling, "and then would come on duty to execute that same ATO. And of course they were in the TACC to take over or hand over for at least a couple of hours before and after. They put in long days." This familiarity with a particular ATO paid huge dividends in the execution. With the experts' aviation expertise and firsthand knowledge of the fight, they made decisions that affected what happened on the battlefield in real time. Because they personally captained the air war from where they sat in the TACC, they were dubbed "Battle Captains." Robling recollected: "There is no doubt that one of the primary reasons the campaign went as well as it did was because of the hard work of these four Marines: Colonels Jeffrey White, Raymond Fox, Mark Mahaffey, and Bill Griffen."

Most of the Marine sorties were directed toward supporting the "grunt" on the ground. The controlling entity for this effort was the

Direct Air Support Center. With the callsign of Blacklist, it was out-fitted much like the TACC except on a smaller scale. With its entire focus on supporting ground operations, the DASC coordinated with the Fire Support Coordination Center (FSCC) that was embedded with the First Marine Division in order to collect and prioritize re-quests for air support. It then parceled sorties as required. War being the great confuser that it is, the "Dascateers" also serviced ad hoc, time-critical requests that came to them outside normal channels. When operations reached deep into Iraq, the longer distances made radio communications more difficult, and the DASC was augmented by a specially configured KC-130 that served as an airborne DASC— the DASC(A). The DASC(A), callsign Sky Chief, helped to ensure better connectivity across the breadth of the battlefield.

The TAOC, or Tactical Air Operations Center, callsign Tropical, was responsible for controlling the air defense effort. In this conflict Saddam's air force stayed on the ground, and there was little air de-fense to control. Although the Iraqis did send rockets into Kuwait, the Marine Corps possessed no missile defenses capable of defending against them; the Army's Patriots took this duty. The Marines who manned the TAOC directed more effort toward routing friendly air-craft toward the various killboxes and TSTs (Time Sensitive Targets) as the situation dictated. With their surveillance radar they also pro-vided good situational awareness and could vector aircraft toward aerial refuelers or other important points.

The final link in the chain that ran from the TACC all the way down to the battlefield was the FAC, or Forward Air Controller. These were Marine officer aviators pulled from flying billets and as-signed to ground units for a year or two at a time. They marched with the grunts, got dirty with the grunts, fought with the grunts, and killed with the grunts. Requesting and controlling the CAS, or Close Air Support, that the ground unit needed was their task. Their familiarity with aviation procedures combined with the savvy that came from having worked with the grunts from the air made them perfectly suited for the job. Their airborne counterpart was the FAC(A)—the airborne FAC. These specially trained F/A-18D crews often ran the deeper fight, but could also control aviation and artillery fires close to the troops.

In practice it worked something like this: A crew would pull the appropriate information for their scheduled sortie from the ATO that the TACC had helped build and was managing full-time. After getting airborne and checking in with the TAOC, the crew would contact the DASC. The DASC would give them amplifying information, change their mission, or simply send them on their way. Ultimately — if the crew were flying a CAS mission — they would contact a FAC, and the FAC would coordinate the support he needed.

Again, these descriptions are simplifications of a process that requires years for professionals to learn well. Still, in the framework of the stories presented here, they help to build an appreciation of how the Marine Corps operates as a complete air-and-ground team.

12

===

Tomato Man

By March 22 the various RCTs had met or exceeded their objectives of the previous day and now concentrated on meeting their remaining assignments while shifting their effort west toward An Nasiriyah and the Euphrates River. To the west, TF Tarawa and RCT-1 moved on An Nasiriyah, where the Army's Third Infantry Division had taken a bridge across the Euphrates. The Army's capture of this link had opened a route over the river; it also allowed them to bypass the considerable enemy forces that waited in the city. These would be left for the Marines to deal with. In the South Rumaylah oil fields RCT-5 executed a handoff of its area with elements of the First UK Division, while to the east, just south of Al Basrah, RCT-7 continued to battle remnants of the Iraqi Army as well as various factions of fighters who wore no uniforms.

That morning probably marked the first time since the war in Vietnam that Marine Corps Cobras had blown up an enemy boat. Lieutenant Colonel "Woodman" Heywood and his four-ship of AH-1Ws had spent much of the first few hours of daylight supporting RCT-7 against targets north of Az Zubayr near Highway 8. After shooting up Iraqi positions inside a set of buildings, Heywood and his second section leader caught sight of two patrol boats trying to escape up a nearby canal. Heywood sent a TOW missile after one of them, and his second section leader launched another TOW. The pair of near-simultaneous explosions were spectacular. "I remember thinking," Heywood said, "that it was a shame that our video systems weren't working that day."

He was leading the four aircraft back south toward Astrodome in Kuwait when he overflew a FARP convoy on the highway. After reversing course and exchanging hand signals with the Marines in the lead vehicle, he brought his division down alongside the road, where each aircrew took care not to land on any of the exposed mines studding the ground. The FARP team Marines stepped around the deadly explosives while they quickly fueled and armed the Cobras. It wasn't long before Heywood's four gunships were airborne again.

This time they were directed to support a CAAT (Combined Anti-Armor Team) working along a canal that ran east-to-west about eight miles from the newly captured Al Basrah International Airport. Pushing north of the canal, Heywood and his flight started looking for enemy targets. It was only a short time later when his master caution light illuminated in conjunction with his CBOX (Combining Gear Box) pressure light. This component combined the power from both engines and transferred it to the aircraft's rotor system; if it failed, the aircraft failed. "I immediately started back south toward the friendlies," recounted Heywood. "Jon Livingston in my backseat kept an eye on the pressure gauge; minimum acceptable was twenty-five PSI, and we were looking at twenty PSI."

The four helicopters swung overhead the CAAT from the north, but Heywood quickly decided that the team wasn't big enough to provide the security he would need if the Iraqis decided that they really wanted his aircraft. With the CBOX pressure now down to fifteen PSI, he headed back toward Al Basrah International where Third Battalion, Fourth Marines was dug in with tanks and other armor. This was very near where he and his division had shot up the Iraqi positions earlier that day. "It was only a few minutes after I landed near the battalion CP when our aircraft started attracting mortar fire," he remembered. "I guess the Iraqis wanted a little bit of payback. Anyway, I watched the rounds start to creep closer and closer. At the same time I started to get some nervous looks from the grunts. I'm not certain that they wanted my Cobra sitting in and amongst them."

Because the CBOX pressure would hardly be relevant if the aircraft was hit by a mortar round, Heywood and Livingston said some quick good-byes and lifted away from the airfield hoping that the helicopter would hold together long enough for them to get somewhere safe. They headed south, still escorted by the rest of their flight, and it wasn't long before they spotted the headquarters element of Third Battalion, Eleventh Marines. Nearby was a CSSD (Combat Service Support Detachment) fueling point.

Heywood and Livingston set their aircraft down and sent the other three crews back to base to help coordinate the maintenance effort that would be required to get the helicopter airworthy again. After a short chat with the battalion commander Heywood crossed the highway toward the CSSD. He recalled: "There were a lot of cars and trucks on the road. Most of the people just stared, but some of them cheered and waved. A young woman—maybe in her twenties—walked by with a herd of goats. She was taking them to feed and water, which was somewhat reassuring as it made me reasonably certain that there were no land mines in the area. She looked at me but didn't say anything and I remember thinking that the only thing these people really knew was war, and that it must have been a brutal existence."

The CSSD Marines readily agreed to provide security for Heywood's aircraft, and after stopping back at the battalion Command Post for a quick MRE he rejoined Livingston at the helicopter. "I amused myself for a while by sending text messages out on the new survival radio—I wanted to know how the recovery effort was going. Nobody answered. So much for combat e-mail." Bored with his radio, Heywood's interest was piqued when an older man and a young boy stepped out of a mud brick hut a few hundred yards away. The two spent some time feeding a handful of goats and then tended to a small patch of tomatoes. Again Heywood reflected on their primitive, seemingly miserable lives.

It was midafternoon when the three-ship of Cobras returned escorting two CH-46Es from HMM-364—the world-famous Purple Foxes. "I sent the Cobras away to go kill stuff," Heywood recalled, "while Gunny Pack and his team set to work fixing my helicopter." It was during all of this coming and going that the CSSD Marines got Heywood's attention. There, coming across the field, was the old Iraqi man and the young boy.

"The Marines were doing their job," recounted Heywood, "but I wasn't convinced that the guy was a threat, so I walked out to meet him." The man was short but walked upright and with confidence. He was dressed in traditional Arab style with a white dishdasha and a red-and-white-checked gutra over his head. And probably because he was a farmer, he was wearing boots instead of sandals. "He was animated and happy," said Heywood, "and he kept gesturing out toward his house. We smiled a lot at each other but had no way to communicate. I looked back at the Marines and they were keeping a close eye on him—no doubt ready to take him out if he made the wrong move."

After a short time the Iraqi farmer and the boy left, but were soon on their way back. This time they were carrying something—a box full of tomatoes. "We gestured some more," Heywood said, "and I figured that he was trying to sell me the tomatoes, so I pulled out my wallet." The Iraqi would have none of it. He pushed the Marine's money away and held the box of tomatoes toward him again.

"It was then that I realized that the man was giving us a gift—he was thanking us for what we were doing. It was an incredible moment standing there in that field with millions of dollars of aircraft and all those armed Marines and this simple farmer and his boy. He really had nothing but a mud house, some goats, and a tomato patch, but he was proud of what he had and was happy we were there. He was giving us what he could in order to thank us. That man showed us the very best of Arab culture, and I think that we all learned a lesson that day."

Heywood thanked the man heartily and the pair of them and the small boy laughed as Heywood made exaggerated gestures—pantomiming how he would eat and enjoy the tomatoes. A little while later the old man and the boy waved good-bye and headed back to tend their goats and crops.

By now the aircraft was fixed. Still feeling good about having made a warm connection across a chasm of culture and language, Heywood couldn't help but reflect on what had just taken place. The irony was still with him as he strapped into his gunship and brought it roaring back to life. On the one hand he was hoping that all would be well with the old man, while at the same time he and Livingston were getting airborne and heading west to kill more Iraqis. It was a kooky world.

The RPG that struck the M88 tank retriever near Al Basrah on March 22 destroyed the vehicle and badly wounded three of the Marines inside. One of the more grievously injured men was Master Gunnery Sergeant Guadalupe Denogean, a twenty-five-year veteran who had emigrated from Mexico with his parents nearly forty years earlier. His younger Marines, also hurt, braved the flames that consumed the retriever and pushed and pulled his broken body out of the wreckage.

Denogean belonged to First Tanks. But when the unit moved on it did so without two Denogeans. Young Sergeant Jovan Denogean, also on First Tanks' roster, stayed out of the fight until he was certain that his father would survive.

But he would be back.

13

===

Cobras Over An Nasiriyah

By the end of March 22, TF Tarawa was already engaged with the enemy in An Nasiriyah. RCT-1 passed through Tarawa's zone two different times in order to secure bridges to the north and west of the city in preparation for the arrival of RCT-5 and -7 on March 23. Those two RCTs completed their handover to the British of that part of Iraq that sat between Kuwait and Al Basrah. Once around An Nasiriyah, RCT-1, -5, and -7 would continue the race north while Tarawa would stay behind to kill enemy fighters who remained in the city. That was the plan, anyway.

It was daytime again and Captain Todd "BT" Miller of HMLA-267 was dusty, thirsty, and assed-out tired. So were the crews of the other three AH-1W Cobras that made up the rest of his flight. "Seeing the sunrise was a lot like taking aspirin for a bad headache," he remembered. "It released a lot of tension." As their division leader, Miller had flown them all over southeastern Iraq during more than twelve hours of night operations. It was the longest night mission that any of them had ever flown; they had taken off prior to sunset the previous afternoon. "We had been flying all night on goggles, shuttling back and forth between the FARPs and the front lines near the Rumaylah oil fields, Al Basrah, and Umm Qasr. We had been working with Marines and with the Brits but most of it had been a bust as we hadn't shot at anything all night."

Now, on the morning of March 23, his four-ship was refueling at the Astrodome FARP just inside the Kuwaiti border with Iraq. Their tasking was complete and they were preparing to return to their base at Ali Al Salem. "We were pretty much done in," Miller recalled. "All the aircraft needed servicing and my dash-two had a mechanical problem that pretty much kept him from doing any more ops anyway."

It was then that the call came: "Sky Chief, the airborne DASC, called us and said that there were friendlies engaged in a pretty heavy firefight up in An Nasiriyah. They wanted us to launch immediately." Miller was responsible not only for making sure that whatever mission the crews were assigned got accomplished, but also for making the correct decisions about the welfare of the men and the aircraft. "Aside from safety considerations—because we had been up all night—I was concerned because some crews had caught hell during the previous couple of days for flying beyond what they were scheduled. As young Cobra pilots we'd had it pounded into us that the grunts get what they want—always. I think that guys were just leaning forward and trying to do the right thing." Unfortunately, this type of commitment was difficult on the tasking cycle. Miller knew that he was supposed to stick with the schedule, and in this case that meant going home.

Nevertheless, he double-checked with Sky Chief and the word came back: They were the only available crews and aircraft, and they were needed straightaway. "I kind of polled the rest of the fellas and of course they were all chomping at the bit to go out and kill bad guys. We put a quick brief together and got airborne in a hurry. I sent dash-two back home to Ali Al Salem; he wasn't too happy about that."

Operating under the callsigns of Orkin 61, 62, and 63, the three crews raced northwest as fast as their hard-worn ships would carry them. Miller was manning the front cockpit of his bird. It was from this station that the Cobra's weapons were typically fired. In the aft cockpit was his good friend Dave "Fuse" Bussel. "Fuse was a great pilot and a really good sounding board for me if I was up against a tough decision," Miller said. "If I was thinking one way I could generally count on his experience and knowledge to validate what I wanted to do. On the other hand, he wasn't afraid to speak up if he thought I was about to do something that might not be too bright. The two of us made a pretty solid crew." The rest of his division was made up of seasoned fliers as well. Captains "Weasel" Weis and Ron "Ike" Canizzo crewed the formation's second aircraft, and Captains Dan "Shoeshine" Sheehan and Brad "Gash" Lagaski rounded out the lineup in the third gunship.

The three ships were flying northwest, parallel with Highway 8, toward An Nasiriyah when they overtook an enormous column of friendly equipment. "It really bothered me," Miller said, "because there would be a break with no one on the road, and then we'd come up on another line of vehicles. Well, until we got close I couldn't tell if they were our guys advancing, or the Iraqis retreating—I was worried about flying straight into an ambush. On the other hand, if they were bad guys I still wanted to be able to kill them."

The column that Miller and his three-ship had overtaken was Regimental Combat Team 5. It had started a two-hundred-mile road movement that same morning, its route also charted to An Nasiriyah.

Miller had other problems besides the long line of friendly vehicles. "We were going like hell and fuel was already a concern. Initially we were going to stop for gas at a new FARP just south of An Nasiriyah, but the closer we got the more it became obvious from Sky Chief that they needed us up there right now." The three crews put together a hasty game plan and pressed on. They decided to skip the refueling stop, shoot up their ammo upon making contact with the enemy, and then disengage to either find the new FARP or set down along the highway and wait for a refueling truck.

The men whom Miller and his crews were coming to aid were part of the First Battalion of the Second Marine Regiment, or "one-two" in Marine lexicon. They were stalled at a highway overpass at the southern approach to the city. Although the Marines were taking heavy fire, they were unable to counter with overwhelming fire of their own—an Army convoy had been ambushed earlier, and there were survivors still trapped in the area.

Miller remembered: "On the radio we were passed through a couple of different FACs until they handed us off to Major Scott Hawkins, callsign Hawk. He was assigned to a tank detachment at the very head of the column." By now things were getting hot; an AAV had already been hit by an RPG and sat smoking on the west side of the road. And whenever Hawkins keyed his radio, the Cobra crews could hear bullets pinging off the outside of his tank. Another factor played into the agitation. The three crews had been so tired when they left the FARP that they had all taken "go pills." These were legally sanctioned amphetamines—speed. They were wired.

The three Cobras slowed almost to a hover as they approached the fighting. From where he was battened down in his tank near the overpass, Hawk was having a difficult time making visual contact with the Cobras. "It was confusing when we got there," Miller recalled. "We could see the tanks in a staggered formation on the highway, and there was a lot of dust and smoke, but we couldn't really see the enemy positions." It was obvious when Hawkins finally caught sight of Miller's formation. A frantic call came over the radio: "You're taking fire! You're taking fire!"

Miller didn't see anything. "I called back, really calmly, 'From where?' and he shouted back, '*Everywhere!*' "

It was then that Sheehan and Lagaski in Orkin 63 took hits in their helicopter's tail boom. Now thoroughly alarmed and without a good idea of what the situation was, Miller wheeled his aircraft around and led the other two Cobras back south and out of range of the enemy gunners. "We fell back and regrouped, and checked to make sure that everyone was still okay. Then Sheehan spotted a heavy machine gun in a fighting hole. He hit it with a TOW and blew it to bits. And as we looked closer, we could see that the entire area on the west side of the highway was built up with trenches and fighting holes. There were bunkers and pillboxes, strong points in buildings, and guys with RPGs running back and forth between the different positions. The place was full of heavy weapons and vehicles—even some half-buried tanks."

Miller and the other two crews tore into the area like mad dogs. "We charged in there and just opened up on those guys. It was kind of a free-for-all; we weren't using the most organized tactics. The smartest thing we did was shoot and shoot and then shoot some more—sometimes from a hover. They didn't stand a chance."

The Cobra crews pummeled the enemy positions for fifteen more minutes. "Hawk was shouting into the radio and calling us onto targets. Fuse and I were shouting back and forth on the intercom, and of course all of us were talking and jamming the radio with all sorts of calls—it was crazy! I remember," continued Miller, "that the go pills had made my mouth incredibly dry; I felt like I had a wad of paper towels wrapped around my tongue." The three crews raced back and forth just above the ground and fired everything they carried, including wire-guided TOW missiles, laser-guided Hellfire missiles, 2.75-inch rockets—both high explosive and fléchette—and 20-millimeter cannon. They used it all to good effect. Miller remembered, "Weasel hit one bunker with a TOW and a dozen bodies literally came flying out of that thing when it exploded. After that I started looking through my scope at a line of trees and could see dozens of guys crawling through it. I opened up with the 20-millimeter and ripped that place to pieces." As Miller shredded the cover with his cannon, Hawk called out that there were army units in the same area. "My heart jumped into my throat—but only for a second. I could see plainly through the TSU [Telescopic Sight Unit] that the guys running for the city were Iraqis and definitely not ours. Hawk came back a moment later and confirmed that I was okay."

The destruction that Miller and Bussel were throwing down was multiplied two more times by the firepower that Weis and Canizzo in Orkin 62, and Sheehan and Lagaski in Orkin 63, were pouring into the Iraqis. Miller remembered that the 2.75-inch fléchette rockets

were particularly effective against troops in the open. Upon detona-
tion, hundreds of tiny metal darts flew in all directions. "Those
Iraqis," he recalled, "actually looked like they deflated when they got
caught by fléchettes; they dropped like they had been hit with a ham-
mer." Finally, out of ammunition and gas, the three Cobras fell back
and turned south to rearm and refuel.

"By now our hearts were really pounding," Miller recalled. "Up to
this point we hadn't gotten into any kind of shooting like this." He led
his flight back down the highway—back past the advancing mass of
men and equipment that made up RCT-5 and toward the spot where
Riverfront, the new arming and refueling point, was supposed to be
located. "On the way back we passed nose-to-nose with another
Cobra on his way up. I don't know who he was, but he asked if he
could join us. I told him that he was welcome, but that things were
hot up north and that they really needed help, so he pressed on
alone." Miller learned later that the crew of the lone ship had found
and laser-designated targets for fixed-wing aircraft; the decision to
press to the fight as a single ship had been a good one.

"We were really low on gas and in danger of flaming out. As we got
close to where the FARP was I actually spotted it because I saw two
army Black Hawks circling to land. I got hold of them on the radio
and told them what was going on and asked them to let us cut in line.
They had no problem with that and waved off to get behind us."

What Miller and the other two Cobras landed into was little more
than a dusty rendezvous point in the desert rather than a fully func-
tioning FARP. Only the fuel trucks had arrived, and they were just
getting set up. "The Marines working that FARP were busting their
asses," he recollected. "As soon as we got down they hooked up the
fuel hoses. Then the ammo trucks and troops started showing up and
they started off-loading all their stuff into the dirt and slapping it onto
our birds. It wasn't even close to being by the book but they just did
what good Marines always do: They made it happen."

While the young enlisted Marines hustled the aircraft back into
readiness, the three crews evaluated their situation and put together
their follow-up plan. "Shoeshine's bird had two holes in the tail

boom, but it was obviously still flyable. I needed him and Gash back at An Nasiriyah and cleared them to fly another mission. We decided to be a little smarter for this next sortie, though," Miller recalled. "Fuse and I discussed it and drew a few things on paper, and then he got out and quickly briefed the other copilots using an expedient dirt terrain model."

The "expedient" model was sand that the fliers kicked and scratched into place. The plan was to put two birds forward and shooting while one stayed back and covered their rear. Then, as the crews shot up the targets, they would rotate positions. "Now that we had all been there," Miller said, "we named a few of the more prominent features so that we could communicate better. Simple terms like *the lake* and *the wall* would bring everyone's eyes to the same spot when things got going hot and heavy."

Within forty minutes of touching down, the three gunships clattered airborne again in a whirling cloud of sand, leaving almost a dozen newly arrived aircraft behind. The word was out: Marines were in dire need of air support but the helicopters from Ali Al Salem couldn't range An Nasiriyah without stopping for gas first. Miller looked over his shoulder at the near-frantic activity at the FARP. "Those young Marines at Riverfront who got us put back together were amazing."

Approaching An Nasiriyah again, Miller's flight was passed on to a new FAC, Captain Dennis Santare, callsign Mouth. The complexion of the fight had changed—many of the uniformed soldiers had fled. "We had to be careful because there were many more civilians running around this time," Miller said. This made things particularly difficult for the Marine fliers, because the enemy had to be positively identified as hostile. "They had to have weapons in their hands before we could kill them," Miller said. This part of the ROE would frustrate Cobra pilots throughout the war—after all, what civilian in his right mind ran around in the middle of a pitched battle? That the Iraqi combatants sometimes didn't wear uniforms exacerbated the problem.

"These people weren't stupid," Miller recalled. "By now, even

though we were still taking fire, most of them were running for the
city. It was a rout, and they were leaving a lot of equipment behind
that we just blew to smithereens." In keeping with the brief he had
put together at the FARP, Miller positioned two aircraft forward while
the third provided covering fire. "Rather than executing a dog-pack
attack like the first sortie had been, this effort was very methodical,
and went just as we briefed," Miller continued. Regardless, the
enemy was still fighting back and scoring hits. In fact, although
Miller didn't know it yet, Weis and Canizzo had been hit, although
not critically.

"The Iraqis had a lot of stuff hidden amongst palms and fig trees
and dry, brushy growth. One by one we picked off anti-aircraft guns,
trucks, heavy machine guns—it was like a smorgasbord of targets. I
can remember thinking that it was like thumbing through the pages
of the recognition books back in training." It was then that Weis in
Orkin 62 spotted a large gun barrel reaching up over a berm next to
an open-pit mine about twenty-five hundred yards north of Santare's
position on the east side of the road. "At first," Miller said, "we
thought it was a large anti-aircraft gun, a 57-millimeter S-60."

By this time a flight of Marine F/A-18 Hornets had arrived on station, and Miller tried to put together a brief so that the fighters could
hit the big gun and whatever was behind it. "But behind the berm it
was difficult even for me to see and I was afraid that at the altitude the
Hornets were flying, unless I marked it really well, they'd put a bomb
into one of several nearby houses. To be honest there wasn't much
left in the area that warranted a thousand-pound bomb. What ended
up happening was that Weis 'lased,' or marked, the gun for me with
his laser, and I fired a Hellfire missile right into it. It went up in a
huge eruption that set off multiple secondary explosions. When we
saw the pieces fly we realized that the barrel had actually belonged to
a T-55 tank. At the same time, Weasel spotted two more barrels, and
I fired three more missiles while he lased. They were all direct hits
with spectacular explosions—mostly due to Weasel's keen eyes and
steady hands."

Now with the tanks aflame, the Hornet pilots—more than two

miles high—had a good fix on the area and were cleared to drop their bombs under positive control from Santare. Ultimately nine T-55s were destroyed. Because of how they were positioned, it is likely that the enemy tanks would have gone unnoticed from the ground and would have been able to execute a flank attack against the advancing Marine column. The casualties could have been enormous.

After shooting up most of their ammunition, Miller and the rest of his flight took a moment to catch their breath and assess the situation around them. The approach into An Nasiriyah was a flaming shambles. The fight between the defending Iraqis and the Marines had gone badly for the defenders. The Iraqi fighting positions, their equipment, their buildings, even their people were burning. More and more Marine ground units—covered by more and more Marine aviation units—were pushing into the city.

"It was time for us to get out of there," recounted Miller. "Our guys on the ground were making some headway and there was finally plenty of help overhead. We checked out with Mouth and headed back for Riverfront." The three ships made an uneventful retrograde back to the FARP, where the seemingly tireless young Marines again hung a new load of weapons and topped their fuel tanks. "While they got our birds ready," recalled Miller, "we got together and discussed the situation. We were exhausted. Two of the aircraft were shot up and all of them needed extensive servicing. Most important, there was now plenty of help at An Nasiriyah. If we pressed back north again the potential for ugly things to start happening was very real and we decided to pack it in."

They didn't say much to each other over the radio on the way back to Ali Al Salem. Normally they would have engaged in a bit of "smokin' and jokin' " during the transit back to base—it helped to keep the mood light. But on this day they were overly tired. Still, Miller couldn't help but smile behind the dark visor that covered much of his face. The three crews had trained for years to do exactly what they had just done. It had been a textbook example of the Cobra community's reason for existence: close fire support for Marines in contact. They had performed well—and with ferocity. "I was smiling," Miller remembered, "because I felt like we had won one for the grunts. Without asking, I knew that the rest of the guys were smiling, too."

When the three AH-1W Cobra crews of HMLA-267's Orkin 61 flight shut down back at Ali Al Salem Air Base in the early afternoon of March 23, it marked the completion of nineteen hours of continuous combat flight operations.

Orkin 61 flight was recognized for putting one of the initial cracks into the defenses that guarded the approach to the heart of An Nasiriyah. Not only that, but the crews had undoubtedly saved the lives of many of their fellow servicemen as well. The men manning the HMLA-267 Cobras that day were officially credited with destroying multiple fighting positions; numerous vehicles including six large Zil transport trucks; four tanks; four ZU-23, 23-millimeter anti-aircraft guns; four ZPU-4, 14.5-millimeter anti-aircraft guns; and approximately sixty enemy soldiers.

The rhythm of the fighting was such that aircrews—especially the Cobra and Huey fliers—were often flying operations that were double or even triple the length of anything they were used to during peacetime. Regardless, it was something that the Marines on the ground required and something that had to be done. In order to keep the crews alert in the event that the lack of rest became an issue, the fliers had the *option* of taking performance enhancement drugs—go pills, or five-milligram doses of amphetamines. The Marines of HMLA-269 were among those authorized to use the drugs. Colonel Robert "Boomer" Milstead, the commanding officer of MAG-29, HMLA-269's parent unit, remembered, "I used to call those crews my 'little crack babies.'"

The counterparts to the amphetamine pills were the downers or "no-go pills." These allowed the fliers to rest when heat, noise, and stress made getting a good sleep impossible. "These were fifteen-

milligram doses of Restoril," explained Milstead. "They weren't allowed in the cockpit; this precluded anyone from taking one by accident." In practice, the careful and regulated use of both the
amphetamines and the barbiturates was a success, and few problems
were reported.

14

===

Huey Shootout Over An Nasiriyah

"It was supposed to be a 'softball' mission—a no-brainer," remembered Major Paul "Goose" Gosden of HMLA-267. The ATO for March 23 called for a pair of UH-1N Huey helicopters to provide command and control support to RCT-5's one-day, two-hundred-mile road march. The huge regimental combat team was scheduled to move up Highway 8 from a point south of An Nasiriyah, up past the city, and northwest toward Baghdad.

"All we were supposed to do was act as a radio relay overhead the RCT. That was why I had no problem when Nick Kulish, an embedded reporter from *The Wall Street Journal*, asked if he could come along," remembered Gosden. "It was also the 'cherry popper' mission for First Lieutenant Mike 'Stroke' Bersky, my copilot and the youngest pilot in the squadron. He hadn't been in Iraq up to this point and this would be a good opportunity to get him wet."

Aside from Kulish and Bersky, the rest of Gosden's crew consisted of his two crew chiefs, Sergeant Rogan McIntyre and Corporal Sarah Wilson. McIntyre was the classic hard-charging "salty dog"; he felt that he could do anything. "And Wilson," Gosden remembered, "we called her Mom. Not only could she do all the crew chief stuff, but she mother-henned us around like we had sprung straight from her loins. She made sure we were clean, warm, and fed. I can still picture her sitting cross-legged in the back of the bird making peanut butter and jelly sandwiches for us with that big K-Bar knife she kept strapped to her leg."

Gosden, his crew, and Kulish were awake by 0300 that morning. They met with the crew of the other ship to brief and coordinate the mission. "My wingman," Gosden recalled, "was Captain Lonnie 'Chivo' Camacho. He was a great guy who also had a really good crew. He had become my wingman only recently because of all the crew swaps that were made before the war." After briefing and grabbing a quick bite to eat, Gosden and the rest of the flight climbed into their aircraft and clattered airborne out of Ali Al Salem Air Base in Kuwait at 0700.

"This was the mission," Gosden said, "when I learned that there is no such thing as too much firepower or too much ammo." His aircraft was armed with an M2 .50-caliber machine gun in the left door with four hundred rounds of ammunition. This was Sarah Wilson's weapon. Sergeant McIntyre operated an M240G 7.62-caliber machine gun in the right door with four hundred rounds. On the outside of the aircraft there was a pod of seven 2.75-inch folding-fin rockets. Also, each crewman had his personal M16 strapped against the transmission wall in the back—with several hundred rounds per weapon. Aside from all these weapons, each of the Marines carried a 9-millimeter Beretta pistol.

Gosden brought his flight into the Astrodome FARP just before crossing the border into Iraq. At Astrodome, the Hueys were topped off and the crews received an intelligence update before getting airborne again. They test-fired their weapons as they crossed into Iraq. "It was a pretty nice day—clear except for a scuzzy film of oil smoke above us. We were cruising at about a hundred knots at an altitude of two hundred feet, with Chivo maintaining a position roughly two hundred feet abeam." After about a half-hour flight the huge column of Marines and equipment came into view. Coiled into a defensive formation, it was more than two miles in diameter.

The RCT's air officer called a "tally" on the two Hueys and talked

Gosden's eyes onto the antenna-covered vehicles that made up the Command Post. Once the crews landed and shut down, the column's aviation tankers set to work topping off their aircraft. While the refueling was under way Gosden met with the RCT commander, Colonel Joe Dunford, and received a quick brief. Essentially the two helicopters were there to provide a communications link for the colonel and his column. On the road the RCT was so long—fifteen to twenty miles—that maintaining radio line-of-sight from the front to the rear wasn't possible. Colonel Dunford also pawned off a radio operator and one of his lieutenant colonels on Gosden and his crew. Assigned to act as the airborne commander, the lieutenant colonel was a reservist and a toy maker in his real life.

Once the column began to move, Gosden stationed his two helicopters overhead in a long, lazy orbit. "I felt like Dad in the family truckster," he remembers. "I was letting the new guy, Bersky, drive, I had a *Wall Street Journal* reporter bouncing around in the back, along with a toy maker, some kid radio operator, and my own crew."

The two Hueys rode herd on the RCT like a pair of airborne cowpokes—prodding the laggards along, relaying radio messages, and keeping the commander updated. They also monitored the radio traffic on the Direct Air Support Center frequency. There was something big going on in An Nasiriyah to their north—parts of Task Force Tarawa were pinned down. "I could hear them talking about casualties, and they were pushing as much air support as they could find into the area."

On the hazy horizon, Gosden and the rest of the flight could make out smoke plumes rising from the Iraqi city. "After we had been airborne for a while I brought the flight back to the rear of the column and we set down. On the ground I briefed the command as to what we were hearing and seeing. By now we needed gas but the RCT's tankers had already rolled, so I dumped off the toy maker and the radio operator and told them we'd be back. After we got airborne I pointed us toward a brand-new FARP they had set up just south of An Nasiriyah."

When they arrived at the FARP, Gosden and his flight found a madhouse of frantic activity. "These guys had literally just set up shop; there was expeditionary matting lying all over the place, a bunch of trucks, stacks of ammo, and people running everywhere. And it was the only game in town. There were six Cobras, two CH-46s, and a pair of Army Black Hawks already in line when we showed up." After a twenty-minute wait, Gosden and Camacho brought their helicopters to the head of the line and shut down while they refueled.

Gosden and the other pilots had stepped away from their aircraft for a few minutes to talk and stretch. It wasn't long before McIntyre ran up to them. The DASC was calling for Opah 76—their callsign. Gosden ran back and got on the radio. "The DASC told me that the boys in An Nasiriyah needed help *now!* I started to think that things were getting pretty desperate if they were calling in a pair of Hueys for close air support."

The two crews scrambled aboard their birds and quickly rumbled aloft, north toward where the fight was. "It was just me and my crew now. I had told Nick Kulish that this was probably a trip he didn't want to be along for and left him behind; he seemed okay with that." The flight intercepted the highway and started right toward the heart of the city. It was ugly. Aside from the smoke, they could make out fires and explosions; there was a pitched battle raging on the main thoroughfare through the town.

What Gosden and his flight were flying into was a fight that had started earlier that morning when elements of the Army's 507th Maintenance Company had gotten lost and been ambushed. The surprise attack had cost them eleven killed and six captured. The Marines of Task Force Tarawa had charged in and now were locked in a pitched clash with hundreds of Fedayeen and other irregular fighters. Gosden listened to the radio like a fan glued to the big game. Just as they reached the southern outskirts he began to jot down the frequencies and taskings that the DASC forwarded to him.

"It was right about then that Chivo called over the radio and said that he was having problems; he was out of fuel. He had taken off without a full bag of gas and on top of that, his auxiliary fuel tank wasn't transferring." Gosden had a tough decision to make. The primary formation element for firepower and self-protection considerations was the section, a flight of two aircraft. No one was supposed to go into combat without a wingman. This was a golden rule, a rule that was written in blood, and a rule that wasn't to be broken. Nevertheless, there were Marines under fire. They were Marines who might die if they didn't get help. They were Marines who needed Gosden to break the rule.

"Almost at this same time the DASC called us and asked for about the hundredth time how far out we were. It was obvious that they needed help immediately, so I made the decision to send Chivo back. Stroke and Mom and McIntyre and I pressed on alone."

With Bersky at the controls and McIntyre and Wilson at their guns, Gosden watched over his shoulder as Camacho wheeled his greasy gray bird back to the south. Turning back to the front he began to coordinate with the DASC to make contact with the Marines under fire. They were at 125 feet and one hundred knots flying up the main highway, straight into the city. "Everything was on fire. I mean everything—tanks and trucks and cars, even buildings. I can tell you right now, concrete burns if it gets hot enough." The inferno had been created by earlier flights of Cobra gunships and Air Force A-10s. Smoke from a refinery that had been damaged added to the choking mess that the helicopter was thrashing through.

The DASC passed Gosden to a Forward Air Controller with the callsign Mouth. The brief from Mouth—punctuated by heavy gunfire in the background—was simple: There were two main bridges on the road, one north and one south. Mouth and his Marines were north of the south bridge on the east side, and the Iraqi combatants were on the rooftops on the west side.

By now Gosden and his crew were taking fire. Streaks of tracers lashed out at them, the individual rounds making sharp cracking sounds as they passed close by. McIntyre answered back with short, staccato bursts from his M240G, while Wilson's .50-caliber gun replied with deeper booming volleys. The burning smell of gunpowder punctuated the stink of the smoke that was already burning their eyes.

"It was total chaos," Gosden remembered. "There were people running around everywhere—guys with guns dressed in jeans and tennis shoes. Some of them were in their traditional robes, and there were also civilians without weapons, but other than our Marines there wasn't anyone in uniform. Tracers and RPGs [Rocket Propelled Grenades] were flying all over the place. Stroke looked over at me with this sort of funny grin and said, 'Do you think we should be doing this?' I put on my best war face and said, 'Stroke, we're going in!'"

Ahead of him near the bridge Gosden could make out the hulks of two burning Marine AAVs—Assault Amphibian Vehicles, or Amtracks. They were only two of seven AAVs that would ultimately be destroyed that day. One had been mistakenly strafed by an Air Force A-10, while the other had been blasted by multiple RPG hits. By now he could also see the friendly positions. They set up an orbit over the beleaguered Marines, and Mouth started calling out targets. The noise of the battle was near deafening, and the chop of the helicopter's blades added to the din. Gosden oriented their runs so that either Mom or McIntyre could get a clear shot. Whichever gunner wasn't shooting would turn around and call out targets for the gunner who was engaged.

The reaction to the Huey's arrival was immediate. "We really started drawing a lot of fire, but at the same time we were shooting the hell out of those guys. By now I'd taken the controls from Stroke—this was a hell of a first mission for him—and was setting up our firing passes and trying to stay unpredictable. Meanwhile Mouth was shouting into the radio cheering us on and we were yelling back and forth over the intercom. It was absolute bedlam."

Mouth's unit was getting shot up from one particular rooftop, and they couldn't bring any weapons to bear. Gosden remembered what happened next: "So McIntyre spotted these guys and started to call my turns so that he could line up a shot. And he calls out 'left' then 'right,' then 'left, more left . . .' and then all of a sudden I hear rounds hitting the aircraft and he starts screaming, 'You're right over the fucking top of them! I can't get a shot!'"

Gosden jerked his Huey away in a hard bank to the left. From behind McIntyre screeched at him: *"Don't-ever-fly-over-that-fucking-building-again!"*

The approach to the rooftops was causing problems for the Huey crew. Running from east to west required Gosden to clear a set of power lines and then bunt the nose of the aircraft down to bring weapons to bear on the rooftops. Nevertheless, after getting shot up on the previous pass the Marine pilot was anxious to neutralize the enemy fighters, and he set the ship up for a rocket run. "I swung back across the road and as I pushed the nose over I could see this guy standing up with an AK-47—shooting it right at me. It really pissed me off and I got ready to give him a face full of rockets. Just when I couldn't get any closer I mashed down on the button . . . and nothing happened! The rocket pod was dead."

Gosden didn't have many choices: He could fly over the top of the building again, or he could turn off early. Either option made his helicopter a juicy target. "I pulled off hard to the right and Mom—all 105 blond pounds of her—opened up with that .50 caliber and cut the bastard right in half."

By now the unit on the ground was breaking loose. The Huey crew could see them standing up and cheering and moving farther up the road. Nevertheless, enemy fire still lashed up at the helicopter. "I was watching McIntyre as he was shooting on one pass," Gosden recalled, "and a bullet came up through the floor of the cabin, between him and his gun. It kind of brushed him back, and he had a startled look on his face. I couldn't help myself and started to chuckle. I shouted back at him that this wasn't like shooting at the tire stacks back home."

All of this had happened in only about ten minutes, but still Gosden and his crew were running low on fuel and ammunition. Mouth called and directed them to move two blocks north to work with a different FAC, callsign Kool-Aid. At this point Gosden wasn't sure he had enough fuel to get back to the FARP. The crew did a quick ammo count as well: Mom had about two hundred rounds remaining, while McIntyre was down to less than a hundred. "We took a sort of consensus and decided to stick around for as long as it took."

Gosden made contact with Kool-Aid, and it took less than a minute for him to set his helicopter over a pair of Abrams tanks stuck in mud just off the highway. They were badly bogged down, and the crews couldn't dig them out because of the fire they were taking. The Huey crew could see enemy bullets hitting the big tanks and knocking off wispy little clouds of dust.

"Kool-Aid kept telling us to take the bad guys out, and I kept telling him that I needed him to mark the target because I couldn't see where the rounds were coming from. He shouted back and said he couldn't mark the target because he was buttoned up inside his tank. This all seemed pretty ironic to me since we were hanging our asses out—literally—over the top of him, while he was snug in his tank.

"Finally," Gosden continued, "the obvious occurred to me. I told Kool-Aid to mark the target with his main gun. There was a dead period for about ten seconds and then all of a sudden a third tank roared up onto the highway, turned south, stopped, swung its turret west, fired, and turned a two-story building into dust."

Gosden banked his Huey toward the rubble and heard Kool-Aid call over the radio, "Okay, it's not that building, it's the one just to the north!" Gosden wondered to himself why his crew was bothering with the building when the tanks obviously could have taken it completely down by themselves. Regardless, they caught sight of the enemy combatants and blasted at them with the remainder of their ammunition. Finished, Gosden called Kool-Aid and told him that they were leaving and that more help was on the way. At the same time he heard a sharp cracking noise behind him. "I turned around and there was McIntyre, God bless him, with his M-16, shooting out the door. Screaming and shouting, he was fighting all the way out."

Having stayed much longer than his fuel allowed, Gosden and his crew made a beeline for the FARP they had left only an hour or so earlier. They landed with no fuel registering on the gauge, having arrived just as the last trucks were packing up to leave. Gosden's wingman, Captain "Chivo" Camacho, and his crew didn't make it back to the FARP at all. They set down adjacent to Highway 8 and stayed there until an LAR (Light Armored Reconnaissance) detachment drove up. After fashioning a water bottle into a funnel, the armored boys off-loaded enough fuel from jerricans to get Camacho airborne again and on his way home.

The fight at An Nasiriyah on March 23 was the sharpest and deadliest clash of the war. Marine losses totaled eighteen killed in action. This number would likely have been much higher without air support.

"We really went all out to support the fight at An Nasiriyah," remembered Robling of 3rd MAW's efforts. "The last week of March was particularly ugly, but we continued to work closely with Task Force Tarawa to give them the support they needed. Each night we'd get a call from Tarawa's commander—Rich Natonski—and he'd thank us for what we'd done that day while he outlined what he'd need the next." Still, it was a frustrating fight for the wing's aviators. Robling recalled the vexation: "An Nasiriyah was our first real exposure to the urban fight, and it highlighted the fact that aviation can't do everything. Unless you're going to level the entire place, individual Marines are going to have to go from house to house and clear the place out."

It is the enlisted Marines who make the Marine Corps what it is, and it is the staff noncommissioned officers—or staff NCOs—who make the enlisted Marines what they are. The staff NCOs are the men and women who started their military lives as privates, and then worked their way up the rank structure. They are the hands-on leaders who turn the officer's orders into action and who ultimately, through their own performance, determine whether their officer succeeds or fails.

Gunnery Sergeant Robert Hulet had proven himself over a career that had spanned two decades as a helicopter crew chief. But at the end of 2002 he was ready to open a new chapter in his life. He'd already submitted retirement papers when he was approached by his Commanding Officer, who wanted to know if he would consider an extension on active duty if the squadron was called up for service in

Iraq. Already a veteran of Desert Storm, Hulet could have easily said no and wouldn't have received the slightest bit of criticism. He was well respected; the fact that he had been asked to stay was indicator enough of his reputation.

Instead "Gunny" Hulet pulled back his retirement papers. When the squadron arrived off the coast of Kuwait on February 24, 2003, he was ready to go ashore and get the unit's aircraft ready for combat. In less than a month they were ready many times over, and so was he. More important, so were the junior enlisted Marines who made up the bulk of the squadron. These were young men and women barely out of high school whom he and the other senior enlisted leadership trained and mentored every hour of every day.

Hulet spent the final two nights before the war sleeping inside his assigned UH-1N on the flight line. He remembered the big raid against the border Observation Posts on March 20: "We were among the last birds to lift off—I had been busy checking ordnance and arming guns so that the rest of the flight could get out on time." During the actual attack Hulet manned the Huey's GAU-17 minigun and put seventeen hundred rounds into OP-3. Nevertheless, the assault on the border post made up only half the terror that night. After slogging through the airborne muck that filled the sky, his aircraft's crew—like most others—had to wave off their first attempt to land. In instances like these, the crew chief played a vital role in guiding the aircraft down. These were some of the very worst conditions Hulet had ever seen. The crew's second effort was even more hairy, but they finally managed to get the aircraft's skids on the ground. Safely down, they buttoned up the ship for the rest of the night.

The next morning, after shooting up an Iraqi truck-mounted, 12.7-millimeter machine gun, the helicopter commander positioned the aircraft over a bedraggled-looking group of Iraqi soldiers. "They were pitiful," Hulet recollected. "They looked up at us and you could tell they were afraid—they were waving a tiny white flag." The crew took compassion on the sorry-looking enemy troops and threw down packets of MREs and bottles of water before flying on to their next mission.

Hulet was also in the thick of the fighting at An Nasiriyah a couple of days later on March 23. Assigned to fly Casualty Evacuation escort for a flight of CH-46Es, the crew aboard his ship was caught in a fierce small-arms firefight deep in one of the neighborhoods off the main highway. Once clear of that hornet's nest, the Huey crew stayed with the CH-46Es until they were safely on their way before returning to the city and posting themselves overhead the front of the fighting. For the moment they were the only air support available. It was then that the wingman called out that his auxiliary fuel tank would not feed—the flight would have to split up, or else leave the Marines unprotected.

Hulet had other ideas and coordinated a plan with the pilots. The wingman touched down in a field not far from where the battle was raging, and Hulet's pilot in turn descended low enough for him to leap clear and run with his M16 and pistol to the other aircraft. After being around Hueys for nearly twenty years, he knew exactly what was wrong; the jury-rigged alligator-clip-and-cannon-plug combination he had in his pocket was just the fix.

After being airborne for so long—an entire career—it felt strange to be running across the dry ground toward the other aircraft. He could hear the sounds of gunfire mixed in with the clapping chop that his helicopter made as it circled in the distance. He was nearly out of breath when he reached the other Huey, but he wasted no time. He popped open a panel on the malfunctioning ship and jumped a broken wire with his field-expedient device. Immediately he felt the system's electric pump churn to life. "You're good to go!" he shouted up at the other crew and in just seconds they clattered away, giving him a thorough dusting in the process.

Hulet felt very alone, but his spirits lifted when he turned and saw his own helicopter descending to pick him up. He ran toward it and with a flying leap was aboard before the bird even touched down. "Automaticall," he said, "I was on my feet and behind my gun. It wasn't even something that I thought about."

The war continued just like that for Hulet. Things broke and he fixed them. Things needed to be shot and he shot them. But most important, he passed what he knew to the junior Marines with whom he flew and fought. Of everything that he did, this was what he was most proud of. "As it happened," he said, "I had waited an entire career to see fighting like this. These youngsters were seeing it all from the beginning. I worked hard to teach them whatever I could because I knew that one way or another I wasn't going to be around much longer."

When Gunnery Sergeant Hulet officially retired later that year, the Marine Corps was better because of what he had taught hundreds of Marines over the course of many years.

The fighting in and around An Nasiriyah continued to be fierce into the night of March 23. Indeed, 3rd LAR was ambushed just after nightfall as it pressed north out of the city. The response from the Marines crewing the LAVs was violent: They ripped into the enemy with 25-millimeter cannon fire and fusillades of 7.62-millimeter machine-gun rounds. Still the effort wasn't enough, and a single-word call for help went out over the guard channel: "Slingshot." It was a radio brevity codeword indicating that a friendly unit was in danger of being overrun; all available aircraft were expected to drop their assigned tasking and respond straightaway. Only minutes later the first of more than fifty sorties of aircraft arrived overhead.

Marine F/A-18D crews took on the FAC(A) role, and it wasn't long before airpower turned the killing into a slaughter. Not only was the immediate threat to 3rd LAR eliminated, but a group of ten Iraqi tanks a mile or so north of the unit was also found and destroyed. The following morning, more than 150 enemy bodies were counted.

An enormous advantage that U.S. forces enjoyed over their Iraqi counterparts was their ability to see at night. For the most part the enemy had no night-vision equipment, and his effectiveness dropped dramatically once the sun went down. This was validated by the experience of Lieutenant Colonel Steve Heywood's HMLA-267, the mixed unit of Hueys and Cobras that ultimately saw twenty-three of its twenty-six craft sustain damage: None had been hit after nightfall. The already huge mismatch of forces and capabilities during daylight grew even greater in the darkness. It was a factor that the Marine Corps exploited at every opportunity.

It was blacker than normal on the evening of March 24—the night following the "Slingshot" response. Major Shawn "Bull" Hughes skirted the west side of An Nasiriyah as he led his two-ship of Hueys toward the spot where 2d LAR was deployed in a defensive circle. The sky over the city was marked by the flashes of heavy weapons, while closer to the ground red and white tracers arced back and forth at each other as Marine and Iraqi gunners traded fire. Near the northern edge of the city Hughes carefully navigated past a battery of Eleventh Marines M198 howitzers—flying through their gun line would be decidedly unwise. Hughes and his copilot, Captain John Jaeski, and the crew aboard the other Huey, commanded by Captain Jeff "Beaver" Gilliland, had been supporting 2d LAR for much of that day. Earlier, from directly overhead the unit, they had silenced enemy gunners who had been laying down fire from nearby buildings. The spent brass from the UH-1N machine guns bounced off the eight-wheeled LAVs below them. The metallic rattle punctuated the fact that Hughes and the two crews were indeed engaged in *Close* Air Support.

Now, despite the darkness, through their night-vision goggles and FLIRs, they could make out where the LAVs were circled just off the western edge of Highway 7, about ten miles north of An Nasiriyah. The drive through the city hadn't gone as quickly as had been desired, and the unit had been directed to wait for everyone else to catch up. At that moment they were the very point of the Marine Corps's spear.

"Their air officer called us and said that they were taking indiscriminate fire from all directions," Hughes recalled. "It wasn't overwhelming or particularly coherent—more harassing." The unit wanted the Hueys to locate and kill the enemy fighters, and the two crews were soon busy rooting around the area. A couple of farming compounds, made up of just a few buildings each, were across the highway to the unit's east and northeast. Atop several of the roofs were people in ones and twos, but it was difficult to tell if they had hostile intent or were just gawking at the assemblage of firepower. From time to time the LAR unit fired at targets to the south, but the helicopter crews could find nothing.

Hughes remembered: "Everyone was starting to get frustrated. We couldn't find anything, but by now the volume of fire had picked up. Also, the Iraqis were signaling back and forth across the road with flares." Hughes was starting to worry that his section would run low on fuel before they would be able to do anything to help the LAV unit. "You could tell by the strain in their voices," he recounted, "that they were starting to get agitated."

The two Hueys had been on station about forty minutes when the crews spotted a pair of headlights about ten miles north of the LAVs on Highway 7. "Of course, because of all the fighting," Hughes said, "there wasn't a lot of traffic on the road, so a pair of headlights was an attention getter." When the driver doused his lights it drew even more attention. As the vehicle continued south down the highway toward the spot where 2d LAR was circled, the fliers could make out that it was a large bus.

"We passed what we were seeing to the Air Officer," Hughes remembered, "and started counting down the distance as the bus got closer." There was no reason for the bus to be on the road—especially given the fighting at An Nasiryah. That is, there was no reason unless it was carrying enemy fighters. The Iraqis had been using Highway 7 to reinforce their garrison in the city, and this was the first time that the Americans had pushed so far north. A clash was bound to occur.

Hughes recollected: "The LAR Marines got ready as the bus closed the distance. By now Beaver and his crew had set up over the farming compound, just northeast of the LAVs. I had been flying a pattern perpendicular to the road and now I stepped off to the east side about a half mile north of their position." Hughes watched the bus and counted down the distance: four kilometers, three kilometers, two . . . one. Now the bus started to run over and around obstacles that the LAR unit had put on the road to slow enemy attackers.

This counted as hostile intent as far as the ROE was concerned, and Hughes passed the word to 2d LAR's Air Officer. The clearance to engage was given and a single streak of fire—probably a TOW missile—rocketed away from the circle of LAVs. "There was a big explosion at the front of the bus," Hughes remembered, "and it slowed to a halt." Immediately about ten adult males hurried to clear the vehicle. Gilliland opened up with rocket and machine-gun fire and 2d LAR's Marines poured their fire into the bus. Hughes moved closer and his crew chief and gunner, Staff Sergeant Gunther and Sergeant Westhoff, opened up with their GAU-17 7.62-caliber minigun and M2 .50-caliber machine gun. The Iraqis tried to take cover in ditches along both sides of the road and to the rear of the bus. It was no use; between the fire that was now coming from the LAVs and the two gunships there was no escape. Through his FLIR, Hughes watched the scrambling enemy go lifeless.

"We spun around and reset again for another attack," Hughes said, "but there was no movement around the bus." All of the enemy fighters had been butchered. They would never make it into An Nasiriyah. They would never shoot at a Marine. Up north along the highway another vehicle—headlights on—stopped several miles away. After a moment or two—headlights still on—it turned around and drove away. Hughes checked his fuel against what Gilliland was carrying. It was time to go home. They checked off station with 2d LAR's Air Officer and made their way back south—careful to skirt the fire that was coming out of the city.

The First Marine Division's history records 2d LAR's engagements on the night of March 24–25 thusly:

Almost immediately after establishment of the perimeter it came under attack. Captain Monclova decisively led his company, integrating direct, indirect fire with close air support, engaging numerous vehicles carrying personnel south toward An Nasiriyah along Route 7 throughout the night. . . . Throughout the entire night the company engaged the enemy. . . . Due to the skillful use of supporting arms and a high volume of direct fire the Battalion was successful in defeating each attempt at penetrating its lines. As the last attack was defeated near dawn, the Battalion collected numerous EPWs and observed between 200–300 enemy Killed In Action. In addition to the Killed In Action and Enemy Prisoners of War, Alpha Company destroyed 2 buses used to carry forces south, as well as 2 trucks and several cars being used as personnel carriers.

"Just at sunup the next day," Hughes said, "we were airborne again overhead 2d LAR." He took the section of aircraft past the shot-up bus. There, in various grotesque positions, were the men they had killed the night before. There were more inside the bus. Too, there were several other vehicles that had tried to come down the highway after they had left. The Marines of 2d LAR had destroyed them, and many more bodies littered the desert.

Hughes recalled: "We set down next to the LAVs and the commander came out and gave me a big bear hug—said that we had saved their bacon not only that night, but all through the previous day. I derived a great deal of job satisfaction from that."

Within twenty minutes they were airborne again and looking for a fight.

15

The FARP

Without them, the Marine Corps advance would have cost more time. Worse, it would have cost more lives. Simply put, the FARPs—Forward Arming and Refueling Points—were very basic airfields carved out of highways along the MEF's line of advance, or set up on captured Iraqi air bases. They were the absolute linchpin of rotary-wing operations within Iraq and ultimately serviced almost every combat aircraft type in the Marine Corps inventory.

Within days of blasting over the Iraqi border, Marine ground forces had fought so far into the country that they were already at the range limits of the Kuwait-based helicopters that were so crucial to the continuation of their assault. Those helicopters that were ship-based in the Persian Gulf were even farther removed from the leading combat elements. It was the FARPs that kept them all in the fight.

Plainly put, the FARPs were force multipliers. Rather than flying a hundred or more miles from Kuwait to the battle and then back, formations of Cobras and Hueys launched from their main base at Ali Al Salem—or from warships in the Persian Gulf—and flew to the FARP located closest to the fight. There they topped off while the crews received the latest intelligence brief. Following the refueling, the crews took off again, joined the battle, fired their ordnance, and then returned to the FARP for more fuel and ammunition before launching back into the fray. During especially heavy fighting crews sometimes passed through a given FARP so many times that they lost count. These quick turnarounds enabled one aircraft to provide the support that would have required two or three or more had the FARPs not been available.

The FARPs in this campaign were largely planned and controlled from within the headquarters element of Marine Air Group Thirty-nine (MAG-39) and fell under the logistics umbrella of Marine Wing Support Group Thirty-seven (MWSG-37). MWSG-37 drew from its various subordinate units and laterally from other commands to piece together robust teams that set up and tore down a number of different sites as the advance through Iraq made its way northwest. Because the FARP teams were essentially bare-bones airfields-on-wheels, all the many and varied specialties necessary for combat aviation operations were represented. There were bulk fuelers, engineers, communicators, intelligence specialists, airfield operations experts, mechanics, and more. When the fighting got hot, the ordnance Marines were among the busiest of all—humping tons of rockets and missiles and ammunition onto lines of Cobras and Hueys that sometimes never seemed to end.

And the Marines who made up these teams were there for the duration. One squadron commander remembered loaning one of his best corporal mechanics to a FARP team prior to the start of hostilities. "It paid dividends for us to send out the cream of the crop," he said. "These were the guys who were going to be dealing with the difficult problems—breakdowns and malfunctions out in the dirt that were going to demand some amount of skill and a good amount of ingenuity." The downside, of course, was that the "borrowed" Marines stayed gone. "We didn't see that poor guy for five weeks," the commander remembered, "and he smelled like a goat when he finally got back to us."

That was because the Marines who worked in the FARPs did just that—work. Major Bernard "Woots" Cernosek commanded FARP Team Bravo and recalled, "We did have established day and night shifts but when things got going heavy—which was a lot of the time— everyone just pitched in and got things done regardless of what shift they were assigned to." This sort of nonstop schedule working in the heat on grime-covered aircraft while living in the dirt made keeping clean a challenge. Hygiene was also difficult simply because of the nature of the FARPs. Many of them were in place for only a few days before they were taken down and moved again. Always on the move, the Marines rarely failed to stay freshly shaven, but laundry and other niceties were problematic, especially when getting the FARP ready demanded so much preparation.

And to a generation of young men and women who had grown up knowing what was happening around the world almost the instant it happened, the isolation was odd and confusing. "Our entire world was the FARP," Cernosek said. "If it didn't happen within a klick [kilometer] of us, it may as well have happened on the moon; we had little news of what was going on beyond our little perimeter. Once in a while," he continued, "we'd get the BBC over the HF [High Frequency] net and find out about a big fight that our Marines were engaged in. I'd plot it out on a map and realize that the shooting we were hearing was what was making the news!" Dirt, inconvenience, and isolation notwithstanding, none of the Marines who manned the FARPs forgot that their brothers doing the fighting had it much more difficult.

Because the landing area was often set up on a portion of road or highway, a suitable stretch had to be identified, surveyed, and closed off to traffic. Once the appropriate length of surface was set aside, it was repaired if required, painted, and "shaved" for air operations. Shaving the length of the highway involved knocking down lampposts, highway markers, signs—anything that could hurt an aircraft. Medians were scraped away until the road surface was as smooth and level as the Marines could make it.

In addition to all the runway preparation, expeditionary lighting was laid out and a provisional "control tower" established. The fueling and arming points were the reasons the FARP existed, and these were set to service as many aircraft at one time as possible. Generally there were eight refueling points, with four of them set up for simultaneous rearming.

Getting the aircraft safely into the FARP—especially at night—was sometimes a challenge for the hard-pressed pilots. Cernosek improvised a lighting system using chem lights: small plastic tubes that emit a fluorescent glow for several hours when the components inside are combined by bending the tube and breaking the seal that separates them. "These were great," he recollected. "They enabled the pilots to see the landing area from a much greater distance than they otherwise would have been able." He recounted how he had tried to second-guess the supply system and ordered fifteen thousand of the disposable lighting aids to get the five thousand or so that he estimated he would need. Instead he ended up with forty-five thousand. "I could have lit the highway to Baghdad!"

Of course it wasn't feasible to take possession of a section of highway and sever the flow of traffic—especially when that traffic had to get forward to fight. This meant that stout detours capable of routing heavy traffic off the highway—and then back on—had to be constructed and maintained. Scraping these out of the desert and keeping them passable was a full-time job—and a dusty one. The dust that this activity created, combined with the natural wind, often made getting in and out of the FARPs a dangerous exercise. This point was driven home when a UH-1N crashed while lifting out of a FARP on the evening of March 30. The vertigo-inducing cloud of dust that enveloped the aircraft was the primary reason for the mishap. Of the four-man crew, only the copilot survived.

The FARP was actually made up of two major components. The first was the MMT—the Marine Air Traffic Control Mobile Team. The MMT was responsible for the actual air operations in and around the site, as well as for ensuring the proper setup of the field. It was headed by an air boss—usually a major or lieutenant colonel aviator. It made sense that aviators would know what other aviators would need. Lieutenant Colonel Joe "Shepard" Strohman was the air boss of FARP Team Echo. A Huey pilot by trade, he was no stranger to expeditionary operations, to include managing a FARP. He had been tucked away on the staff at MAG-29 when his commander called for him only a week or so prior to ATF East's arrival in the Persian Gulf. Strohman recalled: "My colonel said, 'Joe, I'm going to send you in to run a FARP. You're going to take a team of Marines with you. Do a good job and don't get a stick up your ass.' That was it; ten days later we were in Kuwait."

Although there were guidelines for how to establish a FARP team and what was required, the Marine Corps did what it always did with the limited means and materials at hand. It task-organized, or built the teams for the job at hand. *Task organization* is Marine-speak for improvising—making do. "Or," remembered one officer speaking about the campaign in general, "a lot of the time we just pulled it straight out of our ass and made it work." Strohman remembered, "I got my best man, Staff Sergeant Pash, at nearly the last minute because he was the friend of another one of the Marines in my unit. And where my guys found all of the vehicles and equipment we ended up with . . . well, I didn't ask any questions." The makeup of Cernosek's FARP differed from the others: "We ended up with several Army HEMTTs [Heavy Expanded Mobility Tactical Trucks] and their crews because we were supposed to be traveling overland initially, and they were good off-road vehicles. The Army guys were a little bit different but we brought them into the fold and they adapted really well."

Aside from the MMT, the other major part of the FARP team—in fact, the bulk of it—was the detachment from the Marine Wing Support Squadron, the MWSS. These Marines operated and maintained the fuel trucks, the firefighting equipment, the enormous fuel bladders and their associated pumps and hoses and other gear, as well as heavy equipment for runway repair and the tools required for Explosive Ordnance Disposal (EOD). This component of the FARP was really a rough-and-tumble, armed-and-dangerous convention of engineers, truckers, mechanics, and heavy-equipment operators. But above it all, they were Marines. In combination with the MMT they made the FARPs what they were: effective combat multipliers that performed nonstop through the entire campaign.

The FARPs became de facto way stations, or oases, for all manner of traffic. If a helicopter experienced a mechanical malfunction, it more often than not limped into the closest FARP. If an aircrew lost communications or needed new tasking, it stopped at an FARP. Fliers who ran out of crew day or who just needed a rest or a meal took refuge in the FARPs. Even ground units sometimes stopped through the miniature airfields for food, water, fuel, or information. After all, the FARP team was tasked to support; they were a service organization. Strohman reminded his Marines of that fact from time to time. "My rule for the team was: Do it right, do it fast, and give the aircraft that come to our site the best service you can. No one says no but me, and I never say no. Keep it safe because I need every single one of you in order for us to accomplish our mission."

Iraqi civilians, some curious and some on a mission, also found their ways across the boundaries of the FARPs. Strohman recalled one incident: "At Qualcomm FARP we were approached by a group of Iraqis who were trying to enter our area right at the ASP [Ammunition Supply Point]." He strode out to head them off under the cover of about twenty of his armed and ready Marines. Coming face-to-face he found that the Iraqis were affable, and more inquisitive than anything else. "They were led by an older gentleman who had a small boy hanging tightly on to his leg. After a bit of gesturing I realized that they were just trying to welcome us. We smiled a lot and I gave the little boy a small LED flashlight that had been given to me by a visiting female captain only a day or so earlier."

The story's second half took place on April 3 when Lieutenant General James Conway, the MEF commander, was visiting the site. "The overpass that crossed over one end of our position came under RPG attack," remembered Strohman. "Our security force fired back with a Mk-19 and at the same time one of our snipers called out from behind his .50 caliber that he had the RPG shooter in his sights." The RPG rounds stopped and Strohman ordered the sniper to hold his fire while he and a team of Marines climbed into their vehicles to investigate. Under the cover of a pair of Cobras, Strohman and his men drove out to the nearby village. "We didn't find the RPG shooter," he remembered, "but we did find the individual targeted by our sniper—it was the father of the little boy that I had given the LED flashlight to."

Keeping the FARPs in business was a complex task; it involved much more than simply packing up every few days and setting up in a new location. Their business was fuel and ammunition, and the approximately 150 Marines who made up each one of the FARPs dispensed both at prodigious rates. To keep the air wing in the thick of the fight they had to be resupplied constantly. Most of the fuel was trucked in, as was much of the ammunition. Still, CH-53s and CH-46s often serviced the sites. "The 53s could carry fuel bladders externally," explained Cernosek. "The Frogs primarily delivered parts and other supplies." The "Sugar Daddy" who kept the entire logistical nightmare orchestrated, who saw to it that none of the FARPs ever had to turn away an aircraft, was Lieutenant Colonel "Diamond Dave" Lobik from the MAG-39 operations shop. "I was on the Iridium [satellite telephone] with him continuously," Cernosek recalled. "He never let us down." Strohman's separate recollection matched Cernosek's almost exactly: "I was on the phone with him hourly. He did a fantastic job, and whenever he stopped by he'd bring things for the young troops: snuff and candy and magazines—that sort of stuff." Robling praised Lobik even more highly: "That the war went as well as it did was due in no small part to the FARPs. That the FARPs worked as well as they did was in large part due to Lobik."

Aside from helicopters, the Pioneer Unmanned Aerial Vehicle squadrons—VMU-1 and VMU-2—used the FARPs extensively. During the first week in April one of the UAV units set up at Strohman's Qualcomm FARP. There was some grousing because of all the room that the unmanned aircraft and its associated equipment required, but Strohman was firm in his evenhandedness and cut what he believed was a good compromise that included the last two thousand feet of the runway. "From the overpass near our perimeter," he remembered, "I watched one of the UAVs land, take off again, and then smack right into the overpass—not far from where I was standing. I immediately sent word down that they could have the extra thousand feet of runway that they had wanted earlier."

Although their role was support, the FARP Marines—like all Marines—were trained riflemen and encountered some of the same dangers as those troops at the head of the attack. Strohman's team came under artillery fire three different times, once by friendly guns. Another time the team took five EPWs (Enemy Prisoners of War) after receiving RPG and small-arms fire. For his part, Cernosek had to coordinate a CASEVAC for three of his men during the first night of the war; they had driven their vehicle into a tank trap. Those three Marines were among the very first casualties of the ground campaign.

It was near the end of March when the MEF's logistical effort started to show signs of strain. The First Marine Division was charging up Highway 1 straight toward Baghdad and was running thin on fuel, food, and ammunition. The 3rd MAW was tasked to augment the supplies that 1st FSSG was pushing up the Main Surface Routes, and the staffers at the wing put together a plan that called on the KC-130s and CH-53Es to lift seventy thousand gallons of fuel a day to the units leading the attack.

Key to the plan were the FARP teams that prepared the sites to receive the supply-laden aircraft. Hantush was a portion of Highway 1 that was actually designed to serve as an auxiliary airfield for the Iraqi Air Force. It was captured on March 31, and by the next day fuel and supplies from just-landed KC-130s were going straight to the Marines who were carrying the fight forward.

The FARP known as Wrigley Field was made up of a section of Highway 1 south of Hantush. Strohman's team had put it into action only ten hours after starting work. It, too, serviced KC-130s. Major John "Roady" Skinner, who had been the first Coalition pilot to put a fixed-wing aircraft into Iraq, was also at the fore of operations at Wrigley: "The blacktop road that made up the runway was only forty-two feet wide. Well, the book says that a minimum runway width of sixty feet for the KC-130 is 'highly recommended.' " Recommended or not, the Marines approaching Baghdad were running dangerously low on fuel and ammunition. Skinner and his fellow Marine aviators simply shrugged at the narrow road and got on with the mission. "After all," he asked, "what's eighteen feet among friends?"

Skinner and the other KC-130 crews flew nonstop missions into Wrigley for two days. It was a challenging exercise. A forty-foot over-pass crossed the highway just prior to the touchdown point of the short three-thousand-foot section of road that was designated as the runway. Once the pilots put the big ships down and got them stopped, they reversed the engines and backed all the way to the ap-proach end of the runway; there was no place to turn around. There they off-loaded fuel—sometimes as much as eight thousand gal-lons—into bladders set up just off the runway.

If the cargo wasn't fuel it was usually water, MREs, or ammunition. Because there were no forklifts to assist with the unloading, the crews executed "combat off-loads" to empty their aircraft. "We opened the cargo door at the rear of the aircraft and lowered the ramp," Skinner recalled, "and then applied power while we held the brakes." The pi-lots then released the brakes, and the aircraft leapt forward. The pal-lets sitting on the roller system of the aircraft trundled aft and out while the KC-130 essentially moved out from underneath them.

The air-delivered supplies were treasure to the infantrymen. De-pending on the requirements, a KC-130 carried five to six pallets that held either forty thousand MREs, thirty thousand bottles of water, or more than twenty-two tons of ammunition. The MREs were espe-cially welcome; by the end of March some of the Marines at the fore of the fight had been rationed to only one meal per day. The fliers who skillfully delivered these goods were aware of the importance of their effort—and the incongruity. Skinner recalled: "The irony of what we were doing wasn't lost on us. We found a certain humor in the fact that we were using Saddam's own airfields and highways to chase him out of power."

But in a pinch the FARP teams didn't even need captured airfields or prepared highways to execute their mission. During one convoy movement Strohman's Staff Sergeant Pash looked into his rearview mirror and saw a Cobra and a Huey flying low and slow behind the train of vehicles. He immediately established radio contact and found that they needed fuel. Strohman recounted how Pash got the team prepared for the two helicopters: "The time it took from the moment he radioed the aircraft until the time that a safe landing zone was established on the highway was less than three minutes. This included stopping a 120-vehicle convoy, setting up a security block in both directions, getting the crash trucks into position, and having fuel and ordnance men standing by." A short time later the two aircraft were fueled, armed, and on their way—but only after the team's corpsman had treated a crushed finger that one of the airmen had sustained. Stationary or on the go, the FARPs were truly 3rd MAW's convenience store for the aviator who needed service and needed it fast.

Ultimately it was evident to everyone that the FARPs were one of the greatest enablers of the entire campaign. Colonel Robert Milstead, the commander of MAG-29 who had sent Strohman to lead FARP Team Echo, was steadfast in his conviction as to their value. His MAG was afloat for the first ten days of the fighting, and the FARPs were one of the primary reasons that his aviators were as effective as they were.

. . . I want to pile on and say that they were the single biggest contributor to our ability to fight across 450 nautical miles of Iraq! MWSG-37 [and that group's FARPs] was *the* maneuver element of 3rd MAW—no doubt about it.

16

Going Long

The First Marine Division's three RCTs had fought through their own tremendous traffic jams as well as Iraqi forces while making their way around and through An Nasiriyah on March 23. As the following day dawned RCT-5 and -7 worked their ways up Highway 1 while RCT-1 prepared to move up Highway 7. This was the region that had stymied previous invaders. The terrain was treacherous, and Marine commanders were anxious at what they might encounter. Nevertheless, there was still plenty of fighting left to do to their east. Elements of the First UK Division faced considerable Iraqi forces in the vicinity of Al Basrah, and for much of their air support they relied on I MEF's Air Combat Element—3rd MAW.

Captain Allen "Grimace" Grinalds and his four-ship of HMLA-267 Cobras—callsign Opah 15—were on their way back to Ali Al Salem Air Base in Kuwait. It was 0700 on March 24, and they had spent the previous fourteen or so hours shooting up targets in the hellhole that An Nasiriyah had become only the day prior. "I contacted the

DASC(A) for our flight back," Grinalds recalled. "He gave us a quick update on various threats along our route of flight; it was all matter-of-fact, and he didn't seem particularly concerned about any of it. But after reviewing our route and the threats that he had just passed to us, I realized that we would be flying right by a couple of enemy Roland SAM sites. I let him know, and again, he didn't seem as concerned about the threat as we were. This really wasn't unusual, and we had a running joke that the DASC(A) had actually been infiltrated by the Saddam Fedayeen and it would only be a matter of time before they slipped up and broke out in Arabic catcalls over the radio."

After adjusting his heading to avoid the enemy missile sites, Grinalds settled back for the remainder of the flight to Kuwait. For this sortie, as the flight leader, he was strapped into the aft cockpit. In the forward cockpit was Captain Bill "Spyder" Talansky. "Bill was a super pilot," Grinalds remembered, "but he was from New York and no one in the division could ever understand a thing he said." Piloting the second Cobra were Captain John "Barefoot" Garrigan and First Lieutenant Kevin Rusch; the third aircraft was crewed by Captain Drew "Smitty" Aylward and First Lieutenant Mike Blakemore; the fourth gunship was manned by Major Matt "Tinkle" Dwyer and Captain Jim "Bung" Mullin.

The crews were still getting used to each other. The year previously Grinalds had been assigned from HMLA-267 to Marine Aviation Weapons and Tactics Squadron One (MAWTS-1), the Corps's weapons and tactics schoolhouse. For the war he had been reassigned to HMLA-267, but most of the other pilots in his flight had arrived from other units just prior to their deployment to Kuwait.

Before the start of hostilities—because they hadn't had the opportunity to fly together—Grinalds often held class in one of the disused aircraft shelters at Ali Al Salem. It had been badly damaged during Desert Storm, and no one bothered his crews there. Inside, they worked on the very basics. Something as simple as being familiar with the cadence and inflection of a wingman's speech pattern over the radio could mean the difference between success and failure. Because of their lack of experience together, one of Grinalds's main concerns was that they wouldn't be able to anticipate one another's actions—and recognizing the subtleties in a wingman's voice is an important part of that. "With the exception of Spyder's accent, I think we cracked the nut. We would sit there for hours and 'chair-fly' through different situations over and over again, trying to cover every contingency we might encounter. After several sessions they'd start rolling their eyes at me when I would break out my Close Air Support brief for the umpteenth time." But the work paid off, because they would fly together only once before the shooting started.

As the flight rumbled toward the Kuwait border, the DASC(A) asked Grinalds to check in with his flight's status. Assuming that the request was nothing more than a routine query whether they had observed any anti-aircraft fire along their routing, he replied that they had encountered no enemy fire and then passed on the flight's fuel state and weapons status. The DASC(A) responded with an immediate Joint Tactical Air Strike Request (JTAR) tasking in support of the First United Kingdom Division northwest of Al Basrah.

"Lately I had begun to take these 'immediate' JTARs with a grain of salt. We'd get fired up and blast out to make contact only to find that the threat had disappeared or that everyone had gone to bed for the night. In some cases, the 'immediate' JTAR was many hours old and had been overcome by events. My initial thought was that this might be another wild-goose chase. On top of that, everyone, including myself, was pretty much exhausted from flying all night. I was skeptical."

While Grinalds copied the brief, John Garrigan calculated the fuel requirement for them to complete the mission. They didn't have enough on board to make a good effort of it. Grinalds told the DASC(A) that his flight would take the mission but needed thirty minutes to stop in to Busch FARP and take on fuel and more ordnance. On the way to the FARP, Grinalds led the division over

Safwan Hill where he had helped destroy an enemy Observation Post the first night of the war. Shot up as it was, it didn't look nearly as sinister as it had when it was still manned by the enemy.

Once the four gunships landed, the practiced Marine ordnance men set to work slapping more Hellfire and TOW missiles on board the sinister-looking helicopters. The crews kept the engines turning to facilitate a quick departure. At the same time, other FARP personnel darted in and among the aircraft, attaching fuel hoses and checking for damage. "While the ordies were loading us up I went over a quick CAS brief with the rest of the flight—just like we had practiced a million times before in the wrecked hangar back at Ali Al Salem."

All during this period the DASC(A) made repeated calls asking Grinalds and his flight to expedite. Unfortunately one of the aircraft was extremely slow in taking on fuel. With friendly troops in extremis Grinalds couldn't wait any longer and stopped the refueling. Smitty Aylward's bird was left with about twenty minutes' less fuel than the rest of the flight. The ships were each loaded with three Hellfire missiles, three TOW missiles, a pod of nineteen 2.75-inch HE (High Explosive) rockets, a pod of seven 2.75-inch fléchette rockets, and about three hundred 20-millimeter cannon rounds.

The four Cobras stirred up a small storm of gray-brown desert dust as they hurried airborne. The DASC(A) passed the flight more amplifying information, including the fact that they could expect to be fired on by man-portable SAMs and anti-aircraft artillery. He then cleared them direct to Contact Point (CP) Bigfoot, approximately fifteen miles northwest of Al Basrah. Bigfoot was actually a bridge across the Hamar Canal—a fairly wide stretch of water that ran roughly east-to-west. Once they neared Bigfoot they were cleared to contact the FAC, callsign Manila 6, on Iron—a TAD (Tactical Air Direction) frequency.

"I had a hard time talking to Manila on Iron," Grinalds remembered. "The Iraqis were jamming the frequency, and every time Manila or I keyed the mike we'd be overpowered by loud, screeching warbles—it made me want to take my helmet off. I'd key the mike and spit out 'Manila switch Steel' really quickly—trying to get him to switch to Steel frequency. It was almost like a bad joke: 'Uh, Steel! 'Switch Steel! Steel!' Finally he caught on and we all met over on the other frequency and had a good check-in with no interference."

Approaching Manila's position at Bigfoot, Grinalds and the rest of the flight came face-to-face with the grim reality of the situation. The position was taking accurate artillery fire. A pall of dust and smoke covered the area, and the British unit was taking casualties. "My heart sank when I saw what was coming down on them. Everyone was dug in pretty well, but it still looked bad," Grinalds recalled.

Manila 6 was Major Stanton Coerr, a reserve officer normally assigned to a Marine Air Naval Gunfire Liaison Company (ANGLICO). While on active duty he—like the gunship crews approaching him from the southwest—had been a Cobra pilot. He was now attached to the First Royal Irish Regiment Battlegroup, a British army infantry battalion that was part of the United Kingdom's Sixteenth Air Assault Brigade. His job was to coordinate U.S. supporting fires for the British unit.

"Manila," said Grinalds, "was really cool and professional. When he keyed his mike we could hear the arty rounds exploding and guys shouting in the background. But for all it appeared to bother him, we might as well have been having a conversation in his living room— very impressive." Manila briefed the situation while the Cobras set up an orbit away from the artillery barrage. The British unit was primarily holed up at the southern end of the bridge, but had reconnaissance elements across the span to the north. Equipped as they were with relatively small 105-millimeter howitzers, they were being outranged by the heavier Iraqi guns.

Nevertheless, Manila was able to provide a good grid location to the enemy artillery position. These data were derived from a British counterbattery radar system nicknamed, aptly enough, "Cobra." The radar detected the enemy artillery rounds as they came in and, by extrapolating their trajectories, was able to determine where the guns were located.

"After Manila completed his brief," Grinalds continued, "I plugged in the coordinates he had given me and realized that one of us had made a mistake—the target was thirteen kilometers away. He gave me two more grids but they all plotted out at roughly the same location." It was only after talking to the FAC further that Grinalds realized that Manila wanted the Cobras to fly nearly nine miles in front of the British lines to hit the Iraqi artillery tubes.

Grinalds had misunderstood the FAC. He had thought that Manila was briefing his flight to hit Iraqi Forward Observers (FOs) hidden in the nearby area. The accuracy of the fires was such that there was no doubt enemy observers were calling the artillery in. "But that wasn't the case. They didn't know where the enemy FOs were; they just wanted us to go way up forward and hit the guns."

That wasn't a job for Cobras over flat desert on a bright, sunny day. Ranging deep into enemy territory was not how the Marines used their gunships. The Cobras were intended to provide close fire support for ground units rather than ranging deep into enemy territory on hunter-killer missions. As lightly armored as they were, and in such small numbers, they were extremely vulnerable to coordinated enemy air defenses.

Grinalds remembered that he was not happy at all. "I had *zero* interest in going up there after those guns. None. There was a good chance we would get decisively engaged. The weather was great—which was not good for us. And of course we operate right in the heart of just about every weapons envelope out there. If we ran in low, say fifty or a hundred feet, they could knock us down with a big stick or some well-chosen dirty words. If we ran in higher, maybe at a thousand feet, we were perfect targets for shoulder-launched missiles. Those factors in combination with the fact that it was broad daylight and that there was no terrain to hide behind had me very concerned."

Grinalds put Manila on hold and tried to generate some fixed-wing support—either Hornets or Harriers. He was able to raise a single section of F/A-18s, but the two jets wouldn't be able to arrive on station until after they refueled—it would be at least thirty minutes until they were able to lend any help. "I really, really didn't want to go up there without fixed-wing cover. If an aircraft was shot down or disabled, we were going to lose it." If a bird went down, the operating procedure was to attempt to recover the crew, and then destroy the aircraft after zeroizing the crypto equipment in the radios. With a carabiner—a piece of equipment commonly used by rock climbers—the downed crew were supposed to attach themselves to a tie-down point on another aircraft and ride out on the stub wings. It all sounded plausible—in theory. Still, Grinalds didn't want to have to validate it for real.

"After about another minute I said 'we're it' and decided to go. In retrospect, we were going to be either heroes or goats. Sometimes there's a fine line between the two, and the side you land on rides on just a little bit of luck." This was one of those times. Grinalds spread his formation out and pointed the four ships north. Only a moment later Manila aborted their run and called them back. There had been some confusion with the British artillery units, and there was a danger that the gunships might get caught in a volley of friendly fire. Once the miscue was cleared, they were on the way again.

"I spread everyone out into combat spread—about two hundred meters between each aircraft," Grinalds said. "We were clipping right along: 130 knots at fifty feet above the ground." The flight leader glanced to either side of him. The gunships had a sinister look. Clusters of munitions clung to their worn and dirty sides. Slightly nose-down as they scooted toward the suspected target, they seemed terrible and war-like.

The terrain below wasn't the desert they had been used to flying over up to this point in the campaign. Rather, there was more irrigated agriculture—green and brown fields studded with mud brick compounds and sorry-looking herds of livestock. All manner of refugees lined the narrow roads that they dusted with their rotor wash. There were people on bikes, old men and women on foot, entire families pushing carts. The luckier among them rode in small pickups or sedans packed to overflowing. The traffic flow was north and west, away from Al Basrah. "The refugees were like something you'd see on the evening news or in *Time* magazine," Grinalds recalled.

After a short time—at so low an altitude—the gunships lost radio contact with Manila. Their rotors glinting in the sun, the Cobras weaved and banked above the refugees as they checked the first two grids the FAC had given them. They found nothing. "Flying around all those 'civilians' was really making me nervous," Grinalds remembered. "I thought we were really pushing our luck and was ready to call it quits and swung the division back around south to try and reestablish radio communications with Manila." It was then that John Garrigan came up on the radio and reminded Grinalds that there was still one more grid location to investigate. There was a long pregnant pause while the rest of the formation waited to see what Grinalds would do. "Spyder and I talked it over and decided to head back north."

Grinalds wheeled the division around again and headed toward the last grid. After a moment or two it seemed apparent that there were no enemy artillery units in the area. "Then for no reason that I could see, other than our presence, a lot of the men on the road started diving for cover. The pucker factor was really going up as we circled over groups of men that were running while others did nothing and still others waved white flags. We were just waiting for them to shoot so that we could shoot back. We knew that a lot of them were combatants out of uniform and that we were essentially playing chicken—waiting for them to shoot first."

Again Grinalds was ready to turn back, but all the strange behavior was starting to pique his interest. "As we pressed farther north Jim Mullin called out some smoke up ahead. I looked and realized that the smoke was coming from the Iraqi artillery pieces we were looking for." The guns that the Cobra crews had found were Soviet-designed D-30, 122-millimeter towed howitzers.

The battery of guns was in an open field with a high berm at the southern end. The berm stood between the gunships and the enemy. Only three hundred yards from the Iraqi combatants stood a mosque. The enemy was aware of the Coalition's Rules of Engagement relative to cultural and religious sites. Iraqis often took advantage of Western sensitivities to civilian casualties and collateral damage and placed high-value military hardware in or close to mosques, schools, and hospitals. It often complicated Coalition efforts, but it was not going to be a factor in this instance.

By now the helicopters were taking heavy fire. Caught by surprise and with no better plan, the four Cobras charged the field. Aside from the artillery guns, Grinalds and his crews could make out several Zil-type trucks and anti-aircraft guns. Muzzle flashes blinked against their rush, and flak bursts spattered the sky above them. Even in the bright sunlight they could see fingers of tracers reaching up at them. Too, the crews could see armed men below them letting loose volleys of fire from smaller anti-aircraft pieces—even from their AK-47s. The closer the crews pressed in, the heavier and more concentrated the fire grew. Grinalds fired rockets into the field from about two miles and followed them up with running TOW shots at the anti-aircraft guns. The rockets made a short *fsspt* sound, not unlike toy fireworks. The TOW missiles fired with a louder, deeper *whoosh* and then corkscrewed toward their targets.

As they closed inside a mile, the enemy fire became too heavy and Grinalds banked the flight away to the west. "We still hadn't done the job yet. The last two ships, Smitty Aylward and Tinkle Dwyer, had a bit more tracking time and destroyed one of the D-30s prior to me turning the formation away. I didn't want to break contact but I needed about a minute to get the division back together and set up for a more deliberate attack."

Adrenaline was running fairly high among the four crews as enemy anti-aircraft rounds exploded above them and streams of tracers reached out like frightful strings of fire. "Smitty and Tinkle did a great job covering my section as we pulled off on that run," Grinalds said. "I'm sure they saved our lives two or three more times that day."

The four crews shouted instructions back and forth at each other over the radio, and then Grinalds marshaled them for another sprint at the enemy. On this run—still under heavy fire—he pushed the flight farther in, and the gunships destroyed two more of the guns. In his zeal Grinalds was too aggressive and overflew the protective berm.

It was, as Marines like to say, one of those "Oh shit!" moments. As the Cobras passed over the berm they crossed over the top of four T-62 tanks that had been hidden by the earthworks. The tank crews added to the barrage reaching up at the gunships with machine-gun fire from their coaxial mounts.

Caught by surprise, Grinalds turned the division out to the east and then banked back around for a go at the tanks. The volleys of enemy fire continued to arc out at them. That none of them had been hit was a near miracle. The Cobras pushed in and began engaging the tanks from about a mile out. "We took out all four of them with Hellfire missiles. From this point the tide began to turn in our favor and the Iraqis began to break and scatter." Many of the anti-aircraft guns fell silent with no crews to man them.

At the same time, the gunship crews spotted a group of about fifty Iraqis running north in a large group toward the mosque. The Marines ran them down with rockets and guns. "It's sobering to see the expressions of the people you are engaging but the hard fact of the matter is that they are combatants."

After only a few more short minutes of mopping up the area with their remaining ammunition, it was time to go. "Again," Grinalds remembered, "I started to get nervous when I considered where we were and that we didn't have any ordnance left—and Smitty was very low on fuel. We basically pulled max power and jinked all the way back toward Bigfoot. It was a thirteen-kilometer run, which should have only taken about five or six minutes, but that day I think we all felt like we were measuring it with a calendar."

Low on fuel, the flight headed directly for Busch FARP. As they passed within radio range of Bigfoot they made contact with Manila and forwarded their Mission Report (MISREP) and Battle Damage Assessment (BDA). Manila replied that the artillery fire had stopped and that they were evacuating their wounded.

Grinalds's flight returned with some of the most spectacular footage of the war. In it Iraqi troops can be clearly seen running from their tanks. An instant later two Hellfire missiles find their marks and the tanks disappear in spectacular explosions.

In a report after the area had been secured, a British Army colonel noted: ". . . I visited the sites some while later . . . I saw up to four T-62s in hull down positions whacked through the turret. It didn't smell too good and I didn't stray too close. . . ."

Major Stanton Coerr, Manila 6, also had high praise for the Cobras of Opah 15 flight. ". . . It is not an exaggeration to say that the aviators of the Opah 15 division saved my life. We were taking indirect fire but had to hold on to the Hamar Bridge, as three rifle battalions needed that bridge to push north out of the Rumaylah oil fields. . . . Opah 15 got to me just in time to avert what could have been a real disaster."

During the mission, Grinalds's flight had difficulty staying tied in to the command and control system. It was a common problem most often due to the quirkiness that so often bedevils radio communications, and it was a challenge that every aviator dealt with on a constant basis. That being said, it must be remembered that command and control is a two-way street, and the Marines who staffed the various agencies were equally frustrated.

Nevertheless, everyone did what the Marine Corps had trained them to do: got the job done. The ability to improvise—"wing it"—has been a Marine Corps strength since the service's birth, and the men and women who fought in Operation Iraqi Freedom were no different. One Marine who took advantage of the tools he had to get bombs on top of the enemy was Gunnery Sergeant Troy Mohler, who worked in the TAOC, callsign Tropical.

There were occasions when targets needed to be serviced, yet there were no FAC(A)s or other assets to control or direct the aircraft that were available. Using a carefully prepared chart and mensurated coordinates from up-to-date imagery, Mohler would pass target descriptions to aircraft on station and clear them for Type III CAS. It was ad hoc, but effective.

> . . . with the photos and other imagery I had, I would describe the target to the aircrews and direct them to the precise location. They often didn't understand who or where I was and would ask what my position was in relationship to the target. When I replied that I was about 150 nautical miles or so south of the target they seemed amazed at the level of detail I was able to pro-

vide—of course it was due to the imagery I had. Even then, they sometimes didn't understand and would ask me for my assessment of their bomb hits on the target. . . .

Even at this early point of the campaign, Coalition forces were being forced to deal with the maddening trickery of the Fedayeen and Jihadist fighters. Most often these men were not local to the town in which they were fighting and so had no compunction against using civilian homes—or families—for cover. In many cases the Coalition ROE precluded engaging these ruthless criminals. One tactic the enemy fighters adapted early on was to wave white flags when AH-1W Cobras arrived overhead, then resume fighting after they departed. Or sometimes they simply walked away. Although the incident described in the First Marine Division's history of the campaign took place later on, Captain Brian Gilman's recounting of the enemy's reaction to the arrival of 3rd MAW airpower is illustrative:

Whenever rotary wing air showed up these guys would just bug out. It was one of the most frustrating experiences I've ever had watching these guys walk away, but they'd disappear and suddenly reappear with no weapons, wearing civilian clothes. It was tough but the Marines showed incredible restraint. We didn't want more civilians getting killed.

17

===

The Storm

The advance up Highway 1 continued on March 24–25 as RCT-5 and -7 pressed northwest. And at An Nasiriyah RCT-1 pushed north on Highway 7 while Task Force Tarawa stayed behind to continue the killing. RCT-1's northward push would continue to keep the enemy off balance and would serve to keep the attack moving along more than one route.

It was 0530 on March 25, and Lieutenant Colonel Jerry "Badman" Driscoll was worn out. The commanding officer of HMM-268, Driscoll had just led his section of CH-46Es back to RCT-5's headquarters to the west of An Nasiriyah. They had spent the previous several hours evacuating casualties back to field hospitals in the south. Now safely on deck, he made certain that his two crews and their aircraft were settled in then crawled into his sleeping bag and fell immediately asleep.

* * *

Amphibious Task Force (ATF) East transits the Suez Canal under a hazy sky en route to the Persian Gulf. *(Robert Milstead)*

A two-seat F/A-18D from VMFA(AW)-533 in the "goofy bubble" configuration (centerline fuel tank and only one wing fuel tank). This aircraft is armed with two wingtip mounted AIM-9M Sidewinders, two Mk-83 General Purpose 1,000-pound bombs, and four GBU-12 Laser Guided, 500-pound bombs. [VMFA(AW)-533 *via James W. Frey]*

An F/A-18D takes fuel from a KC-130 (not pictured). Aside from laser guided bombs, this aircraft is configured with an ATARS (Advanced Tactical Airborne Reconnaissance System) pallet as indicated by the slight bulge below the nose. The ATARS system takes the place of the 20-millimeter cannon. [VMFA(AW)-533 *via James W. Frey]*

AV-8Bs recover aboard the *Bonhomme Richard*. *(VMA-311)*

An AV-8B recovers aboard the *Bonhomme Richard* as seen through a night vision device. *(VMA-311)*

An AV-8B just prior to starting its takeoff roll. *(VMA-311)*

"Objects in mirror . . ."
A KC-130 follows a support vehicle.
(Joe Strohman)

The close support that helicopter crews could provide to their ground brethren included the ability to land and get face-to-face briefs. *(Stephen Heywood)*

The Hantush (QUALCOM) FARP deep inside Iraq on Highway 1 was crucial to the resupply of 1st Marine Division forces. *(Joe Strohman)*

A door gunner's position on an HMLA-267 Huey. The weapon is an M240G 7.62-caliber machine gun. *(Stephen Heywood)*

AGM-114 Hellfire missiles mounted on an AH-1W Cobra. *(Jonathan M. George)*

A CH-53E with a suspended load. *(USMC via MAG-16)*

A head-on view of an AH-1W Cobra armed with AGM-114 Hellfire missiles, 2.75-inch rockets, and TOW missiles. A 20-millimeter cannon also adds to the gunship's lethality. *(USMC, Jonathan M. George)*

Cobra crews were sometimes away from their bases for days at a time. Crew rest looked like this. *(Todd Miller)*

The front end of Maj. Stephen "Pygmy" Hall's AH-1W Cobra after he was shot up and forced down south of Al Basrah. *(Stephen Hall)*

Again, dust in the takeoff and landing phases was always a hazard for the rotary wing crews. *(Stephen Heywood)*

An Iraqi "Technical" as seen through the weapons system of an AH-1W Cobra. The Iraqis mounted all manner of weapons aboard pickup trucks. *(Stephen Heywood)*

The crew of this Cobra survived after crashing to the ground and then skidding upside down across this Iraqi airfield near Samarra. *(Jonathan M. George)*

The wreckage that was an AH-1W's forward cockpit. Capt. Jeff Sykes survived the crash with only superficial injuries. *(Jonathan M. George)*

Many Cobras—particularly early in the conflict—were operated from ships steaming off the coast of Kuwait. *(Stephen Heywood)*

A VMAQ-1 aircraft and a NAVY F/A-18C wait their turn for aerial refueling. Air Force refuelers were crucial to the effort and serviced the aircraft of both the Navy and the Marine Corps. *(VMAQ-1)*

Looking past the ECMO's position at another EA-6B refueling from an Air Force KC-135. *(VMAQ-1)*

An interesting view of an HMM-162 CH-46E over southern Iraq. Note the barrel of the .50-caliber machine gun protruding from the aircraft's right side. *(Eric Griggs)*

A CH-46E during a CASEVAC effort near An Numaniyah. *(Eric Griggs)*

A VMU-1 RQ-2B takes off with rocket assistance. Note the elevated Patriot air defense batteries in the background. *(USMC via VMU-1)*

The sandstorm of March 25 was a once in fifty years event. Find the VMU-1 support vehicle in this photograph. *(USMC via VMU-1)*

Marines race to unload ammo during the fight at the presidential palace on April 10. *(USMC via HMM-165)*

A wounded Iraqi awaits evacuation aboard a CH-46E during the fight at the presidential palace on April 10. *(USMC via HMM-165)*

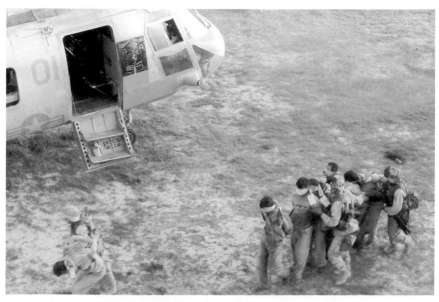

A group of Iraqi prisoners waits underneath the spinning rotor arc of a CH-46E during the fight at the presidential palace on April 10. (USMC *via* HMM-165)

Burning and looting in Baghdad on April 10 as seen from a CH-46E gunner's station. The weapon is an M2, .50-caliber heavy machine gun. (USMC *via* HMM-165)

Looking across Capt. Will Oliver at looting crowds on the outskirts of Baghdad during the fight for the presidential palace on April 10. *(USMC via HMM-165)*

The landing zone at the presidential palace during the fighting on April 10. The area was just barely big enough to handle a single CH-46E. *(USMC via HMM-165)*

A censored view of the FLIR video from Maj. Mark Butler's AV-8B as the Maverick missile he guided in from Capt. Tyler Bardo's aircraft smashes into a tower at the Imam Abu Hanifa Mosque during the fighting on April 10. *(USMC via VMA-214)*

It was hard-charging, hard-working marines like this who kept 3rd MAW in the fight during Operation Iraqi Freedom. Working unheralded in the heat and the dirt, these men and women never let their brothers in the thick of the fighting go unprotected. *(Stephen Heywood)*

An ordnance marine affixes a laser bomb kit to a 1,000-pound Mk-83 General Purpose bomb. When he finishes, the weapon will be a GBU-16, Laser Guided Bomb. *(USMC, Micah Snead)*

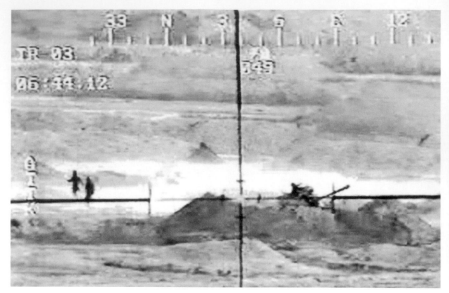

Tank crews run from their vehicles as they come under fire from the AH-1W
Cobra gunships of Allen Grinalds' flight. This engagement took place on
March 24, near Al Basrah. (*USMC via HMLA-267*)

The AH-1W Cobra crews that Todd Miller led against Iraqi fighters at
An Nasiriyah on March 23. From left to right they are: Captains Brad "Gash"
Lagoski, Dan "Shoeshine" Sheehan, Ron "Ike" Cannizzo, Jim "Weasel" Weis,
Dave "Fuse" Bussel, and Todd "BT" Miller. (*Todd Miller*)

One of the advantages of rotary winged operations was that the aircrews could land and communicate face-to-face with the marines they were supporting. Here, Capt. Todd Miller communicates with an FAC. *(Todd Miller)*

The note that Miller and the FAC exchanged in the picture above. Noise levels often made it easier to communicate with pen and paper. *(Todd Miller)*

I think EVAC MISSION WENT. I CAN CALL TACP LCL to CHECK.

WHAT TAD FREQ ARE YOU ON?

OK — LOOK THANKS FOR ALL THE SUPPORT YOU COBRA GUYS SAVED OUR ASSES. "HAWK" TANK FAC.

3rd MAW's wing commander, with his assistant commander and the wing's group commanders. Left to right: Col. Ron McFarland, MACG-38; Col. Mike Anderson, MWSG-37; Col. Rich Spencer, MAG-39; Brig. Gen. Terry Robling; Assistant Wing Commander, Maj. Gen. James Amos; Wing Commander, Col. Mark Savarese, MAG-13; Col. Randolph Alles, MAG-11; Col. Robert Milstead, MAG-29; and Col. Stuart Knoll, MAG-16. *(USMC via Robert Milstead)*

Cpl. Sarah "Mom" Wilson, a UH-1N crew chief, was in the thick of the fighting at An Nasiriyah and proved to be deadly behind her door-mounted gun. *(Paul Gosden)*

Hospital Corpsman Third Class Michael Vann Johnson Jr. was one of the Navy Corpsmen attached to Third Battalion, Fifth Marine Regiment. As a corpsman his duty called for him to be at the fore of the fighting—to provide first aid and to keep his wounded Marine comrades alive until they could be evacuated for more extensive treatment. Caring for the Marines was a duty that Johnson relished, and one at which he excelled. At twenty-five, he was older than most of them and felt a sense of fulfillment when they came to him for advice and guidance. As to his own safety . . . only a short time earlier he had written a letter to his mother telling her that he was going to be all right; that "God had twisted a guardian angel" around him. In the fighting around An Nasiriyah on March 25 the HMMWV he was riding in was struck by an RPG; he was killed instantly. Lance Corporal Quintero, also in the HMMWV, was badly wounded as well.

Driscoll had been asleep just more than an hour when the call came. "We got the word that the Third Battalion had gotten into a firefight and needed a CASEVAC mission immediately. This battalion was the lead element for the RCT so we knew that things might get interesting." Driscoll and the rest of his two crews quickly unbuttoned the two helicopters and in short order were headed north up Highway 1. Driscoll assigned the actual lead of the formation to the commander of the other aircraft, Captain Aaron "Fester" Eckerberg. Not only was it good experience for Eckerberg and his copilot, First Lieutenant Ryan "Jester" Sather, but it also showed his confidence in the junior officers.

"It didn't take us too long to find the battalion CP," Driscoll recalled. "After we landed I had a short chat with Lieutenant Colonel Carl Mundy, the battalion commander, while the casualties were being loaded." The fight was still ongoing. Enemy artillery rounds were impacting just a few hundred yards away, and the racket from the battalion's return fire rang in Driscoll's ears. The still-turning engines of his two aircraft added to the din.

"We put a Petty Officer Johnson aboard our bird," Driscoll said. "He was a corpsman who had been killed only a short time earlier and there was little we could do other than treat him with the respect that he and his family deserved." The wounded Marine was placed on Eckerberg's ship. Only minutes after landing the two CH-46Es were airborne again and headed south.

It was a short time later that the "Storm of the Century" caught up with Driscoll's flight. He recalled: "It wasn't a gradual thing. All of a sudden we were facing what looked like a solid wall of brown. It was really unnerving." The two CH-46Es collided with the storm in a blinding blast of sand and dirt. Clouds of dust made their way into Driscoll's aircraft—he could smell it and feel it. The fine grit even found its way between his teeth. Eckerberg, with the wounded Marine on board, made a dive for the ground and swung away toward the highway trying to maintain visual contact with the desert below. The maneuver was too aggressive for Driscoll to maintain formation. He separated from Eckerberg and immediately transitioned to flying on his instruments; there was nothing but brown to see outside his windscreen.

"Once I was clear of Fester, I started a climb to make sure I was clear of the ground," recounted Driscoll. "Also, I thought that perhaps we might be able to get above the worst of the visibility." All the while he and his copilot, Captain Bill "Spam" Pacatte, were fighting off the disorienting effects of vertigo. Their guts told them they were flying in one attitude and direction while their instruments told them otherwise. Following their guts—the more compelling instinct— would kill them. It took all their concentration to fight against the siren song of their instincts and fly according to their instruments.

Climbing through four thousand feet, Driscoll recognized that he was flying into the heart of the SAM threat; there was no way he was going to get above the shrouds of dirt being flung against his aircraft. He gently descended the helicopter back to two hundred feet while he and the rest of the crew weighed their options. "We discussed setting down in the desert right where we were, but there was a danger that we might land near an Iraqi unit." The hazard was very real. To this point the Marine advance had been concentrated along the roads and highways that ultimately led toward Baghdad. There were unknown numbers of small, bypassed Iraqi units in the desert. "Finally," Driscoll remembered, "I made the decision to feel our way over to the highway. From there we'd make our way down to Pac Bell FARP, to the south along Highway 1."

Using their onboard GPS, Driscoll and Pacatte groped through the flying sand until they reached the highway. "Not only was the visibility awful, but we were fighting a vicious headwind and our speed over the ground was only about twenty-five knots," Driscoll said. At times scooting along at only fifteen feet, just to be able to keep sight of the highway, Driscoll kept the helicopter moving south. "We played by the rules of the road—that is, we stayed on the right side just in case anyone else was playing the same game and flying north along the highway." It was a simple if informal means of maintaining some type of traffic deconfliction. Nevertheless, their biggest threat was the combination of roadside towers and traffic on the highway. Driscoll recounted: "There were a couple of times when we just barely lifted clear of oncoming traffic. It was actually kind of humorous to see the faces on these guys as we passed by each other at almost the same level."

There were times though that the flying sand was simply too much and they were forced to land. "I'll never forget," Driscoll said, "we were setting up to land alongside the highway at one point and we almost set down on top of a poor Marine who had his pants down around his ankles while he tended to his business. There he was a million miles from home, in a combat zone, dirty, hungry, and tired, caught in one of the worst sandstorms of the past fifty years, and he couldn't even exercise a bowel movement in peace and quiet. As it was, he didn't even budge—he just hung on to his toilet paper and finished the task at hand while we landed right next to him."

Finally, after more than two hours, Driscoll and his crew put their aircraft down at the Pac Bell FARP. It was quite literally a port in the storm—an assorted collection of Marine and Army helicopters had already clobbered their way through the blinding wind to take refuge at the ad hoc staging point. Driscoll was relieved. "We covered our aircraft up as best we could and hunkered down against the wind and dust." Later that day a UH-1N Huey came through for fuel, intent on returning to Kuwait regardless of the danger. Driscoll made arrangements to get Johnson's body aboard and back to the rear. "It just didn't seem right to leave him out there in the desert." Later in the day, Driscoll drew some comfort from a message noting that Eckerberg had been able to get the wounded Marine on his way to a field hospital, and the prognosis for his recovery was positive.

In the meantime the Marines moving on Highway 1 were having a devilish time. Not only were the drivers suffering from fatigue, but the blowing sand was making movement almost impossible. In places the visibility had gotten so bad that Marines dismounted to lead the drivers at a walking pace just to keep the columns moving forward. Still, drivers were falling asleep at the wheel; accidents slowed movement even further. One tank crew was lost when the driver either lost sight of the road or fell asleep and rolled off a bridge and into the Euphrates.

One Marine left his HMMWV to answer nature's call. The visibility was so poor he became disoriented and began to wander. As luck would have it he stumbled into a UH-1N at a nearby FARP. The obliging Huey crew took him in for the evening.

The blowing dust was so fine that it got into every crack, crevice, or hole in the body. It was *everywhere*. Marines wrapped bandannas or rags around their faces, or even put up with the discomfort of their gas masks in order to keep from breathing or ingesting the stuff. It made some Marines vomit up orangeish, muddy bile.

Ultimately, Driscoll's crew stayed bedded down at the FARP for two more days. He recalled their wait for the weather to clear: "Mostly we just sat around and talked with the other crews who were stranded out there. It was interesting to see what they had been doing—getting their perspective of the war." A notable aspect of this mission was the fact that Oliver North had been on board Driscoll's ship the entire time. He was a Fox News reporter embedded with the unit, and Driscoll recalled that the former Marine "was truly a pleasure to have around. He was never a prima donna—he ate what we ate, he slept where we slept, and he stayed out of our way and never made any demands. The young Marines loved him; he shared stories with them and never turned down any requests for photos or autographs. He was a true gentleman—I can't say enough good things about him."

It was late on March 27 when the weather cleared enough for Driscoll and Pacatte to bring their helicopter back to Ali Al Salem and put themselves back into the war.

The pilots and staff at 3rd MAW had been briefed that there was a sandstorm coming. "We'd seen them before, and we already knew that they were unpleasant and that they made it difficult to fly and work," Guts Robling recalled. "But we had no idea what was in store for us with this one." The maelstrom of wind and sand and dust that swept into southern Iraq and Kuwait during the morning of March 25 has subsequently been dubbed the "the Fifty-Year Storm," and described as the sort of event that happens only once or twice during a lifetime. Regardless of how often a weather event of this type occurs, this particular storm was vicious enough to virtually shut down helicopter operations—particularly across that portion of Iraq.

On the day it began Robling was en route to the newly captured airfield at Jalibah in southern Iraq in order to sort out some logistical and operational issues. "We wanted to start operating out of there at a pretty good rate, and things weren't quite moving as quickly as we would have liked. Tamer wanted me up there to push things along because . . . sometimes just having a general walking around energizes folks a bit more."

The sandstorm was just beginning when Robling's helicopter touched down. "There was a massive wall of dirt moving down on top of us," he remembered. "It was like nothing we'd ever seen—except maybe as a special-effects gimmick out of the movies." It wasn't long before the storm roared into the area and brought operations to a halt. Wind gusts reached speeds of sixty miles per hour and it became nearly impossible to do anything under the brutal crush of the wind-driven sand. "I was with Colonel Mike Anderson, the commanding officer of MWSG-37, and we didn't do much other than hunker down. Every once in a while the youngsters would run outside and pound the tent pegs back into the dirt, but other than that there wasn't much else that we were able to do."

Robling was stuck. He wasn't getting out of Jalibah that day. Nevertheless, the MWSG-37 headquarters was located only a short distance from the FSSG, and he made his way there to establish liaison with the staff. "I wasn't there long," he recalled, "when word came across that there was a company of Iraqi infantry approaching our position. This could be good; I remember thinking I might actually get into a firefight without having to do it from thirty thousand feet." Robling ran outside the tent and into the storm with his 9-millimeter pistol. He found a platoon of Marines in defensive positions straining to see into the whirlwind of sand.

"I was only out there a moment or two when the sergeant major nabbed me and almost physically dragged me away," recalled Robling. "He wasn't going to let a general officer get shot on his watch." The sergeant major tactfully but firmly brought Robling back from the perimeter while the younger Marines guarded against a threat that never came.

The storm continued through the night. Robling remembered: "I had only planned on being there for just a few hours. All I had with me was my helmet and pistol; I had no razor, no toothbrush, no nothing. Plus, I had my aide and two security kids with me. At that point I probably was more of a hindrance then a help." Ultimately a place was found for Robling to spend the night. The next morning three Army UH-60 Black Hawks were found sitting only twenty-five yards from their tent. "It was a miracle that they had been able to set down in the middle of the storm, and extremely fortunate that they hadn't landed on top of our tents," Robling remembered. "It was even more remarkable that no one had heard them come in."

Three more days passed before Robling was able to hitch a ride back to 3rd MAW headquarters at Al Jaber.

The Marine who had lost his way and was hosted by a Huey crew for a sleepover woke up on the day the storm subsided to find his vehicle less than a hundred yards away.

18

Hercules in Iraq

None of the crew had ever been shot at, but this mission was going to make them the first Coalition airmen to land a fixed-wing aircraft inside Iraq. That being the case, they were going to get shot at a lot.

By the evening of March 24 the Marines had seized the Iraqi airstrip just outside the town of Jalibah and made it ready for operations. Fuel and ammunition brought in to the airfield—now tactically known as Riverfront—would augment the supplies being trucked into Iraq over surface routes. Although it took the aircraft away from other missions, resupply by KC-130 was speedy and responsive.

That night at Joe Foss Expeditionary Air Field, just south of the Iraqi border in Kuwait, was dry and windy. From where they sat inside the tent that served as a makeshift operations and maintenance center the crew could hear other aircraft coming and going on the busy desert runway. It was very late in the evening when Major John "Roady" Skinner cut short the small talk that his crewmen were exchanging and focused their attention on the brief he was about to give. Their mission that night was to deliver thirty thousand pounds of bulk fuel to Riverfront. It was a fairly straightforward assignment; they would fly in to the airstrip, taxi clear of the runway, stop adjacent to a set of rubberized fuel bladders, and then pump their fuel directly into the bladders while saving just enough for their return flight to Kuwait, with a little extra as a reserve.

That is, it would have been straightforward were it not for the fact that they were going to be flying their big aircraft 150 miles into Iraq at night, at an altitude of a hundred feet, at 250 knots, and under a skuzzy layer of oil smoke. The anti-aircraft fire that random groups of bypassed Iraqi troops would send up was guaranteed to make the sortie even less straightforward. There was also the fact that, fifteen hundred feet from each end of the eight-thousand-foot runway, the Iraqis had dug two deep trenches in an attempt to make it unusable. Their effort was wasted. Although the shortened runway would no doubt pose some challenges, the remaining five thousand feet were still enough to conduct KC-130 operations.

"I emphasized what I thought were our primary threats," Skinner recalled. "Aside from the anti-aircraft fire, I was primarily concerned about the extremely low altitude we would be flying at." Ingressing into enemy territory at only a hundred feet would demand the very best from the entire crew. Those crewmen not at the flight controls had to maintain a careful lookout for enemy fire while the pilots had to "keep the aircraft out of the dirt." Additionally, the 133-foot wingspan of the aircraft would require that the pilots actually start a climb before they turned lest they drag a wingtip and fly the aircraft into the ground. In the accident reports these types of mishaps were pigeonholed under the category of CFIT: Controlled Flight Into Terrain. Whatever the name, it meant that the aircraft was accidentally smashed into the dirt. And it usually killed the crews.

Skinner's airmen were fairly seasoned, and the brief went smoothly despite the hazards that they knew were waiting for them. They belonged to VMGR-234, a reserve unit normally based out of Naval Air Station Fort Worth, Texas. Both Skinner and his copilot, Major Kevin "Devil Boy" Cunnane, were reservists who had been recently furloughed from the same major airline. Skinner remembered that it seemed odd: "Only about two months earlier we had been flying passengers in to places like Chicago and Los Angeles while being served by flight attendants. During that time our biggest concern was that the fares traveling in first class might eat all the good desserts. Now, having been activated by the Marine Corps, we were sleeping in cots and eating dirt."

Following the formal brief, Skinner's crew collected their gear and assembled outside in the nighttime air. Each of them snapped a fully loaded magazine into his 9-millimeter Beretta pistol and then checked that the weapon was securely strapped to his chest. Two extra Marines were added to the crew; with their M16s they would provide security on the ground at Riverfront when the defueling operation got under way. "I asked my Marines one more time if they had any questions," Skinner said. "They had none—it was time to get some."

The preflight inspection, engine start, and taxi out to the end of the dirt runway were uneventful. Much more interest in their normal duties and markedly less banter were the only signs that the crewmen appreciated the gravity of the mission. Once the takeoff checks were complete Skinner took one last look down the runway before he and Cunnane pushed the aircraft's four throttles all the way forward. It was 0330 on March 25.

The big ship moved slowly at first as it overcame the gripping inertia of the soft sand that perpetually plagued the expeditionary airstrip. The four huge turboprops spun up with a roar and whipped an enormous cloud of dust and dirt into the air. Skinner could hear the pinging clatter that small stones made as they were lifted from the ground and slammed into the fuselage. The KC-130 picked up speed even as it rose and fell on its big tires into the soft spots that the engineers could never completely scrape away. Finally Skinner and Cunnane hauled the aircraft airborne.

After checking through the Tactical Air Operations Center, the crew dropped the big transport down to the deck and pointed it west toward Jalibah. "I immediately put the rest of the guys to work watching for low-flying helicopters and power lines," Skinner said. "When you consider how many helicopters were operating in what was a relatively small airspace, it's remarkable that we didn't lose any aircraft to midair collisions." The danger from another hazard that Skinner had briefed—being targeted by "friendly" U.S. Army Patriot missiles—faded as the crew made its way deeper into Iraq. The deadly Patriots were a real threat—only a few days before they had accidentally shot down an RAF Tornado, and later in the war they would blast a U.S. Navy F/A-18 out of the sky.

Skinner's KC-130 began to draw anti-aircraft fire as he drove it deeper into Iraq. Still, none of the enemy rounds found its mark. "One of the primary benefits of low-level flight on an extremely dark night is that it is virtually impossible for the enemy on the ground to see you in time even if they are equipped with night-vision goggles," he said. "At such low altitudes the horizon hides your aircraft, and it is not uncommon for the bad guys to be unable to see you even when you fly directly overhead."

Sure enough, the tracer rounds that reached up at the low-flying transport spurted skyward in seemingly random streams that swept back and forth through the blackness. Sometimes that randomness put the enemy fire directly in their path. "We had to force ourselves not to maneuver too aggressively so close to the ground," recollected Skinner. Just a minor miscue brought on by haste would do what the Iraqi gunners could not. There wasn't a man on board the aircraft who hadn't already imagined the fireball that their aircraft and fifteen tons of bulk fuel would make if they should hit the ground.

The KC-130's mass demanded that it be controlled with a combination of finesse and an ability to predict the future. Unlike flying a fighter that responded instantly to even the very smallest inputs, the "Battle Herk" was an aircraft that reacted to the pilot's commands in a comparatively slow and measured manner. Although it responded to the small nudges and prods that came from the pilots on the flight deck, those responses still took time. Flying at a hundred feet above the ground left little margin to recover from a mistake made five seconds previously. Anticipating what control inputs were going to be required was almost an art that was learned only after long and difficult experience.

The big transport also demanded that the men and women who flew it had some muscle on their bones. At times the fliers didn't necessarily fly the aircraft so much as they horsed it around. Even though the controls were hydraulically boosted, big hard turns required big hard muscles. The entire crew—except perhaps the two last-minute security add-ons—knew all of this. Each time Skinner and Cunnane made an aggressive move the fliers in the rear of the aircraft held their collective breath until the big ship was settled back into straight and level flight.

Anti-aircraft guns weren't the only threat that worried Skinner. "Our ASE [Aircraft Survivability Equipment] gear kept chirping at us—warning that we were being tracked by Iraqi missile batteries." Nevertheless, the low-altitude profile that he was flying made it impossible for the enemy systems to achieve a solid firing solution, and no missiles were launched at the huge target that the KC-130 presented.

There were obviously no established instrument approaches into the newly captured airfield. Instead Skinner's navigator, CWO-5 Kevin "Rock" Lampe, had earlier devised a "self-contained approach" that would rely on the aircraft's Global Positioning System. Executed as designed, it would set Skinner and Cunnane up for a five-mile straight-in approach to the runway. However, as the crewmen completed their checklists and readied for landing, a wicked fusillade of tracers erupted from a point just three miles out from the end of the runway.

It was enough to keep them from continuing the approach. Skinner remembered: "There simply wasn't an opening in the solid line of AAA [Anti-Aircraft Artillery] that would allow us to line up on the runway and land. Instead we actually descended farther, accelerated, then maneuvered to set up for a landing from the opposite direction." At the same time, Lampe drafted a quick approach and passed it forward to the two pilots. By now it seemed that every single Iraqi in the desert surrounding the airfield was wide-awake and anxious to shoot down an American aircraft. The night sky was laced with streams of tracers that reached out in all different directions.

After a few minutes Skinner had the aircraft set up on the new profile that Lampe had devised. "To minimize our exposure we stayed at fifty feet for the final three miles of our approach to landing," he recollected. "The anti-aircraft fire was directed much higher than where we were flying, and most of it arced over the airfield." It was obvious that the Iraqis did not have an exact fix on the KC-130. This was good; Skinner now needed to devote the greater part of his attention to the task of actually getting the aircraft safely on the runway. With a full load of fuel the aircraft was heavy—150,000 pounds—and would be landing faster than normal, which in turn would require every bit of runway available. Also, the heavy load was stressing the airframe to near its limits; a hard landing could tear the wings from the fuselage.

Through his night-vision goggles Skinner picked out the subdued infrared lighting that delineated the trench the Iraqis had cut across the runway. Marines on the ground had put it in place only hours before. He double-checked his alignment, angle of attack, and airspeed. Maintaining the exact airspeed required was critical. "On the limited landing surface available, a smooth landing on the touchdown point would have been worthless if we carried even ten knots of extra airspeed—we simply wouldn't have been able to stop the aircraft prior to the trench on the other end of the runway."

Through his long career Skinner had seldom had to work so hard. Finally, just a few seconds before touchdown, he and Cunnane pulled the controls back toward their laps. "I could feel the sweat dripping down the side of my helmet as I flared the aircraft for landing," he recalled. The infrared lights marking the trench disappeared under the nose of the KC-130 as Skinner felt for the runway with the landing gear. A gentle shudder announced that the wheels had made contact with the asphalt. The two pilots brought the throttles back to flight idle, hesitated a moment to ensure that the big, square-bladed propellers were spinning properly, then pulled the throttles farther back into reverse and jumped on the brakes. The rapid deceleration that followed threw the crew forward hard against their shoulder restraints, but still the far trench was approaching rapidly. Nevertheless, Skinner was able to hold the shuddering aircraft under control. As the big transport slowed below fifty knots he engaged the nosewheel steering, bled off more speed, and then turned the aircraft off the runway toward where the fuel bladders were stationed and waiting. At the edge of the runway he could make out small groups of Marines guarding against an Iraqi counterattack. Looking skyward, he could still see trails of Iraqi tracers arcing over the field. The enemy gunners had no idea that he was safe on deck.

The importance of the thirty thousand pounds of fuel that Skinner's crew off-loaded that evening cannot be overstated. It was enough to completely fill the tanks of 176 HMMWVs—the ubiquitous vehicle that seemed to move the entire Marine Corps. His was the first sortie into Jalibah, but many, many more would follow. Particularly as additional Iraqi units were bypassed in the race for Baghdad, and as attacks on supply convoys became more common, air transport would bridge the gaps between supply and requirements. These sorts of operations boldly underscored the fact that the Marine Corps was a complete air-and-ground team.

19

The Prowler

The storm that swept over the region on March 25 had slowed the advance up Highway 1 by RCT-5 and -7. RCT-1, however, had better weather, and after pushing out of An Nasiriyah encountered stiff resistance from Fedayeen and Republican Guard fighters in the town of Al Gharaff, only about ten miles north along Highway 7. The enemy sprang a number of ambushes on the RCT's main body after letting the armored elements that made up the lead pass through town toward Ash Shatrah. The fighting became especially fierce when elements of the attached artillery support began receiving extremely heavy fire from very close quarters. Without missing a beat the Marine "cannon cockers" lowered several of their guns and fired directly into the buildings from where the Iraqis were shooting. This demonstration was quite effective.

At the southern edge of town Captain Jason Frei, an artillery battery commander, was hit by a Rocket Propelled Grenade while leading an advance party. His hand was severed by the blast. Nevertheless he improvised a hasty tourniquet from a radio handset cord and continued to lead his Marines against the enemy ambush. An hour later he was evacuated, near shock, after having suffered a massive loss of blood. Storm or not, the fighting that day was fierce along Highway 7.

By March 26 the worst of the storm had passed, although visibility was still difficult and the sunlight that passed through the airborne dust turned everything a freakish orange color. RCT-5 and -7 concentrated on eliminating Fedayeen elements in the vicinity of Ad Diwaniyah while RCT-1 continued its running gunfight north on Highway 7.

The fliers in 3rd MAW—particularly the fighter and attack types— continued to support the RCTs regardless of the weather. This was possible in part because the storm didn't effect Kuwait nearly so badly as the region of Iraq along Highway 1. On the other hand, helicopter support was sometimes spotty, depending on the visibility near the ground.

The United States has been the dominant military aerospace power since World War II for a number of reasons. One of the most important of these has been the nation's ability to execute airborne electronic warfare on a grander and more effective scale than any of its opponents. Since 1971 one of its most potent tools in this aspect of the art has been the EA-6B Prowler.

It's ugly. When I was earning my wings during the early 1980s (mind you, I'm one of the vainest people on earth), I lived in constant terror of being assigned to fly one of the unattractive, four-seat "family trucksters." Its redeeming factor—a facet that transcends appearances—is the undeniable fact that it is and has been the most effective aircraft of its type by a wide margin. Its primary role is SEAD—Suppression of Enemy Air Defenses. Looks aside, degrading or destroying the enemy's capacity to attack friendly aircraft is a capability that has endeared the EA-6B and its crews to the pilots of sexier aircraft, and has made the Prowler a "must-have" when striking into heavily defended territory.

The EA-6B executes its mission primarily through the jamming of enemy SAM radars or by destroying those radars with HARMs—High Speed Anti-Radiation Missiles. A discussion that goes beyond the generalities of how the aircraft is used is outside the scope of this book and might easily slip into the classified arena. Nevertheless, it is commonly known that the aircraft can provide jamming cover for a strike while actually part of that particular group of aircraft, or from a distance—at a point that allows a single EA-6B to cover one or more different strike groups. Naturally a number of factors dictate the tactics; these include, among others, the enemy threat and his capabilities, the number of EA-6Bs available, the geography, and the friendly situation. It should also be understood that the effectiveness of the platform is such that enemy SAM crews often will not operate their systems if they believe that there are EA-6Bs in the vicinity. Staying alive is a priority, even among the nation's opponents. In pilot-speak this very desirable effect is called a "soft kill."

Derivations of the Grumman A-6, Navy and Marine Corps EA-6As flew protective sorties during much of the Vietnam conflict and were ultimately replaced by the EA-6B, which began service at the tail end of that war and has since undergone massive and continual upgrades. During the early 1990s, following Desert Storm, the U.S. Air Force retired its own tactical jammer, the EF-111, and the EA-6B was left to take up the role for the entire Department of Defense. To better facilitate the increased tempo that operations over the former Yugoslavia and the Persian Gulf demanded, the Marine Corps's single large squadron, VMAQ-2, was divided into four smaller units: VMAQ-1, -2, -3, and -4.

During this campaign the Marine Corps's Prowlers were based in Saudi Arabia at Prince Sultan Air Base. The Saudi installation carries the international identifier of PSAB and is universally known among the military aviation community as "Pee-Sab." "The EA-6Bs were a strategic asset, and we put them down in Saudi Arabia with other strategic resources," Robling remembered. "We had to list them all as excess sorties so that the ATO staff could use them as they saw fit. But General Moseley was good to his word—whenever we needed our own Prowlers we got them."

Captain Dave "Shoe" Mueller was a pilot with VMAQ-1, one of

the two Marine EA-6B squadrons at the base. Already in his career he
had flown missions over Iraq in support of OSW and ONW during
two different periods. During OIF, however, the pace had been much
more hectic. He remembered his workload as the month of March
drew to an end: "During the previous week my flight time was approximately double the amount of time I spent sleeping. I was aver-
aging seven hours a day in the air and only about four in the rack." An
advantage that the Prowler enjoys over most other tactical aircraft is
that it doesn't have to rearm to execute its mission. If the aircraft and
its systems hold up, and if there are refueling aircraft available, and if
the crew can stay awake, there is no reason for the aircraft to return to
base. Because of this the crews were often pressed to their limits.

The mission of March 26 was one that would tax Mueller and his
crew beyond what they had ever experienced. Although the "how and
what" are classified, an outline of the mission's conduct gives an idea
of the effort the crew put into that day's sortie.

The fliers had already been at work for about five hours when they
made their way to the flight line. Briefings began four hours prior to
takeoff. That didn't include the time that went into preparing the
brief beforehand. Fortunately some efficiencies were gained by keeping the same four-man crews together during the majority of the campaign. "This could be a blessing or a curse, depending on who a guy
ended up with," remembered Mueller. "I got pretty lucky; Major Bob
'Hadji' Bader was the XO [Executive Officer] and one of the most
tactically proficient ECMOs [Electronic Countermeasures Officers]
in the community. Captain Chris 'Smokey' Robinson was another ex-
pert ECMO. Our crew was rounded out by First Lieutenant Matt
'Cess' Poole. He had joined the squadron in those last few hectic
weeks before we had deployed. He had no combat experience but
was a sharp guy with a good attitude; he was a quick learner." Although Mueller was the pilot, it fell to the three ECMOs to run the
complex systems that made the Prowler what it was: the best tactical
jamming aircraft in the world.

Aside from being a pilot, Mueller also served as the squadron's aircraft division officer. As the flight went through the maintenance

shop to sign for the jet, he took a few minutes to catch up on what was going on in his department. "The guys were as tired as we were. They'd been working nonstop since we'd come into theater and were performing miracles to keep the jets flying." Indeed, the squadron was in the midst of setting a new monthly flight-hour record for a five-aircraft Prowler unit: more than seven hundred hours for the month of March 2003. "That I had been blessed with competent Marines made me extremely happy," Mueller remembered.

He and his crew got airborne uneventfully and headed north through Saudi Arabian airspace. After a quick rendezvous with an Air Force refueler, Mueller topped off the aircraft's tanks and then pointed the crew into Iraq for their first mission. The visibility at altitude was outstanding, but blowing sand blocked their view of the ground below. "From all the action that was being relayed over the radio it seemed that the Close Air Support aircraft were having a tough time working through it, but they were still trying," recalled Mueller. Fortunately, the Prowler's electronic tools were essentially impervious to the blowing dust. The support the crew provided to I MEF and its aircraft was just one more component that was supporting the drive north out of An Nasiriyah.

It was sometime during this early portion of the flight that the aircraft's navigational system decided to take a hiatus. "It was disconcerting to hear a Persian controller come up on the radio and accuse us of encroaching on the 'Iranian Empire,' " said Mueller. There is nothing quite like being lost while traveling at several hundred miles per hour. "We got on our basic instruments and got headed away from Iran," Mueller recalled, "and then got the Air Force AWACS to give us a vector to the tanker." During the trip to the refueler Mueller and Poole got the navigational system realigned and working properly.

"Actually," recounted Mueller, "we were at the end of our scheduled mission and were looking forward to heading back to PSAB and getting some good Air Force chow in our bellies." But the situation had changed. The deteriorating weather had scrubbed the launch of the aircraft that was supposed to relieve them. Furthermore, a

B-1 bomber had just checked in and was headed for "downtown"—
Baghdad. The Air Force aircraft needed jamming protection, and
Mueller offered up the crew's services.

During the years after Desert Storm, the Coalition had effectively
eliminated most of the SAM threats in those sectors of Iraq covered
by OSW and ONW. Baghdad, however, had remained essentially un-
touched during all that time. On paper, at this time in the campaign,
the defenses over the capital city looked formidable. So fearsome
were they postulated to be that the area over and around the city was
demarcated as a "Super MEZ"—a Super Missile Engagement Zone.
On maps it was crosshatched with overlapping red circles that depicted a system of SAMs so seemingly deadly that any aircraft that
dared to penetrate it would face certain annihilation.

After all, the enemy SAM system operators had learned a great deal
during the previous decade and were considered a real threat to aircraft that dared penetrate into the heart of Iraq. On the other hand,
the Iraqi operators had also learned that their counterparts in northern and southern Iraq who had actively tried to engage Coalition
aircraft had ended up dead. Basically, at this point in the war, there
was still no good idea of how severe the anti-aircraft threat over Baghdad was, and it was more prudent to treat it with respect than with dis-
regard.

In this particular instance the coverage provided by Mueller's crew
was sufficient to ensure that the Air Force bomber completed its mission unscathed. The effort went well, and the EA-6B was soon on its
way back to the aerial refueler as night cloaked the battlefield. After
topping off with gas another time Mueller took his crew back over
Iraq for a mission in general support of ongoing operations. Nevertheless, those operations were dropping off in volume as the sandstorm that was stymieing the ground advance was also frustrating the
support that could be provided from the air.

Finally, their obligations complete, Mueller's crew prepared for
the return trip to PSAB. They were quickly informed however that
the Saudi base was closed because of foul weather; they would have
to divert into Ali Al Salem in Kuwait. "This was not what I expected

or wanted," said Mueller. "The Marine Corps flew helos out of there and the Brits operated some jets, but I would have preferred to have diverted into Al Jaber—about fifteen miles south of Al Salem. That's where most of the Corps's fixed-wing assets were based."

Ultimately it didn't matter. Just as the crew was descending into Ali Al Salem they were called back for another mission into Iraq. Again they refueled and provided jamming. Finally, they were ready to return to base. The weather at PSAB was still marginal, though, and it looked like the Air Force controllers were going to send them away again. "We really didn't want to divert into anywhere other than our home base," Mueller explained. After some slick talking they convinced the controllers to allow them to head back to Prince Sultan Air Base. "We had missions to fly the next day and our jets could better help them from PSAB rather than from some outlying base where we had no maintenance troops."

Their luck went sour about 150 miles from the Saudi base; the Air Force controllers there turned them away and directed them to head back to Kuwait, where the weather was supposedly better. "I all but begged them to let us continue to PSAB," remembered Mueller. "I even called back to the squadron and asked them to make our case, but it was all in vain." Finally, realizing that their pleas were getting them nowhere, Bader called up to Mueller from the rear of the aircraft: "Okay, Shoe, turn the jet around—they don't want us here." Mueller reversed course and drove the crew back toward Kuwait. The salt in the wound came when they heard the Air Force controllers clear an Air Force aircraft for the approach back to PSAB.

When Mueller finally brought the EA-6B back to Ali Al Salem, he found that the weather there was worse than it had been at PSAB. Still, in degraded visibility, he brought the jet in for an uneventful landing. More than nine hours after having taken off from their base in Saudi Arabia the Marine fliers crawled out of their jet. "Actually, once we landed," Mueller recalled, "the Air Force treated us pretty well." The crew was provided with the gear they would need to spend the night in reasonable comfort and given a good meal to hold them over until morning when they would launch on another day full of missions.

For Mueller, the icing on the cake was the sleeping arrangements the Air Force provided for the evening. It was obvious that they had had to contract from civilian vendors for much of the bedding. "The Hello Kitty sleeping bags looked like they had come straight from a little girl's slumber party," he recalled. "They put the first smile on my face since we had walked to the jet the previous morning." That night—snuggled into his little pink sleeping bag—Mueller got the best sleep he'd had since the war started.

The next day, March 27, proved that although the services were getting better at joint operations and more comfortable at crossing boundaries and allowing their own boundaries to be crossed . . . the process was not yet perfect. Ad Diwaniyah sat in that nether region just astride the line that separated the Army's area of operations from that of the Marine Corps. Technically it belonged to the Army. Marine Lieutenant Nate Boaz headed a HUMINT Exploitation Team in the vicinity and was approached by an Iraqi who informed him that the city's stadium was a staging area for the Fedayeen and their weapons. Just that moment it was supposed to be occupied by hundreds or more of the fighters.

Boaz immediately passed this information to the First Marine Division's intelligence section, which in turn directed a Pioneer UAV from VMU-2 to investigate. Iraqi informants were often unreliable, but that wasn't the case in this instance. Imagery from the Pioneer confirmed the presence of armed Fedayeen inside the stadium. Because the target actually fell inside the Army's battlespace, however, the division had to pass the request for an air strike up through the MEF, which was obliged to pass it farther up the chain to the CFLCC (Lieutenant General David McKiernan's headquarters). The Coalition Forces Land Component Commander sent the data down to the Army's V Corps headquarters.

The V Corps staffers felt compelled to confirm the validity of the report themselves and sent a Hunter UAV overhead the stadium. Sure enough, the Fedayeen were still there in numbers. Finally the target was passed through the CFACC and ultimately the Air Force. The stadium was struck and scores of enemy fighters were killed. The success illustrated the fact that too much bureaucracy can still prevail over an ignorant and foolish enemy.

20

A Million Ways to Die

It was a war that relied on speed to confuse and demoralize the enemy. Where and when the Iraqi commanders decided to challenge the Coalition hardly mattered; by the time the decision was made, the Americans had already overrun that point and more. Over and over, though, the Americans were learning that bypassed pockets of Iraqi fighters had to be neutralized. All the tools in the Marine Corps's chest were used to complete this task—including tactical jets.

They had been flying their missions on the "night page" for several days now. Sundown was their sunrise, dinner was their breakfast; like vampires they crept back into their sleeping bags before the sun rose too high above the horizon. Captain Neal "Rudy" Rickner and First Lieutenant Chris "Sparky" Clark of VMFA(AW)-225 crawled out of bed in the early evening of March 27 anticipating a hot shower and some decent chow. The two young officers had gotten a decent amount of rest because by now arrangements had been made to provide the MAG-11 aircrew with sleeping quarters inside air-conditioned shelters. The setup didn't endear them to some of the young enlisted men and women who were sweating it out in canvas tents open to the environment; on the other hand, it didn't make sense to put fatigued, red-eyed aircrews into the cockpits of fifty-million-dollar aircraft loaded with tons of high-explosive bombs.

"After we showered and ate," recalled Rickner, "Sparky and I divided the work that needed to be done before we went out on our mission—scheduled for early the next morning." Rickner was assigned as the section leader that night, and Clark was his WSO. Because the fight was moving so fast, the positions of friendly units needed to be replotted on their charts and the latest FSCMs (Fire Support Coordination Measures) needed to be studied. The daily SITREP (Situation Report) that Major General James Mattis wrote was also a "must-read," as it delineated his highest priorities and guidance to his subordinate commanders. Additional data were collected more informally from face-to-face meetings with other aircrews and through an archive of e-mails that listed lessons learned from mistakes made on previous sorties.

Planning for their particular mission began with a review of the Air Tasking Order. The ATO was made up of hundreds of pages and covered all the fixed-wing sorties that the Coalition was scheduled to fly for the given period. Amplifying information was provided for each individual flight as well as special instructions that encompassed myriad topics. It took training and time to navigate through the cumbersome document, but it was essential to the conduct of the air war. Still, because the war never stopped, and because it was built on a projection of what the battlefield would look like during a given period, it often required adjustments. Those adjustments—as often as not—took place once the crews got airborne. "We found our mission in the ATO and planned to all the relevant data but we were still prepared to flex to something different if directed," Rickner said. "It had happened several times during the previous week."

Assigned the callsign of Waxen 67, the two-ship of F/A-18Ds had been detailed to conduct AR (Armed Reconnaissance) in a killbox near Al Kut. Simply put, they were to proceed to the last known position of the Baghdad Division of the Iraqi Republican Guard and destroy what they found. "Our intelligence shop provided us some more definitive coordinates to look at, as well as some very dated satellite imagery," Rickner said. After briefing with the other two Marines who would man the second aircraft in their section, Rickner and Clark and the other two fliers headed for their aircraft.

Rickner led his section airborne at 0350 on March 28 and pointed northwest toward Al Kut, approximately two hundred miles distant. Clark worked the radios and brought them through the several different controlling agencies that would ultimately authorize the flight to operate in the battlespace. To extend their time over Al Kut, the ATO had fragged the two Waxen 67 birds to take on two thousand pounds of fuel each from a KC-130 orbiting over southeast Iraq. The extra ten minutes or so this would give them in the killbox could be valuable.

Once the nighttime refueling evolution was complete, Rickner eased his formation away from the tanker and then pointed northwest again, climbing to save gas. It was only a few minutes later, though, that they were contacted by the TACC: A high-priority target had just been discovered, and the pair of Hornets were needed to kill it. "Task Force Tarawa was taking harassing artillery fire at An Nasiriyah," recounted Rickner. "All of us were very aware of An Nasiriyah because of the fighting that had taken place there on March 23. A lot of Marines had been killed." He turned his aircraft south toward the Iraqi city and was directed to switch frequencies and contact a FAC, callsign Pooh.

Rickner remembered: "As soon I heard his voice I realized that Pooh was Major Robert 'Pooh' Warshell. We had worked regularly together during the previous year back at Miramar, in San Diego." In fact, Rickner had seen Warshell working in the TACC in a nonflying billet at Al Jaber only a week earlier. But Warshell was eager to get into the fight, and after the casualties were counted at An Nasiriyah he was assigned to a unit in the field.

"Pooh gave us a set of coordinates that defined an area he wanted us to search," Rickner said. "Although he didn't have eyes on the Iraqi artillery he had a general idea of where the gun or guns were." After making certain that Waxen 67 flight knew where the nearby friendly units were located, Warshell turned Rickner's two Hornets loose.

"I put our wingman above us in a high-cover position to watch for SAM launches or AAA," he remembered. "At the same time, we dropped lower and Sparky started searching the area with the FLIR." It took only a few short minutes before Clark discovered an artillery tube in a revetment not far from the coordinates that Warshell had passed. A lower pass overhead the gun confirmed that it was indeed what the FAC was after.

This was exactly the sort of target that was vexing the Coalition forces. Both the Army and the Marines had been passing through the city since March 22, and although it hadn't yet been completely secured the appearance of heavy artillery fire must have caught the Marines of Task Force Tarawa by surprise. It wasn't the first time and it wouldn't be the last time that the various Marine units were surprised by forces that had been bypassed or ignored.

Clark read the coordinates of the newly found artillery tube back to Warshell, who subsequently cleared the flight to engage it as well as any other targets in the immediate vicinity. Rickner recounted: "We offset about ten miles to the southwest and then turned back inbound." Traveling at almost five hundred knots, the two fliers dropped their single GBU-16 at a range of about four miles from the target. Both of them anxiously watched the FLIR display waiting for the explosion that would mark the thousand-pound bomb's impact into the enemy gun. Instead, they were disappointed to see a sad little puff of dust where their bomb dudded into the edge of the revetment.

With no more precision-guided ordnance on board, Rickner brought his wingman down to play. Although the second aircraft wasn't equipped with a FLIR, the crew could drop on a set of coordinates while Clark and Rickner guided the bomb into the target with their own FLIR. "We repositioned and then pushed our wingman out in front of us while we followed in trail," Rickner remembered. Once the second crew called that they had released their GBU-16, Rickner and Clark again gave their full attention to the FLIR display. They weren't disappointed; the Iraqi gun disappeared in a brilliant explosion.

Knowing that there had to be other targets in the area, the two Hornet crews continued to circle overhead while they searched. "It was the worst time of the day to go trolling for targets," recalled Rickner. "The sun was just starting to rise so that we were constantly flipping our goggles up if we ran to the east, or snapping them down if we headed west." Regardless of how they tried to compensate, it was still difficult; it was too bright to see well with the goggles on and too dark to see well with them off. Too, the temperature differential between potential targets and the surrounding terrain had decreased to the point that the FLIR was becoming less and less effective.

Warshell was getting impatient on the ground and advised Rickner that he was ready to push two AH-1W Cobras into the area to see what they could find. Clark got ahead of the game and told the gunship crews to enter the area and describe what they found. Almost immediately the Cobras reported that they had the destroyed target in sight as well as three large military trucks parked nearby that appeared to be unscathed. "They tried talking our eyes onto the trucks but the visibility was hopeless," explained Rickner. "As high as we were, and with the sunlight reflecting off of the haze and dust, we just couldn't see much of anything. Even the Tigris River was barely visible."

The Cobra crew advised Waxen 67 that they were going to "mark" the target for them with a Hellfire missile. Rickner rogered the call and positioned himself to watch for the Hellfire. It was only a moment later that he saw a missile apparently arcing skyward. "It startled me. I instantly put out chaff while I started to defend. I should have made a professional call for the section to react but instead the only thing that came out of my mouth was: 'Uh . . . hey, do you see that!' Almost immediately Rickner realized that the SAM he thought he was defending against was the Cobra's Hellfire. He recovered his wits as he watched the missile tip back over and detonate into the ground. Keeping the explosion in sight, he rolled in from fifteen thousand feet to deliver a string of three unguided thousand-pound Mk-83 bombs.

The accuracy of Rickner's bombs caught the Cobra leader off guard. He remembered the gunship pilot's radio transmission: "Waxen 67, we're going to . . . *Holy!* [radio microphone unkeys then rekeys] . . . Waxen, those were direct hits, those trucks are gone and there are secondary explosions all over the place. *Nice hits!*" It was likely that the trucks had been carrying ammunition for the gun that the flight had destroyed earlier.

It was only a short time before the Cobra crews found another set of trucks. This time they fired a Hellfire for Rickner's wingman to use as a mark. After Waxen 68 spotted the explosion and called that he was in his dive, Rickner and Clark watched as the Hornet continued to drop toward the earth. Finally the nose of the other aircraft started back up, and continued up. Confused, Rickner and Clark watched for the set of three explosions that should have marked their wingman's bombs. There were none. "Our wingman's nose continued up until it looked like he was flying almost vertically," Rickner said. "Finally we saw the aircraft slice back down toward the horizon." When the other jet appeared to be fully recovered, Rickner called him over the radio: "They said that they were fine, but bingo—low on gas and ready to go home."

After checking out with Warshell, the two Hornets headed back to Al Jaber. On their way they enjoyed a spectacular sunrise; the distant mountains in Iran were beautifully silhouetted against the reddish orange ruddiness of the rising sun.

"After we got back we found out what had happened to our wingman," Rickner explained. "While he was in his dive his NVGs [night-vision goggles] came off his helmet and got jammed in the control stick, forcing it aft. What was worse was that he had to pull the stick further aft in order to dislodge them. Then, when they broke loose, they slid forward and he had to grope around his feet to get them out of the way before the control stick would move again."

The incident underscored the fact that every aviator lives with: There are a million ways to die in an airplane.

21

≡≡≡

Convoy Escort

The Iraqi Army was notable during the campaign for the incredible fact that it never really showed up. I could find no account that described an encounter against a unit even so modest in size as a fully organized and equipped battalion. Many of the Iraqi soldiers simply shucked their uniforms and deserted as the Marines closed on their positions. It should also be noted that American airpower vaporized a great number of Iraqi formations before they could even start toward the fighting, while some enemy units just chose not to do battle and never left their garrisons.

Instead, most of the fighting that Marine ground units became engaged in took place in the urban environment against small army units or bands of Fedayeen or foreign fighters. The Iraqis, to their credit, realized that their forces were far from a match for American firepower on the battlefield. Rather than getting slaughtered in the open, many of those who chose to fight gravitated to the villages, towns, and cities. All of the population centers were situated on major roads, and the American advance moved along those some highways. The built-up areas along these routes were perfect for setting up ambushes. Throughout the entire war, these attacks were the only con-

sistently effective way the Iraqis found to slow the Marines' sprint toward Baghdad.

A number of factors made the urban areas good ambush sites. Foremost was the fact that the roads funneled the Marines into very narrow and predictable avenues of advance. Once caught in an urban
attack, often between multistory buildings, there was little room for
the heavily mechanized units to maneuver or escape. Disabled vehicles and concentrated fire compounded the problem. Another factor
that the Iraqis used to their advantage was the very nature of the "terrain" itself. Concrete structures offered tremendous protection
against small-arms fire as well as multiple points from which to carry
out an attack. As one infantryman put it: "Every window and every
door was a potential fighting hole for the bad guys." It wasn't unusual
for Marines clearing urban areas to find stacks of guns, RPGs, and
extra ammunition stashed under several different windows in the
same building. With this arrangement a single enemy fighter could
shift from position to position, shooting as he went.

Another problem that confounded the Marines as they pushed
through the towns or cities was that it was difficult to distinguish the
enemy fighters from noncombatants. Many of the Iraqis didn't wear
uniforms; instead they clothed themselves casually in slacks and sport
shirts. An unarmed man who dashed from one side of the road to another in the middle of a firefight very likely could have been an
enemy soldier in civilian clothes who was simply moving from one
armed strongpoint to another. Or he could have been a worried father
trying to get back to his home and family.

Unfortunately, killing combatants holed up in a building often
meant demolishing the building, and this often meant killing the
noncombatants who were also inside. It was unavoidable, but it
stirred up hatred in a populace that otherwise might have been more
welcoming. And it made for bad press in the Arab world and beyond.
Additionally, it could take a toll on morale; it wasn't hard for a Marine
to empathize with people whose houses and belongings—and perhaps their loved ones—were little more than bits of rubble in the
street.

Add to this the fact that anything that moved in the street during a firefight, hostile or not, became a target. This guaranteed that families riding in civilian vehicles were accidentally targeted and killed. That this happened was the fault of the enemy fighters; they typically traveled in private automobiles for the simple reason that anything that looked remotely military rarely survived even a few minutes after being detected.

Finally, the urban fight often took away the option of using fixed-wing aircraft for CAS. With restrictive ROE, fighters such as the F/A-18s and AV-8Bs were tools that frequently could not be used. Employing even the relatively small five-hundred-pound bombs was typically not an option because the fighting took place at such close quarters that friendly troops were in as much danger as the enemy, and also because of the enormous damage that the bombs generally wrought. The targeted building might go down, but so might two or three other nearby structures.

Attack helicopters, on the other hand, could be more useful. Their ability to stay low and slow, although it made them more vulnerable, also made it easier for them to find and destroy enemy targets. That aside, the weapons they carried were less destructive and more suitable for fighting in pent-up areas. These attributes were readily recognized by the ground commanders, who often requested that their movements through urban areas be covered by AH-1W Cobra support.

"Daaaamn," Captain Kristian Pfeiffer thought out loud to his copilot, Captain Doug "Sweaty" Lindamood. They, and the other three HMLA-169 Cobra crews he had been leading since before 0600 on the morning of March 28, were tired. Not just tired—exhausted. They had been flying in support of the convoy below for nearly twelve hours, and now it was almost dark. They were scribing a slow lazy orbit in the sky overhead Highway 7 while the command element of the two-hundred-vehicle convoy decided what it wanted to do. The Marines who manned the huge assemblage of trucks, fuel tankers, and HMMWVs were charged with moving north as rapidly as possible. The supplies and equipment they carried were essential to RCT-1 and its drive north.

Personally, Pfeiffer wanted to go back to one of the FARPs and get some rest. Already his flight, Clancy 31, had made five different refueling and rearming stops and had escorted the convoy through the notorious stretch of An Nasiriyah that, even this early in the campaign, had been dubbed "Ambush Alley." The line of support vehicles had then pushed twenty-four miles farther north into the small town of Ash Shatrah. There the lead elements had already reached the far side when vehicles in the middle began taking mortar, RPG, and heavy machine-gun fire from fighters hidden in and among the buildings that made up the center of the town. The Iraqi defenders, perhaps in a display of loyalty, had chosen to make their stand under a garish mural of Saddam. But rather than smashing through the attack, the convoy commander had somehow—and for some reason— turned the long snake of vehicles back upon itself and beat a retreat back through the attack to the south. Pfeiffer and his flight of Cobras had engaged the enemy defenders with Hellfire missiles and gunfire, but there was no way to tell if they had been routed.

Regardless, the convoy commander received orders that reiterated the critical nature of the mission; there was no choice but to continue north immediately. Accordingly, the formation was repositioned and poised for a new attempt. "I was hoping that there would be another flight of Cobras sent out to take over for us," Pfeiffer recalled, "but there was just no one else available." The convoy's FAC desperately wanted the flight of Cobras to cover the next effort to smash through the town. "I told him that we needed fuel and that he needed to sort it out immediately, or we had no choice but to leave," said Pfeiffer. "Actually, I held the flight there longer than I should have—getting all the way back to the FARP with the fuel we had would have been a very near thing." Finally a voice rang out over the radio net: "We've got your fuel, sir!" Sure enough, Pfeiffer spotted a break in the middle of the line of vehicles where a pair of fuel trucks was being positioned to service the Cobras. A hard-charging staff NCO had taken charge of the situation. "The way the trucks all made room, and the way people were rushing back and forth to get ready for us, well, it kind of reminded me of the parting of the Red Sea," Pfeiffer remembered.

"We set down next to those trucks and started taking on fuel right there along the highway," he went on. "We were forced to break just about every rule in the book as far as putting pins in our weapons and maintaining the proper distances and things of that nature. And we actually gravity-refueled with hose nozzles straight into our open tanks while our engines were running." Regardless, this was combat and Pfeiffer was anxious to make things happen. After twelve hours in the cockpit, he was fatigued to the point of being punch drunk.

"While they were putting fuel in my bird," he remembered, "I got out and made a quick 'leak check' while I stretched my legs. I was starting to get frustrated with the whole thing. The convoy had started through this nasty little town and then it had turned back. Then we had hit the enemy, and now—several hours later—we were still waiting around while higher headquarters tried to make up their minds. Any surprise or momentum we may have had was gone. If we didn't get relieved it was going to be a very long night."

While he tried to shake twelve-plus hours of kinks out of his tired body, the Cobra pilot made small talk with the young Marine who was refueling his aircraft. It was at that point that Pfeiffer experienced an epiphany. "It was your classic 'Hallmark Moment,'" he remembered. "Here was this young kid with a very serious look on his face, but it was obvious to me that he was trying to mask the fact that he was very scared. He was the driver of that particular truck. It was a big, fat, multiwheeled, bag-of-fuel, high-explosive target and in just a short time he was going to be taking it into a known ambush and was going to burn to death if he got hit. Frightened or not, he was a very brave young man." It was at that moment that Pfeiffer decided that regardless of how tired he was, he was going to see the convoy all the way through.

He and his division of Cobras did just that. After getting airborne in the dark, they set up to the southwest of the town and watched the line of vehicles advance. Just as the Marines on the ground reached the southern edge of Ash Shatrah, Pfeiffer's gunships salvoed two Hellfire missiles into an enemy bunker that guarded the approach. A plume of dust, smoke, and fire marked the spot. It was dead. The convoy continued past the Iraqi position toward the point where the original ambush had forced the entire column into retreat just hours earlier.

By now a second flight of three gunships had arrived to augment Pfeiffer's division. Combo 43 was assigned to cover the rear of the effort while the original four Cobras provided protection for the forward elements. Tonight more firepower was better than less.

The enemy was still there, but he didn't take the Marines under fire until the lead element was nearly clear of the town. This time several segments of the long line of support vehicles came under fire at once. The Marines returned fire and pressed ahead. There was little sense in turning back—the convoy had to get through, and if not then, when?

Corporal Garrick Tracy was one of the Marines on the highway below Pfeiffer. He was at the wheel of a Mk-48 LVS (Logistics Vehicle System)—essentially an enormous, diesel-powered truck, or power unit, with a long, heavy flatbed trailer. On this night he was carting two huge bulldozers. During normal driving the Mk-48 is about as fast and maneuverable as a strip mall. Hauling two bulldozers, it was even less so, and now with the convoy taking heavy fire he was wishing he was somewhere else. Mortar rounds dropped close by, and machine-gun fire and rocket grenades ripped into the vehicles from both sides of the road. He could hear the sharp ping of bullets ricocheting off the bulldozers behind him. "We were just punching through it—hauling ass," he remembered. "There were blown-up semis and buses in the road. It was like a slalom course going through there. I was running off the road left and right."

The column was made up of more than two hundred vehicles manned by Marines just like Corporal Garrick.

It was very dark now, and Pfeiffer watched the screen of Iraqi tracers lace through the gloom and into the caravan of Marines. The volume of return fire from the Marines increased until at times the lines of tracers almost made up a solid sheet. Pfeiffer didn't watch long before he threw his Cobras into the fight. He called for a cover-the-break, or trail, attack and brought the four ships in from the south on a northerly heading that paralleled the highway. "It was a madhouse down there. The bad guys on the east side of the road were pouring all kinds of fire into the convoy."

The Cobra crews dived toward the enemy shooters, but even with night-vision goggles the low-light conditions made it difficult for the pilots to make out individual targets. "Finally Sweaty was able to find these guys on the FLIR," Pfeiffer recalled. The four gunships let loose a fusillade of 2.75-inch rockets and 20-millimeter cannon that tore into the buildings and fortified positions that lined the eastern side of the road. The *whoosh* of the rockets and clattering staccato booms of their cannon added a new dimension to the chaos.

Pfeiffer turned his ship hard to the west and watched the other three Cobras come out of their firing runs. From the east side of the road he could see parts of the curtain of tracers lift skyward as the Iraqis shot up at the Marine helicopters. None of the enemy rounds found its mark, and Pfeiffer called for another attack. Again the four Cobras dived down on the east side of the road, and again the white-bright flash of rocket fire split the night sky. Red streaks of 20-millimeter tracer fire followed the rocket trajectories. Pfeiffer and Lindamood pressed to within two hundred yards of the enemy fighters and sprayed cannon rounds until there was no return fire. "They either stopped shooting, or we killed them all," Pfeiffer said, "because the only shooting that was being done was coming from the supply column—it was all one-sided."

The flight of Cobras reset to the west of the highway to regroup. Stoked by the excitement of obliterating the ambush, it was time for the crews to take a moment to calm down and plot their next move. "Right about then," recalled Pfeiffer, "my 'Spider Senses' started to tingle." Out of the corner of his eye he caught sight of a towering structure and realized that he was leading the flight directly into a course of enormous power-line stanchions—not just the spindly sort that fed the local power supply but the massive, multilegged monsters that suspended the enormous cables that powered the national grid. In the low light there was a better chance than not of one of his crews smashing into either the cables or one of the towers. They wouldn't have survived. Pfeiffer remembered: "We got lucky; the cables had already been knocked down, and we managed to stay clear of the stanchions themselves." Still, he realized that a moment of inattention had nearly done to his flight what a town full of Iraqi fighters hadn't been able to do.

The shootout at Ash Shatrah was only one of several that Pfeiffer's flight fought during a nearly twenty-four-hour period that covered most of March 28 and stretched into March 29. He candidly says that trying to accurately recount the numbers and types of weapons they fired and the targets they engaged is near impossible. They were airborne too long. Following the escort through Ash Shatrah, his Cobras covered the convoy through another ambush at the small town of Ar Rifa. Finally, when the entire line of vehicles was safely within the protective perimeter of RCT-1, Pfeiffer and his crews returned to the FARP at Camden Yards after logging a total of twenty-one hours of "ass in the seat" time and fourteen hours of actual flight time—a heretofore unheard-of stretch. "After spending so much time with that supply column we actually developed a sort of emotional attachment," said Pfeiffer. "We had adopted it and simply couldn't stand the idea of leaving them unprotected. You just don't leave your comrades."

One Marine was lost during the movement of the convoy. Although it was amazing that more weren't killed, that fact is little solace for the friends and family of Sergeant Fernando Padilla-Ramirez of MWSS-371 whose truck was overturned near the tail end of the caravan. For reasons that still are not clear, although other Marines on the truck escaped to safety, Padilla-Ramirez was left behind. He was taken by the Iraqis. His body was recovered in early April.

* * *

The period encompassing the last few days of March to the first day or so of April came to be known as the Operational Pause. Having blitzed across the border and plunged much deeper into Iraq than planners had anticipated, the forces were tired and logistics efforts were hard-pressed on both the Army and Marine Corps sides. This isn't to say that the forces were not fit for combat—they were. And for their part, the Marines insisted that they were ready to press on; there was no need to halt, no requirement to regroup and refit. Their fuel tanks were topped off, they had plenty of ammunition, the equipment was holding up, and most important the troops were itching to get on with it. Mattis was decidedly unhappy about stopping; he was anxious to take advantage of weaknesses in the Iraqi defenses and was fearful that the enemy generals might fix them. Nevertheless, McKiernan ordered his land component commanders to stop in order to consolidate their gains and secure their lines of communication. Part of the consolidation was particularly distasteful to elements of RCT-5. They had pushed up Highway 1 all the way to Hantush and had captured the airstrip there. When the order came they were extremely reluctant to abandon their hard-won prize.

The idea of a pause wasn't necessarily bad. Certainly the troops would benefit from a few days of rest, and there was no doubt that pockets of resistance—such as those in bypassed towns like Ash Shatrah and Ar Rifa—had to be cleared. But it was the way that it was reported in the press that galled the Marines the most. After having gained so much territory in such a short time, they were disgusted to hear terms such as *bogged down* and *quagmire*. It was almost as if some segments of the media took a perverse pleasure in seeing the fall of Baghdad delayed for a few more days.

It didn't help, either, that the administration and the Pentagon played semantics. Denials that there was a "pause" were constant when in fact—for whatever reason—the advance had been reined in. Still, it wasn't as if the fighting stopped completely. Bypassed enemy forces *were* cleared. And although RCT-5 and -7 generally stayed put along Highway 1, RCT-1 continued to advance toward Al Kut on Highway 7.

All of that aside, what didn't slow down was the air campaign. If nothing else, the pause was a great opportunity to methodically shape the battlefield rather than trying to keep up with the lightning-quick pace the ground forces had set in their race to Baghdad. I was a guest on the Fox News Network on March 30 and was questioned by show host Laurie Dhue as to what I believed was taking place. I took the opportunity to describe the beating that I thought the enemy forces were taking from the air. More specifically, I stated that Coalition aircraft were "turning the Iraqis into hair, teeth, and eyeballs." The network did not invite me back.

In fact, that description is exactly what took place. Coalition aircrews kept up around-the-clock attacks all through the pause and until the fall of Baghdad. Saddam's divisions were smote from above—almost literally out of existence. There were no massive armor-on-armor battles or earthshaking artillery exchanges because none of the Iraqi armies survived. Most of their equipment was blown up, and their troops ran away or were killed.

22

Fuel Bladder Rodeo

The aircrews call the giant CH-53E helicopter "the Shitter." This odd but affectionate appellation is derived from the big, boxy shape of the aircraft; it is reminiscent of an old-fashioned outhouse. Also, the official name—*Sea Stallion*—is a bit too pretentious for the hard-core pilots who finesse it through just about every assignment the Marine Corps can give a helicopter.

The three-engine CH-53E is the largest rotary-wing aircraft in service with U.S. forces. Capable of lifting thirty-two tons, the huge helicopter can hoist and transport an M198 howitzer, an LAV-25 armored vehicle, or even another CH-53E in the event that one of the big machines becomes disabled in the field. And despite its size, with a top speed of 150 knots it is one of the fastest military helicopters operating today.

The two huge CH-53Es rumbled through the dusty dark only a hundred feet or so above the desert. Suspended below each were three five-hundred-gallon fuel bladders. Their destination was the Fenway

FARP, near Qalat Sakar, not far from where RCT-1 was moving north along Highway 7. Fighting at nearby Al Kut had been ferocious during the previous couple of days, and FARPs like Fenway were keeping the Cobra gunships fueled, armed, and in the thick of things. In turn, the FARPs had to be kept fully stocked; aside from resupply by truck transport, they also relied on supplies brought in by helicopter.

On this evening, March 30, Captain Andrew "Gus" Byrd was leading his section's two CH-53Es at a speed of 120 knots. At faster airspeeds the fuel bladders slung underneath the aircraft became unstable. "Visibility," he recalled, "was only about a mile or so—very crummy. There was a lot of dust and haze and very little moonlight. Even though we were wearing goggles, the featureless, flat desert blended right into the sky and it was very difficult to keep from getting vertigo."

Crossing the Kuwaiti border into Iraq, Byrd cleared the flight to execute its weapons checks. A moment later the blasting report of his ship's two .50-caliber machine guns boomed above the combined growl of the three engines and the enormous seven-bladed rotor. To his right, and slightly aft, the tracers from his wingman's guns blossomed in his night-vision goggles as they streaked downward and slammed into the desert. He and his copilot, Captain "Cletus" Rich, ejected chaff and flare decoys, checking that their ALE-39 dispenser was ready to spoof enemy radars and missiles by ejecting chaff bundles or flares.

Although their route of flight took them over territory that was technically under Coalition control, the reality was that the Coalition forces only controlled the highway routes up toward Baghdad, a few towns, and little or none of the countryside. There were small units of bypassed enemy fighters scattered all across the desert.

"Flying low like we were enabled us to stay undetected by most of the radar-guided anti-aircraft guns and missile systems that were still out there," recounted Byrd. "On the other hand, it also made us vulnerable to the smaller, more mobile weapons if we happened to fly to close to them. Other aircraft had been ambushed this way. It also required us to keep up a really good lookout to ensure that we didn't get scraped out of the sky by power lines or radio towers." All of these threats, in combination with the poor weather, were demanding the most of the two crews.

Byrd's goggles magnified what little natural light there was and showed the black murk in front of him as a greenish glow. As the helicopters powered their way through dust of varying density, the light level fluctuated, and the scene glimmered and scintillated—exacerbating the vertigo he was fighting. It took every bit of attention he had to watch for obstacles and enemy fire while at the same time checking his charts and cross-checking his instruments. At the speed and altitude he and Rich were flying it would take only an instant of inattention to smash the big machine into the dirt. The fuel they carried on board and in the bladders slung beneath them would ensure a merry funeral pyre.

The two transports were about sixty miles inside Iraq when it happened: "All of a sudden the nose pitched way up, while at the same time the aircraft yawed and rolled about thirty degrees to the left." The helicopter was out of control, and Captain Andrew Byrd wasn't sure that he wasn't going to die. "At that instant the only goal I had in my entire life was regaining control of that aircraft. I climbed away from the ground to gain some altitude as a safety cushion while I tried to steady it. [Captain Rich] called out my altitude and backed me up on the instruments." Byrd, Rich, and the rest of the crew were little more than passengers on what had just become a deadly carnival ride, courtesy of the United States Marine Corps.

A quick glance at the aircraft's caution/advisory panel told the two pilots that the Automatic Flight Control System, the set of computers that made normal control inputs possible, had gone out. Along with it the hydraulic servos that provided boost to the flight controls—the equivalent of power steering—had also failed. It was akin to trying to control a large ship with a canoe paddle. A large flying ship with more than five tons of fuel swinging crazily under the belly.

"After about thirty seconds or so, I finally got it settled down, more or less," Byrd recalled. "The guys in the back, Staff Sergeant Brady, Corporal Sablar, and HM2 Davenport, were really hanging in there.

They had no control over whether they were going to live or die, but they remained professional the entire time." During the wild gyrations that followed the system failures, the fuel bladders had started to swing well beyond limits. Nevertheless Brady kept Byrd apprised of their disposition and called up directions until the oscillations began to dampen. Meanwhile Sablan and Davenport checked what mechanical components they could in order to troubleshoot the emergency.

Byrd remembered, "By the time it occurred to me that maybe I ought to jettison the fuel bladders, we were out of immediate danger. Besides, if I dumped the fuel it would never make it up to the FARP. If the FARP didn't have fuel, our guys on the ground might not get the support they needed."

Good intentions aside, Byrd knew that he'd never make it up to Qalat Sakar with the aircraft malfunctioning as it was. In fact, he still wasn't certain that he wasn't going to crash. "Without the servos it took about forty pounds of force to move the controls an inch or two. But without the Automatic Flight Control System the aircraft was so sensitive that just the smallest input caused huge control deflections. I'd try to push the nose down a degree or two, and we'd end up pointed into the ground. When I tried to counter that, I'd accidentally overcorrect and we'd start climbing toward the clouds." Still, Byrd and Rich continued to wrestle the big ship until they had it pointed back around toward their base at Ali Al Salem. "After I grew used to it," Byrd recounted, "I started to think that maybe we wouldn't ball it up after all."

Byrd's wingman, Captain Chris "Rudy" Dalton, was also one of his closest friends. "Rudy made a good call, and offered to take the lead and fly in front of us. His aircraft out in front would give me a good visual reference point in the haze—I'd have one less thing to worry about." Byrd agreed, and Dalton powered his aircraft into the lead.

The immediate danger was over and a decision had to be made as to where to recover the sick bird. "The airfield at Jalibah was closer than Ali Al Salem, but if we landed there it would take a while to get mechanics and tools and parts flown in to fix it. And it would be

longer still before we'd be able to deliver the fuel to Fenway." Ultimately Byrd decided to fly the bucking rhinoceros his aircraft had become all the way back to Ali Al Salem.

"By now," he said, "Cletus had gotten part of the Automatic Flight
Control System back online. All we had to worry about was the
tremendous control forces. These were wearing us out. My arms were
burning and at one point I called up Rudy and told him that I wasn't
sure we were going to make it. He called back that we looked steady
as a rock."

Finally the two CH-53Es rumbled over the boundary fence at Ali
Al Salem and detached the fuel bladders into the loading zone. Once
safely on the ground Byrd and his crew grabbed their gear and clambered out of the traitorous ship. "I was fired up," Byrd remembered.
"That aircraft had just tried to kill me and I wasn't going to have any
part of it. I immediately asked for another bird and within an hour we
were on our way again."

Now on board a different helicopter, Byrd and Rich lifted off and
headed to the pickup point on the north side of the airbase. There
they hovered in place while Brady lowered the tethered hook and the
crew on the ground attached the sling that held the fuel bladders.
After a few minutes they were on their way back into Iraq.

Except for a few "tickles" indicating enemy anti-aircraft activity on
their radar warning receivers, the transit across the desert was uneventful. Although the visibility was still poor, the terrain changed as
the formation continued north. Rather than flat and barren, the landscape became dotted with more trees and brush; the extra terrain relief was less difficult to pick up with the night-vision goggles, and
navigation became easier.

Nevertheless, in this case easier than very difficult was still difficult.
As the formation rumbled up to the small airstrip that made up the
Fenway FARP, Byrd had a tough time identifying where he was supposed to drop his load of fuel bladders; it didn't help that there was no
response to his repeated radio calls. Communications in this austere
environment were problematic and would remain so throughout the
conflict. Finally Byrd spotted a collection of vehicles and equipment
and slowed the two-ship formation.

"As we got closer, I detached Rudy and he set up an orbit east of the FARP while I transitioned to a hover," Byrd said. The huge CH-53E whipped up a whirling shroud of dirt as the two crewmen settled it toward the ground. Watching out the right-side window, Byrd picked up a reference point on the runway and tried to hold the helicopter steady in the swirling dust as he settled the load of bladders on the ground. When Brady called up that the bladders were safely at rest, Byrd called for the load to be released.

Nothing happened.

The release mechanism failed, and Byrd and Rich were stuck in the hover. The release mechanism was tried again. Again, nothing happened. Byrd—or any pilot, for that matter—could only hold the aircraft steady for so long. Sand and dirt thrashed against it, obscuring his view and making it impossible to hold a solid hover. Vertigo started to take hold. Recognizing his limitations and afraid of rolling the helicopter into the ground, Byrd applied collective and lifted the aircraft and its load up and away.

The night just seemed to get longer and longer. Byrd and Rich briefed over the intercom with Brady and set up for another run. Again, the helicopter gently settled the badly needed fuel bladders on the ground. Again, the big, seven-bladed rotor's downwash created a miniature dust storm. And again, the external load failed to release.

"I couldn't believe it," Byrd recounted. "I really wanted rid of that load. I thought about sidestepping the bladders once they were on the ground, and then landing alongside, but the combined sling and tether were only about twenty feet long and there just wasn't enough room." Feeling himself falling victim to vertigo once more, Byrd yanked the load away a second time.

On the next attempt the crew briefed for an emergency release. An explosive charge would shear the bolt that attached the cable to the bulkhead inside the aircraft, just under the transmission in the "roof" of the big ship. Byrd made a third approach and set the bladders on the ground while holding a hover in the maelstrom of dust that once more threatened his vision and sense of equilibrium. When he was certain that the load had made contact with the dirt, he gave the command and heard a sharp pop as the charge fired.

His helicopter was free of the bladders. Byrd lowered the nose of the aircraft, flew forward a hundred feet or so, and set down. It took only a moment or two for Brady to run out of the aircraft, collect the bird's suspension rigging, and climb back aboard.

Byrd hauled his helicopter airborne and made room for Dalton to drop off his fuel bladders. Like Byrd, Dalton also fought with the storm of dust. Unlike Byrd, he was able to shed his load on the first try. Within a minute, the two aircraft formed and started for home.

Regardless of the fact that the two crews had completed their mission, everyone on board was aware that this fact mattered not at all to enemy gunners and bad luck—they could get just as dead on the way home. For that reason Byrd kept up a sharp watch. "We headed south, almost on a heading direct for Ali Al Salem," he remembered. "And we stayed fast and low—about seventy-five feet."

As much as he tried to steer clear of the built-up areas along their route, there was no way that Byrd was going to be able to stay away from every little village and farming compound. And where there were buildings, there were people. And often the people had guns they wanted to shoot at Americans. The flight was about twenty miles northeast of An Nasiriyah when the bright staccato flash of heavy machine-gun fire surprised them from ahead and slightly to their right. Byrd recalled, "I was able to make out two or three guys huddled around a technical [armed civilian pickup truck] with a big machine-gun mount. I called out, 'Two o'clock low, cleared to fire!' "

Only a second or two passed before the starboard gunners in both ships opened up with their .50-caliber machine guns. Wicked-fast ropes of tracers and armor-piercing rounds sliced down into the truck and the foolish men who crouched near it for cover. After several seconds of the high-velocity rounds there likely weren't any enemy combatants left alive to see or hear the two helicopters arcing away from the site of the abortive ambush.

Byrd's bad luck held. Only a moment later, again from in front and to the right of their flight path, the two big ships were taken under fire. "I could see a cluster of guys around a mud hut and flashes from larger weapons, and some smaller ones as well," he recounted. Once again he cleared the flight to return fire. This time only Dalton's gunner opened up. As the tracers ripped into a small band of enemy fighters Byrd could make out another set of men rushing out of the mud hut. "Rudy's gunner adjusted his fire and walked those guys right back up to the house and through the door—really shot them up. Then he sprayed the hut and the entire thing burst into flames."

Byrd wondered at the ignorance of the enemy troops. "I can't believe that they could have seen us that well in the dark. As far as we knew they didn't have any sort of night-vision goggles. I'm almost certain that they just reacted to the noise and fired in our general direction—they truly had no idea what they were up against."

Except for some heavier Anti-Aircraft Artillery flashes in the distance, the rest of the trip home was uneventful. Byrd was glad to put the big ship safely on the ground. It had been nearly nine hours since he had first gotten airborne. After wrestling with an emergency in nighttime weather that alone could have killed him, and getting shot at twice—not to mention the fuel bladder rodeo at Fenway—getting back on the ground seemed like a good idea.

"I remember getting down out of the aircraft and stretching. It was just dawn and the sun was a beautiful yellowish pink. HM2 Davenport walked up from the back of the airplane with a great big smile on his face. He said, 'I guess we earned our pay on that one, didn't we, sir!' "

Byrd returned his crewman's smile: "That we did, Davenport, that we did."

By this time in the fighting, at least on the aviation side, the routines were getting more settled, the coordination was going more smoothly, and familiarity with the plan and the players was becoming more ingrained. Captain Anthony "Curly" Bolden was a WSO with VMFA(AW)-225, and his daily schedule had him conducting FAC(A) missions each day beginning right at first light. These sorties required him to coordinate with the FACs or Air Officers embedded with the various ground units. Many of them were dear friends, and he couldn't help but worry about them and pray that they were safe even though he knew that they were smack in the middle of harm's way:

The worst of it is the uncertainty as we make our way north each morning. Did everyone make it through the night? Who is going to answer the radio when I call? I can only imagine that I feel just a tiny bit of what our wives and families go through every time the phone rings or the doorbell chimes. Is someone going to tell them that their husband or father or son isn't going to be coming home? My God, what a torture. Fingers Feringa, Hamster Hobson, Peg-Boy O'Connell—these are just a few names of very dear friends that right now are on the ground slugging it out with the enemy. These are the Marines that we talk to every day. These are the Marines who are our link to the thousands of other Marines that are down there. Each and every morning that we fly the dawn patrol, our greatest fear is that we will make that first call and someone that we don't know will answer.

23

Napalm

"Nape." *Napalm*. The word was a marriage of two other words: naphthalene and palmitate, the two major components of the earliest mixtures. It was the fiery, skin-cooking weapon that robbed men of oxygen as it roasted them alive. Napalm was first used during World War II, but it wasn't until the Vietnam War that the terror that was napalm was seared into the wider American consciousness. The evening news showed canisters of the stuff tumbling from screeching fighters as they raced low over the enemy. The small, silver containers burst as they skipped across the ground, and the combustible mixture of jellied fuel that erupted from them—still traveling at hundreds of miles per hour—splashed across an area the size of a football field in a great, horrible fireball.

Krispy Kritters was the macho-morbid term attached to the flaming, flailing, soon-to-be-dead troops—or civilians if mistakes were made—able to stumble out of the roiling firestorm. A United Nations convention banned napalm in 1980. The United States was not among the signatories, but the last U.S. stockpiles of the corrosive inflammable were destroyed in California during 2001.

At Kuwait's Ahmed Al Jaber Air Base, the F/A-18D crews that were crowded into the alert tent that evening were chattering more than normal when Captain Dale Douglass* pushed back the flap and stepped inside. The Air Tasking Order for the night of March 31 directed a preplanned, preemptive strike prior to RCT-5's advance across the Tigris River in the vicinity of An Numaniyah. Douglass remembered: "This was an on-call mission, which meant that a flight of crews briefed it and stood by to execute until they got the call to launch or until they ran out of crew day. If it didn't go, it was passed on to another flight. We were the third batch of crews to pick up this mission, and most of us thought that it would be canceled before it was flown."

The excitement was centered on the assigned ordnance. In addition to the normal load-out of two external fuel tanks and multiple air-to-air missiles, each of the four F/A-18Ds was loaded with three Mk-77 Firebombs. The five-hundred-pound Mk-77 canisters are derivatives of the napalm weapons used during Vietnam. The primary difference is the mixture inside; rather than gasoline, the flammable component is jet fuel, which has a higher flashpoint and is moderately more stable. Regardless, in practice it crashes, it splashes, it flashes. It is a frightful weapon.

"Our target was a checkpoint or troop concentration at a bridge that crossed a canal to the northeast of RCT-5's position," Douglass remembered. "The attack had a number of objectives. First, it was intended to clear the area of Iraqi combatants prior to our Marines getting there—and without damaging the bridge; second, it was believed that napalm would frighten and demoralize any enemy troops who remained; and finally, all that heat and fire and noise—right in front of our own troops—would remind our guys that the wing was committed to doing what they needed, when and where they needed it."

The order to launch came just as Douglass and the rest of his flight came on duty. "We briefed the bare basics in about twenty minutes. It

*Not his real name. Because of the very strong emotions that surround the use of napalm and napalm-like weapons, the pilot asked that his name, the names of the other participants, and the squadron number not be identified.

was evident from the start that the calendar and the weather were going to work against us. The moon was down during that part of the month. Worse, the visibility was horrible and there were cloud layers from five thousand to twenty-three thousand feet." This meant that Douglass and his comrades would conduct their attack using night-vision goggles at low altitude in very low-light conditions. Such dangerous flight would have been prohibited during peacetime exercises, but it was a requirement for this mission.

"Our brief included the targeting assignment for each aircraft, the attack heading, altitude, and formation. We also went over the contact frequency for RCT-5's FAC. The plan was to contact him just prior to the attack for any last-minute coordination." Preparations complete, Douglass, his Weapons Systems Officer, and the other three crews made their way out to the flight line to preflight their jets in the dark.

Dark is different. The simplest tasks take longer, and the smallest misstep can cause grave errors. With this in mind, Douglass and the others combed their aircraft and the loaded weapons, intent on making certain there was nothing that could sour the mission. With their checks complete, the four crews taxied their jets to the end of the runway. "We took off at ten-second intervals," Douglass recalled. "After getting airborne, we snapped our goggles down over our faces, but getting joined up in that weather was still a circus. Aside from the clouds, there was a lot of haze and sand in the air. Visibility wasn't more than a couple of miles." Through their goggles the aircrews looked for the greenish blob of light that was the aircraft in front of them. Finally the flight joined and punched its way through the clouds. "As we climbed out we fumbled through a phone book's worth of radio frequencies and finally got clearance to press toward the target area," Douglass said. "The different agencies we checked through made sure that we didn't run into other Coalition aircraft. They also made sure that we didn't get engaged by friendly air defenses."

The westbound fighters finally powered above the weather and spread out into a tactical formation. The lead pilot and Douglass positioned themselves a mile abreast, while their respective wingmen tucked themselves close. "The target was only about 250 miles from our base at Al Jaber, so it wasn't long before we were closing the formation back up so that we could drop through the clouds together. It was about this time that we got word about a suspected SA-3 antiaircraft missile site southwest of the target. We altered our course accordingly," Douglass recollected.

"After starting down we switched frequencies to check in with the RCT-5 FAC. As soon as we made contact, I recognized him as an old squadron buddy. I could even tell that he had a cold! Anyway, he filled in the last couple of details for us and we chatted for a moment or so as the flight made its way down through the mess that the weather had become."

Thick clouds made it extremely difficult for the formation to stay together. To make matters worse, the enemy SA-3 radar was tickling their warning systems as they descended. The idea that they might be engaged by one, or perhaps more, of the big Soviet-made missiles while they were slogging down through the murk put them all on edge.

Douglass lost sight of the formation leader for a moment then regained it when the four jets popped into a clear area between cloud layers. "Then my wingman lost sight as we were passing through the last layer," Douglass recalled. As close as they were to the target, there was no time to maneuver in an attempt to get the fourth aircraft rejoined. "The rest of us turned to the final attack heading, spread back out to a tactical formation, and pushed our airspeed up as we leveled off at five hundred feet. All the while my wingman was trying his best to get back into the formation."

By now Douglass, his WSO, and the other three crews were racing just above the desert floor at more than five hundred knots. "We were hauling ass at about twenty miles out from the target. It was really bumpy now, too. We were being jolted up and down by the same turbulence that was kicking up all the dust and creating all the weather." At the speed it was making, the formation was only about two minutes from releasing its firebombs; the crews started their final checklists.

The mission was a dangerous combination of contrasts. Douglass and the other crews were snugly strapped into the close confines of incredibly complex machines that were rocketing just barely over the dirt and dark and cold of the oldest nation-state on earth, a land that had been the domain of the camel for thousands of years. Snug or not, as low and fast as they were hurtling toward the target, the crews were only an instant of inattention away from death. Douglass went over the weapons checklist with his WSO, step by step. At the same time he executed all those instinctual tasks that kept his jet from splattering across the desert in a thousand flaming pieces: A quick scan outside through the grainy green-black of the goggles to check his position in the formation; a split-second glance at his Heads Up Display to make a minute altitude correction; a peek under his goggles at the barely illuminated checklist strapped to his knee; back outside at the formation; minute throttle and stick corrections that came without thinking; another look back to the HUD—even through the goggles he couldn't make out anything in front of him; another check outside at the rest of the formation; a hurried glimpse at his digital displays to check his weapons; a split-second look at the navigational display that glowed up at him from between his legs. All of this and more was automatic to Douglass and the other three crews; it came almost intuitively after years of training.

By now the lost wingman had regained contact and was hurrying to catch up. In front, Douglass and the rest of the formation pressed on. "It got pretty hectic as we got to about ten miles from the target," he recalled. "We made one last check with our radar for enemy aircraft and then switched into the air-to-ground mode. It reminded me a little bit of the first *Star Wars* movie, when the good guys were flying across the Death Star." Douglass's WSO slaved the radar to the target coordinates, and both of them tried to make out the objective, albeit without much success.

"We were getting pretty busy; we were less than a minute from the target. By now it was obvious that our wingman wasn't going to catch up, so he was ordered to stay clear and out of the way. We couldn't risk losing the crew if they flew through our bombs while trying to drop their own. From the tone of their reply it was obvious that they were disappointed."

Coming up on the target, it was apparent that the Hornets had gone undetected. Other than the glow coming from isolated homes and outposts, there were no lights—no anti-aircraft fire, no SAMs. Nothing. In the dark the outlying Iraqi posts received no warning of the Hornets' presence beyond a chest-rattling roar as the aircraft swept overhead and then disappeared into the night.

"By now," Douglass recalled, "we had given up on the radar and switched to our Forward Looking Infra Red pod, our FLIR. We were right on the target coordinates. At four miles out—about twenty-five seconds—I started counting down the range as my WSO kept scanning with the FLIR. Finally we could make out what looked like a small building and some vehicles." Douglass refined his steering and—with his right thumb poised on the bomb release button—watched as the release cue marched down the steering line glowing on his HUD. As the aircraft reached that point in space where all the appropriate physics reached a perfect convergence he mashed down on the button and felt the aircraft jump as the three five-hundred-pound canisters fell away.

"Just then, through the FLIR, we could make out a group of men running in the target area. I could only imagine their terror as they looked for somewhere to hide." By now the bombs were in midflight, whistling toward the earth, only a second or two from exploding into scorching, all-consuming fireballs.

Douglass watched with a sort of detached, fearful fascination as the enemy troops raced across the FLIR's field of view. Rather than running away, fate directed the Iraqis directly into the center of the designated impact area. "I saw a bright flash as our bombs exploded," Douglass remembered. "It was foolish of me to watch for the explosions, because my goggles washed out completely. I nudged the stick back slightly to make sure that I was climbing away from the dirt. At the same time, I looked for the rest of the formation and got blinded again when their bombs exploded."

Douglass hadn't been the only one who had made that mistake.

Blinking to regain their vision, the crews climbed and banked their jets away from the target. In his disappointment the last wingman — who had been unable to drop his bombs — broke radio discipline: "Fuck, fuck, fuck . . ." carried over the airwaves.

Douglass reflected on the mission. "Once we got back on top of the clouds I started to calm down. This was the first mission where I knew for certain that I had killed people — because I saw them. I felt good knowing that my friends on the ground might be able to push through that area with little or no resistance and I also wondered what the Marines would find in the target area. To this day, I still don't know."

In press briefings Pentagon spokesmen consistently denied that napalm was used against the Iraqis, while knowing full well that journalists were asking about the instances when Marines had employed Mk-77 Firebombs. Although technically they were correct, the Pentagon denials were hairsplitting absurdities. This was particularly true when the Marines had no compunction against telling the truth. Colonel Randy "Tex" Alles, the commanding officer of MAG-11, declared in direct terms that the approaches to the bridges across the Saddam Canal at An Numaniyah were "napalmed." He went further: "They were Iraqi soldiers there. It's no great way to die."

Napalm. Firebomb. To the Iraqis who burned to death that night, the semantics were irrelevant.

24

Precision Strike

It was the very first few minutes of the last day of March, and the Marines of VMA-311 had been flying their Harriers in support of their infantry brothers for more than a week. With the rest of 3rd MAW they had concentrated on prepping the battlefield in front of the RCTs as well as helping to clean up the pockets of enemy fighters who had been bypassed. They would continue to play a valuable role in this effort. Lieutenant Colonel Mike Hile, the Commanding Officer, was pleased that his squadron had settled into an effective battle rhythm. Operations afloat were always a challenge, but the young men and women that made up his maintenance department aboard the USS *Bonhomme Richard* were keeping the jets in good condition. Jets that were in good condition were jets that could fly more sorties. More sorties flown meant more targets engaged. More targets engaged meant more enemy killed. More dead Iraqis meant more live Marines.

His pilots were becoming more effective as well. During the first few days of the fight a number of factors including the weather, the ROE, the command and control system, and their own limitations had kept the fliers from being as effective as Hile would have liked. Nevertheless, that period was past and more and more the Harrier crews were demonstrating to the Iraqis and to the rest of the Coalition what an effective attack platform the aircraft was.

Hile and eleven other pilots, five from VMA-311 and six from VMA-211, had finished a quick late-night breakfast and were listening to the normal series of pre-mission briefings. First was the weather forecaster; he reviewed the latest satellite pictures over Iraq as well as the forecast conditions for the northern Persian Gulf during the scheduled launch and recovery periods. The stifling sandstorm that had clobbered the area a few days earlier had cleared, and now meteorological conditions were much more favorable. The operations brief followed and included an update of the friendly situation on the ground and that day's active control measures. Although the MEF's advance had been reined in for several days, the Marines were preparing to march on Baghdad while at the same time hunting down and crushing pockets of resistance to their rear and flanks.

Next up was the intelligence brief. It covered the disposition of the Iraqi forces as well as potential threats. These were mostly SAMs and anti-aircraft guns—the Iraqi Air Force hadn't been heard from since the start of the war. Last were the instructions from the Landing Signals Officer. He was responsible for choreographing the twelve-aircraft ballet that would launch and recover as part of the *Bonhomme Richard*'s first wave of the day.

Before the LSO could finish, the senior watch officer interrupted the brief and relayed the fact that new orders had just come in from the MEF. The two squadrons aboard the ship were being retasked to hit critical targets in the town of Ash Shatrah, about twenty-five miles north of An Nasiriyah. Details about the objective were still coming in across SIPRchat. Except for the fact that it was secure and protected, this computerized tool—the Secret Internet Protocol Router— was not much different from the typical Internet chat rooms that a normal eighth-grader might visit. But rather than sharing gossip about boyfriends and girlfriends, the SIPRchat was used by the Coalition's planners and operators to help execute the war.

It wasn't long before the MEF's intent—and the specifics of the target—became clear. In preparation for an assault to clear out Ash Shatrah, the MEF wanted the Baath party headquarters in the center of the town destroyed by a predawn strike. Although American units had advanced well beyond Ash Shatrah by this time, convoys and smaller units were still being ambushed. Late on the night of March 28 a Marine had been dragged from a convoy of support vehicles and then later killed and dragged through the streets. It was becoming apparent that the Baath party was playing as big a role in fighting the Coalition as was the Iraqi military. With this strike and other preparatory fires—and a subsequent raid into the town by elements of RCT-1—the MEF hoped to cut off the head of the Baath party snake.

AV-8B Harriers were selected for the mission because their Litening targeting pods provided the fidelity required to surgically attack specific points without destroying sensitive structures nearby. Hile took the role of mission commander and planning began immediately. "The MEF wanted eight targets hit, and we intended to do that with eight aircraft. I didn't waste any time and assigned Major Will Price—MAG-13's WTI [Weapons and Tactics Instructor]—to begin the target area analysis. This meant that with my guidance and concurrence he would construct the actual plan of attack—who, what, when, where, and how."

Without in-flight refueling the mission would take the AV-8Bs near the limits of their range. In order to stack the deck in their favor, Hile needed to ensure that he took advantage of every bit of help that the *Bonhomme Richard's* commander could provide. "I sent Captain Matt Heafner, one of the more experienced LSOs, to coordinate the ship's location and heading for the scheduled takeoff time." Not only would the ship's location at the commencement of the launch be crucial, but the ship would also have to maintain the same heading until all the aircraft were airborne. If the *Bonhomme Richard* had to reposition midway through the effort, the attack would fail. In the constricted and shallow waters of the northern Persian Gulf this would not be an easy task. Hile also charged Heafner with devising a compressed launch scheme so that the aircraft would burn as little fuel as possible at the start of the mission. Like every portion of the plan, these seemingly mundane details were crucial to success. If even the simplest thing went awry, the operation could unravel before it got under way.

Hile tasked Captain Thomas Hodge, MAG-13's intelligence officer, to get the latest available imagery for the targets and to plot the exact DMPIs, or Desired Mean Points of Impact. These were precise points on specific targets—for instance, the northeast corner of a targeted building. For this sort of operation, a photo was absolutely essential. The pilots were being tasked to hit certain portions of individual buildings, and expecting them to execute their mission in the middle of the night against targets they had never seen was unrealistic.

On the flight deck the maintainers from both squadrons looked over their aircraft with even greater care than usual. The ordnance load for each aircraft was hung and inspected. The lead aircraft of each section would carry only a Litening pod and a thousand-pound GBU-16, while the wingmen would carry two GBU-12, five-hundred-pound LGBs. The intent was for only the wingmen to drop, with the bombs on the lead aircraft available as backup. The tanks that held the distilled water so crucial to getting optimum performance out of the Harrier's engine during takeoff and landing were double-checked full. Also, because they would be operating so far from the ship, arrangements were made to have the aircraft topped off with fuel after they had started but just before taking off.

Within a short time the plan began to take shape. Hile wasn't particularly worried about what he and his Marines could control; it was what they couldn't control that bothered him. What was of particular concern was that two of the DMPIs were close enough to sensitive structures or areas that there were CDE, or Collateral Damage Estimate, concerns. This meant that the targets would have to be approved at the theater commander's level; CENTCOM would be making the ultimate decision as to whether or not Hile's mission would go. He had seen much simpler challenges pull a plan to pieces.

Once complete, the plan was briefed to the crews. A short time later they pulled on their flight gear and headed topside. With the preflight inspections accomplished they climbed into their jets and started their engines. In the dark, the flight deck was the scene of a seemingly chaotic commotion of confusing lights and arm waving and running about. Appearances aside, everyone had a role and knew it well. Plane captains in their distinctive brown shirts checked the exterior integrity of each aircraft; troubleshooters in green jerseys stood by to fix any last-minute discrepancies; the ship's refuelers, nicknamed "grapes" because of their distinctive purple shirts, topped off every aircraft before it taxied toward the rear of the ship; and the flight deck handlers, or "yellow shirts," directed each aircraft into position as the time for launch approached. Ten minutes prior to takeoff Hile called over the radio: "Gator Tower, Waxen flight up and ready. Eleven point zero on the fuel with a full bag of water." The *Bonhomme Richard*'s control tower rogered his transmission, and the yellow shirts tending his jet broke down the tie-down chains that tethered his aircraft to the deck. Hile followed their signals and taxied into launch position at the stern of the ship. His wingman, Captain Jason "Bearclaw" Duncan, and the rest of the flight followed.

In the meantime one of the Harriers developed a problem that couldn't be fixed in time to meet its takeoff window. Fortunately Hile's plan had considered this possibility: the spare pilot and aircraft—already briefed and started—took the broken jet's place.

At the back of the ship Hile went through his last-minute checks. Everything was in order except for what most concerned him: Clearance to hit the CDE targets had not yet arrived, and it would be one more thing for him to worry about once he got airborne. Only a moment or so before launch Hile felt the ship heel over to port as the *Bonhomme Richard*'s CO, Captain Jon Berg-Johnsen, brought her into the prevailing winds. A quick look down at his aircraft's moving map display reassured Hile that the ship's crew were executing their portion of the plan perfectly.

Once safely airborne and with Duncan in position off his left wing, Hile started for Ash Shatrah. As he made his way northwest to landfall, across Kuwait and into Iraq, he went through the usual communications drill. After switching from the *Bonhomme Richard*'s frequency he contacted Green Crown aboard one of the ships that controlled a given sector of the airspace over the gulf. With its radar Green Crown verified that Hile's Identification Friend or Foe equipment was "sweet," or in working order. From Green Crown, he was directed to contact Red Crown—another ship—and then Karma, the AWACS aircraft that controlled the airspace over southern Iraq. All of the switches went smoothly and finally Hile—as the flight lead of Waxen 25—was directed to contact Tropical, the MEF's Tactical Air Operations Center.

Hile was growing impatient. There was no word yet that his strike had been approved, and he didn't want the hard work and planning of his Marines to have been for nothing. He checked in with Tropical: "Tropical, Waxen 25 airborne as fragged." The answer came back: "Waxen, Tropical, we have you sweet and sweet. You are cleared to switch to terminal control. CENTCOM approval for your targets has been received. Good hunting."

Finally, the last piece of the planning process had fallen into place. As he led Duncan deeper into Iraq, Hile looked down at the landscape below him. Because his night-vision goggles enabled him to see even the barest bit of illumination, he could pick up flashes of light that may or may not have been fighting as well as the steadier illumination that marked the towns and villages still enjoying electrical power. At last, north of An Nasiriyah, he set up a left-hand orbit fifteen miles to the north of Ash Shatrah and waited.

Just as briefed, the following three sections of Harriers checked in at ten-minute intervals. The plan called for the four pairs of aircraft to establish themselves in four separate holding patterns at cardinal headings—north, south, east, and west—from the target at a distance of fifteen miles. There would be one section of two jets in each orbit. To further deconflict, each section was assigned a different altitude; this would reduce the chances of a midair collision should one pair of aircraft stray out of their assigned airspace.

At 0458, exactly two minutes prior to their planned TOT or Time on Target, the eight AV-8Bs accelerated out of their holding patterns toward the Baath party headquarters at more than 450 knots. Each section leader slaved his Litening pod to his assigned DMPI and compared what he saw on his display against the photo that he had reviewed during the earlier brief. Hile recalled: "Acquiring a specific target in an urban environment is particularly difficult. When the FLIR display is a mixture of greens and blacks, one building looks very much like another. It's one thing to review a satellite photo in the ready room and quite another to correlate it against something you're looking at on a cockpit display in the middle of the night while you're racing toward a target with only seconds to make the correct decision."

The decisions made by the *Bonhomme Richard*'s pilots that night were right on the money. Hile, like the other section leaders, concentrated on locating his assigned DMPI. Duncan, like the other wingmen, ensured that his laser-guided weapons were ready to drop. At the correct moment the wingmen released their GBU-12s while the flight leaders guided them into their targets. Within thirty seconds each bomb had found its mark; three of the four shattered a building or portion of a building. The fourth failed to detonate.

Wasting no time, the eight jets all swung around in a hard right-hand turn back toward their orbit points. Turning away from the target in the same direction was another safeguard against a midair collision. The time it took to travel back to the push points was minimal, but it allowed the smoke to clear enough so that the last four DMPIs could be found and struck. Only four minutes after the first bombs had hit the target the eight jets streaked back toward the center of Ash Shatrah. Just as before, the four sections delivered four more bombs, and just as before all four scored direct hits. Coincidentally, just as before, one bomb failed to detonate.

The failure of bombs to detonate was one that had plagued and would continue to plague both the Harrier and Hornet communities through the entirety of the conflict. At any rate there was nothing Hile could do about it. He called for a check-in over the radio and marked off all eight pilots as they responded. Satisfied with how the mission unfolded—and doubly satisfied that Ash Shatrah's Baath party headquarters was in ruins—he headed back toward the *Bonhomme Richard*.

*   *   *

Ash Shatrah was taken that same day in a battle that left scores of Iraqis dead and the region's Baath party officials—those who were still alive—on the run. The attack Hile led was a direct contributor to the success of that effort. The First Marine Division's record recognized the excellence of Hile's attack and recorded it thusly:

> ... the nominated targets were struck, and 7 of 9 were destroyed. The precision of the strikes marveled the local populace, who turned out into the streets in droves to witness the demonstration of both firepower and restraint.

25

POW Rescue

At first sniff, the tasking stank. It stank badly. The only thing that kept it from stinking worse was the fact that it had come through Guts Robling at 3rd MAW headquarters. Guts was good at putting up a commonsense screen against some of the . . . less well-considered schemes that the wing was sometimes saddled with. Nevertheless, Colonel Stuart "Pitbull" Knoll, Commanding Officer of MAG-16, didn't like the sketchy details that accompanied his orders.

As the leader of one of the three Marine Corps rotary-wing air groups, or MAGs, in the theater he was being directed to support a high-priority effort to rescue a POW somewhere in the vicinity of An Nasiriyah. His MAG was headquartered aboard the USS *Boxer*, an LHD now steaming in the northern reaches of the Arabian Gulf, just east of Kuwait. Distanced as he was from the wing headquarters, Knoll didn't know much more about the mission; supposedly the POW was a Marine lance corporal or private first class. That didn't make much sense to him—he wasn't aware that any Marines had been captured. Neither did it make sense that this was supposed to be a joint operation with the Army, the Air Force, and the Navy's SEALs.

The whole thing smelled more than slightly like the disastrous attempt to snatch U.S. hostages out of Iran in 1980. After months of planning, that effort had failed while killing eight of his fellow servicemen, and wounding many more. Some of them were men he had known. Knoll still remembered the shock and embarrassment that settled over the entire nation after that debacle. All that aside, his Marines were already heavily committed to supporting the division's drive toward Baghdad, and this rescue operation would only detract from their ability to meet that all-important mission.

It was afternoon now, 1530 on March 31, and the rescue was scheduled to kick off the following night. In less than two days Knoll and the rest of the participants would be either heroes or goats. Being a goat wasn't an option that he or his Marines could stomach, and with that in mind Knoll started to make things happen immediately.

"I put myself in charge of this thing right from the start," he recalled, referring to MAG-16's component of the overall effort. "Not because my aviation skills were indispensable, and not just because it's my style to lead from the front, but I wanted to make sure that we had enough horsepower to say no if the folks putting the plan together started to get stupid."

Straightaway Knoll selected Lieutenant Colonel Gregg Sturdevant as the assault flight leader. Sturdevant—a veteran of recent combat in Afghanistan—was the CO of HMM-165. He would be tasked with the hands-on planning and flight lead duties for the helicopters of the Marine force, while Knoll would maintain overall command responsibility of the same force. By 2130 that evening Sturdevant and three other planners were piloting two CH-46Es to Tallil Air Base.

Tallil, about a dozen miles west of the heart of An Nasiriyah in southeastern Iraq, had been captured only a few days earlier. A former bastion of the once formidable Iraqi Air Force—bristling with MIG fighters—Tallil had been heavily hit during Desert Storm twelve years earlier. Stifled by the Coalition's Operation Southern Watch, the Iraqis hadn't been able to do much with the base since the end of that earlier conflict. Now the planning for the rescue operation was being led from one of Tallil's shattered aircraft shelters.

More information filtered through to Knoll and his staff during the remainder of that day and into the next. As it turned out, the POW was an Army private first class who had been injured in an ambush and was being held at the Saddam General Hospital in embattled An Nasiriyah. The city straddled the Euphrates as well as the main supply route the Marines and Army were using to advance northwest toward Baghdad. During the previous week the Marines from Task Force Tarawa, a brigade-sized unit, had been engaged in fierce combat with irregular elements of the Iraqi Army as well as Fedayeen and Baath party forces. The close-quarters fighting had been the most ferocious of the war to that point—more Marines had been killed at An Nasiriyah than anywhere else. Ultimately a route had been punched through the city, although most of the environs of that route— dubbed Ambush Alley—were still infested with hostile elements. Every convoy that made its way through An Nasiriyah encountered various levels of enemy fire. Those areas of the city off the main route were still considered "Indian Country." And Indian Country was where the POW was being held.

At 1600 on April 1, Colonel Stewart Knoll swung his CH-46E into a left-hand arc and watched as the last of his four wingmen lifted away from the *Boxer*. With all the helicopters of his flight safely in tow, he banked his aircraft west and started for Tallil. Cruising at three hundred feet above the water, Knoll led his formation across the muddy coast of Kuwait near the spot where the Euphrates bumps up against Bubiyan Island before it dumps into the gulf. Once past the delta he turned the formation on a more westerly heading and dropped the flight down to only a hundred feet above the desert floor. Although his aircraft were pushing into their fourth decade of service, more recently installed GPS systems helped him to navigate. Still, his backup system was his own set of eyeballs—in combination with a set of charts, a compass, a clock, and his airspeed indicator. The principles of navigation hadn't changed much since the days of the sailing ship.

In the diminishing light of late afternoon, the gray-brown desert had a dirty concrete sort of look to it—barren except for the straight lines of rusting oil or gas pipelines, and the occasional shepherd camps surrounded by bands of camels or dusty sheep, and piles of windblown garbage. A low berm, and not much else, marked the border between Kuwait and Iraq. Deeper into Iraq, and closer to the Euphrates River, small villages and mud-walled farming compounds became more numerous. It was from these types of small farms that Knoll and his units had taken hostile fire during the previous week. "Usually it was small-arms stuff," he recalled. "Some nineteen-year-old asshole with an AK-47 firing from the doorway. There was nothing to keep us from killing them, but we weren't going to level a house and wipe out an entire family just because some idiot kid was taking potshots at us. They were just ignorant—they didn't know what we were about."

Knoll took his formation into the captured Iraqi airfield at Jalibah, where they unloaded an engine for one of his MAG's other CH-46Es. After a quick squirt of fuel they clattered airborne again and continued on their way. It was dusk when Knoll's five helicopters touched down at Tallil Air Base; in the distance they could see An Nasiriyah, only a dozen miles away. After shutting their birds down, the Marine pilots went straight to the small cinder-block building where the plan was being fine-tuned. The enlisted aircrews—two Marines in each bird—stayed behind on the disused high-speed taxiways where they had landed, and immediately turned to the task of preparing the helicopters for the mission.

"Except for a four-hour break, Lieutenant Colonel Sturdevant and the other planners we had sent out the day before had been working nonstop to help put the operation together," Knoll recalled. "It was clear to them that our piece was only a part of what was a very complex operation and that no matter how good the preparations were, there were a lot of points at which this thing could unravel." Within a few minutes of landing, Knoll and the rest of the Marine contingent received an overview of the plan then set to work putting on the finishing touches.

Knoll's officers were correct: The plan was complex, and there were any number of opportunities to fail. The participants included contingents or representatives from Delta Force, the Marine Corps, the Navy's SEALs, the Army's Rangers, and various government agencies including the CIA. "There were all sorts of different haircuts running around the planning spaces," remembered Colonel Knoll. "And there wasn't much socializing going on. I got the names of some folks, but it was obvious that I wasn't going to get the names of others. Or even what organization they were representing."

The forces that were being put together fell under the mantle of Task Force Twenty. Task Force Twenty was charged with specialized operations in Iraq to include finding and capturing political leadership, locating weapons of mass destruction, and other important but sensitive missions. The air component for this mission was extensive and included a Marine EA-6B Prowler jet aircraft to suppress enemy air defenses; two Air Force AC-130 gunships to provide high-powered aerial cover; ten USAF A-10 Close Air Support aircraft on strip alert—just in case; two Marine AH-1W Cobra helicopter gunships; several Marine AV-8B Harriers; four Army AH-6 "Little Bird" helicopters augmented by four more MH-6 helicopters; five Army MH-60s; and finally Knoll's six CH-46Fs and three CH-53Es, intended to provide the force's heavy lift.

The actual rescue force—those troops who would be put onto the ground—included approximately 60 Special Forces personnel and 280 Army Rangers. It was the Rangers whom Knoll's helicopter crews would be charged with inserting into the Landing Zone, or LZ. The Rangers, in turn, were tasked with securing the perimeter around the hospital and repelling any counterattacks the enemy might mount.

Midnight on April 1 was designated as L-Hour. This was the moment when the Task Force Twenty Special Operations troops would be landed atop the hospital. From there they would descend into the building until the POW was located and evacuated. The plan required supporting and diversionary fires from the Marine Corps's Task Force Tarawa. The Tarawa Marines were already engaged in blasting out the enemy forces in and around An Nasiriyah. The barrage would serve to draw attention away from the hospital during the actual rescue, and was to be initiated following a strike at L-Hour minus twenty minutes by the Marine AV-8Bs against one of the main highway spans across the Euphrates.

Once the AV-8B strike was complete and Task Force Tarawa's artillery barrage was under way at L-Hour minus fifteen minutes, the two Marine AH-1W Cobra gunships were to set up a clockwise orbit around the city. The Cobras were loaded to suppress enemy fire as required, but their primary mission was to make noise—to desensitize the Iraqi combatants to the sound of helicopters and mask the approach of the main force. They were rotary-wing attention getters.

At L-Hour minus five minutes electrical power to the city was to be cut. The entire city would be plunged into black except the hospital—assuming its emergency generators operated properly. This would not only disorient any sort of organized resistance, but also make it easier for the helicopter crews to find the hospital—the only lighted structure in the city.

At L-Hour minus two minutes the AH-6 gunships would tear overhead, ripping the night as required with their miniguns—prepping the zone in advance of the MH-60s. Then, in the pitch black while the defenders had their heads down, the MH-60s would sweep in to insert the Special Operations forces precisely at L-Hour.

"Our job was to put the Rangers in place," Knoll remembered. "We were scheduled to land the first wave of 135 Rangers at L-Hour plus five minutes, and at L-Hour plus thirteen minutes. After dropping off the first wave, we were tasked to go right back to Tallil, pick up the next 153 Rangers, and bring them back.

"There was one part of the early plan that I hadn't liked," Knoll continued. "Originally, we were supposed to land right in front of the hospital. Well, we had been briefed that there were Baath party fighters billeted on the hospital grounds, and I could easily imagine us getting shot up just as we were coming in to land. As important as this mission was, it wasn't important enough to risk putting relatively defenseless helicopters—helicopters full of troops—right in the middle of a potential ambush. There were concerns about the number of helicopters that would be operating in the area, too; this had the potential to get very dangerous in and of itself. Earlier I had passed my concerns to Sturdevant and I was glad to see that the planners had made adjustments more to our liking."

The three CH-53Es of Knoll's force arrived at Tallil about two hours after he had brought in the five CH-46Es. "Originally, the planners had called for using only CH-53s because they carry a lot more," Knoll said. "But as vulnerable as most transport helicopters are, the CH-53 is even softer—it has absolutely no armor protection whatsoever. So the plan was to put the CH-46Es in first. They've got some armor, and in the event that the LZ was taking fire the first few sticks of Rangers in the CH-46Es, along with the other assets we had, could clear the place out so that we could follow up with the CH-53s, or land them somewhere else."

After everyone became comfortable with the plan, there was a short period during which the Marines were able to relax. Most of them took the opportunity to heat up something to eat—an MRE. Nevertheless their commander was still harboring some nervous skepticism. "To be quite frank," Knoll recalled, "I kept waiting for the call to cancel this thing. So often, with an operation as delicate as this, a mission that is contingent on so many different parts, it ends up being overtaken by circumstances and terminated. I was really surprised that the call never came."

With mealtime over, the intensity of the preparations increased as the hour of execution approached. Crew chiefs checked their aircraft once, twice, and three more times. The Rangers and Special Operations troops likewise went over their gear and, more important, reviewed and rehearsed their plan. Last-minute coordination was made with those units supporting the operation from outside the air base. The final air mission brief got under way at 2100.

"I can remember thinking to myself that this was something straight out of the movies," Knoll said. "There were Navy and Army guys, and Marines, and all sorts of Special Ops guys and civilians with long hair. We were gathered around a makeshift briefing board with charts duct-taped onto it, and bare lightbulbs overhead. It was just like something off of a Hollywood set."

Immediately after the main briefing, Sturdevant reviewed the lift plan for the Rangers, and then Knoll gathered the Marines around him. "I told them that what we were about to do was important. If we pulled this off we were going to be part of the first POW rescue since World War II. By now I was fully committed to the plan; if we could save the life of one of our own—and do it without killing anyone—this would be a fantastic feat. Then I tried to put it all back into perspective. What we were doing was just a simple insertion, something that we had all done many, many times before. There was nothing sexy about it, nothing slick. There probably wasn't going to be any need for heroics, and if we just executed our portion of the mission we'd be just fine."

As it happened, the night was perfect for the mission. The level of illumination was near zero, and the Iraqi fighters would have a hard time detecting, let alone tracking, the elements of Task Force Twenty. "We could have landed just about on top of the bad guys and they wouldn't have been able to see us. It was a black, dark-ass night," Knoll remembered. On the other hand, Knoll's Marines were equipped with ANVS-9 Night Vision Devices. With these goggles they would be able to see well enough through the dark to execute the entire mission without any external lighting—lighting that might attract the enemy and mark them as targets.

The operation, complex as it was, depended simply on everyone completing their assignments—as basic or difficult as they might be. Once the final briefs broke up, the men set off to do just that. They had no choice but to trust that their teammates did their jobs, and their teammates likewise had no option but to trust that they did theirs. All of these tasks, as Knoll had noted earlier, were potential failure points.

Knoll's lead element of three CH-46Es was formed up into an echelon, with Sturdevant's bird in the lead. His own aircraft was offset to the right side where he could monitor the progress of the overall mission and "watch Sturdevant's back." The three helicopters had lifted off precisely at L-Hour minus seven minutes with their fully armed complements of Rangers.

Just as planned, two minutes after the Marines had gotten airborne, the city went dark at L-Hour minus five minutes. Whoever had been charged with taking down the power grid had completed their task. The diversionary barrage that Task Force Tarawa was throwing against targets on both sides of the Euphrates was well under way now. Bright flashes from bursting artillery rounds ripped the black night and backlit the An Nasiriyah skyline. Under the onslaught, buildings and bunkers and vehicle hulks blazed with a brilliance that lit the way for the approaching helicopters. "The illumination from the high-explosive rounds alone was giving us what we needed to navigate by," Knoll recalled. "Added to that were mortar and machine-gun rounds, as well as shells from the unit's armored elements. This was a classic no-holds-barred display of combined arms firepower—it was awesome." Above it all orbited a section of AV-8B Harriers. Their specially modified Litening pods videoed the operation and linked it to the various commands in real time.

Three minutes later the Special Forces AH-6 Little Birds arrived on station ready to let loose with a wicked fusillade from their M134 7.62-caliber miniguns. "Once the Little Birds arrived on station they started sweeping the area with their infrared pointers. These showed up through our goggles like bright pencil beams—really dazzling, almost otherworldly," Knoll remembered.

Here and there comparatively feeble flashes twinkled back at the Marines, but the Iraqi defenders were putting up nothing to effectively challenge the overwhelming firepower that was ripping the area apart. It was easy to mark Tarawa's position from the volume of fire pouring out from its units. Aside from the big artillery rounds and the mortars, heavy machine guns rained what appeared to be nonstop torrents of red and white slugs into the Iraqi positions. These high-velocity rounds ricocheted out of the impact area in all directions in a Fourth of July display of terrifically hot firepower.

Approaching the city from the southwest, Knoll's helicopters navigated a gauntlet of obstacles at an ingress height of two hundred feet. This altitude was a compromise to keep them away from obstacles rising from the ground, yet it was still low enough that they could navigate easily and stay out of the employment envelopes of a variety of anti-aircraft weapons. Still, a collection of radio towers rose like stilettos from the desert alongside the Euphrates. Each one of those towers was held erect by a web of cables, any one of which could bring down a helicopter. There were no accurate charts that showed all of them; Knoll and his crews were depending on what little information they had, their Night Vision Devices, and luck.

The first three CH-46Es made it across the Euphrates and over the city without incident. In front of them the Marine pilots could see the Special Forces AH-6s, MH-6s, and MH-60s grinding overhead the hospital in a circular pattern. It was a carefully orchestrated ballet that saw the various helicopters come dangerously close to each other as they all met their assignments. Squads of men were already making their way down toward the second floor where the POW was being treated. Knoll and the other Marines found their designated Landing Zone—a section of floodplain separated from the rest of the city by a low dike. "Now that we were closer, the light bloom from all of the different explosions was so bright that it was washing out our goggles," Knoll said, "but as we slowed and approached the LZ, we were able to see well enough to get in." Then, just as the colonel was about to settle his bird full of Rangers onto the dirt, he spotted a wrecked vehicle immediately underneath his aircraft. He quickly sidestepped the obstacle, put his helicopter down, and turned to watch as the Rangers raced off the exit ramp and rushed into the city.

It was then that the shout rang out over the radio: "I think I've just been hit by a SAM!" The call came from Captain William "Fester" Oliver, who was flying in the echelon of CH-46Es behind Knoll. An impact had rocked Oliver's aircraft, rolling it violently to the right. The young captain and his copilot, Shannon "Cookie" Fields, wrestled against the controls and brought the stricken bird back upright. In the rear of the aircraft, the Rangers—who had bungee-corded themselves to the floor of the aircraft rather than buckling in—were struggling to disentangle themselves from each other and their gear.

Knoll's heart was in his throat as he strained to hear more information over the radio. "Getting hit by a SAM on a black night like that was one of the few things I wasn't overly nervous about. My biggest concern had been an ambush in the zone, and right after that my chief worry was that we might kick up a bunch of dust in the Landing Zone and roll a bird over, or run into each other in the dark—a midair collision. After that, I was troubled about all the damn towers and wires that were out there—obstacles we didn't know about. But getting hit by an SAM was way down on my list."

In the meantime Oliver and his copilot had gotten the aircraft flying toward the objective again, seemingly none the worse for wear. After checking the engine instruments and verifying that all was normal, Oliver noted the large number of towers that his formation was flying over, under, and through. And he realized that rather than being struck by a SAM, he had hit a guy wire, or cable—one of the many dozens strung back and forth across their flight path.

Later inspection would show that the aircraft's landing gear had indeed caught a cable. Fortunately the helicopter had enough mass and energy to snap it before it had been thrown inverted. Had Oliver snagged the cable anywhere else, it is likely that he and his crew and their cargo of Rangers would have ended the mission in a fiery ball on the desert below.

Knoll whooped a silent sigh of relief when Oliver called out that he had actually struck a wire and that the aircraft was still flying. With the Rangers now out of his own aircraft, he and the other two CH-46Es in his formation rumbled back into the air and cleared the zone for the following echelon. They had been on the ground for less than sixty seconds.

By now the POW had been found and the Special Forces troops were rushing her to an MH-60 specially prepared with medical equipment. Clearing the rest of the hospital, they found that Iraqi combatants had fled only hours before and had left behind arms, equipment, maps, and other documentation—evidence that they had been using the hospital as a headquarters from which to fight the Marines. Although the Rangers and Special Forces troops outside the hospital were taking sporadic fire, no one but the medical staff remained inside.

It was someone from this staff who helped the Special Forces to their second objective—the bodies of eight other Americans. These Army soldiers had been killed in the same ambush that the POW had been captured from. Six of them were buried in the dirt outside, while two more were in the morgue. Without shovels, the Special Forces attacked the ground with their bare hands and raced to retrieve the bodies of their fallen comrades.

Meanwhile the follow-on formations of Knoll's CH-46Es and CH-53Es had finished the insertion of the first wave of Rangers without any further problems. Knoll and the rest of the first echelon egressed back to Tallil at three hundred feet, hoping to stay clear of the cables that had nearly turned the mission into a disaster. Once safely on the ground at Tallil, the colonel looked back over his shoulder as the second wave of Rangers came on board. Just a short time later the flight was airborne again and completing a second uneventful insert. Within an hour of delivering the first Rangers, all the Marine helicopters were back at Talil waiting for the call to return to the city.

The sky toward An Nasiriyah was still punctuated by the flashes from Task Force Tarawa's intense bombardment. Knoll was back aboard his aircraft, readying it for the extract flight. Here at Tallil he could barely make out shadows racing about in the dark, readying for the next part of the mission. His two enlisted crewmen were hurriedly checking the aircraft, just as others were doing on their own birds.

Finally, as the time approached to retrieve the Rangers, Knoll reached up to the overhead console to start the Auxiliary Power Unit, or APU. This small turbine engine provided the power to start the larger main engines. With a practiced hand he lifted and threw the switch and listened for the familiar thrumming whine as it came to life.

It didn't happen. The APU responded with a weak moan and fell silent. Immediately Knoll's two enlisted crewmen, Corporals Joseph Gerard and Stephen Metzger, leapt up and took turns pumping a hydraulic piston in order to build pressure in the APU accumulator for another start attempt. The entire aircraft rocked gently with each

muscled stroke that the Marines forced into the system. A few minutes later, with the APU fully charged, Gerard gave Knoll the go-
ahead to throw the switch. Again, a teasing hum, then silence. The
helicopter sat dark on the ground with the crew inside struggling to
bring it to life. It was useless. "We must have tried to get that thing
started six or seven times," Knoll said. "My poor crewmen were a
sweaty, worn-out mess by the time I told them to give it up."

Knoll had a decision to make. "I could have jumped into the spare
bird that was already crewed and ready to go, but I decided against it.
The spare crew knew the brief, and they were trained and ready—
they were just as capable of executing as I was. If I had booted them
and taken the bird myself it probably would have caused more confusion than good. Plus, this was a historic mission; I wanted as many
people as possible to be able to participate. As hard as it was, I told
them to press on without me."

It was difficult. "I felt like the general—Gregory Peck plays him—
in the old movie *Twelve O'Clock High*. You know, where he sits in
that control tower and counts each aircraft as it comes back home.
This was perhaps the most important mission of my career and now I
couldn't do anything except wait and pray, and try to take some comfort in the fact that my men made up some of the best aircrews in the
world. Still, I didn't like it."

He didn't like it for the better part of another hour. With the POW
safely out of the hospital, the Special Forces finished pulling the last
of the bodies out of the dirt. The Marine aircraft arrived on time; the
execution went as planned. "I counted the aircraft back to Tallil two
times that night," Knoll remembered. "It was still so black that I actually missed the last bird back, a CH-53. I was nervous as hell; it would
have been an awful note to finish up on." Nevertheless, before dawn
every aircraft was safely on deck at Tallil with every Ranger who had
embarked. Likewise, every man in every other element of every other
service made it back; there were no casualties. Most important, the
POW was now in safe hands. The mission had been accomplished.

The celebration was tempered by the nature of the mission. Despite the successful rescue of the POW, the exhumed remains of the

fallen Army soldiers were a grim reminder of what the ultimate sacrifice really was. "I went to shake the hand of one of the Special Forces first sergeants," Knoll recalled. "He hesitated, and then told me, 'Colonel, I apologize but I've had my hands all over dead people—I'd rather shake your hand later.'"

The dramatic rescue of Private First Class Jessica Lynch received publicity and scrutiny well beyond what any of the participants had imagined. This surprised and to some extent embarrassed Knoll. "With some good planning and attention to execution—along with a healthy dose of luck—we did our job. That's all; we just did our job. People like to say that we're heroes. I don't see it that way. If this was the Super Bowl, we were just the bus drivers that drove the team to the playing field. We got them there and back in a safe and efficient manner."

Modesty aside, Colonel Knoll and the other Marine Corps elements who played a role in the rescue can take a certain measure of pride in their performance.

26

The Son Goes Back to the Fight

Major General James Mattis, the commander of the First Marine Division, had had enough of waiting by the time March turned into April—it was time to kick off the next phase of the campaign. In reality, his forces had not been entirely idle but had been aggressively "pausing" along Highways 1, 7, and 17. They just had not made any all-out moves toward the Iraqi capital. Now it was time for those moves.

Rather than continuing to push toward Baghdad on Highway 1, the plan called for RCT-1 to attack north up Highway 7 and keep the attention of Iraqi forces in Al Kut. In the meantime RCT-5 seized the highway airstrip at Hantush on March 31; this allowed 3rd MAW to start reinforcing the division with supplies brought up from Kuwait. RCT-5 and -7 would then race up Highway 27 and prepare to punch through An Nasiriyah and across the Tigris.

The battlefield had been well prepared by 3rd MAW. During the previous several days the wing had taken advantage of the pause to systematically obliterate everything that could be found around An Nasiriyah, Al Kut, and Baghdad. The Al Nida Republican Guard Di-

vision was hit hard, and intelligence estimates concluded that 80 percent of the Baghdad Republican Guard Division's heavy weapons
had been destroyed. This was all good news to the Marines on the
ground.

Captain Jim "Morris" Isaacs had been leading a section of UH-1N
Hueys most of the morning of April 1 in support of RCT-7's attack
through the city of An Numaniyah. Around and above him other aircraft tore through the air like great armored birds over a huge, burning trash heap. Iraqi combatants and civilians alike scuttled through
the streets as they ran either to or from the fight. A long, snaking line
of vehicles, most of them green but a few of them tan, moved in fits
and starts toward the river. Smoke rose in gray and black pillars that
dirtied the sky as RCT-5, trailed by RCT-7, smashed its way through
the confines of the city.

Isaacs's mission was to act as the RCT's eyes. He led the two ships
in a protective orbit around the Marines on the ground and checked
for the enemy at intersections, rooftops, alleyways—anywhere the
Iraqis might set up an ambush. Although he knew that what he was
doing was essential, it made him edgy. Certainly the helicopters enabled the two crews to move quickly from place to place, and to see
into positions that were hidden from the troops on the ground; on the
other hand, they were also loud, tempting targets. The noise they created as they clattered from point to point made certain that their presence was no secret.

Still, though, things had gone well up to this point. They had shot
up some artillery and AAA pieces earlier—the Iraqi crews had already
fled—and had provided suppressive fire with their .50-caliber machine guns whenever the RCT had called for it. Aboard his aircraft,
Isaacs was carrying RCT-7's assistant operations officer Major Andrew
Petrucci. Petrucci knew the RCT's scheme of maneuver; getting a
good look at the ground that the unit would be traversing only a short
time later was invaluable. It was like peeking at another player's poker
hand.

Once the RCT had pushed across the Tigris, Isaacs brought his two helicopters down alongside the Command Post. Here he and his copilot, Captain Mike "The King" Lawlor, and the pilots in the other Huey, Captain Pat "Puc" Gallogly and First Lieutenant Keith Thorkleson, received a face-to-face brief from the RCT staff. It delineated the planned route of advance and further tasked the Huey crews for road reconnaissance to the southeast of An Numaniyah along Highway 6 and the Tigris River toward Al Kut.

After a quick trip back to Qualcomm FARP for fuel and ammunition, the two helicopter crews made their way back to An Numaniyah and then struck out ahead of RCT-7's lead trace along the route they had been assigned. "We tried to stay in between the river and the highway," Isaacs remembered. Offset from Highway 6, they were less likely to take fire from Iraqi units that might be moving toward the fighting at An Numaniyah. Flying southeast at a height of only fifty feet, they scanned the area for anything that might threaten the RCT's coming advance. Below them they saw civilians walking along the highway or working in the fields, but there was very little traffic on the road and no sign of the Iraqi Army.

Until they approached the mosque. "It was sort of a mud brick color with a shiny, turquoise-green dome," Isaacs remembered. "Puc was the first one to see the artillery pieces." The mosque was a mile or so to their front and offset just slightly to their right, toward the river. Gallogly talked Isaacs's eyes onto the long tubes of the Type 59 130mm guns. These were Chinese copies of the Russian-made M46 and had exceptional range (seventeen miles) and hitting power. They were exactly the type of threat that the Hueys had been sent to uncover.

There were three guns and two trucks arranged in a line that started literally from up against the northeast side of the mosque and reached toward the highway. After taking a quick look at the enemy position from a distance, Isaacs wasted little time in getting the flight positioned for a run at the artillery pieces. He set Gallogly up about 150 feet away and slightly in trail on his right-hand side and double-checked that his two gunners were armed and ready. After scanning the area one more time for anti-aircraft guns or ambush positions, Isaacs dropped the flight down to twenty-five feet and took up a heading that would put the right-hand gunners of the two Hueys in a position to fire on the truck and gun that were farthest from the mosque.

"As we got into range," recalled Isaacs, "we could see guys running away from the guns—some of them ran toward the river and others went straight into the mosque. None of them were wearing uniforms." That so many enemy fighters had stopped wearing uniforms was a frustration that continued to vex American forces. An Iraqi in uniform was clearly identifiable as a bona fide target. An Iraqi in slacks and a sport shirt was not a legal target unless he was actually firing on Coalition forces. The gunners in Isaacs's flight did not shoot at the fleeing enemy.

Instead the fire that erupted in a booming chatter from the two guns sent hundreds of Armor Piercing Incendiary rounds into the closest gun and its tow and ammunition truck. Traveling at greater than three thousand feet per second, the ounce-and-a-half projectiles smashed into the targets with a fantastic force that tore the truck to shreds in just seconds. The artillery gun, although its barrel was too thick to penetrate, was rendered unserviceable by the rounds that tore into its breech and operating mechanisms. As it turned out, this ancillary damage was moot. The incendiary characteristics of the bullets caused the ammunition in the truck to go high order. "The truck went up in a fantastic explosion with massive secondaries that took the gun with it," recounted Isaacs.

Still worried about the possibility of an Iraqi trap, Isaacs pulled his aircraft hard around in a left-hand turn away from the mosque and reset the formation to the west. The truck and gun were still burning when he pointed the two Hueys back toward the mosque. The stink of expended ammunition lingered in his nostrils despite the fact that virtually the entire aircraft was open to the outside. Looking back into the cabin, he could see his two gunners readying for the next pass. Petrucci—who likely was seeing more action than he had anticipated—was straining to see out past the gunners while still trying to stay out of their way.

The second pass saw the middle Type 59 absorb the entire weight of the fire from the guns of the two ships. Although it didn't disappear in a blinding flash as the first one had, it was wrecked by the hard-hitting projectiles. There was one gun and one truck remaining.

Because he was reluctant to make a third predictable pass from the same direction, and because the last gun was so close to the mosque—less than five feet—Isaacs crossed the Tigris and put Gallogly back in a trail formation. Ever watchful for enemy anti-aircraft guns, Isaacs arced the two aircraft back over the river and commenced a final run against the Iraqi position. Flying in low from the south, the two Hueys popped up over the top of the mosque just at the last moment. For the final time that day the gunners let loose with a fusillade of API rounds that turned the truck into tatters and wrecked the remaining artillery piece.

Isaacs continued on the northerly heading, crossed over the highway, and pulled the nose of his aircraft up to clear a set of power lines. Just at that instant the warning light illuminated. "It was the airframe fuel filter caution for the right engine," he recalled. "It operates on the same principle as a filter for a car engine. And just like with a car, if the filter gets clogged or blocked the engine is going to stop." Isaacs wasn't particularly keen on the idea of losing an engine at just that moment. While the UH-1N technically has some capacity to maintain flight on a single engine, it is marginal—and it certainly wasn't a capability that Isaacs wanted to test in and among folks that he had just been shooting up.

And it wasn't just the one engine he was worried about. "Earlier, we had taken bulk fuel straight from a 970 [M-970 refueling truck] that wasn't necessarily configured and tested for aviation fueling. I was worried that we may have been loaded with a contaminated batch of gas and that I'd lose both engines.

"We immediately turned straight back up the highway—northwest toward the lead trace of the RCT," he continued. While he and Lawlor went over their checklists and discussed their options, Gallogly and Thorkleson in the second aircraft kept an eye on their ship. Warning light notwithstanding, the engine continued to produce power. Isaacs and Lawlor took care not to overtax it while the distance back to the lead trace continued to narrow.

"When we finally got there I set down on the highway right be-tween a HMMWV and a tank. I was damn happy to be there," Isaacs remembered. The two crews got out and discussed their options. Now that they were back among friendly forces the consequences of losing an engine were less dire than they would have been had they still been out in Indian Country. The crews decided to press back to Qualcomm FARP. There they would have a better chance of getting the ship repaired, and the RCT wouldn't be burdened with providing security for their sick aircraft. After a short hop to drop Petrucci back at the RCT-7 CP, the two Hueys made their way south and were back at Qualcomm by late in the afternoon.

Sergeant Jovan Denogean made his way toward the two helicopters; they might be able to give him a ride back to First Tanks. He had hitchhiked this far, and the Hueys might be able to take him the rest of the way. His father, Master Gunnery Sergeant Guadalupe Denogean, was going to survive despite the fact that he had sustained a massive head wound, the loss of parts of his hand, and injuries to his back.

For Jovan's part, he wanted to get back to his comrades and into the fight.

"Sergeants Moore and Merson got to work on the aircraft as soon as we got on deck," Isaacs said. "Although they were gunners, the great majority of their work and experience was actually oriented toward maintaining the aircraft; during peacetime there's a lot more main-taining to do than there is gunnery." The two Marines got into the guts of the aircraft, and it wasn't long until they had pulled out the suspect filter.

"There wasn't anything wrong with it," Isaacs recollected. "In ef-fect, we had screwed ourselves. The packing that seated the filter and kept it from leaking was broken when it was removed, and of course we didn't have a replacement. We made contact with the squadron back at home base but they weren't going to be able to help us anytime soon."

It was at this point that Denogean approached Isaacs. "A young sergeant came up to me and introduced himself as 'Sergeant Dino,'" recalled Isaacs. "He was a real nice, outgoing guy who was headed back to his unit after having spent the last week or so watching over his dad. His father had been hit pretty hard at the beginning of the war near Basrah." Isaacs told the enlisted man that indeed they were anxious to head back toward where the fighting was but that they were stuck waiting for a part. Denogean stayed close by the two crews as day turned to night. Moore and Merson meanwhile had traced the warning light to a chafed wire, which they quickly repaired. Nevertheless, they still needed a packing to reinstall the fuel filter.

Isaacs recollected that Denogean approached him as the hunt for the vital component went on: "He asked me, 'Sir, what's a packing?'" The pilot explained that it was similar to an O-ring, something that would ensure a tight seal between the filter and the rest of the components that fed fuel into the engine.

Denogean blinked at Isaacs. He was a tank mechanic; he knew all about gaskets and seals and O-rings. "He looked at me like I was stupid," Isaacs said, "and he pointed out toward where long lines of vehicles were driving past the FARP and told me that a lot of them were carrying repair kits that would probably have something close to what we needed." It was a revelation. But it was also late. Isaacs gathered the crews and put together a game plan for the next day.

Early the following morning Isaacs and Gallogly hooked up with a pair of MPs with a HMMWV. "We made our way over to the highway and started chasing down a convoy. It was like trying to cut cattle from a herd—they weren't stopping for anything. I guess you just don't stop a hundred-vehicle convoy in the middle of a war." Eventually, though, the line of vehicles halted for some other reason and the HMMWV pulled up next to an AAVR7, the recovery version of the tracked AAV7. These amphibious tracked vehicles are workhorses.

They give the Marine Corps the ability to make a beach assault by carrying troops from larger ships to the beach—and obviously well beyond.

"We banged on the hatch," said Isaacs, "and a crusty old staff sergeant stuck his head out. It took some talking to convince him that what we were doing actually made sense. Anyway, we showed him the broken packing and he came up with a couple of parts that looked like they might work." With their hard-won prizes in hand the two pilots climbed back aboard the HMMWV and had the MPs take them back to their aircraft.

As it developed, it didn't take long for Merson and Moore to adapt the AAV parts to the Huey. Denogean watched over their shoulders. Isaacs remembered: "They had to do a little cutting and it wasn't quite a perfect fit. But somebody had the smarts to augment the AAV part with some rubber bands and in combination it all provided a pretty snug fit. In fact, it didn't leak at all."

By midmorning the two Hueys were airborne and en route to support RCT-7 for the remainder of the day. Along the way they stopped at First Tanks to reunite Sergeant Jovan Denogean with his unit—a small detour that was well worth it for the help he had given. "I really liked him," Isaacs said, "and was glad for him that his father was going to survive."

At a ceremony almost two weeks later at the National Naval Medical Center in Bethesda, Maryland, Master Gunnery Sergeant Guadalupe Denogean, father of Sergeant Denogean and brother to 170,000-plus other Marines, became a citizen of the United States of America. President George W. Bush and First Lady Laura Bush were there for the tearful proceedings. Afterward, Denogean was embraced by the president and thanked for his service. The president also recognized and thanked Denogean's family for their sacrifices: *"Gracias a ustedes."*

27

Destruction By FAC(A)

Al Kut was rumored to be where Marine forces would encounter Republican Guard units for the first time. "Consequently," remembered Captain Fred "Chewy" Pierce of VMFA(AW)-225, "we had been bombing the shit out of it all week." Dawn of April 2 found Pierce and his WSO, Major Karl "Grumpy" Hill, orbiting overhead Al Kut while lead elements of RCT-1 worked their way north on Highway 7 toward the city. The ground units had just left the smaller town of Al Hayy a short time earlier with the objective of fixing—or trapping—the Baghdad Division of the Republican Guard in Al Kut. This would allow RCT-7 to attack the city from the west. The Iraqis would have nowhere to escape.

To this point, the mission hadn't been overly busy for Pierce and Hill. They were flying as a single-ship Forward Air Controller (Airborne); Pierce had earned his FAC(A) qualification a few weeks earlier, just before the fighting started. As the sun rose farther above the horizon they both released their goggles from where they were mounted on the top front of their helmets. Reflexively the two fliers reached up to massage their necks—at the same time shrugging and flexing their shoulders. It would take several minutes to work the knots out; the few ounces that the Night Vision Devices weighed felt like twenty pounds after a couple of hours.

They had launched out of Al Jaber at 0300 that morning. It was the time slot that they were normally assigned, and they were starting to get used to it. Still, they enjoyed a chuckle before the brief when they noted their randomly assigned callsign on the ATO for that day: Awake XX.

"During the previous couple of weeks we discovered that particular time of day was never predictable in terms of what sort of action we might see," Pierce said. "It was either dead calm or all hell was breaking loose. We rarely experienced much in between." On that morning it seemed very quiet. They had been maintaining radio contact with Lieutenant Colonel John "Jake" McElroy for much of the flight. Pierce recalled: "He was the regimental Air Officer and was keeping us updated on the situation on the ground. I had never met him, but we had heard about him from other guys. He had been an F/A-18 pilot who had left the Marine Corps years earlier. Then he ditched his civilian job to go back into the Marine Corps—just for this fight. We thought that was honorable."

From where Pierce and Hill were guarding it—several miles overhead—the long column of vehicles that was the lead trace of the RCT seemed to be moving almost in slow motion. Ahead of them a bridge crossed a canal that marked the southern outskirts of Al Kut. On either side of the highway were bunkers and fighting positions. Some of them had weapons ready to be manned, but there was no one in sight. The Iraqis had either not yet "arrived for work" so early in the morning, or had decided to stay home altogether. Suddenly McElroy's voice crackled over the radio: "The lead tank just hit a mine, boys . . . this ain't good." Almost immediately a swarm of civilian vehicles—including a white bus—appeared out of nowhere and converged on the bridge. The bus turned itself broadside and blocked the northern edge of the span. Behind it a large group of cars came to a stop, and soon a crowd of Iraqis mobbed the northern end of the bridge; they were waving white flags.

Pierce and Hill watched the action below with renewed interest. "The situation made us nervous as hell," Pierce remembered. "We had been over An Nasiriyah about a week before when the Iraqis had pretended to surrender and then shot up a bunch of our Marines. Then, we had been helpless to do anything, and now it looked like we were going to be set up for a repeat." On the highway the RCT stopped to consider the new situation. If the bridge was blown up or destroyed, it would slow their advance significantly.

To engage the flag-waving Iraqis without provocation would be murder. But the RCT wasn't about to do something so foolhardy as dropping its guard. Regardless, the crowd had to be dispersed and the bridge had to be crossed. McElroy's next call over the radio echoed the thoughts of the crew circling overhead: "Oh no, I think this is going to be bad."

"I believe that we all thought the Iraqis were going to try to lure the RCT into close quarters with a false surrender and then try to drop the bridge," Pierce recollected. Reinforcing that theory was the fact that groups of Iraqis were now crawling over and around the structure that supported the span.

Then an idea occurred to Pierce. He called to McElroy over the radio: "Jake, Awake." It rhymed.

"Send it," the Air Officer answered.

"Do you mind if we take a look around there before you push up?"

"Have at it."

Pierce looked down through the bright morning sky at the bridge and the glint of the green canal that passed underneath it. The white object that was the bus stood out in keen contrast to the dusty black asphalt of the road beneath it. A very slight hint of haze failed to dull the sharp-edged relief of the landscape below. From where he was flying northbound—and west of the highway—he rolled over into a tight right-hand turn and let the nose of the fighter drop toward the ground. Simultaneously he pushed the throttles up to, but not through, the afterburner detents.

The jet accelerated quickly in the steep dive despite its load of two Mk-82s, a single Mk-83, a single GBU-16, and two external fuel tanks. As it picked up speed the aircraft began to shudder slightly and became almost hypersensitive to control inputs. "Jake," Pierce called out, "are there any helos down there?" A low, supersonic pass over a helicopter could tear it to pieces.

"Negative" came back the reply.

The nose of the Hornet pitched down ever so slightly as it powered through the sound barrier and continued to accelerate. "We're supersonic, Grumpy."

Hill didn't answer. He looked through his binoculars at the crowd on the bridge—only a couple of miles distant. For their part, there was no way that the Iraqis would have been able to see the fighter hurtling down at them.

Pierce leveled the aircraft just above the green foliage that lined the north side of the canal—as low as he dared go. He had never been so fast so close to the ground. The faint green glow of the digits on his HUD displayed his airspeed: 1.28 Mach. Behind him he could see the shock wave from his aircraft ripping across the Iraqi countryside. Dust and debris were torn from the earth in a single, great whirling tornado.

The Iraqis looked up just in time to see the gray, twin-tailed fighter rocketing only barely over their heads in seeming silence. An instant later the concussive energy of the shock wave broke over them with a wickedly loud *kaaa-raaack* that rang their ears and overpressurized their sinuses; it felt as if they'd been dealt a collective punch in the nose, and their guts literally trembled from the effect. At the same time a shower of glass exploded from the windows of the vehicles in a tremendous, glittering eruption. Over the radio Pierce and Hill could hear McElroy and his Marines shouting and laughing.

Pierce snapped the stick of the Hornet back and felt seven g's of gravity smash him down in his seat. Established in a thirty-five-degree climb into the sun, he looked back over his shoulder. "The cars and people all began to scatter. One car started back north and was T-boned by another. The bus took a turn too hard and flipped over. It was pure pandemonium down there."

A short time later McElroy called up his thanks and congratulations; RCT-1 was making its way across the bridge toward Al Kut. "We found out later," Pierce said, "that the bridge had been rigged with explosives."

When night came on April 2, the First Marine Division was on the north side of the Tigris at An Numaniyah. Enemy forces in the south of the country, particularly in Al Basrah, were now wholly and completely cut off from Baghdad. Al Kut had also been isolated, and although there were still small groups of fanatical fighters hiding out in various small towns, resistance in the south was being gradually and systematically squashed by Task Force Tarawa. All the way to the east, the British maintained a stranglehold on the area around Al Basrah.

After fourteen days of fighting, the F/A-18D crews of VMFA(AW)-533 had found their stride. By April 3 the rough edges that had slowed the air wing's command and control procedures during the first few days of the campaign had been honed smooth and operations were moving apace. Lieutenant Colonel L. Ross "Migs" Roberts and Major John "JP" Farnam were airborne at the very start of this day on a single-ship Forward Air Controller (Airborne) mission north and west of Al Kut. It was 0100—their favorite time to fly. By now Iraqi military units had learned that the only time they had any hope of moving and still surviving was at night. This made for good, clean hunting for the Coalition aircrews. It was good hunting because it was the time the enemy chose to leave his hiding places. It was clean hunting because there was very little civilian traffic late at night; odds were that a line of vehicles moving during these hours was made up of Iraqi fighters.

The F/A-18D FAC(A) crews existed to hunt and to kill. The Marine Corps's only two-seat tactical jet, the F/A-18D was well suited to the mission, and its crews were the only Marine jet aviators who practiced it. Specially trained, only the most experienced pilots and WSOs earned this qualification. For instance, Roberts and Farnam together brought more than five thousand hours of F/A-18 flight time into the cockpit. When it is considered that most sorties during peacetime are only an hour or so in duration, the breadth of their expertise becomes obvious. The most junior aircrews in VMFA(AW)-533 that Roberts, the squadron commander, had allowed to be qualified possessed more than two thousand combined F/A-18 flight hours. Further increasing the effectiveness of Roberts's crews was the fact that he kept them teamed together. This helped eliminate the "getting-to-know-you" friction that sometimes took a while to smooth out when the makeup of the crews was constantly changing. That Roberts also kept them flying during the same part of the twenty-four-hour cycle increased their efficacy even more. The other two F/A-18D squadrons in theater followed the same practices for good reasons.

Prior to the war the FAC(A) aviators of MAG-11 had spent a great deal of time working with the staff of the First Marine Division. The division had key billets filled with experienced aviators whose job it was to coordinate and control air support requirements with the wing. Understandably the division's plan was influenced to some extent by the capabilities that the wing would be able to provide. This interface between the wing and the division was invaluable: Not only did the aviators become intimately familiar with the planned ground scheme of maneuver, but in many instances they also knew the names and faces of the ground commanders who would be executing that same scheme of maneuver. This benefit inherent in the Marine Corps's unique organizational structure is difficult to quantify but can hardly be overrated. In fact, it would be a key component of the successes that were ultimately won on the battlefield.

It was nearly 0500 now. Roberts and Farnam, as callsign Degree 60, had spent the previous four hours directing a series of Marine and Air Force aircraft against an Iraqi armored battalion that had been hiding in a grove of date palms. The train of air-delivered munitions had pummeled the enemy unit into a shambles. One pair of Air Force

F-15E Strike Eagles alone had dropped a total of eighteen GBU-12, five-hundred-pound Laser Guided Bombs.

With just a few minutes of fuel remaining, Roberts decided to do some reconnaissance along Highway 6, the east–west road that ran between Al Kut and Baghdad. This was just in front of where RCT-5 had stopped the night previously only a few miles west of Al Kut. "Looking through my NVGs," Roberts recollected, "I spotted five groups of closely spaced lights on the road heading east toward RCT-5." Describing to Farnam what he had spied, Roberts put the Hornet into a thirty-degree dive from where they had been cruising at fifteen thousand feet. It was still very dark, and there was not enough light for him to identify the vehicles with his NVGs. He carefully designated a group of the lights through his HUD, and Farnam was subsequently able to capture the targets with the FLIR. Farnam called up over the intercom from the rear cockpit: "Let's make this a good pass, Skipper, it looks like it might be artillery." It was important to make the identification early; multiple passes consumed precious fuel and provided more shooting opportunities for the enemy.

As the aircraft streaked down the road over one of the several groups of lights the two Marines counted five trucks, each towing a Type 59 artillery piece. These particular guns were capable of firing chemical shells. The division commander, Major General Mattis, had made it clear that he believed there was a good possibility that the Iraqis might use chemical weapons as the Marines pushed past Al Kut and toward Baghdad. The two Iraqi divisions that now stood between Mattis's Marines and the capital city were the Al Nida and the Baghdad—perhaps the most loyal of Saddam's units. And the most likely to start chemical warfare.

Roberts pulled the aircraft skyward and started a left-hand turn to circle back toward the Iraqi convoy. He and Farnam could both see that the trucks had pulled off the road, most likely spooked by the noise of the twin-engine jet. Roberts remembered: "After they pulled off the highway they turned off their lights. They probably had no idea that we could still see them with our FLIR and that we had already marked their position with the GPS." Still, there wasn't much

that the two fliers could do to the enemy procession. They were
nearly out of fuel and had only eight 5-inch rockets; unguided, these
were practically useless at night. Farnam made a quick call back to
Blacklist, the Direct Air Support Center, to confirm that there were
no Marine units this far forward. After making sure that there were no
friendlies in the area, Farnam made another call to the division's Fire
Support Coordination Center to secure clearance to engage the target—it was in the division's zone of responsibility.

In the meantime the Iraqi artillery battery had taken to the road
again. Keeping one eye on the Iraqis and another on their remaining
fuel, the crew arranged for a rendezvous with a Marine KC-130 to
take on more gas. Just as they raced off to the east—toward the big
tanker—they marked the spots where the enemy vehicles had again
pulled off the road and into an adjacent field on the south side of the
highway. Roberts, who had previously served as an artillery officer,
recognized what the Iraqis were doing. It wouldn't be long before
they began to emplace in preparation to fire on the RCT. On the
other hand, they wouldn't be difficult to find when he and Farnam returned.

While Roberts worked the radar and coordinated the rendezvous
with the tanker on one radio, Farnam arranged with Blacklist to get
armed aircraft sent their way. "As we were joining on the left side of
the tanker we could see that there was a section of Harriers, callsign
Demob 67, finishing their refueling on the right-hand hose," said
Roberts. "They hadn't seen any action yet and were still carrying their
normal complement of bombs; the lead aircraft was loaded with a single GBU-16 and a Litening FLIR pod, and the wingman had two
GBU-12s." Once more Farnam worked his radio magic and got the
two AV-8Bs assigned to his new target. He passed them the coordinates and cleared them to strike the target on their own. Both he and
Roberts watched as the two little attack jets sidled away from the
tanker and arced west back toward the Iraqi position.

"We knew that their three bombs wouldn't be enough to kill that
target," said Roberts, "but just one good hit would cause the rest of
the Iraqis to lose their guts and clear out." It wasn't long before the jet

had taken on a full load of fuel. He backed it out of the refueling basket, turned away from the tanker, and started after the AV-8Bs. He
recollected: "While we were still fifteen miles out from the target we
watched through the FLIR as the howitzer in the center of the battery
exploded just as it was being detached from a truck." The Harriers
had found their mark. Along with the gun, the truck that had been
towing it disappeared in a blindingly brilliant blast that continued to
flash and erupt as the ammunition that it was carrying reached high
order. Wingo 32, a pair of Air Force A-10s that had been sent to help,
called out the fireworks from forty miles away.

"The Harriers had scored a nice hit," Roberts remembered, "but
they weren't responding to us on the radio." Had they been the only
aircraft working the target this would not have been much of a problem, but there were two A-10s inbound and it was the F/A-18D crew's
job to coordinate the attacks. This lack of communication with their
fellow Marines was a concern for Roberts and Farnam; a slapdash
grope-fest in the nighttime sky might very well end in disaster. Again,
through their FLIR, they watched two more bombs fall from the Harriers and onto the Iraqi artillery. One fell short, and the other failed to
detonate. A moment later the two AV-8Bs reported up on the frequency. They were out of ammunition and headed home.

It was time to put the A-10s to work. The awkward-looking aircraft
had been put into service during the 1970s at the height of the Cold
War. Designed to take on Soviet armor in the event of a Warsaw Pact
invasion of Western Europe, the slow but heavily armored aircraft was
practically a bomb dump truck. It carried all manner of munitions
and was designed around the 30-millimeter GAU-16 cannon. The
GAU-16 was a fast-firing brute and could take on anything the Iraqis
could field. Unfortunately the A-10 hadn't been updated with the latest in nighttime targeting devices. This would create work for Roberts
and Farnam, but it was work that would be well worth the effort.

The section of A-10s checked in: "Degree 60, Wingo 32 checking
in with four Mk-82s, two IR Mavericks, and a thousand rounds of 30-
millimeter each."

Farnam knew that the A-10s had seen Demob 67's bombs hit earlier. He answered: "Wingo 32, Degree 60, understand you have the target area in sight, stand by for updated target coordinates."

"Wingo 32 is ready to copy."

Farnam passed the coordinates and then built a verbal picture of the target in relationship to the still-burning artillery piece. The lead pilot of Wingo 32 flight declared that the brightness of the burning truck was washing out his Maverick display, but he could make out a dark form approximately fifty yards to the east of the fire. Farnam confirmed that the shape Wingo was describing was another Iraqi artillery piece and cleared him to engage.

But Wingo 32 was taking no chances. A-10s had mistakenly killed several Marines earlier in the campaign, and this pilot wanted to make doubly certain that the target he was about to engage was indeed hostile. "Wingo called for us to mark the target with our hand-held infrared designator," remembered Roberts. The designator, or IZLID (Infrared Zoom Laser Illuminator Designator), emitted a very precise beam of energy much like the laser beams popular at rock concerts. The difference was that night-vision goggles were required to see the beam. Roberts continued: "I held the aircraft in about a fifty-degree angle of bank in a left-hand turn while JP pushed the rubber boot of the flashlight-sized designator up against the canopy. Once he had it positioned he fired the beam and tried to steady it on the target." It wasn't as simple as all that, though. Light from the designator spilled back into Farnam's cockpit, washing out his goggles, and he had to rely on Roberts to fine-tune the aim point. "It was like trying to get my wife to scratch the right spot on my back," Roberts said: "Up a little . . . a little right, up, up, no that's too far . . . oooohhh . . . yeah, that's *just right*."

A moment or two later after confirming that the IZLID beam was illuminating the form he saw on his Maverick display, Wingo 32 lead repositioned his aircraft and called the target in sight. Farnam cleared him to attack.

"Wingo 32, in hot," the A-10 pilot answered. A few seconds later he followed that transmission with another: "Rifle." A bright flash erupted from underneath the aircraft's wing as a Maverick missile streaked toward the Iraqi artillery tube. The missile found its mark, and the big gun and its attached truck disappeared in a dazzling burst of white-hot fire.

There was a downside to the successful hit, though. The illumination caused by the brightly burning fires made it almost impossible for the A-10 pilots to discriminate anything else in the target area. It was too bright for their goggles and Mavericks, but not bright enough to bomb with unaided vision. They would have to rely on the Marine FAC(A) crew to talk them onto more targets.

After an abortive attempt to mark more of the enemy artillery pieces with the laser designator in their aircraft's FLIR pod, Roberts and Farnam decided to use the rockets they were carrying to provide the A-10 pilots a visual reference point. With a new set of Iraqi guns captured in the FLIR, Roberts pointed the nose of the jet down toward the burning fires. Like the A-10 pilots, his goggles were rendered near useless by the light; he relied solely on the data projected onto his HUD. Behind him, Farnam had the FLIR centered on a line of Iraqi vehicles. Passing through seven thousand feet Roberts mashed down on the red pickle button and tried not to look directly into the white-bright motors of the four rockets that whooshed away from the jet. An instant later he reefed the nose up hard away from the ground and felt the blood start to leave his head as seven g's of gravity pulled hard at his body.

The rockets hit just north of the line of trucks and artillery pieces. Almost immediately Wingo 32 called out, "Contact mark!"

Farnam answered without delaying. "From the mark, northwest one hundred. I want all four of your bombs in a string—fifty-foot spacing—oriented from east to west."

"Wingo 32's rolling in, contact mark."

"Wingo 32, you're cleared hot," Farnam answered.

Roberts and Farnam watched the ungainly A-10 roll in from the east. The infrared reflective strips that ran across the aircraft's wings flashed up at the pair of Marines as they followed the attack. As he dived, the pilot of Wingo 32 ejected a series of flares to preemptively decoy any enemy missiles.

The four bombs hit the ground in rapid succession but missed to the south by a hundred yards. Farnam wasted no time and contacted the A-10 wingman: "Wingo 33, call contact lead's hits."

"Wingo 33 is contact lead's hits."

"Okay, Wingo 33," Farnam replied, "from lead's hits I want your bombs on the same line, east to west, but move it a hundred meters north."

"Wingo 33's in from the east."

"Wingo 33," Farnam answered, "you're cleared hot."

With his lead's hits as a visual reference, Wingo 33 set his aircraft up on the same heading but adjusted his flight path slightly to the north. Pointed at the gray-green void that was the ground below, he had little to rely on but the guidance the Marines had passed. At just the right moment he released his bombs and felt the aircraft shudder as small explosive charges slammed the four bombs down and away from the jet. At the same time the aircraft seemed to jump—suddenly lightened of two thousand pounds of deadly ordnance.

Roberts and Farnam had their eyes glued to their FLIR display. Suddenly four bombs appeared on their screen—almost like minnows in formation. An instant later they slammed exactly into the line of vehicles, setting them all on fire as red-hot shrapnel ripped through them at incredible velocities.

Farnam called out over the radio: "Wingo 33, that was right on target! *Great hits!*"

Wingo 32 came back on the net: "Degree 60, Wingo 32, we've got enough gas for one more pass. Do you mind if we saw things up a little with the cannon?"

Farnam cleared the two A-10s to let loose into the same area with their big guns. It was like shooting a dead man, but the show was spectacular. The heavy depleted-uranium rounds slammed into what was left of the Iraqis with incredible results. Molten metal shot high into the night sky.

A short time later Wingo flight declared themselves bingo and Farnam cleared them to depart the area and passed them their BDA, or Battle Damage Assessment. This was an estimate of the number of vehicles the flight had damaged or destroyed and was part of the FAC(A) duties.

Just as Wingo flight departed, Muddog 14, another section of A-10s, checked in with Farnam. "Do you have the target area in sight?" the WSO asked.

"Affirmative, from forty miles." Night-vision goggles were almost like magic.

Roberts and Farnam quickly discussed their worsening fuel situation and decided that they could afford to remain on station for about ten more minutes. They put together a hasty game plan that would target a truck–gun combination a bit south of the others, farther from the brightly burning fires.

Using the FLIR, the two Marines derived accurate GPS coordinates. "Muddog," Farnam called over the radio, "advise when ready to copy target coordinate."

"Muddog's ready."

"Grid Alpha Tango 23412 98345, elevation two hundred feet. Attack from south to north. I want your IR Maverick first followed by your wingman's. We've got just enough fuel for your first pass. Once you've got the target we'll hand the area to you."

"Muddog copies—we'll be there in two minutes."

A minute later the A-10 flight lead called out: "Muddog 14 has one truck and artillery piece just south of the fire."

"That's your target," Farnam answered. "You're cleared hot."

"Muddog copies, ten seconds . . . Muddog 14, rifle." Again a Maverick missile crashed into its target and the Iraqi Army had one less artillery piece in its inventory.

"*Great hit, Muddog!*" The A-10 pilot had done an outstanding job, and now it was time for Roberts and Farnam to head back to Al Jaber. "Muddog, you have control of the target area. Be advised there's one more gun to the west of the center fire."

"Muddog copies, thanks for the work."

Roberts and Farnam landed about an hour after sunrise—it had been a very long night. The weary fliers climbed down from their jet and high-fived their ground crew while they described their latest exploits. A small crowd followed them into the maintenance spaces where Roberts had earlier arranged for a video machine to be placed. "It was important that the squadron's Marines were able to see the fruits of their labors," he said. "This paid huge dividends in keeping them focused on their jobs. They were typically putting in sixteen or seventeen hours a day on the flight line, and being able to watch the mission tapes reinforced to them the importance of what they were doing. Watching the success of our combined efforts as a team was a tremendous satisfaction to them."

This type of continuous destruction of the Iraqi Army from the air—well in front of the advancing Marines—was an undeniable factor, indeed perhaps the most important factor, in the success of the ground effort. Controlled much of the time by F/A-18D FAC(A) crews such as Roberts and Farnam, Coalition airpower was an unrelenting and unstoppable force. Quite simply put, the Iraqis were never able to mass in units large enough to slow the American advance. This fact was sometimes lost on ground commanders whose awareness of the battlefield was often no more than what they could see from the road. They had little or no idea that the deserts and fields around them were littered with much of the Iraqi Army—units that they would have had to kill themselves if not for their brothers who flew overhead on an around-the-clock basis.

The killbox system was an outgrowth of a command and control measure that had first seen widespread use during Desert Storm. Since that time it had been refined, and it became one of the predominant means for controlling CAS and interdiction flights. The KI (Killbox Interdiction) system was a matrix of grids demarcated by drawing lines along the 00- and 30-minute lines of longitude and latitude. These lines produced approximate squares measuring roughly thirty-five miles per side. Each one of these squares was in turn subdivided into nine smaller squares such that it resembled a telephone keypad.

A row of killboxes was given a numeric designator, such as 84, while a specific killbox was given a two-letter designator, such as AW. Then the individual keys were numbered.

With the advances in navigation both on the ground and in the air, this system was supremely useful to all of the various fire support control entities. For instance, killboxes could be shut down in their entirety, or just certain portions of the keypad could be put off limits. Airborne FACs could direct supporting aircraft to proceed to a given key on the keypad and await further instructions, or could use the system to help describe a target: ". . . a pair of T-72s just north of the road intersection in the northeast corner of 84AW-9." As the concept related to Close Air Support its use was cleverly dubbed "KIck CAS."

The system wasn't foolproof, as had been dramatically illustrated earlier in the campaign on March 27. One of RCT-1's command groups was mistakenly attacked by an Air Force A-10 near the intersection of Highways 7 and 17. An RCT-5 unit caught up in a firefight had requested air support, and somehow during the process an incorrect grid zone designator was passed to the Air Force pilot. As fate would have it, the RCT-1 command group was located exactly at the bogus grid designator. Somehow the Air Force pilot identified the friendly unit as enemy and received clearance to engage. He tore up the Marine unit with his 30-millimeter cannon—but amazingly no one was hurt. It was while he was climbing to reengage for another attack—this time with bombs—that someone came up on the frequency and aborted his run. In the meantime the RCT-5 Marines were wondering what had happened to their air support.

Stupid things happen during war. This war was no different. Hours after Roberts and Farnam had landed, a pair of VMA-311 Harriers was working with an F/A-18D FAC(A) near the Tigris when they discovered a row of fighting positions dug into the bank. The positions were empty, but there were several cars moving suspiciously up and down the line. Curious, the crew aboard the Hornet dropped low to investigate.

Reacting to the diving fighter, the Iraqi cars scattered—several of them at high speed down the wrong side of a road that ran alongside the river. The pilots aboard the Harriers watched with an interest that turned to dark humor as the lead car struck oncoming traffic head-on. The resulting jam trapped the cars that followed, and traffic soon built up behind the wreck. Out of fuel, the Harriers turned for home without dropping their ordnance, but with an interesting story.

28

===

CAS on Highway 6

By April 4 all three RCTs were on the north side of the Tigris. The race for Baghdad was back on. After Al Kut had been taken on April 3, RCT-1—in one night—had backtracked south down Highway 7, turned west onto Highway 17, then north onto Highway 27 to join RCT-5 and -7 on Highway 6. Saddam's forces were now caught between the pincer that was the Army attacking from the south and the Marine Corps attacking from the east.

"The ATO had us scheduled to go plinking in a killbox just to the east of Baghdad," remembered Lieutenant Colonel Kevin "Wolfie" Iiams. *Plinking* was a term that 3rd MAW fliers used to describe those missions where they were turned loose to destroy whatever they could find within a set of geographic coordinates. Usually it was a low-tempo effort that allowed them to work on their own terms without exercising a great deal of coordination with their ground counterparts.

A seasoned veteran of Desert Storm, Iiams was now assigned as the

MAG-11 operations officer. As Colonel Alles's right-hand man, he was charged with coordinating and facilitating the combat operations of the five Marine F/A-18 squadrons at Al Jaber, as well as the twenty-four KC-130s that daily ranged back and forth across the theater. On this day, April 4, just as he did nearly every day, he was taking time off from those duties and flying an F/A-18C from the VMFA-232 Red Devils. As wingman to Captain Byron "Shreck" Sullivan, he would be able to get a firsthand look at how the fight was progressing. "On the way up there," Iiams explained, "it was pretty quiet and we surfed through the different TAD [Tactical Air Direction] nets looking for an old Red Devil buddy of ours."

They didn't find their pal, but on one of the frequencies the two Marines made contact with an F/A-18D FAC(A) from VMFA(AW)-225. The two-seater crew had found a battery of guns that were in a position to threaten RCT-5's advance west along Highway 6. "The FAC(A) gave us a quick brief on the target area and the threat; they had been shot at by a couple of MANPADS [Man Portable Air Defenses] and some AAA but otherwise it wasn't a big deal," Iiams recounted. Almost immediately the original FAC(A) was out of fuel and was relieved by another F/A-18D crewed by Captains Matthew "PWOC" Shortal and Anthony "Curly" Bolden.

"We set up in a lazy left-hand circle," recounted Iiams, "and started dropping Mk-83s on the guns." Sporadic bursts of AAA marked the sky around them, but the fire was poorly aimed and not yet a great menace. To their east along Highway 6 the pilots could see the RCT hurtling west toward their ultimate objective: Baghdad. Hundreds of green and desert-tan vehicles sped along the highway, weaving through and around obstacles, but always moving—and fast. "Those guys were hauling ass," Iiams recalled. "I mean they were driving like they were late!"

The Scout Platoon of Second Tanks was leading that racing column of vehicles. The head of any attack or patrol is the most dangerous place in the world. After two weeks of combat the men at the van of

RCT-5 knew it firsthand. Just the day prior, the Scout Platoon commander, First Lieutenant Matthew Zummo, had been seriously wounded and evacuated.

The ambush they encountered was fierce. An excerpt from the First Marine Division's history of the campaign describes what happened next:

> Second Tanks continued the attack along Highway 6 with the Scout Platoon in the lead. In the vicinity of the 65 easting, the scouts uncovered another enemy ambush. In the process of engaging the enemy, the new Scout Platoon Commander, First Lieutenant Brian M. McPhillips, was killed by an enemy sniper.

The two single-seat Hornet pilots had each dropped a pair of Mk-83s on the artillery pieces when a call for help came over the radio from a FAC traveling with RCT-5. Iiams recalled: "Evidently, all hell had broken loose down there. The lead elements on Highway 6 had run into an ambush and been hit hard. Marines were wounded and they were taking heavy fire. When the FAC keyed his mike we could hear machine-gun fire and shouting in the background."

Sullivan and Iiams in their two aircraft, and Shortal and Bolden in the F/A-18D, quickly posted themselves over the top of the now halted train of combat vehicles. "You could tell that things were getting amped up down there," Iiams said. "There was a lot of chatter on the radio, and down on the ground we could see smoke from where the lead element was engaged." Approximately three hundred yards to the east of the fight the rest of the RCT, led by Second Tanks, began to herringbone off to both sides of the road. The strain in the ground FAC's voice telegraphed the intensity of the fighting to the aircrews orbiting overhead.

"We were eager to give the guys some help," Iiams said, "but the fighting was too close. The enemy was holed up only a few meters off the northeast side of the road." Dropping their thousand-pound Mk-83s on the Iraqi positions would certainly obliterate them, but doing so would also kill the Marines they were trying to protect. There had to be another option.

"The ground FAC came up and told us to stand by," explained Iiams. "He said there was a section of Cobras on the way." The Hornets arced overhead in a loose orbit that contrasted sharply with the tight anxiety gripping the men who were flying them. The fighting below was growing in intensity, and there was no sign of the gunships. A few minutes later the word was passed that both Cobras had taken fire; one had been forced down, and the other was too damaged to continue the mission. The F/A-18 crews were desperate to do something. In the meantime Shortal and Bolden had descended to a thousand feet in order to get a complete picture of what was happening. Going as fast as the aircraft's two engines would push them, they scanned the road, trying to locate the epicenter of the ambush. Bolden remembered: "As we reached the convoy we could see a bunch of men in recently dug trenches behind the only tree line for miles—only about fifty meters off the road."

Iiams looked down in frustration at the enemy fighters in their positions. "It was right about that time," he remembered, "that someone pointed out that we could probably use our guns." Figurative lightbulbs illuminated above the heads of every flier over the RCT. The crews had been operating under the restrictive ROE for so long that they had nearly forgotten about the five hundred or more rounds of 20-millimeter high-explosive incendiary ammunition each aircraft carried. The firefight below met the criteria to waive the rules that prohibited them from descending below five thousand feet. "We had Marines in contact with the enemy, and they were in danger of getting overrun," said Iiams. "That was all the reason we needed."

The ROE allowed aircrews to do what they needed to help ground forces in extremis; this was one of those instances, and the Hornet crews were anxious to get into the fray. Bolden, the WSO in the two-seat aircraft, quickly coordinated with the RCT FAC to set up the strafing runs. In addition to their 20-millimeter ammunition, he and Shortal were carrying 5-inch rockets; they dropped down to mark the target for Sullivan and Iiams. "By now the anti-aircraft fire was starting to get pretty heavy," recalled Iiams. "Along with the AAA bursts we could make out muzzle flashes on the ground, and see tracers reaching up toward us."

Shortal dived down and sent the rocket on its way. It was right on the mark, but still so close that it threw shrapnel against the vehicles of the lead Marine element. The FAC(A) crew asked for—and received—the initials of the ground unit's Commanding Officer. This was a requirement when employing ordnance "danger close." This was deadly, deadly business; killing friendly troops was a gut-wrenching tragedy with consequences that ranged well beyond the deaths themselves.

"We lined up for our strafing runs so that we were parallel to the highway on the north side—flying from east to west, diving in from over the top of the RCT," explained Iiams. "As long as we kept our rounds on the north side of the road, we would be sure not to hit any friendlies." Shortal made the first pass, with Iiams watching from above. "The stupidest thing entered my mind right about then," he recalled. "I realized that everyone else in the flight was the son of a Marine Corps general! PWOC's dad had worn a star or two, maybe more, and had flown more than three hundred F-4 sorties in Vietnam. Shreck's dad had also been a fighter pilot, and again, had also flown F-4s in Vietnam. Likewise, Bolden's father had flown A-6s in the same war before going on to become a fairly famous Marine Corps astronaut. Hell, my dad was an insurance guy from Louisiana."

Iiams quickly decided that the relevance of military legacies in the flight was not something that needed to be considered at just that moment. He dived on the enemy position from eight thousand feet and watched his airspeed quickly accelerate above five hundred knots. He made certain that his dive was steep—thirty degrees rather than the more typical ten or fifteen. This would guarantee that his rounds would clear the edges of the holes from where the enemy was fighting. Had he been in a shallower dive, the explosive bullets would have hit more dirt and fewer Iraqis.

Iiams concentrated on putting the pipper of his gun sight just on the northern edge of the enemy emplacements. At approximately three thousand feet the cueing on his HUD flashed IN RANGE. Iiams squeezed off a one-second burst, letting the pipper wander just slightly over the enemy positions in order to get better coverage. In front of him he could see the black swarm of cannon rounds racing for the ground.

After pulling back on the stick and putting out a salvo of chaff and flares, he had his aircraft heading skyward again. He checked where his cannon fire had hit—a hundred or more small dusty-gray plumes of smoke rose from the ground where the Iraqis had been firing. Behind him Shortal and Bolden plunged toward the ground in another rocket run. With the weapon on its way they, too, climbed back to altitude. "We continued taking turns for several more runs," recollected Iiams. "PWOC and Curly cleared us 'hot' each time but we didn't hear too much from the ground FAC." It soon occurred to the F/A-18 crews that the FAC was likely shuttered up in his vehicle and fighting for his life.

Shortal and Bolden were just pulling out of a run when they caught sight of the anti-aircraft fire that had by now developed into a virtual wall just north of the fight. If they executed a normal pullout they were going to be shot down. Shortal brought the stick hard toward his gut, slammed it to the left, and virtually pivoted the aircraft in midair. Bolden simultaneously called Sullivan out of his dive to keep him out of the same ambush. A few seconds later both aircraft were clear of the enemy fire, having only narrowly escaped flying into the trap.

"By now we were all pretty excited and breathing hard," Iiams said. "Along with all the AAA, there had been a couple of MANPADs launched our way. All of that in combination with the fire on the ground and the chatter over the radio had gotten our adrenaline pumping pretty good." Once more the three fighters cruised overhead the RCT while the crews caught their breath. Below them they could see that a group of vehicles from the main body of the RCT had pushed forward to the engagement.

"We got the call then," remembered Iiams, "that they had the fight under control but that there were wounded Marines who needed an emergency CASEVAC." Bolden and Shortal immediately got on the radio and started coordinating the effort. The buzz of anxious radio calls among multiple players continued back and forth until a call came from the RCT that numbed the Hornet pilots. The RCT asked that the priority for the CASEVAC mission be changed from urgent to routine: The most badly injured of the Marines were dead.

"Every one of us in that mission fought back the urge to puke," Iiams said. Their entire raison d'être was to support those Marines on the ground; they felt a sense of failure. Worse, what if they had caused the casualties? What if they had shot up their own brothers with their wickedly effective fusillades of 20-millimeter fire?

Iiams remembered: "We came up on the radio and asked if they needed any more help. They thanked us and said that they had everything under control." Getting low on fuel, the three aircraft pushed to another objective area near Salman Pak to drop their remaining bombs before they returned to Al Jaber. There, Iiams started a massive fire when he blew up a fuel tanker. Sullivan also destroyed a heavy truck. Neither felt any satisfaction, and the return flight felt longer than usual.

Back on deck Iiams gathered all the participating crews together for a thorough debrief. "We went over what we thought we might have done wrong, or what we could have done sooner or better," he recollected. "After all, it wasn't too often that we heard, 'Thanks, but they're dead,' come from the guys we were supporting. When they die . . . well, I guess you have self-doubts and tend to second-guess everything you're doing." Nevertheless, the review of their flight revealed no significant mistakes or failures.

Knowing that word of the casualties would get back to Alles, and that Alles would have to be ready with answers, Iiams walked to the MAG-11 headquarters tent and gave the MAG-11 commander a face-to-face report. Alles in turn sent him to debrief Major General Amos and Brigadier General Robling. Robling recalled the meeting: "I saw Wolfie coming and told Tamer, 'Here's a guy that needs to be pumped up.' " The two generals had already gotten word from Major General Mattis that the division had lost an officer in action and that the Hornets had done a great job helping to get the situation under control. "Tamer immediately picked up on Wolfie's distress," said Robling, "and reassured him that the flight had kept a bad situation from getting much worse. Tamer was really good at this; the way he understood and dealt with his Marines was one of the key reasons he had so much respect and credibility from his subordinates." The wing commander's message from the RCT helped assuage some of the earlier sting that Iiams and his comrades had taken back with them from the sky over Highway 6.

Meanwhile, RCT-5 kept barreling toward Baghdad. This fight was all about speed, and the deaths of two Marines weren't going to stop it.

There were two squadrons of Marine F/A-18s fighting in the campaign that did not fall under 3rd MAW's command. VMFA-323 and VMFA-115 fought from the decks of the *Constellation* and the *Harry S. Truman*, respectively. Because the Navy lacks the wherewithal to adequately equip its aircraft carriers with its own squadrons, it has increasingly drawn on the Marine Corps to make good its shortcomings. The aviators from both of these squadrons fought alongside their Navy comrades with distinction.

29

"We're Not Going to Get Shot Up . . ."

"Today, we're not going to get shot up." It was the way Major Jason "Droopy" Adkinson of HMLA-267 always started his pre-mission briefs. Not that it had made much of a difference; in the two weeks since the war had started he'd already brought home two Cobras that had been holed by enemy fire. Nevertheless, he was a positive thinker, and he liked the simple declarative nature of the statement.

On this particular day, April 4, he had made the same proclamation. Now, leading a division of three AH-1Ws and headed north from Three Rivers FARP at An Numaniyah toward where RCT-5 was charging west on Highway 6, he wasn't so certain. Only about twenty miles southeast of Baghdad, the lead trace of the RCT, Second Tanks, was pushing through built-up areas along the highway toward where Iraqi elements had set up an ambush site. On the TAD frequency he recognized the voice of Captain Kristian "Penguin" Pfeiffer, a fellow Cobra pilot from his sister squadron, HMLA-169. Pfeiffer and his wingman were working with the Second Tanks FAC to root out the fighters dug in along the road ahead of the armored unit. Both the Cobras and the tanks were taking heavy fire. Just moments earlier, two of Pfeiffer's wingmen had staggered clear of the area, too shot up to stay and fight.

Adkinson remembered the scene: "We crossed the Tigris River and angled up to the highway, then paralleled it on the south side heading west. The radio chatter was kind of a garbled mess and rather than contacting the FAC, I spoke directly with Penguin, who was just about out of fuel and had to leave." The two flight leaders conducted a battlefield handover; the departing ships egressed eastbound on the north side of the road while Adkinson led his flight west on the south side. "I remember," recalled Adkinson, "that Penguin just matter-of-factly mentioned that he had been taking 'heavy small-arms and AAA fire and that there had been RPG launches and possible MANPADs.' He sounded like he could have been talking about the weather."

Approaching the lead trace of Second Tanks, Adkinson swung his flight into an orbit while he assessed the situation. He could see the M1A1s shooting their heavy 120-millimeter main guns into targets along the highway, including into the high berm that paralleled the north side of the road. Muzzle blasts from small-arms fire marked the positions of the enemy fighters where they hid along the top of the berm, and in and among the buildings that lined the highway. Farther west he could see where two burning black fire trenches intersected the road from the north and south. Behind these trenches was where additional elements of enemy fighters were dug in. On the road, almost in between the two trenches, an Iraqi tank sat burning— the loser of a duel with the Marines on the ground.

Adkinson didn't like the setup. "The RCT was pushing straight up the highway and was by no means clearing the villages and towns that ran alongside. This meant that there were plenty of folks with AKs, and AAA, and RPGs who could target us on our run-in to the target." Almost as bad for the crews were the 150-foot-high power lines that sagged along and across the highway. These and the towers that supported them could easily drag a helicopter out of the sky. Too, they forced the crews to fly higher than they wanted—where it was diffi-cult to dodge behind a building or a grove of trees. In effect, the wires forced the gunships up high where everyone could see them. And shoot at them.

Regardless of the threat, Adkinson's Cobras were charged with sup-porting the RCT as it moved toward the ambush site. He set the flight up to attack the enemy positions behind the northern fire trench; he would lead the flight in from the east, south of the highway. "I had my wingman, Captain Erik 'Slats' Bartelt, on my right side because we were going to pull off to the left after the firing run." Covering the two lead ships from behind were Captain Dave "Spanky" Moore and his copilot, Lieutenant Colonel Brad "Woody" Lowe. Adkinson's copilot, Captain Jason "Jekyll" Gibson, and Bartelt's copilot, Major Pete Calogero, had gone facedown into "the bucket." This was the TSU—the Telescopic Sight Unit. They had already picked out targets through the smoke and fire behind the northern trench and were waiting for their lead to take them close enough to launch their weapons.

"By now," Adkinson said, "the Second Tanks FAC had cleared us to engage. This was Type III CAS—he was buttoned up in his vehi-cle against the enemy fire, and too far back to get his eyes on the am-bush site. The best he could do was confirm that we knew where the friendly forces were and where the enemy was, and then clear us to engage."

The plan was for Adkinson and Bartelt to attack the Iraqi positions with TOW missiles, 20-millimeter cannon fire, and 2.75-inch aerial rockets. Moore was expected to follow them from above and behind, and to call out and suppress enemy fire as the first two ships launched their weapons and turned hard away from the target. From a point just a hundred yards or so beyond the lead tank and only about a mile from the burning trenches, Adkinson rolled his Cobra into the attack. Bartelt was close behind on his right side.

The enemy rounds smashed into their ships almost immediately. "It was like someone was hitting the aircraft with a baseball bat," re-called Adkinson. The helicopter shuddered; in the front cockpit he

saw Gibson—startled by the sudden impacts—pop his head up out of
the TSU. Shooting weapons had just dropped far down their list of
priorities.

Hit on the right side, Adkinson broke the ship into a hard left descending turn, at the same time calling over the TAD frequency that
he had been hit and was still taking heavy fire. Bartelt, hit badly as
well, matched his turn and followed him south away from the highway. Finally, over an open area and out of range of the enemy guns,
the two crews assessed the condition of their ships. Adkinson's aircraft
was rumbling more than it should have but it seemed flyable for at
least the next few minutes. Bartelt's bird, however, was in trouble.
"His transmission was seriously damaged; the temperature was up
and the oil pressure was down. If it failed he was going to crash.
Spanky, in the other aircraft, didn't appear to have been hit." In fact,
Moore's ship had taken two hits although they weren't critical.

Realizing that Bartelt's Cobra wasn't going to stay airborne for
much longer, Adkinson led the flight straight back to the highway
and turned east down the line of advancing Marines. About three
miles down the road Bartelt found a patch of dirt and landed literally
only a few feet away from the column of friendly vehicles. Almost at
the same time he shut the engines down, hoping to save the transmission before it cooked itself beyond repair. Adkinson set his helicopter down adjacent to Bartelt, but left his engines turning. Moore
and Lowe continued to circle overhead in a protective orbit.

"Slats hopped out of his aircraft and walked over to mine," Adkinson remembered. "His face had blood on it where a 7.62-millimeter
round had gone through his canopy. The shattered Plexiglas had cut
his cheek up." Calogero—in Bartelt's front cockpit—had also had a
close brush. His head had been down in the TSU when the device
was hit by another round. Fortunately he hadn't been injured. Bartelt
looked the lead ship over and signaled that it was a mess. Adkinson
shut it down and crawled out. There were 7.62- and 12.7-millimeter
holes all up and down the tail boom and in the belly. The number
two hydraulics system behind Adkinson's head had also been shot up,
as had the right-hand engine. As damaged as the tail boom was, it

didn't appear that anything that would keep the aircraft from flying had been hit hard. Adkinson climbed back aboard, intending to get it back to the FARP for repair, rather than leaving it alongside the road in Indian Country. It didn't happen; the Iraqi bullets had shot out the start relays in the belly, and the engines wouldn't even turn. He was going nowhere.

"So Jekyll and I got out of the aircraft and kind of stood there for a few minutes with Slats and Pete Calogero, watching all the Marines drive up the highway. I looked over at Slats—at his bloody cheek—and joked that I was going to put him in for a Purple Heart. He just kind of glared back at me and said that he'd shoot me if I did."

Moore and Lowe, still circling overhead, relayed to the DASC that the two aircraft were down with battle damage and that a recovery effort needed to be put together. Then, low on fuel, they departed. A few minutes later a UH-1N Huey from their squadron landed next to the two Cobras. The Huey's crew chief, Gunnery Sergeant Alvarado, was also qualified as a Cobra mechanic. He looked the two ships over and reported back: "Shit, sir, you guys aren't going anywhere." Unbeknownst to Adkinson, one of his control tubes was nearly shot in half. It had been a blessing that the aircraft wouldn't start. Otherwise he might have ended in a ball of flames somewhere on the route back to the FARP.

It was becoming evident that the two crews and their aircraft would be stranded for a while. The RCT had punched through the ambush site and was continuing west. As big as the column of Marines and vehicles was, it would eventually pass. They would need protection. "Pete Calogero," Adkinson said, "ran out and flagged down a HMMWV and got on the radio with the Blue Diamond Forward Command Post. They chopped a CAAT Team—four anti-armor HMMWVs out to our position to provide security until a platoon of LAVs came out and set up a perimeter around us. The sight of those Marines in their armored vehicles made us feel quite a bit more secure."

By late afternoon the bulk of the RCT had passed and the road became heavily trafficked by Iraqi civilians on foot and in buses, cars, vans—even on donkeys. Almost all of them waved a white T-shirt or sheet to mark their status as noncombatants. Ironically, the two Cobras had landed across the road from an Iraqi military compound, and the civilians on the highway soon started looting it. The crews watched as furniture, generators, air conditioners, even refrigerators were ripped out of the buildings and thrown into trucks and vans.

The two damaged aircraft also attracted a few Iraqis. Most of them were simply curious, but one man attempted to engage them in a debate. Adkinson recalled: "He only had one leg. He said that he'd lost the other during Desert Storm. Anyway, he was arguing pretty forcefully that we were only in Iraq to kill civilians and that we should go away. He actually spoke very good English and that kind of surprised us." Eventually the commander of the LAR platoon approached the man, and he and the others soon dispersed.

Finally, near sunset, a CH-46E landed nearby; the DASC had sent the transport to pick up the Cobra crews. Adkinson was reluctant to leave his ships behind. The CH-46E commander told him that he could do what he wanted, but that he was getting low on fuel and was going to leave regardless. "We were probably just number five or six on that guy's 'to do' list," Adkinson recalled. After making certain that the LAR platoon would be remaining with the two Cobras until a recovery crew arrived, Adkinson and the three other fliers boarded the CH-46E. Moments later they were airborne and en route for Three Rivers FARP.

Despite his pre-mission declaration, Adkinson's flight had indeed gotten shot up. Reflecting on the sortie, Adkinson summarized: "When I think about it, I guess that was a fairly unsuccessful mission—we got defeated by the bad guys and we didn't even fire a shot."

Still, it had been only one mission. During a total of thirty-four combat flights over the course of the campaign, Adkinson and the crewmen who manned the rest of his division got their share of licks in and then some.

30

CASEVAC

A cross the Tigris and with no organized threat behind them, the men of the First Marine Division looked northwest toward Baghdad. Although the campaign thus far been a series of short, sharp fights, it was thought that the battle for the capital could turn into a long, protracted, and bloody siege. Saddam's divisions had failed to materialize in any coherent form, and it was believed by some that the men who made up their ranks had been withdrawn into the city where the American dominance in advanced weaponry could not play so big a part in the coming clash. Perhaps the Iraqis were preparing to make the Coalition pay for Baghdad house by house in a grueling urban brawl.

There was another factor worrying the Americans. During Desert Storm the Iraqis had huge stockpiles of chemical weapons, but had failed to use them. The Coalition had destroyed great caches of these weapons immediately after that war during 1991, and the UN required that Saddam divest completely himself of them. But no one in his right mind believed that the chemical weapons were completely gone. That being the case, was it possible that the Iraqis would choose to use them now as the Marines and the Army approached Baghdad's gates? The men in the field—in chemical protective suits that they had worn for more than two weeks—wondered at the possibility.

The fighting on the morning of April 4 had been furious. Almost from the time that Second Tanks had rumbled across the Line of Departure about six miles west of Al Aziziya on Highway 6, the unit and those who followed were caught up in constant combat. The enemy was a mixed bag of remnants of the Al Nida Division of the Republican Guard combined with Fedayeen and Jihadi fighters from all over the Middle East. Casualties had been heavy; there were scores of wounded Marines and several dead. The enemy was tenacious and clever. A Syrian combatant hiding underwater in a canal had emerged to ambush and kill Corporal Erik Silva. Silva's comrades bayoneted and shot the Syrian to death.

Now, only ten or so miles from the edge of Baghdad, the fighting was especially intense.

"We had spent the night before in an Iraqi school," remembered CH-46E pilot Major Michael "Gogo" Gogolin of HMM-268. "It was interesting. I remember that all of their Saddam stuff—the paintings and banners and flags and such—was all kept in a special closet, sort of like we would have stored holiday decorations back home. It was obvious that they only brought it out for extraordinary occasions."

On this morning Gogolin and Major Michael "Flash" O'Neil— the commander of the other aircraft in his section—were briefing with the RCT-5 staff at their headquarters on Highway 6. The southeastern edge of Baghdad was only twenty miles or so to the northwest. Colonel Joe Dunford, the RCT commander, passed his plan for the day. The bulk of his Marines were already heavily engaged and advancing, and he intended to move his headquarters by midmorning. Following Dunford's brief, the two pilots returned to where the rest of their crews were waiting with the two aircraft. Gogolin recounted:

"We were in the middle of a cup of coffee awhile later when we got the word that there was something happening farther up the road and that we needed to get ready immediately." Gogolin and O'Neil grabbed their charts and other planning material and hurried back to the RCT headquarters while their crews prepared the aircraft for the mission.

"We were given a grid location, a frequency, and a callsign," Gogolin recalled. "They didn't have much else to pass other than that there were Marines in contact and casualties that needed to be moved." After the two pilots raced back to their helicopters, it was a matter of only minutes before the two birds were spun up and readied for takeoff. After a quick update from the RCT, O'Neil—the section leader that day—led the flight airborne. At seventy-five feet and 120 knots the pair of CH-46Es, callsign Grizzly 40, paralleled the divided highway while offset slightly to the northeast. An excerpt from the justification for the award the crews earned that day reads as follows:

Approximately three minutes into the flight the section avoided a possible missile launch from a building on the southwest side of Highway 6. A tank round that was fired from below on Highway 6 simultaneously destroyed the building.

Gogolin and his copilot were flying just behind and to the right of O'Neil's ship. "There was a big flash from the top of one of the buildings to our left. Major O'Neil broke hard right across my front and we followed." After wheeling over into an aggressive turn, their rotor blades clawing at the air, the two aircraft continued to head away from the explosion at only a few feet above the ground. After about fifteen seconds they started a turn to the northwest and eased back alongside the highway.

The route was littered with numerous destroyed enemy antiaircraft artillery pieces, armored personnel carriers, and artillery pieces from RCT-5's advance. There were numerous power lines ranging from 30 feet to 200 feet along Highway 6. The visibility was hindered due to numerous large black plumes of smoke created from oil trenches set on fire along Highway 6. Both aircraft expended multiple flares on ingress. . . .

It was obvious that there had been recent fighting along the route. "We were dodging in and out of plumes of oil smoke," explained Gogolin, "and could see all sorts of Iraqi equipment that had been shot up or abandoned. And although the visibility was fairly good that day, the smoke made things a little difficult in places." This was especially true because both sides of the road were fairly built up with homes as well as industrial buildings. Power lines and light posts further cluttered the highway. The crews kept a sharp lookout for bypassed enemy fighters—a well-aimed RPG or a shoulder-fired SAM could bring down one or both of their ships.

A series of sharp flashes and a thin wisp of smoke marked the right side of O'Neil's aircraft as the gunner engaged an Iraqi BMP with his .50-caliber machine gun. An instant later Gogolin spotted a corresponding set of flashes as the rounds slammed into the enemy vehicle. Below them the road was clear, but the fliers could still see civilians watching them from doorways and windows—no doubt alarmed at the clatter of their rotors and the occasional bursts of gunfire.

Fox Company, Second Battalion, Fifth Marines—attached to Second Tanks—was ambushed at an intersection along a route that led into Baghdad. Unknown to the unit's Marines, the sector they were fighting in held a huge cache of enemy ammunition and arms. In the exchange of fire there was a spectacular explosion and the company's first sergeant, Edward Smith, was wounded in the head.

Smith, thirty-eight, was a twenty-year Marine whose retirement had been put on hold by the service. Despite a promising new career as a police officer he had taken his orders to Iraq in stride; he was proud to serve his country and his fellow Marines. Now he was on the ground mortally wounded. His fellow Marines worked feverishly

under fire to save him, but their heroic efforts were not enough. The
wound was too severe. First Sergeant Smith died and left behind a
wife and three children.

The flying that Grizzly 40 flight was doing, especially right down a
major urban highway, would have gotten them jailed back in the
States. In Iraq it was how they survived; their low altitude thwarted
most SAMs, and their speed made them a difficult target for small-
arms or RPG fire. Nevertheless it was hard, loud, and busy work.
"Somewhere along the way we had let ourselves get left behind on
the radio during one of the frequency changes," Gogolin remembered. "As we got closer to the LZ I knew it was too quiet on the frequency and I had no idea what was going on." Using their second
radio, some mental gymnastics, and the "number of the day," the
flight managed to get together on the same frequency as the FAC who
was running the landing zone.

"Pita was the callsign of the FAC," Gogolin said. "He talked our
eyes onto the LZ as we approached from the southeast. There were
vehicles all over the place, but south of a major road intersection
there was a cluster of HMMWVs in the right-hand lanes not far from
where an Abrams tank was parked in the median." O'Neil swung the
flight across the highway to the west then banked back around and
approached the LZ from the north. He realized almost immediately
that the zone was too small for both ships. Goosenecked light poles
reached out from the median, and power lines ran along both sides of
the road. O'Neil sent Gogolin to orbit over a field to the southwest
while he took on the first load of casualties.

At the intersection, RCT-5's commanding officer was in contact
with enemy forces from three HMMWVs circled in the center
of the intersection. He and his Marines covered the section's approach into the LZ. The landing zone had 30- to 50-foot power
lines along both sides of the road, friendly tanks approaching
the intersection from the southeast along Highway 6 and light

poles in the center of the road on the northwest side of the intersection. The section received enemy small-arms fire as they
entered the southwest side of Highway 6. . . .

Gogolin hooked away from O'Neil, dropped his aircraft down to
only twenty-five feet, and started an orbit. The field was lined by
buildings on three sides and was only about 150 yards in length;
hemmed in as he was, he could maintain no more than about ninety
knots. "I tried to make us as difficult a target as possible. After a few
orbits I decided to mix it up a little and we started flying figure eights.
When we'd flown a few of those I just started turning the aircraft in an
unpredictable profile." As tiring as it was keeping up the crazy gyrations in the constricted confines of the field, Gogolin decided against
simply setting down. The stationary helicopter would have been an
easy target, and, separated from the Marine-controlled highway as
they were, there was no guarantee that help would come in time if
they were hit.

"Every once in a while," Gogolin recalled, "we'd pop up to about
fifty feet or so and peek over the buildings to see if Major O'Neil was
still in the LZ."

Grizzly 40 was on deck for eight minutes as the casualties were
loaded onto the aircraft. The crew of Grizzly 40 evacuated four
urgent, three priority, and one routine from the initial LZ. There
was numerous small-arms, crew-served weapons, and Rocket
Propelled Grenades being fired around the LZ to the northeast
side of the intersection. Grizzly 40 departed the LZ. . . .

"I climbed just a little bit and was able to see Major O'Neil's aft
rotor as he started to lift off," remembered Gogolin. O'Neil got airborne and headed south with his load of wounded Marines while
Gogolin brought his ship out of the field and arced around to approach the LZ from the north. "Initially they had told us that there
were nine casualties," explained Gogolin. "I knew that Major O'Neil
had taken eight and figured that there was one more left for us."

Gogolin's crew chief had the corpsman operate his .50-caliber machine gun while he helped guide Gogolin and the copilot clear of the different obstacles and into the Landing Zone. "It was tight," Gogolin recalled, "very much like an approach at the ship except with power lines, lampposts, and buildings." And shooting. Although he was too busy with getting into the Landing Zone to pay much attention, the RCT was still fighting for control of the intersection to his north.

After a delicately executed approach that required him to sidestep into the zone, Gogolin put the aircraft down. Immediately the crew's corpsman leapt out of the aircraft to coordinate getting the remaining casualty aboard. But there was none; all of the casualties had been evacuated by O'Neil's crew. Gogolin recalled: "I got on the radio with Pita and he confirmed that there were no more injured. Rather, there was a KIA [Killed in Action] to our north and east along another MSR and they wanted us to recover the body. We weren't on the deck even ninety seconds. I got the corpsman back aboard and we lifted off and headed north."

In the meantime O'Neil was retracing the flight's earlier route back toward RCT-5's headquarters. There, procedures directed that they would transfer the wounded Marines to a pair of waiting Army UH-60 Black Hawk "Dust Off" helicopters that would relay them the rest of the way to the "Good Hope" Shock Trauma Platoon south of the Tigris River on Highway 1. On arrival, though, the UH-60s weren't able to accomplish the transfer, and O'Neil lifted off again and sprinted south. In the rear of his aircraft the crew tended to their regular duties as well as taking care of their stricken comrades.

The casualty evacuation corpsmen worked diligently in the back of the aircraft providing life support services on the urgent care casualties and priority care casualties during the 35–45-minute, 80-mile transit to "Good Hope." The injuries included a gunshot wound to the jaw and neck, another through the neck, an abdominal wound, a chest wound, a back wound, and two more gun shot wounds to Marines' hands. Their performance during a highly stressful evolution provided the injured Marines with a calming effect that had a direct impact on their survival.

Anxious to get to where Fox Company was still engaged at the very front of RCT-5's advance, Gogolin set off in a dash straight up Highway 6. They were headed for the heart of Baghdad. And it was the wrong way. "I had gotten confused about the grid location and my copilot made a good catch and got us turned around." Because the new landing zone was still "hot," Gogolin and his crew were assigned an armed escort: Deadly 33, a section of AH-1W Cobras. After reversing course back to the south and then turning northeast at the contested intersection, Gogolin and his crew were on their way.

One of the Deadly 33 Cobras pushed out in front of the CH-46E slightly offset to Gogolin's right, while the other covered him from behind and to the left. Gogolin kept the aircraft exactly over the road at only twenty-five feet. "Pita had warned us to stay over the MSR—that the enemy was still fighting from positions on either side." As fast as he was pushing it, the rattling rumble of Gogolin's ship no doubt startled the drivers of the Marine vehicles that he overtook from behind—only barely clearing their rooflines.

Major Gogolin flew at 25 feet above the ground and 120 knots over the HMMWVs on the road between 30-foot power lines on both sides of the road, having to bunt over several sets of power lines that crossed perpendicular to the road. There was a HMMWV shooting TOW missiles and others shooting .50-caliber machine guns into the buildings on the left side of the road. Deadly 33 broke off and began to prosecute targets in the trees to the left of the main MSR as Major Gogolin arrived at the LZ.

"Pita had briefed us that the unit with the KIA was located on the road near a smokestack," Gogolin said, "and it wasn't very long before we spotted it as well as a group of HMMWVs on the road nearby."

The LZ that had been laid out was small—sixty by two hundred feet—and circumscribed by power lines on all four sides. But as undersized as the zone was, the immediate vicinity was still in contention, and Gogolin didn't want to take the luxury of slowing down for a more fastidious by-the-book approach. Doing so would make the ship easier to shoot down. Instead he reduced power and at the same time brought the nose of the aircraft up while holding the rear down. In this cocked-up attitude, with the belly of the helicopter acting as a huge speed brake, Gogolin slowed the aircraft from 120 knots to almost nothing very quickly.

There was some risk to the technique, however. "If I started the maneuver too early, I wouldn't have enough energy to clear the near wires," he remembered. "On the other hand, if I started it too late, there was a good chance I would have flown us into the far set of wires, or even into the group of vehicles and Marines beyond."

Nevertheless Gogolin and his copilot brought the ship in perfectly. Immediately a group of four Marines hurried toward the helicopter with the body of First Sergeant Smith strapped to a stretcher. Their leader, their friend, he was gone now. "After less than a minute my crew chief called up 'good to go,' " Gogolin remembered. He checked that the area around him was clear and applied maximum power. Once clear of the wires he lifted the aircraft away from the embattled Marines and swung back around in a right-hand turn to the southwest and back over the road. The two gunships that made up Deadly 33 joined in escort, positioned at his ten and two o'clock. At the intersection with Highway 6 the Cobras detached to engage a target. Gogolin made a hard left turn and pointed himself, his crew, and the body of First Sergeant Smith southeast away from the heaviest fighting.

> . . . displayed extraordinary courage under fire, exercised unhesitating life-saving actions in the face of enemy fire, and demonstrated superior tactical airmanship.

It was one of the deadliest days of the war, with several dead and scores of wounded. That more of the injured didn't die was due in part to the aggressive and skillful flying of the CH-46E crews who evacuated them back to safety.

He'd been a warrior for more than twenty-five years. War killed and maimed. But like many aviators, Guts Robling had never really been close to the killing and the maiming. Airmen kill from a distance. They kill well, and they kill a lot, but they rarely see the bodies and the blood and the wounds. Rather, these gruesome sights and experiences are the burden of the ground warrior.

The tent at the Three Rivers FARP sheltered a Level II Casualty Treatment Center. Whereas Level I care includes first aid on the battlefield, Level II care is more intensive. Staffed with physicians, nurses, and other medical care professionals, one of the Level II facility's objectives is to treat life-threatening injuries so that the wounded can be stabilized and transported to a permanent hospital for more complete care.

Robling was at the Three Rivers FARP to help troubleshoot part of the tactical operation. There was always something that needed attention. The fighting on the approach to Baghdad was getting more fearsome, and there had been significant casualties. Some of those casualties were being treated in the tent he was about to enter.

This side trip to see what was going on with the Level II folks was almost an afterthought—made more out of curiosity than anything else. "I wasn't ready for what I saw when I stepped through that tent flap," he recounted. "It was like something out of an old M*A*S*H episode. There were wounded all over the place. Surgeons and nurses were working frantically. Right at my feet there was a Marine sprawled out on a poncho—he was missing a leg. There was blood all over the place. And it wasn't like he was being neglected; he was just in line behind other Marines who needed treatment worse than he did."

Robling didn't tarry long inside. At that moment his presence wasn't doing anything for anyone and he felt more like an intruder than anything else. After making his exit and taking a few moments to digest what he had seen, he realized that the wing played an important supporting role in what was taking place inside that tent that very instant. If not for the efforts of the wing's helicopter pilots, many of those wounded Marines would be dead Marines—Marines who would have no use for a Level II Casualty Treatment Center.

31

Lost Heroes

Lieutenant Colonel Steve "Woodman" Heywood fell into his cot at the main helicopter base at Ali Al Salem in Kuwait. As the Commanding Officer of HMLA-267, he was apprehensive. Less than two weeks into the war twenty of his twenty-six aircraft—a combination of Cobras and Hueys—had been hit by enemy fire. Through skill or luck or both, not a single one of his crews had been injured. Nevertheless, as much as he wanted the squadron's good fortune to hold, he knew that the odds were against it. This was especially so in light of the fact that the Coalition was quickly moving to encircle Baghdad.

In fact, six HMLA aircraft had been hit that very day, April 4. Only several hours earlier two Cobras had been shot up so badly that they barely made it back to friendly lines before they had to put down along an advancing column of ground forces. Essentially the Iraqis had shot them down, although they'd made a half-assed job of it. Making sure that the crews were unharmed and arranging for the repair and recovery of the two ships had consumed much of Heywood's day, although after a week of chasing after the same tasks it was quickly becoming "business as usual."

He was dog-tired that night and due to go back out on combat operations the following day. After a short time, he was asleep.

The three Cobras rumbled north above the desert and through the dark murk that made up the sky over Iraq in the very first few minutes of April 5. The blackness that was the ground below was marked by the bright orange flares of burning wreckage, and by bursts of occasional gunfire. In the distance a refinery burned more brilliantly than the rest. All of it blossomed and flashed in the grainy green of the pilots' night-vision goggles as they flew toward areas where Marines were engaged with the enemy at the very approaches to the Iraqi capital.

There was another bright explosion on the ground, but this one was different. Major Andrew Groenke, the flight leader, called over the radio for his two wingmen to check in.

Only one of the crews answered.

One of the pilots who made up that crew was Captain James "Pinky" Finnegan. It was Finnegan who had written about the emotion that he and his friends had felt as the *Dubuque* steamed out of sunny San Diego Bay with them aboard more than two months earlier on January 17.

"It was shortly after midnight when my cell phone rang and woke me up," Heywood remembered. "It was Major John Wilson over at the MAG and he didn't have good news. There was a Cobra down near Baghdad, and it looked like it was one of mine." After pulling on his flight suit and lacing into a pair of boots Heywood quickly made his way over to the headquarters tent.

"Information was already streaming in," he recalled. State-of-the-art information technology on the battlefield was no longer just a glossy advertisement in a defense magazine; it had become a reality in the thick of combat. "Very accurate facts were coming in very quickly via Microsoft Chat from units in the field," he remembered.

"The basics were that one of the crews had gone down and that there was a fireball. The rest of the flight had circled the crash site, but there had been no radio calls indicating that anyone was alive."

Heywood had previously been in units that had lost crews, but not during combat and not while he had been the Commanding Officer. He knew that the next few days would be some of the most difficult of his life. "The most important thing I needed to do right that moment was get word back to the wives and families as quickly as I could." This was crucial because technology and journalistic insensitivity combined to make certain that bad news traveled fast. Another squadron, HMLA-169, had lost three Marines in a Huey crash a few days earlier. Secretive word began to filter back to the wives about who *hadn't* been killed. Those families who hadn't received surreptitious phone calls or e-mails went through a horrible hell of waiting until the official notification took place.

"We called back and passed the details to the notification team," Heywood recounted. The Marine Corps, during peacetime and war, has specially trained personnel called Casualty Assistance Calls Officers (CACOs) standing by to notify the next of kin in the event that a Marine is killed or seriously injured. These personnel often include chaplains and senior officers—and usually the wives of the senior officers. This was particularly difficult as the spouses were part of the Marine Corps in the sense that they usually had many years of experience because of their association with their husbands, but they still had no official role or authority. In this case Heywood's wife, Rosanna, went with the team to take on some of the dreadful burden. It was a horrible, life-wrenching task that shook the strongest men and women.

The two dead men were Captain Travis A. Ford of Ogallala, Nebraska, and Captain Benjamin Sammis of Rehoboth, Massachusetts. Both were married. Ford had a two-year-old daughter. "These were both outstanding officers and Marines," Heywood said. "Travis was the classic, stoic, hardworking midwestern kid. Ben was a little more outgoing and animated—he was one of our WTIs [Weapons and Tactics Instructors]. Together they made up a great crew and they both had a lot of friends." By now morning had arrived and Heywood had his sergeant major, Phil Freed, bring the squadron together for a formation; he needed to pass the word.

Three months earlier, during the transit out to the Persian Gulf and then again just before the war started, Heywood had briefed the squadron to be prepared for this very eventuality. They were going to war, and no matter how capable the enemy was, or was not, his men—and women—could hardly hope to come out of the coming conflict without taking casualties. It was to be expected and they needed to be prepared. Now it had happened.

"After the sergeant major formed the squadron, I put them at ease and ordered them to gather around me. I told them as much as I knew—that we had just lost two good warriors. And I reminded them of that lecture I had given them on the way over, and that as painful as our loss was, it wasn't unexpected. And I told them that they should be prepared for more. We talked about how it was okay to grieve but at the same time they needed to stay focused—we had a war to fight. Working on the flight line was still a dangerous job. Flying missions was still a dangerous job. Everything we were doing was dangerous, and there were plenty of ways to get hurt if a person didn't give 100 percent of his attention to his work. Most important, I reminded them that we were closing on Baghdad and that the fighting would get worse before it got better. Now more than ever I needed them at their very best."

Talking to the troops was difficult. Writing letters to the families was heartrending and perhaps the most difficult thing he had done in his life. The letters were private and not something that Heywood wanted to recount.

There now were myriad details to attend to. "By now it had become obvious that I wasn't going back out on operations for a few days, and I rescheduled Captain Al Grinalds and his division to go out in place of mine," Heywood said. "After flying and fighting hard during the previous couple of days he was already out on the flight line getting ready to go again. He had been very close to Ben Sammis, and the family asked that he write a eulogy to be read at the service that was scheduled for back home." Heywood had a difficult decision to make. "I felt horrible," he remembered. "I was pulled between my loyalty and sense of obligation to Ben and his family, and by my responsibility to Al as his commanding officer."

The commander made his way out to the flight line, where he found Grinalds already in the cockpit of his Cobra. "It was awful. Here the poor guy had just returned from combat and I was sending him right back out to get shot at and to kill people. He'd lost his good buddy to boot. And then I dumped this load on him." Grinalds, an exceptional officer, took it in good stride and promised Heywood that he'd pen a memorial to his fallen friend sometime during the next couple of days.

More information continued to come in from the crash site. The aircraft had fallen near the town of Al Aziziyah, near the Tigris River, southeast of Baghdad. By now it had been secured by headquarters personnel from the First Marine Division—they were waiting for the wreckage to cool before they attempted to recover the bodies. "We learned that Travis and Ben hadn't been shot down—they'd flown into a radio tower," Heywood recounted. "Whether or not they had reacted to enemy fire and had accidentally turned into the tower, or had just been flying straight and level when they had hit, was unknown." The structure had been camouflaged—painted the same tan color as the surrounding sand. In the night it had been almost impossible to see. Still, the crash had been a very near thing. The tower had been 394 feet tall, and the Cobra had struck it at the 370-foot mark. "They lost about three feet of rotor blade, and it looked as if they tried to control their crash by turning into the wind. It probably just wasn't doable."

It was late that day before the bodies were brought back to Kuwait and Heywood was faced with more difficult issues. "I had to send escorts back with the bodies. Again, I was torn in a dozen different directions. Treating the remains with all the compassion, honor, and dignity that they deserved was a foremost consideration. And an escort was absolutely essential for that. But we were still fighting a war—right that very instant we were flying combat ops and now I had to give up two pilots as escorts. And of course the pilots I chose were also conflicted—they wanted to honor their buddies, but they wanted to fight, too."

In the end Heywood sent Captain Aaron Marx to escort Sammis's body, and First Lieutenant Brian Grant to escort Ford's remains. "Those young men did a tremendous job. They traveled around the world to be available to the families in order to answer questions and to help them through their grieving. You can just picture how the emotions must have been running. I'm proud of how such young men acted with such wisdom and understanding. When I heard back from the next of kin about how Marx and Grant gave so completely of themselves, it made me very proud—and glad of the decision I had made."

Personal effects also had to be gathered, packaged, and shipped. The downed fliers' friends completed this duty with care and reverence. However, receiving the personal items that were recovered from the wreckage was a more delicate task—one undertaken by the commander himself. "It bothers you . . . to handle the wallet, or helmet bag, or whatever another person had with him when he was killed. It's something you'll never forget. In this instance all of it was burned in the crash—even the pistols. Those I had to return to the armory even though they were useless."

Aside from letters to the wives, there were letters that needed to be written and sent to the parents. And of course it took Heywood time to write exactly what he wanted to say to each of them. Even then, despite the effort he took and the emotions he spent, Heywood couldn't help but feel that the letters were inadequate for the loss he knew the families felt. All of this took time from Heywood and his duties as the squadron commander. Still, he felt that treating the families and the tragedy with all the dignity and caring he could muster was what was most important.

Technology has made the job of dealing with casualties much more difficult for the commander. During World War II, for example, there was no instantaneous communication with the next of kin. They might not know for weeks that a loved one was killed or missing.

And seldom, if ever, were the bodies of aviators recovered. If they were, they weren't sent home—there was no need for escorts. The fallen were usually buried in the land where they fell. It says much for the preeminence of the American military that the nation now can afford to honor her fallen servicemen in such a manner.

It was four days after the crash before Heywood was able to even fly past the wreckage. It wasn't that there was anything he could do or find that hadn't been done or found already. Rather, he felt it was his duty to put his eyes on the place where his Marines had died. Already the unit that had secured the area had moved on. Although Coalition forces had fought through several days earlier, they hadn't stayed or mopped up. The vicinity was still considered dangerous. After flying over the site, peering down at the tower, and trying to imagine the last few seconds of Ford's and Sammis's lives, he had seen all that he wanted. The practical side of him noted those elements that would cause him to adjust his unit's future tactics.

It is impossible to quickly accept the sudden loss of a comrade or loved one—habits and expectations die only in fits and convulsions over time. It hurts to remember and it takes time before a person stops expecting to see the lost face among the rest. Still, a squadron at war has little time to reflect and mourn. Each individual handles losses differently, and life just goes on. Eventually the relationship with the lost friend or loved one is cleaned and cataloged and put in a special place in the heart from which it can be retrieved and reviewed and loved and wondered at from time to time.

The squadron held a memorial service on April 7. Heywood returned to flying combat operations on April 9. On that day he met up with Al Grinalds; Grinalds still had not written Sammis's eulogy. Heywood remembered: "At the Three Rivers FARP I met up with Al. The poor guy had been flying almost continuously. When I caught up with him he had just finished a series of sorties where he had been shooting off his weapons as quickly as they could be loaded. He apologized for not having written the eulogy, but the memorial service was scheduled for later that day back in the States. We chatted for a bit, and then I sat with him while he put pen to paper. When he finished we found a computer out there in the field and e-mailed it home. It was magnificent—after the service Grinalds was told that it could not have been more perfect."

Heywood spent the next six days flying combat operations—killing Iraqis. Taking lives, despite the fact that they were enemy lives, meant something different to him now.

32

The Pioneer

"It's a small point but it's one that really got my Marines fired up," recalled Lieutenant Colonel Scott Mykleby, the commanding officer of the VMU-1 "Watchdogs," one of the two Marine Corps UAV squadrons deployed for the war. "What happened too often is that we would run a great mission and the video would show up on CNN or some other news channel. That was fantastic, but invariably it would be described as having come from the Air Force's Predator UAV."

Mykleby's Marines' sensitivities were victimized by the ignorance of the media and the steamroller that was the Predator's public relations effort. In fact the UAV, or Unmanned Aerial Vehicle, that stood the Marine Corps in such good stead throughout the campaign was the RQ-2B Pioneer, a modification of a design that was first fielded in 1986. In unmanned aircraft terms, 1986 is practically the ice age, but a series of improvements and a lot of hard work have kept the Pioneer at the forefront of tactical UAV operations.

* * *

The Marine Corps became serious about UAVs during the early 1980s. The simple, relatively inexpensive platforms available then offered great potential at low cost without putting Marines at risk. The early intent was for them to scout ahead of ground units to discover and coordinate fires onto emergent targets. For instance, upon discovering an enemy tank column, the UAV operators could fix its position, then coordinate with friendly assets—artillery, air, or naval gunfire—to destroy it. Indeed, equipped with a camera capable of providing day and night imagery, these early UAVs promised a very flexible surveillance and reconnaissance capability.

The Pioneer design actually evolved from an even earlier Israeli aircraft. It combines a pusher propeller, a single two-piston, two-stroke engine, twin tail booms, and a conventional wing, to carry an Electro Optical/Infra Red (EO/IR) video camera in the nose section. Small, it measures barely fourteen feet in length, while its wings span just less than seventeen feet; it tips the scales at 450 pounds. The simple engine/fixed-pitch propeller arrangement delivers a cruise speed of seventy knots while a full load of fuel can keep the aircraft aloft for a maximum of four to five hours depending on how hard it is flown. Although the aircraft can execute a conventional runway takeoff, it is normally hurled airborne with a pneumatic launcher that looks like a cross between a heavy rail and a catapult. Rocket Assisted Takeoff (RATO) units can be affixed to improve performance and reliability; these are nearly always preferred. Although a simple net system was used by the Navy to recover its aircraft back aboard ship, the Marine Corps nearly always lands its Pioneers using the aircraft's tailhook and a set of cross-runway arresting gear pendants.

The Army and the Marine Corps used the system extensively during Desert Storm in 1991 to provide battlefield surveillance and reconnaissance, as well as post-strike Battle Damage Assessments. Launched by the Navy from the battleships *Wisconsin* and *Missouri*, the Pioneers also delivered invaluable service as naval gunfire spotting platforms. In fact, there was a well-publicized incident that had Iraqi troops surrendering to a Navy Pioneer—a UAV first. Since that time the Army and Navy have retired their systems, while the Marine

Corps has implemented improvements to its own and intends to operate them until at least 2009.

Major General James Amos, the 3rd MAW commander, knew that he wanted the capability his VMU squadrons could bring, but he also knew that the normal operating and logistics footprint to support the UAVs was outsized—more than he could afford to lift into theater. "Essentially," Mykleby said, "he told us to do what we had to do in order to trim our size so that we could still give the MEF commander the capability he wanted, but with the ability to stay on the move so that we could support the division as it advanced." The VMU-1 Marines did just that. They developed a new scheme of employment and a revised squadron structure that in combination was dubbed "Scoot Tactics." It provided a robust tactical competency while enabling the Marines to break down their system in less than four hours, convoy it through hostile areas, and then quickly set it back up for operations—again, in less than four hours. And it worked well. VMU-1 flew a record number of flights during the campaign at a rate that was more than seven times the normal pace.

After arriving in theater in early February, VMU-1 started flight operations out of Tactical Assembly Area Coyote in north-central Kuwait. Their missions by doctrine were reconnaissance, surveillance, target acquisition, indirect fire adjustment, Battlefield Damage Assessment (BDA), and rear area security support. After a few sorties to unlimber the systems, VMU-1 Pioneers began operating in earnest to support OSW. Information was also collected to support the coming campaign—to include a detailed reconnaissance of southern Iraq.

The camera that the small aircraft carries is perhaps the heart of the system's capability. An Israeli device, the POP-200 sensor provides color optical video imagery for daylight sorties and infrared imagery for nighttime operations. "The fidelity of the optics was pretty good," said Mykleby. "We were able to count individual road wheels on a tank from more than seven kilometers [approximately four miles]."

Nevertheless, it wasn't road wheels that VMU-1's imagery analysts were counting during a daytime sortie on March 20. On that date, the start of the offensive was still scheduled for March 23. "Sergeant Matthew Venaleck, one of our imagery analysts, observed several wellheads on fire in the Rumaylah oil fields," Mykleby recounted. "One of the chief objectives—all the way up to the White House— was preventing an economic and ecological disaster similar to what had happened when the Iraqis torched the Kuwaiti oil fields during Desert Storm." Certain that the wellheads were afire, VMU-1 immediately transmitted the alarming information to higher headquarters, where it evoked an instant response. The military equivalent of an *Are you sure?* immediately came back down to the unit. There was no doubt. Venaleck quickly reassessed the imagery and confirmed that the Iraqis were destroying their own oil fields. This crucial piece of information—from a Marine UAV unit—was a key part of the decision that started the ground campaign the following day. This two-day head start likely saved much of the region's environment from the same sort of calamity as the 1991 catastrophe—a tragedy that has left lingering impacts throughout the Persian Gulf.

Once the war was under way, the nature of the Pioneer's contributions became more tactical. The crews became especially adept at ranging out ahead of the advancing RCTs, finding targets, and then coordinating artillery strikes against them; these were called hunter-killer missions. Typical was a sortie on March 27 in the vicinity of An Nasiriyah. Two separate batteries of Iraqi Type 59-1 130-millimeter artillery guns were detected by a VMU-1 Pioneer. Using the system's GPS, the UAV crew quickly fixed the locations of the two batteries and called for a fire mission from the Eleventh Marines' M198 guns. In short order the heavy Marine weapons delivered several barrages of Dual Purpose Improved Conventional Munitions that devastated the Iraqi batteries.

The nature of the Pioneer system, with its ability to provide real-time corrections for friendly fires—without placing Marines at risk— made it particularly useful. Further, the capability to capture and transmit live images of a target being destroyed—also called real-time

BDA, or Battle Damage Assessment—made it the darling of the MEF's G-2, or intelligence, cell. The video from the system was so detailed that the imagery analysts could not only confirm the damage or destruction of a target but also count the wounded and the dead. Mykleby recalled: "We got so efficient at finding targets and coordinating fires against those targets that we often received priority from I MEF when it came to the allocation of artillery fire missions."

This hadn't always been the case. "Back in the States," recounted Mykleby, "we were kind of the half-forgotten, ugly stepsister. The joke within the squadron about the way we were treated by the rest of the Marine Corps was always 'VMU? VMU who?' But once they saw what we could do, they couldn't get enough of us." This scramble for support from both VMU-1 and its sister unit, VMU-2, created some conflict up and down the chain of command. The units technically belonged to 3rd MAW and as such were tasked via the ATO just as any other squadron would have been. However, because their day-to-day missions invariably had them flying just in front of the many different components that made up the First Marine Division, various staff elements from both the division and the MEF often yielded to the temptation to try to task the UAVs directly. "We would be in the middle of executing one mission," recalled Mykleby, "and then some staff officer—who was in no way connected to the current sortie— would send voice or e-mail tasking telling us that his particular mission was now more important. This happened all the time; people would try to retask us right in the middle of a mission without coordinating through the TACC." Mykleby's unit couldn't comply with these "requests out of nowhere," and it created quite a bit of friction when attempts were made to get the rogue requesters to route their requirements through proper channels. Ultimately the pressure for support outside established doctrine became a real distraction. "There was a lot of fighting over us," said Mykleby, "and people from outside 3rd MAW seemed to forget that the MEF had other reconnaissance and surveillance assets available—such as the F/A-18s and AV-Bs."

Indeed, the MEF's G-2 personnel became so enamored with the UAVs that they tried to insert themselves into the maintenance and supply issues that the VMU squadrons dealt with on a daily basis; the staff wanted to ensure the maximum availability of the system. This was wholly beyond their purview, but it further illustrates how important UAV support had become to the MEF. The capabilities of the system and its importance to the ground commanders remained a very emotional issue, and ownership and tasking were never wholly settled to everyone's satisfaction.

The two VMU units became so adept at destroying emerging targets that their presence alone often was enough to neutralize Iraqi units. On March 28, near Suq Ash, a Pioneer discovered an Iraqi D-30 artillery battery in the process of displacing. As the UAV got closer the Marine operators could tell exactly when the buzz of the aircraft's unique two-stroke engine reached the ground; the faces of the Iraqi soldiers immediately turned skyward. The crew of one Armored Personnel Carrier dismounted and began to fire toward the UAV. Having no success, they clambered back into their vehicle and raced out of the area. Recognizing the Pioneer for what it was, the remaining Iraqis—those who were quick enough—climbed into whatever transportation was close at hand and also cleared out. Essentially, nothing more than the sight and sound of the single UAV had rendered the Iraqi battery useless. Regardless, a Marine artillery strike—cued by the Pioneer crew—followed almost immediately, destroying the guns and the remaining Iraqis.

"There was another incident during late March when things were hot in An Nasiriyah," Mykleby recalled. "On this particular evening one of our crews spotted a group of Iraqi paramilitary fighters assembling on a street. There was no real way to get at them with aircraft or artillery right at that moment so the crew brought the aircraft down to about seven hundred feet and flew right over their heads. They scattered, and didn't get back together that night." As the campaign progressed this type of reaction by the Iraqis became more and more the rule rather than the exception.

On April 5 the Marines of VMU-1 worked with artillery units of the Eleventh Marines to accomplish a military first. Mission commander Major Sal Cepeda and his crew discovered an Iraqi MIG-23 fighter parked on Al Rashid Air Base on the southeastern outskirts of Baghdad. After calculating an accurate geo-location, Cepeda coordinated a fire mission with the Eleventh Marines. With the Pioneer UAV orbiting a short distance away, the VMU-1 Marines watched their screens and waited. Only a moment or two later they saw the Iraqi jet explode in flames as the big rounds from the Marine M198s found their mark. It was the first-ever kill of an aircraft by a UAV–artillery combination.

The nature of the campaign kept the unit moving constantly; it was ceaselessly on the heels of the First Marine Division as the race for Baghdad gathered momentum. In total, from the time the campaign began until April 15, VMU-1 operated from six different locations—mostly sections of road or captured Iraqi air bases. These movements demanded the most of every Marine. Aside from the work and skill that went into breaking down and packing the aircraft, ground control vans, and various support equipment, the squadron's Marines and Sailors (VMU-1 had a small contingent of Navy personnel) had to move all of the common logistics material that every combat unit needs to operate: food, water, ammunition, and, in their case, 100LL AVGAS for the UAVs. Before each move Mykelby conducted a thorough tactical convoy briefing that included everything from the scheme of maneuver to the preplanned CAS targets along the route. Briefing complete, all vehicles were topped off with fuel, radio checks were accomplished, and weapons and ammo were inspected. "I was really proud of those Marines and Sailors," Mykleby recounted. "By the end of the campaign, they became so adept at performing the tactical breakdown, movement, and setup procedure that we were routinely able to tactically displace within two and a half hours of receiving orders. Once we stopped, we were able to set up and get a UAV back in the air, again, in less than two and a half hours. This was an all-hands effort that came about only after a lot of training and experience."

Of course, moving the squadron through hostile territory without losing people or equipment was a feat in itself. As has been described before, the Marine RCTs often punched through an area without clearing it of the enemy. Units that followed often had to fight their way through the same territory. "We made ourselves as fearsome a target as possible," said Mykleby. "All of our squadron vehicles were hardened with sandbags to protect against land mines and RPGs. Everyone rode facing outboard with M16s at the ready, and several of our larger vehicles were sandbagged and armed with .50-caliber machine guns and the smaller 7.62-caliber M240G machine guns. Each Marine had been trained in his own specialty, but foremost, each and every one of them was a rifleman. We looked formidable—during all of our movements the enemy never chose to engage us." A testament to VMU-1's ability to execute its recently developed tactics was the fact that the unit traveled more than fifteen hundred self-escorted convoy miles and still—working in concert with VMU-2—the RCTs rarely went without UAV coverage.

Although it executed its hunter-killer missions primarily with artillery units, VMU-1 worked with F/A-18s and AV-8Bs on occasion as well. During the April 10 battle in Baghdad—the shootout that encompassed the fight for Saddam's palace, as well as the clash at the Imam Abu Hanifah Mosque—Pioneer UAVs flew overhead to help support the CAS effort. Although there are certain airspace challenges associated with operating UAVs and manned aircraft in the same piece of sky, this rarely posed a problem for the Marines. Mykleby remembered: "Most of the time we flew above the helicopter traffic and below the fixed-wing guys, so we were rarely in the way. And for the most part we were fully integrated into the Marine Corps's command and control system. We were also quite often flying in and out of the same forward operating bases that were being used by manned aircraft; these operations posed few, if any, problems."

Iraqi Freedom will probably be marked as the first campaign in which the UAV made major contributions through the whole of the effort. Mykleby, an AH-1W Cobra pilot during most of his career, has little doubt as to the importance of the role that the Marine Corps's own RQ-2B Pioneer system played. "I would state unequivocally that the VMU squadrons proved Pioneer to be an *essential* system, one that was a key contributor to the MEF's many battlefield successes in

Iraq." As to the future, he sees armed UAVs complementing manned aircraft with the ability to not only guide the munitions of other systems, but also to carry their own weapons in the event that a freshly discovered target must be neutralized immediately. "VMU-1 crews, time and again, saw the need for this type of immediate attack capability when fleeting, high-value targets were detected but ultimately escaped because we couldn't get attack aircraft or artillery on them in time."

There can be little doubt that future UAV systems and tactics will add a dimension of warfare only hinted at by the experience gained during the campaign in Iraq.

33

Death on the Diyala

By April 5 the Marines were hard up against Baghdad and looking for a place to enter the city from the east and north. The chief obstacle to their crossing was the Diyala River, which ran from north to south before joining the Tigris in southeastern Baghdad. Although there were two bridges in the southern part of the battlespace that might be usable, those spans were also likely to be heavily defended, and the division wanted the option of crossing from somewhere farther north. Elements of the Army had already raided the Saddam International Airport on the southwest edge of Baghdad, and the Marines were anxious to get into the city from their own area of operations in order to keep the pressure on the Iraqi capital.

Major Randy "Fester" Nash had been an F/A-18 pilot for more than ten years. But on the afternoon of April 5 he was serving as an FAC with Weapons Company, 1st LAR Battalion, RCT-5. Instead of rocketing through the sky in one of the sleek, twin-tailed fighters that he knew so well, he was perched atop an LAV-C2—the command and control variant on the LAV-25 Light Armored Vehicle. From his vantage point on the eastern bank of the Diyala River he looked over the water and scanned the far side for enemy activity. Here, east of Baghdad, the battalion was taking part in the encirclement of the Iraqi capital.

He had received orders for a quick nonflying stint just the previous year and had anticipated that he would be staying close to home in San Diego, but timing and circumstances had dictated otherwise. The buildup for the assault on Iraq started shortly after he had reported aboard Camp Pendleton. Just before the campaign began Nash was given the opportunity to serve as a very senior FAC with a front-line unit. He jumped at the chance.

He remembered that day on the Diyala: "We had been moving most of the night before, and now we were tasked with scouting ahead of the main effort to find a place for the division to cross the river. The Iraqis were sending over sporadic mortar fire from the far side and the company commander, Captain Dave Hudspeth, had ordered his Marines to seek out and engage the enemy while he and the executive officer, First Lieutenant Steve St. John, studied a potential crossing site." From where he sat in the LAV—screened by a canopy of low-hanging palm fronds—Nash listened to the radio net while he kept an eye on the far bank.

The murky water that made up the river stretched about thirty yards across. The banks rose steeply up both sides and were covered with a combination of reeds, high grass, and scrubby palms. A road paralleled the river on the far, or western, side. This landscape was markedly different from the desert topography RCT-5 had traversed in southern Iraq only a week or so earlier.

A motion on the western bank caught Nash's attention. There, just a across the river, a squad-sized element of Iraqi soldiers was patrolling on foot. "These weren't Fedayeen fighters dressed in black, or guys in blue jeans and tennis shoes with AK-47s, these were Republican Guard soldiers in full uniform." Nash caught St. John's attention. "St. John," Nash recalled, "headed up the company's Fire Support Team [FST] and he immediately got a mission under way for the 81-

millimeter mortars." An accurate grid position was passed, and it was only a moment later when a salvo of mortar fire dropped right on top of the enemy patrol. "Five of the Iraqis went down immediately, while the rest ran toward a palm grove. They fired sort of indiscriminately across the river at us while they ran," Nash described.

In the meantime the enlisted Marines assigned to Nash's LAV had quickly formed a fire team and climbed to the top of a bluff overlooking the river. Nash continued to monitor the radio net and kept alert for anything that might require the harder-hitting punch of airpower. At the same time Sergeant Clayton Blankenship from Nash's LAV opened fire on the enemy soldiers who had escaped the mortar barrage. Clayton recalled his shooting: "As I saw them advancing to the main tree line I didn't waste any time putting rounds downrange. I noticed the first three impacts a bit low and adjusted my aim. As I fired again I watched one [Iraqi soldier] fall down immediately, then I waited for the next one to pop up." After a short time Blankenship and the rest of the team had dispatched the remaining enemy soldiers.

Nash tracked the company's fight visually and over the radio. Since the start of the campaign he had controlled several air strikes, and although he was anxious to play a part in this particular clash, he knew that employing any sort of airpower would be overkill in the short, sharp engagements that were going on around him.

It was almost a case of déjà vu when a small white pickup truck drove up, then stopped nearly at the same point where the Iraqi foot patrol had been taken under fire. These small white pickups—usually Toyotas or Nissans—served as modern-day camels for the Iraqis. Ubiquitous, they were used for hauling everything from sheep to melons, but lately they had been carting Fedayeen and mortar rounds. Three Iraqis dressed in civilian garb climbed out of this particular vehicle. When they saw and heard the fighting they rushed back to the cab of the truck, where they each pulled out an AKM assault rifle—a more modern version of the AK-47. Just as the three fighters were stepping away from the truck they were caught up in a volley of fire from one of the Marine LAVs. Nash watched as the explosive 25-millimeter rounds tore into the Iraqis and dropped them where they stood. Another short burst blasted the pickup truck. It subsequently exploded as some sort of inflammable cargo—probably ammunition—caught fire and reached high order.

Still, there was no real need for Nash to call airpower into the fight. He watched the Marines around him use the right tools for the task at hand. To the south of him, only fifteen hundred yards or so, a pair of LAV-ATs (Anti-Tank variants) let loose with a TOW missile at an Iraqi T-72 that was moving toward the engagement. The missile found its mark and turned the enemy tank into a huge fireball that burned and burned as the ammunition inside continued to cook off.

It was just about this time that Nash and some of the other Marines caught sight of a Navy F-14 Tomcat arcing low overhead. Nash checked his Tactical Air Direction frequency and attempted to contact the friendly crew. There was no reply to his repeated calls. Nash recognized the Navy pilot's intent and became anxious as he watched the F-14 circle the area and make another pass over the Marine LAVs. "As a pilot myself I knew that they were trying to figure out if our LAVs were friendly or enemy; they wanted to drop their bombs, and from the air our unit must have looked like a very attractive target." Nash quickly switched through several different frequencies as he tried to establish contact with the F-14 fliers. The tragedy of fratricide, or casualties caused by friendly fire, was a nightmare familiar to every FAC. Although he didn't know it at the time, several Marines had been killed by an Air Force A-10 at An Nasiriyah only a week or so earlier when their AAV had been misidentified as an Iraqi vehicle.

Nash wasn't the only one who was getting concerned—other calls came in over the net asking about the F-14. Still, there was no reply to his urgent calls. The big, swing-wing fighter swept into another turn and pointed down toward the LAVs again. This time a five-hundred-pound GBU-12 fell clear of its underside.

There was a loud, chest-rattling *ka-ruuummmp,* and the two LAV-25s that had just destroyed the Iraqi T-72 disappeared behind a cloud of fire, smoke, and dust. The sound of the blast sent Nash's heart into his throat. Amazingly, the two vehicles, still intact, emerged from the dissipating shroud of airborne debris left behind by the explosion. The bomb had hit just between the two LAVs, but a few yards to their right behind a berm that paralleled the road. The earthen rise had absorbed most of the blast; other than ringing eardrums, a gash to the forehead of one of the Marines was the only injury.

The chatter over the radio net turned more desperate, and the unit was ordered to ensure that air panels were deployed atop all vehicles. These pinkish orange stretches of fabric were intended to be easily recognized from the air and to mark the displaying units as friendly. By now Nash had finally made contact with a section of F/A-18Ds, who in turn were able to establish communications with the F-14 crew. When told of the near calamity the Navy fliers slunk off beyond the horizon and were not heard from again. They were never identified.

Several minutes later Nash's heart was still racing. He was furious with the Navy crew and knew that luck was the only thing that had kept those aviators from killing several of his fellow Marines. Using airpower casually or indifferently was akin to handing a toddler a loaded machine gun. It made everyone nervous and was a danger to all and sundry. Nevertheless, it was nothing he could afford to dwell on. The company's skirmish with the Iraqis was ongoing, and when the current fight was finished the unit would be busy making preparations for the assault into Baghdad. He needed to ensure that he was able to bring on the air assets that would be required.

It was on this day that MAG-16 moved its helicopters ashore to the airfield at Jalibah. The distances from the Persian Gulf to where they were needed deep inside Iraq were beginning to become too problematic to effectively operate from the ships. It was classic Marine Corps doctrine: the seizure of advanced bases in order to conduct wider operations.

34

Al Basrah Adventure

The British commitment to Operation Iraqi Freedom included nearly a third of the land forces—an affirmation of the traditionally strong alliance between the United States and the United Kingdom. Since the start of the war, the UK units had swept across the Al Faw Peninsula and into Umm Qasr, clearing that port so that humanitarian supplies could be brought into Iraq. They had also helped to secure the strategic Rumaylah oil fields alongside their Marine Corps counterparts. By the end of the first week of April they controlled all the approaches to Al Basrah and were making raids into the city whenever and wherever they desired. For a variety of reasons the Coalition leadership did not want to commit the British to a full-blown siege of Iraq's second-largest city. Not the least of these reasons was that the UK forces might be required if the battle for Baghdad became overly costly.

Before they had been briefed earlier that morning—April 6—they had checked Mattis's SITREP on the First Marine Division's webpage. Most of the action had been centered on Baghdad, so the four AH-1W Cobra crews of HMLA-169 were a little surprised when they got airborne out of Ali Al Salem and were assigned two separate JTARs (Joint Tactical Air Strike Request) to work with British armored units in Al Basrah. The flight's leader, Major Stephen "Pygmy" Hall, remembered that by this time in the conflict, the ATO for the Cobras had essentially become a recurring "cut-and-paste" set of twelve lines that essentially told them when to launch and who to contact for tasking once they had done so. There was seldom any clue as to what they'd actually be doing on a particular day.

"We split up into two flights as we approached Al Basrah," Hall recalled. "The two columns we were supporting were at the north end of the city." He sent Lieutenant Colonel Lloyd "Shooter" Wright and his wingman, Rich "Astro" Lawson, to work with the easternmost column while he took his own wingman, Captain David "Slant" Blassingame, to work with the western group. Hall remembered their tasking: "The Brits were playing a sort of cat-and-mouse game with Iraqis that had been sniping at them and taking them under rocket and mortar fire. They suspected that the bad guys were holed up in neighborhoods in the north and northwest of the city. They wanted to use us as armed reconnaissance. Essentially we were supposed to be their eyes out in front—and they wanted us to kill whatever we found that might affect their movement toward the Shatt Al Arab River at the northern end of the city."

Hall led his section on a series of hard-turning sweeps a mile or two out in front and to the flanks of the British tanks. Flying below two hundred feet and at speeds in excess of 130 knots, the two gunships made a tremendous racket as they clattered just above the mix of industrial and residential neighborhoods that made up that portion of the city. It was a beautiful day and Hall could see his helicopter's shadow racing along the ground then leaping on top of buildings and then back to street level again. Except for the startled looks that the noise and commotion from the two Cobras generated, there appeared to be nothing threatening or even out of the ordinary. Still, the two crews stayed alert, and Hall ensured that they never repeated their passes from the same direction. Staying unpredictable in this environment was a key to surviving.

"After nearly two hours, we hadn't seen a thing," Hall recalled. "We got joined up with Shooter's section and then headed over to Safwan to get more gas." Safwan was a joint British–Marine Corps FARP that serviced much of the rotary-wing activity around Al Basrah. While the four aircraft were refueled Hall rebriefed the crews, and before long they were airborne again.

After checking in with the DASC(A), they were again directed to support the two British armored columns. "When we showed up," Hall remembered, "we found that they hadn't gone more than a hundred meters since the time that we had left." This reluctance on the part of ground units—even armored columns—not to advance without helicopters to scout ahead was vexing for the Cobra crews. "It wasn't that they were afraid," Hall said. "It was just that the towns were full of noncombatants and the ROE made it very easy for the enemy to set up ambushes." Indeed, the armored units could have gone anywhere they wanted and leveled everything in their way while killing anyone they wanted, but doing so would have created more enemies. It is difficult to convince a people that you have come to liberate them after you have killed their families and destroyed their homes. Having the Cobras available to scout ahead made the job of the men on the ground easier and cleaner.

Still, none of the Cobra pilots—in their relatively flimsy helicopters—liked to operate in the urban environment; every house or building hid a potential ambush. "Everything we were ever taught," Hall said, "told us to beware the fight in the city. But when our 'earth men' brothers call for help, there is often a very fine line between two decisions. One of those decisions can result in a person being accused of 'being a cowboy' and taking on too much risk. The other decision can result in a person being called a coward. We all would prefer to put on the ten-gallon hats."

Hall coordinated with the British column, and moments later his section of Cobras was scouting the British flanks as well as the way ahead. To the west, Wright and his two gunships were doing the same. This time they were tasked with investigating a group of stadiums that made up part of a sporting complex. The helicopters hunted and pecked around the area and came up empty-handed. It was while Hall and Blassingame were away from the column that things began to happen. "We had made about two or three sweeps and were a couple of miles out—near the Shatt Al Arab River—when we got a call that the Brits were 'taking RPG and heavy machine-gun fire,'" Hall remembered.

He turned the section south back toward the column and almost immediately gained sight of the smoke and fire that now marked the British position. "The FAC with the Brits called out that they were taking fire from their north—from a tall white structure with a distinctive, shiny black roof," recounted Hall. The FAC was correct. The building was unique—almost Oriental in appearance—and Blassingame picked it out quickly. "At about the same time that I gained sight of this place, Slant called out that he could see small-arms fire coming from the building, and almost simultaneously Shooter, who was about two or three miles to our west, called out the same thing."

Hall formulated a plan of attack. "After we passed the building—headed south—I turned east to make room for our firing run—I wanted to run at it from east to west." When he had created about two miles of separation from the target, he started a climbing left-hand turn through the north and back to the west in preparation for his attack. It was while he was leading Blassingame through this turn that his master caution light illuminated. He took a quick look down into the cockpit and noted that his transmission chip light was on. This was an indication that slivers of metal had been detected in his transmission, which was in danger of coming apart. During peacetime he would have aborted his run immediately. This was not peacetime. "I checked and the engine was indicating about 108 percent torque. Normal was 85 to 100 percent." Hall pressed his attack.

"I was in about a twenty-degree dive headed toward the building. I came back on the power to extend my tracking time, and put the pipper of my HUD just below the building while I looked for a good aim point." Hall's plan was to put a pod full of 2.75-inch rockets into the building and to follow that up with a good dose of 20-millimeter cannon fire.

What he saw didn't match up with what he had planned. "I saw nothing," he said. There were men and women and children walking around as if everything was normal—people with groceries in their arms. It was Mister Rogers' neighborhood. Not wanting to fill the scene below with the thousands of razor-sharp fléchettes that the rockets would unleash, Hall broke off his attack, added power, and started a hard left-hand climbing turn to back to the east. "I watched for Slant, who had been offset to my right, and he pulled off target without firing as well."

Hall continued his turn back toward the east and rolled wings level while he gained separation again and tried to formulate his next move. It was then that his ship was hit.

"It was as if someone had taken a bouquet of those giant party balloons and started popping them right in front of my face," he remembered. "We were getting hit hard in the nose section, and the NTS [Night Targeting System] caught fire and the cockpit started filling with smoke." Hall was worried about his copilot, First Lieutenant Dale "Amish" Behm. "At least I knew he wasn't dead," he recounted. "He was shouting like hell up there, but the intercom had been shot out and between that and all the explosions and the caution tones and the radio noise I couldn't understand a word he was saying."

It wasn't just an isolated burst of fire that caught Hall's aircraft. "We kept getting hit mostly in the front section but also in the main fuselage and tail boom—at one point I could feel the rear of the aircraft skid to the left as if a giant hand had swatted it." Hall couldn't tell where the fire was coming from and didn't know whether to turn away to one side or another, or reverse course. "In that sort of situation," he said, "our tactics call for us to just keep driving straight through the ambush, and that's what I did. It was a helpless feeling— kind of like being in a dark room and being beat up with a baseball bat. I was sure we were going to crash right there."

Hall finally brought the Cobra out of the trap. Although the cockpit was full of smoke and most of his engine gauges were shot out or reading zero, the aircraft was flying surprisingly well. "I looked out my right side," he remembered, "and could see Shooter about two miles away flying parallel to me. I took a deep breath, found my best 'he-man' voice, and called out that we had been hit pretty hard." Wright rogered his call and "helpfully" pointed out that Hall's ship was smoking fairly heavily.

Hall managed to get his Cobra pointed west toward the British armored column. Blassingame—whose aircraft had also taken several hits—was in tow but not nearly as heavily damaged as Hall. "I managed to find the road that the Brits were on," he remembered, "but there were power lines all along both sides and I couldn't find a place to put down." The road was built up above the marshy terrain it ran through, and he followed it south until he found a break in the wires. Hall felt doubly relieved when he saw a British Challenger tank posted at the same point. He slowed the stricken helicopter, turned into the wind, and set down in the middle of the road only a few yards from the tank.

He recounted: "I shouted up at Amish to get out and take a look at the bird—see how bad it was." Behm lifted his canopy, crawled out, and made a quick turn around the Cobra. The look on his face told Hall that they were lucky to have made it as far as they had. Behm made a slicing motion across his throat with one hand; it was the signal for Hall to shut the aircraft down.

As the Cobra's two engines wound down, Hall climbed out and joined Behm in a quick survey of the damage. "For Bell Helicopter I'll do advertisements, commercials, infomercials . . . whatever they want, for free, for the rest of my life. To me it was impossible that that airplane flew for as long as it did as well as it did—it was unbelievable." The front of the Cobra had been shot up and had multiple holes all through it. That Behm, in the front cockpit, had nothing more than a handful of metal shavings thrown into his lap was a near miracle. There were holes in the belly of the aircraft, in the engine casings, in the tail boom, in the main and rear rotors—virtually everywhere. Especially unnerving was a huge hole where nearly half of the driveshaft to the rear rotor had been torn away. Fuel drained onto the pavement, and the entire left side of the aircraft was covered in oil.

"At that point I was pretty relieved," Hall said. "I was glad the whole thing was over." He walked the few yards to the British tank and introduced himself to the crew. "They were nice enough but they seemed pretty much indifferent to the whole thing. They didn't even get out to take a look at the aircraft, but they did agree to stick around and give us some security and to try and get word out so that we could get some sort of aircraft recovery organized."

It wasn't long before Wright and Blassingame landed their Cobras next to Hall's ship. Wright's wingman remained overhead to provide high cover. "Shooter and I looked over my airplane again and we started putting together a list of parts that would be needed in case we had to fix the thing right there. I started to feel bad—it was *really* shot up, and technically the schedule for that day had Shooter listed as the mission commander even though I was leading." After the two fliers had tallied the list of spares, Wright gave Hall the two magazines of ammunition he was carrying for his M4 carbine and wished him luck. The handful of extra rounds was a wake-up call for Hall; they reminded him that he wasn't exactly in friendly territory. A few minutes later Wright and Blassingame lifted off, and Hall and Behm were left behind with their new British best friends.

"It was then that I started trying to recall all the infantry stuff that they had taught us when we were second lieutenants back in TBS [The Basic School]," Hall said. Both he and Behm retrieved the M4 carbines they kept stowed in the aircraft for just this sort of emergency. Hall sent Behm over to the eastern edge of the road, where there were what appeared to be some neglected fighting positions. From there the copilot could see across the marsh that ran adjacent to that part of the road. Hall posted himself on the west side. There was nothing to do but wait.

The southern edge of Al Basrah was about two miles north of the two Marines and their crippled bird. That portion of the city was built up about thirty feet above the wetlands that abutted it to the south.

Hall could see crowds of people standing on the high ground looking and pointing at where he and Behm were sitting. *Curious onlookers,* he noted to himself.

It was maybe half an hour later when he saw that the crowd was getting bigger. Not only that, it was starting down the road toward him. "We're not talking forty or fifty folks," he remembered. "This crowd was huge—probably seven hundred of them. There were kids, old men, women, young men—it was the entire neighborhood!"

Hall started getting nervous. What would he do? How would he stop the crowd? Could he fire warning shots? "During the last few days we had seen news reports that described suicide bombers and talked about how the Iraqis were using women and children as shields. There was no telling what these people intended—there could have been a hundred guys in there with RPGs." He started going over the ROE in his head. A war crimes trial was not something that interested him. He counted his ammunition. "I had 112 rounds. It wasn't nearly enough if I had gotten into a shooting match." He thanked his lucky stars that the British tank was still backing him up.

It was then that Wright and the other two Cobras showed up overhead. The three gunships made low, threatening passes over the crowd for the next ten minutes but with no effect. The people from Al Basrah trusted the Coalition ROE too much—not that it mattered anyway. Wright and the other two ships had shot up most of their ammunition at Iraqi armor during the time since they had left Hall on the road. After a short time they were out of fuel and gone.

And the crowd kept coming. Hall remembered: "I wasn't sure what their intent was, but when they got inside of about five hundred meters I climbed up onto the tank and told the Brits to stand by to destroy our aircraft and haul our asses out of there. They said that would be fine, but again didn't seem particularly concerned. Of course there was the simple fact that they were sitting inside one of the best MBTs [Main Battle Tanks] in the world." Hall jumped back down to the road, and he and Behm returned to their respective sides of the road and watched the crowd press on. There was no sense standing out in the open where a sniper might have been able to pick them off.

The Iraqis continued to rally south down the road, and Hall was about to write off his aircraft when the roar of two British Scimitar tracked armored vehicles caught his attention. They raced up from behind in a line-abreast formation, split their formation as they passed the Challenger and Cobra on either side of the road, then stopped about a hundred yards in front of the Iraqi throng. "A couple of guys got out with engineer stakes and police tape and strung off the road," Hall recollected. "And it worked—they crowded up against it and didn't pass."

It actually worked for only a few minutes. Hall was startled by several bursts of 30-millimeter cannon fire: *boom-boom-boom!* The British Scimitar gunners put four salvos of three rounds each into the road just ahead of the mob of Iraqis who had broken through the tape. The guns were more effective than the tape, and soon the rabble was milling in retreat.

"It was then that somebody in Al Basrah started shooting mortars at us. The rounds weren't hitting very close, but that didn't mean that they couldn't make corrections," Hall recalled. Only a few minutes later the British upped the ante a notch when they targeted the mortar positions with 155-millimeter counterbattery fire. Things were getting interesting.

"I was starting to wonder if anyone had gotten the word out that we needed a little bit of assistance. I had known Shooter for fifteen years and was pretty sure he wouldn't have left me hanging," remembered Hall. "I had expected a recovery team by that time." Instead he was faced with a potentially dangerous mob while he babysat a shot-up aircraft under the middle of an artillery duel. Fortunately he had firepower on his side.

It was at about this time that another vehicle rumbled onto the scene. The British had sent a tank retriever to grab Hall's helicopter. "This thing was pretty neat," he recalled. "It had a crane-like arm that swung out from the bed—it was really heavy-duty." The engineer in charge of the operation was all business and started his crew to work immediately. "At first he wanted to put a couple of straps under the bird and lift it up," remembered Hall. "But the aircraft would have crushed itself under its own weight, so I explained to him that when we had to, we lifted it up from the top by the rotor head." The British engineer took a quick look at the arrangement and within twenty minutes had fashioned a rig that bolted straight into the American fitting. A short time later Hall's aircraft was safely aboard the bed of the retriever and tied fast.

It was time for Hall and Behm to leave. "We thanked everyone," Hall said, "and said our good-byes. The Brits really had done some pretty good work for us, and now I was fairly certain that the day's excitement was *really* over." By and large it was. The Cobra and its crew were trucked down to Safwan and turned over to the Marine Corps detachment there. A few days later Hall and Behm were back in combat.

35

Gunning Down the Fedayeen

By April 8 the First Marine Division was across the Diyala and inside the outer limits of Baghdad. Although the RCTs were ready to plunge into the heart of the city, various considerations at a level higher than the MEF were holding them back. For their part, the aviators of 3rd MAW continued to provide support—flying whatever missions their grunt brothers required. Nevertheless, as the enemy's territory shrank, so did the number of targets that required servicing by 3rd MAW's fixed-wing jets. As the Army and the Marine Corps strung a noose around Baghdad, the physical proximity of their units to each other grew closer and closer.

Originally the section of two F/A-18Ds was scheduled for FAC(A) duty south of Baghdad on the morning of April 8. "But an A-10 had just been shot down and we were assigned to act as a radio relay for the low-flying Air Force HH-60 Pave Hawks that were en route to pick up the pilot," remembered Major Jay "Chewy" Frey, of VMFA(AW)-533.

An Iraqi SAM, most likely a Russian-built SA-16, had hit Major Jim Ewald's aircraft, an A-10 of the USAF's 110th Fighter Wing. Ewald remembered looking over his shoulder as the aircraft disintegrated around him. Well after the fact he joked: ". . . I could see little parts falling off the engine and I thought, *I really don't know what that is, but I think I need it.*" A short time later he ejected from the mortally stricken aircraft.

Frey and his pilot, Major Scott "Weeds" Wedemeyer, along with their squadron mates in the other Hornet, reconnoitered the area where the Air Force jet had been downed as well as the route that the rescue helicopters would take out. Traveling at nearly five hundred knots at ten thousand feet, this was a difficult task. Even using their FLIR pod they couldn't guarantee that the route was clear.

In the meantime Ewald had parachuted to the ground and taken cover in a dry canal. He could hear engine noise as vehicles approached; nevertheless he stayed hidden, as he knew that there were enemy troops in the area. It wasn't long before he heard voices; they were speaking in English, but he couldn't be sure that they weren't Iraqi. Then there was a shout: "Hey, pilot dude! Come out. We're Americans." Ewald realized that this group most likely wasn't made up of Iraqis who spoke good English. He had indeed been found by the good guys. Within minutes he was scooped up by soldiers from the Army's Fifty-fourth Engineer Battalion.

Finding nothing threatening, Frey and Wedemeyer passed their information to Warhawk—the Army's Air Support Operations Center. Warhawk assigned a pair of Air Force aircraft to relieve the two Hornets and directed the Marines to contact Bullet 39, an Army FAC attached to a convoy stopped in Al Hillah. Bullet 39's convoy was taking rocket and mortar fire from a pair of compounds on the north side of the highway that ran to Karbala, twenty miles or so to the west.

"Bullet 39 and his convoy were under attack," Frey recalled, "but he couldn't tell from where." The area was a mix of residential and industrial structures—a jumble of buildings, any one of which could have held squads of enemy soldiers. Here and there earthen berms had been scraped up around blocks of buildings. These were obviously intended to serve as defensive positions for the Iraqi Army.

Bullet 39 could do no good without being able to put his eyes on the Iraqis who were firing into his convoy. Likewise the Hornets couldn't help him if they couldn't see the enemy. Finding the Iraqis from above was proving to be difficult; there was a broken layer of clouds at about six thousand feet, and it was hazy below. "Bullet asked us to come down and take a look," Frey recalled. "Weeds left our wingman up above the cloud deck and took us down; we raced up and down the highway looking for the bad guys." Although they still were unable to spy the enemy, Bullet 39 reported that the incoming fire had stopped. Perhaps just the sight and noise of the F/A-18D was enough to cause the enemy troops to cease their shooting.

"By that time we were running low on fuel and had to bingo to the tanker track," remembered Frey. "We promised Bullet that we'd be back, and then headed out to get gas. At about the same time, an Army OH-58 Kiowa scout helicopter showed up. We passed what little information we had to those guys before we left."

The Marine KC-130 that the two F/A-18s rendezvoused with was nearly out of "give." There was only enough fuel to top off one of the birds, and Wedemeyer sent his wingman back to Al Jaber. Better to provide help for a reasonable amount of time with just one ship than to show up with two and leave almost immediately.

After filling his aircraft, Wedemeyer backed the jet out of the drogue, retracted his refueling probe, edged away from the big tanker, then descended and turned back toward Al Hillah, sixty miles distant. Frey switched frequencies immediately. "As soon as I checked in, the Kiowa crew came up on the radio and told us that they'd been hit by an RPG and were clearing out of the area. Even though they had been hit, they had located the enemy and managed to pass us a decent grid location." Not only had the Army helicopter been shot up, but the convoy was taking fire again as well. Frey immediately started formulating a plan with Bullet 39. He passed their estimated time of arrival overhead the enemy position, and the FAC agreed to try to mark it with a mortar just a few seconds prior to their arrival time. This would help to give them both a common point of reference.

"Just as we approached the grid location that the Kiowa had passed, a mortar round hit on the north side of the road, right between two bermed compounds," recounted Frey. "I called out the mark and Bullet 39 responded that our target was the westernmost of the two compounds."

Wedemeyer wrapped the Hornet around in a hard left descending turn and brought the ship down over the compound. Frey remembered: "We could see two white pickup trucks with mortar tubes mounted in the beds. These were the kind of vehicles that the Fedayeen favored, and there were a couple of dozen of them in and around the trucks. We could see their faces turned up and looking at us as we flew over the top of them."

Wedemeyer snapped the jet into a steep climb while both he and Frey looked down behind them through the haze to keep the enemy position in sight. On the main highway to the west of the Fedayeen compound Frey could make out the twenty-five or so vehicles that made up Bullet 39's convoy. He called the Army FAC as Wedemeyer increased their altitude. "Bullet 39, Anubis 45, I have you in sight. In the western compound I've got eyes on two technicals and multiple enemy personnel. We're going to conduct Type III CAS on that target." Bullet 39 rogered Frey's call as Wedemeyer leveled the Hornet at approximately eight thousand feet and then swung the aircraft around in a right-hand turn in preparation for a rocket attack.

Type III CAS was the most permissive of the three variants. Essentially, once the pilot or aircrew was certain of the enemy's position and the positions of all nearby friendly troops, he was cleared to execute his attacks at his own discretion. There was no further requirement for him to get approval to employ weapons.

"While we were climbing we watched some of the Fedayeen get into the trucks while a bunch of others ran into one of the buildings," remembered Frey. "Weeds brought us back around in another right-hand turn and started a dive from the north directly toward the two pickups." For this attack Wedemeyer had decided to shoot four 5-inch

HE rockets. Streaking earthward in a fifteen-degree dive at nearly five hundred knots, he steadied the illuminated pipper in his HUD on the two closely parked vehicles. The rockets were unguided—not much different from the aerial rockets that had been used during World War II. They could find their mark only if skillfully aimed by the pilot. Wedemeyer waited until the jet passed through six thousand feet before he mashed his thumb down on the control stick's red bomb release button; the same button was used to fire the aircraft's rockets. Four of the rockets *whoosh*ed out of the pod on the jet's right-hand wing. At the same time, Wedemeyer pulled back on the aircraft's control stick and pointed the jet skyward again.

"Weeds was right on," recounted Frey. "He didn't miss too often, and both of the trucks were hit and caught fire." A commotion ensued on the ground; it was as if someone had stirred up a nest of rats. The two Marines could see more Fedayeen climbing out of fighting positions and running into two of the bigger buildings.

"By now the weather had improved," recounted Frey. "There was a scattered-to-broken layer at about five thousand feet, but it was clear above and below. Our attack pattern evolved into a sort of cloverleaf. We would hit them from one direction, then come off target and turn ninety degrees to get some separation. Then we would reverse course with a 180-degree turn and come right back at the target for another run."

This time Wedemeyer climbed the Hornet up to twelve thousand feet before leveling off. He and Frey both checked for anti-aircraft fire or missiles before rolling over into another attack. Their target was one of the two buildings the Fedayeen had scuttled into for safety. However, the structure would offer little protection from the five-hundred-pound GBU-12 that the two fliers were going to put into it.

In a thirty-degree dive Wedemeyer watched the enemy compound grow bigger as he carefully steered the jet until the building was exactly under the fluorescent green pipper that glowed in the HUD atop the jet's glare shield. Wasting no time, he pressed down on the target designator cursor on the right-hand throttle and started a pull out of his dive—at the same time following the steering line that appeared in the HUD.

Immediately upon Wedemeyer designating the target through his HUD, the Hornet's FLIR pod automatically slaved directly to the same target. In the rear cockpit Frey took control of the pod and squinted into the gray-green display to confirm that the device was actually looking at the correct building. Only a very few seconds later he felt and heard a *thunk* as the GBU-12 dropped clear of its wing station. At the same time, he heard Wedemeyer call out, "One away," and then felt the onset of the four-g pull that Wedemeyer put on the jet as he started climbing back to altitude again. On the ground Bullet 39 waited and watched for the bomb to drop into the compound.

With the building positively identified, Frey used his hand controller to keep the FLIR display's steering diamond exactly centered. Simultaneously he squeezed the trigger that fired laser energy from the pod straight at the target. In the same instant the seeker head on the bomb detected the energy reflecting off the structure where the Fedayeen were hiding and started guiding to it.

Frey's control was perfect. "The place disappeared in a massive explosion," he remembered. "Fire and smoke and dust—I don't know how anyone could have survived that blast."

Before the smoke even began to dissipate, Wedemeyer pulled the aircraft back around and dropped the nose down toward the compound once more. Again he designated the target and dropped a GBU-12, and again Frey's control of the bomb was flawless. "The second building was destroyed just like the first had been—there was nothing left of it," he remembered.

When the smoke cleared Wedemeyer dropped the jet down low and made a high-speed pass over the compound. He and Frey both spotted a group of about half a dozen Fedayeen running out of the complex and toward the wall of another compound about two hundred yards to the west. Frey contacted Bullet 39 and asked him what he wanted the two Marines to do with the small group. "Kill 'em" was the call that came back.

Keeping sight of the enemy soldiers was difficult, and Wedemeyer worked hard to keep the aircraft close enough so that he didn't lose them in the dust and haze. He reached up to his left-hand display and selected air-to-ground gun as his weapon. Checking for enemy anti-aircraft fire, he wrenched the jet over into another right-hand turn and put the pipper of his gun sight over the small group of fleeing Iraqis. Their black uniforms contrasted sharply with the tan terrain.

"If Weeds was good with rockets, he was even better with the gun," Frey recalled. "He set up the first run very carefully—we didn't want any of them to get away." Flying in a very shallow dive, Wedemeyer waited until he was almost too close before he squeezed the trigger on his control stick. He held it for only a second. The six-barreled M61 Vulcan cannon responded with a *vrrrrrrrrr* that buzzed through the aircraft and sent a hundred 20-millimeter, high-explosive rounds at the small group. The pattern of projectiles tore into the running men; only three of the enemy fighters emerged from the cloud of smoke and dust.

Mindful of the fact that their morning had started with a rescue effort for a pilot who had been shot down, both Marines kept a lookout for enemy missiles and anti-aircraft fire as Wedemeyer set them up for a second run. "There was only one guy left after that pass," Frey said.

Their third and final gun run killed the remaining Iraqi.

Bullet 39 reported that all fire against his convoy had ceased and that he was continuing west along the main highway. He thanked the two Marines and cleared them to switch frequencies.

Meanwhile the encirclement of Baghdad ground on. Major Randy "Fester" Nash, the senior FAC with 1st LAR, peered from atop his LAV at the object in the distance. It was a body, clad in a traditional black dishdasha. Nearer to the dead man he realized his mistake. The lifeless Iraqi had no clothes on; the black robe had instead been a cloak of thousands upon thousands of flies.

As a Marine aviator this was something that separated him from his fellow Air Force and Navy fliers. Rare were the occasions when they saw firsthand the gruesome effects of their handiwork on the battle-

field. To be honest, it wasn't an "every-career" occurrence for Marine
aviators, either, but the nature of their service put them in a position
to do so more frequently. Having been in the thick of much of the
fighting, Nash had seen many bodies on the march up to Baghdad.
He recollected his thoughts and feelings:

> I can never recall feeling repulsed or any sense of remorse. It
> was mostly indifference—other than trying to make sense of
> why that particular Iraqi would stand and fight. Although I will
> admit that if and when there was time to reflect, I often won-
> dered about that individual, if he was only caught up in circum-
> stances—perhaps it was his best attempt at earning a living for
> his family, or more likely he was forced to fight. This of course
> may not have been the case with the Fedeyeen who seemed
> more than happy to fight. There were also thoughts of his fam-
> ily, his children, especially. Being the father of a four-year-old
> demanded that I at least consider that.

36

===

Fight for the Palace and Mosque, Part I

The first couple of days after the Marine Corps's entry into Baghdad were a wild roller-coaster ride. Like the Army's soldiers in western Baghdad, the young Marines fought through firefights with the Baathists and Fedayeen at one turn, and were cheered and mobbed as liberators at another. Robling remembered watching the famous video of Saddam's statue being torn down by a jubilant crowd on April 9. "Tamer and I were in the TACC watching CNN when that thing came down. I can remember that we looked at each other and agreed that we had reached the end. It was all over. Of course we had no idea that it would drag on like it has."

It was on April 10 that all the Regimental Combat Teams were able to meet across the borders of their various zones of responsibility. The fierce defense of the city by organized elements of Saddam's armies never materialized; instead the Americans were hit by Fedayeen irregulars and scattered regime loyalists. Simultaneously the celebrations by the long-oppressed population erupted into widespread looting by citizens and criminals alike. The division's Marines were at a confusing crossroads. Liberators and victors they may have been, but there was a crying need for someone to simply maintain law and order.

And still a need for someone to fight.

The streets and alleyways were so narrow that there was no option other than to crush everything in the way. Stair railings and steps, bicycles, and small market stands were destroyed; even air-conditioning units were snagged and ripped out of their window mounts. The line of tracked mechanical dinosaurs was made up of the tanks and AAVs of the First Battalion Fifth Marines. It was bound for Saddam's Azimiyah Palace on the banks of the Tigris, in the heart of Baghdad.

From where he was standing in the troop compartment of "Track 109," Captain Shawn "Spaz" Basco squinted through his night-vision goggles at the doors and windows of the buildings that pressed in on both sides of the column. Five Marines, weapons ready, lined each side of the long open hatches at the top of the heavy beast. It was just shy of 0200 on the morning of April 10 and it was very quiet. Too quiet, it seemed.

Basco had been trained as an F/A-18 pilot, but his initial instruction, like that of all Marine officers, included infantry training and tactics. That was long past now, and he had spent the last several years rocketing through the sky far from the wet and dirt that marked duty in the field. Still, when the call came for volunteers to fill FAC billets, Basco put his hand up. He was due for a stint in a nonflying position anyway, and doing time as a FAC appealed to him. It was a duty that could only be held by a pilot, and as a FAC he would be responsible for coordinating air support missions for the ground unit to which he'd be assigned.

Basco's previous three weeks of combat as the FAC assigned to Bravo Company of the First Battalion had opened up an entirely new world to him. It was an environment that had called for every skill the Marine Corps had taught him. Just the previous day he had shot an Iraqi through the head as the man—dressed in polyester slacks and a sport shirt—had raised an RPG launcher to fire on the company's command vehicle.

Basco turned in the dark to say something to the company gunnery sergeant. It was at this very moment that the night turned to day. "It was the most enormous explosion I'd ever seen or heard," he remembered. "An RPG slammed into a tanker [fuel truck] and erupted into a huge mushroom cloud of fire that swept up and down the alleyway incinerating everything in its path." An instant later the burning shock wave smashed into Basco's AAV. "When I regained consciousness I was on the floor of the track in a pile with everyone else and flames were cascading down through the hatch. We were going to die."

In the dark hull of the AAV more than a dozen stunned Marines writhed in the dark, gasping for the air that the fireball had consumed. It was a hellish nightmare of a scene. Basco recalled: "After about thirty seconds—it seemed like forever—I was finally able to catch my breath. However, I couldn't hear anything, and the flash from the explosion had blinded me in one eye. I was a mess; my goggles and helmet had been blown off and my M16 had been thrown to the forward end of the troop compartment." The Marines inside the AAV, dazed and disoriented, stumbled over each other trying to regain their bearings. Outside, a solid sheet of machine-gun tracers stretched up and down the alley; white tracers marked the Iraqi fire. The American rounds burned red. There were more white than red.

Fiery trails of RPG rounds also blasted down from the windows and rooftops. Many were shot from such short ranges that they failed to fuse and explode. "Rather than blowing up," Basco recounted, "they just hit and burned. Sometimes they hit our rucksacks—we had them fastened to the outside of the vehicle—and just burned our stuff up."

In the tight confines of the alley, there was nothing that air support could do for the fight. Still unable to hear, and having trouble getting his eyes to focus, Basco grabbed a spare M16 from where it was strapped to the AAV's bulkhead and added his fire to the maelstrom.

The Rasheed Fedayeen Military Complex on the southern edge of Baghdad had been a training base for some of Saddam's most elite fighting organizations. That had been before the war. Now, less than three weeks into the campaign, it was serving as the First Marine Division's Forward Command Post. Like bees to honey the Marines had staked out their CP on the complex's lush playing field—the first real grass they had seen since leaving the United States.

Gunfire rattled from somewhere far off in the dark. Inside his CH-46E near the CP, Captain David Hurst rolled over in his sleeping bag. Crewing on the old transport helicopter had its benefits; the men were able to use the onboard medical stretchers as cots and stay up and off the floor of the aircraft. It was still several hours before daylight and he blinked into the dark, not able to see much. He could smell, though. The old bird stank of jet fuel and hydraulic fluid and thirty or more years of Marines and their cargo. It wasn't a bad stink.

Hurst and his friend Captain Larry Brown were on CASEVAC alert. Larry was asleep just a few feet away, as were the rest of the crew. And although he couldn't see it, Hurst knew that only about fifty feet or so from their own helicopter squatted the other aircraft in their section. Inside it, Captains Will Oliver and Jeff Dansie and their crew were also catching up on sleep.

To this point the campaign had been a wearying grind for the crews of HMM-165; they had flown day and night nearly nonstop on a wide range of missions. Some of the sorties had been dangerous; some of them had not. Still, Hurst was tired. For that matter, everyone in the squadron was tired. He yawned and went back to sleep.

It was daylight now, and Bravo Company of the First Battalion had fought their way out of the ambush and into the Azimiyah Palace grounds. It was a twenty-acre development with a grand palace for Saddam and two lesser palaces for his sons Uday and Qusay. Situated on the east bank of the Tigris River, it was surrounded by a twelve-foot wall.

Outside the walled compound, elements of Charlie and Alpha Companies were engaged in a deafening battle against hundreds of Fedayeen and foreign fighters. Concussions from heavy guns rattled Basco's chest; machine guns and RPG blasts added to the din. He had recovered sight in both of his eyes, and his hearing had come back as well. Not that his hearing was very useful at this point. "It was so loud that in order to communicate, you had to grab a guy by the head, put your lips against his ears, and shout—and I mean literally shout," Basco remembered.

It was time for Basco-the-FAC to put his aviation expertise to work. Casualties were heavy; some of the men were going to die if they weren't evacuated. "Several Marines had been brought up to our track by then. Two of them were really a mess. Corporal Diwani and Corporal Shevlin had been hit in the face—one of them by shrapnel from an RPG," Basco recalled. "I was afraid they would bleed to death. I had watched others die the same way and I wanted to get them to an aid station as quickly as possible."

Basco's biggest challenge was making contact with someone who could help. The buildings in an urban environment block the transmissions of the standard UHF (Ultra High Frequency) radios the military uses for communicating with aircraft. Generally a clear line-of-sight is required; otherwise the range of the radio is significantly shortened. Basco remembered: "I went through every frequency I had trying to raise someone and it just wasn't happening."

Nevertheless, the FAC knew that eventually air support in the form of helicopters would be brought in, and he needed to prepare a Landing Zone for them. The compound was studded with date and palm trees, and Basco couldn't find an open area large enough to safely land the helicopters he knew would come. He remembered: "I grabbed Gunny Jenks and had him go to work clearing an LZ. I told him that I didn't care how he did it, but that we needed a space cleared ASAP. Sure enough, within a couple of minutes Jenks was roaring back and forth in one of the tracks knocking down Saddam's palms." The scene was wild: From inside and outside the palace Marine tanks and AAVs exchanged fire with enemy fighters holed up in the facing buildings. And only a few blocks away another battle was raging at the Imam Abu Hanifah Mosque where Saddam himself had reportedly been sighted. In the midst of it all the twenty-six-ton AAV was playing Paul Bunyan with Saddam's palm groves.

Meanwhile Basco frantically worked his radios, trying to find some sort of air support. "I could see the casualties mounting up and everyone I ran across kept telling me that we had a bunch of Marines that needed to get evacuated—as if I needed reminding." He had given up on using the standard air direction frequencies and instead started transmitting over Guard frequency, an emergency channel that all aircraft and aircraft control entities are required to monitor. Finally he made contact with Copter 65. Copter 65 was, of all aircraft, a Navy E-2C Airborne Early Warning aircraft. Its primary mission was to vector fighters against other fighters, but it had a powerful communications suite and—most important—it was the only aircraft Basco could talk to. "I told these guys that we were in downtown Baghdad and that we needed air support immediately," Basco recounted. "They asked for my precise location. Normally you don't pass that kind of information over an open net because you don't want the bad guys to intercept your transmission and start hitting your position. Well, the snap of bullets flying over my head was a pretty good indication that the gig was up. I was pretty damn sure the enemy knew *exactly* where we were. I referenced the cheap little GPS unit I had bought at Wal-Mart before the war and passed our location to the E-2C guys." Copter 65 assured Basco that he would make the necessary coordination and that help would soon be on the way.

Captain Aaron "Sulu" Locher was the FAC assigned to Charlie Company of the First Battalion. Like Basco, Locher was an aviator, but rather than F/A-18s he had flown UH-1N Hueys. This was his second tour of combat—he'd already seen more fighting than he'd wanted in the tribal hellhole that was Afghanistan. Charlie Company had been ordered to detach from the rest of the battalion before it reached the palace. Recent information sent them instead on a hunt for Saddam and his son Qusay near the Imam Abu Hanifa Mosque.

"We were hauling ass down those narrow streets—gang-fighting the whole way," he recalled. At the objective the Marines disembarked from their AAVs and engaged in fierce house-to-house fighting, slowly advancing from one block to another. "It was really odd," Locher said. "The place was empty except for the Fedayeen and foreign fighters. They had staged RPGs and other weapons on the rooftops and at windows and doors. They'd shoot, drop their weapon, run to another vantage point, grab another weapon, and shoot again. They were like cockroaches; we couldn't stomp on them fast enough. Our guys were really tearing them up but we were still catching hell."

Locher had deployed his Fire Support Team in and among some buildings where they could get a good look at the fighting. Now he was futilely trying to coordinate some air support from where he sat inside his AAV. Charlie Company's tracks were jammed together, almost touching each other in line, or "nut-to-butt." It wasn't a good situation, and Locher sensed an ambush.

"First Lieutenant Tavis McNair was one of our indirect fire guys—mortar and artillery—and he really didn't have anything to do in an urban fight," Locher recounted. "So he was sitting up on the lip of the left forward hatch shooting his M203 grenade launcher. I kept shouting at him to get down, but he wouldn't listen to me—he just kept shooting." Locher's fears were realized when a black-clad Fedayeen fighter stood up on the roof above them. "I could see him just over Tavis's shoulder—almost directly above us. He had a red-and-gold RPG launcher and fired it right at Tavis."

The RPG shot down at the Marines with a characteristic *pop* followed by a low, rumbling bellow. The men watching the rocket shooting down at them felt as if they were in a slow-motion nightmare. "RPGs," said Locher, "appear to move so slow that you almost feel like you can step out of the way."

There was no stepping out of the way of this particular projectile. The rocket exploded against the top of the vehicle and blew McNair back out of his hatch. Locher and the other ten or so Marines inside the AAV were knocked off their feet. "I went down hard against the back of the bench seat. I could smell the stink of gunpowder and I could feel that my face had been burned, but I couldn't see anything," he remembered. "It was all black smoke and arms and legs and I couldn't hear."

A moment later the Marines regained their senses in an uneven sort of hysterical reaction. "The back ramp wouldn't open and some of the guys panicked and jumped out through the escape hatch. A couple of the Marines were crying—it was really messed up," Locher remembered. "I had to grab and pull them back inside because we were taking heavy fire from the Fedayeen. We had a French reporter in the track with us and he had completely frozen. On the other hand we had a retired British Army color sergeant with us—he was some BBC reporter's bodyguard—and he was absolutely awesome. He loaded magazines and kept everyone fired up. He was money."

Locher couldn't get any air support. "I couldn't raise anyone on the radio—it's tough in a built-up area. Earlier I had specifically asked for Hueys and AC-130 gunships. Unfortunately they had been tasked to what were at the time considered to be more important missions. Both of them could have given us the type of surgically precise fire support we needed."

In the meantime McNair was bleeding heavily—he had taken the full brunt of the impact of the first RPG and his face, neck, and head were ripped by jagged shrapnel. Huge shards of it jutted from his neck. There were other wounded Marines as well, but Tavis McNair was in critical condition. It wasn't certain that he was going to live. "I remember," Locher said, "that the two corpsmen who were working on him kept shouting, 'We gotta get him out of here!'

"I tried like hell to raise the company commander on the radio," continued Locher, "but the buildings were eating up the radio and there was no way I was going to get through." Locher prepared to do the unthinkable. "All I knew was that I had to get McNair back to safety, so I briefed the young enlisted Marines—I told them that I was going to disembark and go find the company commander on foot. They kept telling me not to go, that it was crazy. I remember thinking to myself, *No shit, but someone's got to do it.*"

He told the junior Marines to cover him, jumped clear of the AAV, and raced through the alleyway dodging bullets and rocket fire. Machine-gun rounds slammed into the ground at his feet and whipped past his face and buried themselves in mud walls as he ran crouching through the battle. He was utterly exposed. "I felt like I was truly all by myself," he recalled. When he reached the company commander, Captain Sean Blodgett, he advised his fellow captain that McNair was in critical condition and needed to be evacuated immediately; it would take a pair of AAVs to fight back to the palace. Blodgett was still consolidating his position and couldn't spare them. Sound tactics told him to keep his company together; some of his men were still clearing houses, and he couldn't leave them behind. Locher persisted. Finally, knowing that McNair's condition was critical, Blodgett relented—Locher would lead two AAVs back to the palace. "Once that decision was reached," Locher remembered, "I was overcome by an odd feeling—a guilty sense that I would be leaving the fight and abandoning my brother Marines."

Locher sprinted back through the gauntlet to his AAV, stationed everyone into position, settled the wounded, and sent the driver roaring toward the palace. He had the only map in the vehicle, and it was hopelessly inadequate—failing to detail any of the small alleyways and back streets that zigzagged through the neighborhood. "Frankly," he remembered, "it was a shitty map." Regardless, Locher led the two armored brutes on a wild run, simultaneously navigating, coordinating with other units, and firing his weapon.

"I always said that if it ever got to the point where a FAC was doing any shooting, then things had gone from bad to shit." Nevertheless, the Marine captain stood out of the observer's hatch clutching his radio handset in one hand and firing his M9 pistol with the other. "It was insane," he remembered. "We were smashing into cars and over guardrails and I was shooting the whole time. I shot guys in the face through windows from four feet away. I shot guys in bushes and doorways and cars. Our poor radio operator was beside himself. He was reloading for me; I kept yelling 'Faster! More!' and he just couldn't keep up."

The fighting was still raging at the palace and the mosque. "Gunny Jenks," Basco recalled, "had done a pretty good number on the trees when PFC Davis ran up to me and said that he had found a better LZ—it didn't need any preparation." Basco followed Davis toward the rear of the estate near where it ended in a low bluff on the east bank of the Tigris. Just as the young Marine had said, next to an exquisite swimming pool there was a clear area that looked large enough to hold at least one helicopter.

"I grabbed Davis," Basco recalled, "and we went running across the pool deck. As we ran, we came under fire from snipers hidden in a grove about a hundred meters across the river." Chunks of plaster from the palace were knocked loose on top of the two men, and rounds chipped pieces of concrete out from under their feet. The two Marines crouched low as they investigated the new LZ. The snipers never let up.

Basco couldn't set up the zone while the enemy sharpshooters had him under fire. He scurried back to the other side of the palace and made a deal with the company commander, Jason Smith, to provide a Squad Automatic Weapon (SAW) gunner to give him protection. "Every time I ran out or exposed myself, I had that guy pop up and spray the trees across the river. Things got a little easier after that." Basco and Davis continued their work on the LZ; it was just barely big enough.

That was proven just a short time later with the arrival of two CH-46Es from HMM-268—callsigns Grizzly 41 and 42. Basco was ecstatic. "I directed the lead aircraft to pass north of the palace westbound over the river and then execute a left, 270-degree turn to come into the LZ. I told the second aircraft to tear the hell out of the palm groves across the river from where the snipers were shooting at us."

The mission commander of the two CH-46Es was Major Donald "Lando" Presto. Problems with his navigation equipment had forced him to pass the lead to the commander of the second aircraft, Captain Armando "Vato" Espinoza. Espinoza and his copilot, Captain Chris Graham, slowed and approached the LZ from the south, then pulled abeam and sidestepped over the ground from west to east before gingerly putting the helicopter's wheels on the ground. "These guys were either cool professionals or they had no idea how much fire they were drawing," remembered Basco. "Tracers were flying right by the cockpit and they didn't even flinch. Rounds were going through their rotor arc—it was unbelievable that they weren't getting hit."

Basco rushed up to Grizzly 41 to talk with the crew and help coordinate getting the wounded aboard. "While we were getting them loaded, I noticed that one of their crew chiefs looked a little bit older than the standard, run-of-the-mill crew chief," Basco recounted. "I got a little closer and realized that it was Oliver North! I said, 'What the hell are you doing here?' and he answered that he was there doing a war film. I figure he picked the right spot."

Locher was still in the race to save McNair's life. "When we were out a distance from the palace I saw a pair of Frogs [CH-46Es] coming in to land. It was absolutely crazy; they were taking all kinds of fire. I could see RPGs arcing up past them!" Closer to the compound's walls he shouted into the radio: "Hold those 46s! I've got severely wounded on board! Hold the 46s!" Seeing the AAV careening toward them—under heavy attack—the Marines behind the palace wall threw open the huge, heavy gates. Once the bullet-scarred brute bowled through they slammed them shut again.

Locher climbed out as the track ground to a stop. "My hands were shaking—I couldn't stop them. Lieutenant Colonel Fred Padilla, the battalion commander, came over to see what was going on. I was almost black from smoke and burns and covered with blood from all the wounded Marines—I was carrying one of them. And Tavis was obviously in horrible shape. I looked down and saw that the colonel's hands were shaking, too, and I didn't feel so bad—he was the best commander I had ever seen."

Stoked on adrenaline and fear and anger, Locher had reached the mental state that only the most distressed ever experience. "I was almost out of control—beyond furious," he remembers. Anxious to get the wounded Marines on their way, he stormed aboard the helicopter and shoved the man he thought was the crew chief out of the way. Once again, it was Oliver North. "I meant no disrespect to him," said Locher, "but I was . . . working!"

*   *   *

While the wounded were being loaded aboard Espinoza's aircraft, Presto held south of the LZ over the river at about seventy-five feet. Nevertheless, he was still taking heavy fire and moved to a covered position in between the river and the walled embankment that protected the palace. There he held a ten-foot hover and provided covering fire. Over the radio he could hear Basco call out that the LZ was getting hit hard by snipers and RPGs. From his vantage point Presto determined that the snipers were likely hiding on the rooftops of a row of four buildings located two hundred yards to the northwest. He lifted the CH-46E into a thirty-foot hover and swung the nose left, at the same time calling for the right door gunner to target the rooftops. The sniper fire ceased after a withering shower of .50-caliber rounds slammed into the buildings.

Locher stood over McNair in the LZ just prior to loading him on the helicopter. He turned to walk away, and the wounded McNair grabbed his arm and gurgled through the blood in his throat, "Thanks man, I owe you one." Locher turned back around. "No, don't mention it, you would have done the same for me."

The wounded were quickly hustled aboard the Grizzly bird. Before the flight could leave Basco shoved the pilots a note he had hand-scrawled on a chunk of cardboard from a water-bottle box. The message asked that as much ammo as possible be lifted into the palace grounds immediately.

A short time later the casualties were en route to better treatment. "As I watched the helicopters depart, any uncertainty or doubt I had felt about leaving the battlefield disappeared," recalled Locher. "I knew right then that I had made the right decision to get Tavis and the other wounded Marines out of that shit hole!" With the CASEVAC helicopters out of the LZ, Locher turned back toward the battle and thought to himself that it was time to get back to work.

37

===

Fight for the Palace and Mosque, Part II

Back at the Rasheed Military Complex, Dave Hurst and Larry Brown lolled alongside their CH-46E. They were still on CASEVAC alert. Although he felt only marginally better than completely worn out, Hurst would still have rather been flying than sitting. But again, considering that the section's mission was the evacuation of wounded Marines, he supposed that not being put to work was a good thing. Likewise, Brown and the rest of the crew—two enlisted crew chiefs and two Navy Corpsmen—probably felt the same way.

"We were just hanging out," Hurst remembered, "when an RCT-5 Air Officer—a major—walked up and said that there was business to be had if we wanted it. Larry and I reminded him that if he used our two aircraft . . . he wouldn't have any CASEVAC capability. He kind of brushed that off and said that what was going on right that instant needed immediate attention."

The major briefed Larry Brown and Will Oliver that the First Battalion was taking heavy casualties and needed ammo "right now."

They were directed to proceed straight to an Ammunition Supply Point just a few miles to the east. From there the safest route to the fighting called for a northerly transit along the east edge of the city, then a left turn west across the top of the city, and then another hard left turn, straight south, down Highway 2 into the heart of town.

Within minutes Hurst, Brown, and the rest of their crew were airborne as Inchon 40, with Oliver and Dansie and their own crew in formation as Inchon 41. They had little difficulty finding the ASP, and it wasn't long before the two helicopters set down to start taking on the badly needed ammunition. That they had gotten there in a hurry didn't matter. As ready as the two helicopter crews were, the Marines at the supply point weren't. To make matters worse, once things got under way, the loads they tried to put into the old aircraft were so heavy that both winches broke and the ammunition had to be lugged into the helicopters by hand. "Larry and I were getting extremely frustrated," Hurst recalls. "I knew that while we grab-assed around trying to get the ammo loaded, there were Marines getting shot. What was worse was that it was taking so long that we weren't going to have enough fuel to finish the mission!" Finally Larry Brown—the section leader—called a halt to the loading, urged the ASP Marines to get their act together, and then took the two ships to Yankee FARP to top off their fuel tanks.

At the Azimiyah Palace there was growing concern about the rate at which ammunition was being expended. Fighting at both the palace and the mosque was at a fever pitch. It was like nothing that anyone in the battalion had seen before. "If we didn't get more ammo in there soon," Basco said, "we were going to be in big trouble."

Brown and Hurst led the section of CH-46Es back to the ASP and settled them into the zone to finish the loading. "By now," Hurst recalled, "we'd given up on the winches and everyone just turned to the task at hand—lifting, pulling, pushing, and shoving the ammo into the bird. I'm not sure that the weights and distributions were by the book, but we got the stuff in."

Finally, after what had seemed an eternity, the two helicopters roared airborne out of the ASP and started for the fighting. "We flew as fast and low as we could. This made us a very difficult target, but it was also a huge challenge just to keep from running into something." There were plenty of somethings to run into. At nearly 150 knots, the two ships wound their way through the grid of buildings and streets that made up suburban Baghdad. Clattering through cast-concrete canyons of multistory buildings, the two ships just barely cleared television antennas, light posts, power lines, and even clothes strung across the streets. Regardless of whatever else was happening below them on that bright, sunny morning, the sheer rush of racing through the urban tangle—only a sneeze away from disaster—was exhilarating.

Back at the palace Locher stopped at the AAV that served as the battalion Command Post. Alpha Company had been sent to the mosque, and Locher knew that the area was dangerous—too dangerous. In fact, the unit was already fighting for its existence. "I was still fired up and I kept shouting at them to get Alpha Company out of there—that it was too hot. Mostly they just kept working—Alpha Company was in a bad way and I wasn't helping them out with my yelling."

By this time multiple sections of bomb-laden fighters were stacking up high above the city. A-10s, F-14s, F/A-18s, and even RAF Tornadoes orbited overhead, ready to provide CAS to the hard-pressed Marines. With an unobstructed line-of-sight to the high-flying aircraft the battalion Air Officer, Major Ed "Auto" Green, was able to establish good communications with the crews aboard the fighters. As they checked in, he passed them to Ray "Spanky" Lawler, the FAC for Alpha Company.

Lawler targeted a pair of A-10s against a set of buildings from which enemy fighters were pouring down fire on the company. Days before, these had been apartments and shops, but now they were Fedayeen fighting holes. The ungainly, straight-wing jets dropped down and poured a deadly stream of 30-millimeter cannon shells into the area that Lawler had marked. The enemy gunmen fell silent and the Marines of Alpha Company—only sixty-five yards from the spot where the cannon fire had hit—pushed on toward their objective.

F-14s followed the A-10s with thousand-pound bombs that rattled the men from "danger close" distances. As more aircraft joined the fight Lawler used the company's attached M1A1 tanks to mark targets with their 120-millimeter main guns. Soon the Marines were clearing the mosque of the Fedayeen.

The two CH-46Es continued their race toward the palace. It had been several days since the first American troops had entered Baghdad, and the city was clear of organized resistance from the Iraqi Army. In fact, the majority of the city's populace had been celebrating the arrival of the Americans for a couple of days. However, there were still pockets of defiance where hard-core loyalists and foreign fighters held out against the Coalition. The First Battalion Fifth Marines was heavily engaged against just this sort of opposition.

On the other hand, abundant fighters, hoodlums, thugs, and ne'er-do-wells were still spread all across Iraq's biggest city. Many of them were simply Iraqi Army regulars who had shed their uniforms. And without the manpower to force a presence on every street corner, the Americans were unable to do much when Iraqi jubilation turned destructive. Gangs of armed men turned to looting their own neighborhoods, and they had a tendency to shoot at anything that moved.

The two Marine helicopters were especially attractive, if fleeting, targets. "The scene below us was nonstop bedlam," Hurst recalled. "People were rioting and fighting—carrying stuff through the streets. Buildings were on fire, and hopeless traffic jams bottled the whole mess up. And lots of people were shooting at us."

The temptation to let loose with their .50-caliber machine guns against the ill-aimed fire that reached up at them was terrific. "Staff

Sergeant Clausen and Corporal Gerard each manned machine guns that could easily have made a bloody mess out of the crowds below us. But it would have been just plain wrong to open up with those big guns against the idiots who were taking potshots at us." Hurst was right. The heavy, high-velocity rounds would have punched through entire buildings—there was no way of telling what or who might get hit. Moral aspects aside, American .50-caliber rounds smashing into an Iraqi family huddled in their apartment away from the rioting would not have made a good public relations story.

Brown considered the situation and decided to allow the two Navy Corpsmen perched on the helicopter's rear loading ramp to return fire with their less powerful M16s. "Larry made a good decision," Hurst said. "We just wanted to let those knuckleheads know that we weren't going to take that nonsense lying down."

By now Aaron Locher had set up his FAC position atop the main palace. From his perch seven stories above the ground he could see that casualties were still coming into the compound. "I saw this young Hispanic Marine; his hand was shot clear through and was folded almost in half back on itself. But this kid wouldn't sit still, he was mad as hell and bound and determined to go back out and fight. Finally his staff sergeant had to order him to sit down and shut up."

Locher was watching the fight at the mosque when the second set of CH-46Es checked in with the battalion's Air Officer, Ed Green. They were directed to contact Locher—callsign Sulu—for final co-ordinating instructions.

Brown turned the formation hard left and followed Highway 2 south, straight into the city. In the distance they could make out the blue-green dome of the Imam Abu Hanifah Mosque. Smoke rose from the immediate area, marking the heavy fighting that was raging inside and around the temple. "We established communications with the FAC at the palace as we approached the mosque," Hurst recounted, "and he popped a green smoke grenade as we got closer so that we could see exactly where we were supposed to land and at the same time get an idea of what direction the wind was coming from."

With Locher's green smoke in sight the pilots wheeled into a hard right turn and caught sight of the Azimiyah Palace on the near bank of the Tigris. Marines raced back and forth across the once well-manicured grounds. The place was covered in battle trash—disabled vehicles, shell casings, loose gear, and ammo boxes lay strewn about. Fire and smoke billowed from the east side of the palace grounds where Marines were defending their newly seized prize. "As we slowed and set up for landing it became apparent that there was only enough room for one of us at a time," Hurst recollected. "Larry detached Will Oliver to orbit at a distance while we continued into the LZ." The rumbling of the two ungainly helicopters announced them as fresh targets, and they soon received the full-blown attention of the enemy gunners.

"The setup was awkward. We had to stop and then sidestep into the LZ," Hurst recalled. "When we finally touched down, we were swarmed by Marines who grabbed the ammo and rushed it toward the fighting. At the same time, Clausen and Gerard and the two corpsmen pitched in." It took less than two minutes to unload the aircraft, but still Oliver—orbiting at a distance—called for Brown and Hurst to step up the pace; his ship was taking heavy fire from where it was holding along the Tigris.

Although their aircraft was unloaded in near-record time, the crew had to wait while cargo of a different sort was put aboard. "We took some wounded Marines on, and also an Iraqi family—a mother, a father, and a small child. The woman had been hit in the buttocks. She was bleeding pretty badly, but was still moving under her own power. The little girl had a bandage over her head but didn't seem too badly hit. The father was just there for moral support. They threw another young Iraqi man on board, too. I don't know if he was an enemy fighter or just some guy who had been caught up by accident, but he had a big bloom of blood spreading across his shirt from a stomach wound and wasn't any kind of threat to anyone."

Finally loaded, and with the corpsmen treating the wounded, Brown and Hurst lifted their helicopter clear and made room for Oliver's ship. It took only a moment to understand why Oliver had been so anxious to get into the LZ and unload. "We were getting shot at from every direction," Hurst said. "Thankfully, we weren't as easy a target as we seemed to be—just as long as we kept moving." Still, the helicopter's crew breathed a sigh of relief when Oliver's aircraft finished taking on its load of wounded and lifted clear of the palace.

During interviews Hurst acknowledged the heavy enemy fire only when pressed: "It might be misconstrued as bragging," he said, "and our community is not made up of braggarts." He continued, "I always thought Larry Brown said it best. He used to say, 'Just do your job. Treat it like you've been in the end zone before. No bragging, no boasting . . . just doing your job.' " I can attest that Hurst's humility almost got in the way of capturing the real flavor of the story.

"We either had some of the luckiest helicopter crews in the world or the Iraqis had some of the worst gunners in the world," Shawn Basco recollected. "Every time one of the helos lifted off, an Iraqi machine gun would open up and I'd see large-caliber white tracers slice down the right side of the cockpit as the ship edged away to the left. And the gunner would never quite catch up." Basco emphasized his amazement: "I'm not talking once or twice or three times—this happened *every single time!*"

Nevertheless, not all of the Iraqi fighters were poor shots. It was almost noon and Basco was seeing off a CH-46E from his little LZ when, just as before, white tracers ripped down the right side of the helicopter as it sidled to the left and rose up and away. The rushing boom of the RPG racing toward him from behind was only so much background noise. That background noise turned to a roaring explosion as the rocket slammed into the pool deck only a few feet away from where Basco was standing. The explosion knocked him to the ground with a force that sent him tumbling. Finally, he realized, the odds had caught up with him. "I wasn't sure how badly I had been hit. I had dirt and concrete and glass plastered all over me—I hurt in about a hundred places," he remembered. "It wasn't until I started looking myself over that I realized that I'd taken a pretty bad hit in my right shin. Blood was gushing out, but the odd thing was that it was the only place on my body that didn't hurt." Basco didn't realize it at the time, but a piece of shrapnel from the RPG had severed a nerve, an artery, and a vein. Nevertheless, when he stood on his injured limb, he found that it still worked. He continued to coordinate the CASEVAC effort even as the wound continued to dump his blood onto the ground.

The two helicopters threaded their way back toward the ASP through the riotous free-for-all that Baghdad had become. They would unload the casualties while they took on more ammunition. In the rear of the aircraft Clausen and Gerard manned their guns while the two enlisted Navy men tended the wounded. "Our two Navy Corpsmen, HM2 Pitts and HM2 Thomas, were not your standard pudgy little pill dispensers," said Hurst. "These guys were studs. They were as much in shape as some of our best Marines, and just as handy with an M16 as they were with a syringe. And they didn't shy away from hard work, either. When it came time to start hucking ammo boxes around they were in the thick of things."

After a short stop at Yankee FARP to refuel, the two CH-46Es landed at the ASP and off-loaded the wounded. This time around the Marines at the supply point were better prepared, and the ammo-into-helicopter equivalent of a bucket brigade was formed. In short order the two aircraft rumbled airborne again and started back to the palace.

Their mission complete, the Marines of Alpha Company started back to the palace from the mosque. Now it was Locher's turn to control the fixed-wing jets that had started to arrive in force. He directed most of the bombs against enemy fighters in the mosque and surrounding buildings. The ROE protecting religious and cultural centers had been nullified since early that morning when the Iraqis had used it as a base from which to launch their attacks.

Locher's control of the jets was smooth and deadly. "I had a 'Viper' kit," he recalled. "It was a set of binoculars with a laser range finder that I kept plugged into a GPS unit. This thing gave me a ten-digit grid location that I in turn passed on to the aircrews—it was extremely accurate."

Protecting Locher—and taking advantage of the field of view provided by the palace roof—was a combined team of Marine and Army snipers. Locher recounted: "The Army Special Forces soldiers had been attached to the battalion for a while. You could tell the Army guys from the Marines; they were the shooters running around in blue jeans and beards. Still, they were great soldiers—very professional in all other respects." Locher used his Viper kit to provide precise ranges to the snipers. "I can still remember the range from our position to the mosque: 972 meters."

Still en route, Hurst and Brown aboard Inchon 40 monitored the DASC(A) frequency to track the action. What they heard was a pointed example of how quickly the command and control of a fast-moving fight—particularly a fast-moving fight with a lot of moving pieces—could get overwhelmed. Hurst recalled: "We kept hearing the DASC(A) referencing the battle up at the palace and the mosque. They were trying to drum up air assets to get into the thick of things and they mentioned how Inchon 40 could be put into action if required. Finally, when there was a break in the chatter, we came up on the radio and told them that we were already on our second run up to the palace. There was kind of a stunned silence for a moment or two, and then they told us to continue."

If anything, the looting and rioting and shooting was worse on the second trip as the warm morning sun climbed higher into the sky. Again the pilots caught sight of the mosque as they turned south into the city on Highway 2. And again, abeam the dome, the lead ship turned right and set up for another landing in the tiny LZ. Just as before, Oliver and Dansie took their ship toward the Tigris to try to stay clear of the enemy's weapons.

Once safely on the ground, the familiar swarm of Marines helped the helicopter's crew drag the precious ammunition out and rushed it into action. Hurst took a moment to take in his surroundings. "It was obvious that the palace had once been a very beautiful place. It was a modern design with kind of an Arab twist and it was flanked on one side by a little park with trees and walking paths and lampposts. There was even a nice swimming pool behind the LZ." Of course it was no longer as lovely as it had once been. A bomb had blown a gaping hole in the southwest corner of the main building, and many of the other smaller structures were damaged and pockmarked by small-arms rounds.

Rather than setting up an orbit while he waited for Brown and Hurst to get their aircraft unloaded, Oliver found a small sand spit just under the bluff where the palace grounds met the Tigris. The steep bank provided cover from the fighting that was taking place around the palace and was situated to afford some protection from the enemy snipers across the river. Oliver let the other crew know about his new "hidey-hole," and when the time came the two helicopters swapped positions.

Hurst remembered catching his breath when his aircraft settled onto the spit. "As much as I knew that what we were doing was incredibly dangerous, and that there were people getting blown apart just on the other side of the palace, the entire experience was still an unbelievable adrenaline trip. This is what we had been training for—it was what we were all about. Had one of us been badly hit or wounded I'm certain that my attitude would have been different, but at that moment it was just a wild rush."

The fight continued through the afternoon. The two CH-46Es of HMM-165 led by Brown and Hurst continued their runs, alternately bringing in ammunition and carrying out wounded. Captain Shawn

Basco was one of the last casualties put aboard one of the last sorties of the day. Because much of his blood had leaked out onto the ground, and because the air support situation had improved, he was more or less ordered to evacuate. He was on his way home. And it was his birthday.

In total the two CH-46E crews made five runs into the Azimiyah Palace that day. The last load they lifted out included enemy POWs—blindfolded, gagged, and zip-tied. The crews were exhausted, particularly the enlisted crew chiefs and corpsmen. Fighting fatigue and dehydration, they continued man their station.

"It was almost dark when we finally got back to the division CP," Hurst remembered. "We were on the edge of being completely worn out. In fact, Staff Sergeant Clausen was stabbed with an IV just to keep him hydrated. But people came out of nowhere and swarmed us like we had just won the Super Bowl. It was a great feeling knowing that we had been able to help our brother Marines at the palace."

The two CH-46E crews of Grizzly 41—the first helicopters to land at the palace that morning—also had much to be proud of. After running three missions into the palace LZ that morning, they subsequently flew three more missions that night and finally shut down just before midnight.

One of the enlisted aerial observer-gunners in the Grizzly flight that day had been Corporal Amanda Hoenes. Manning a heavy, .50-caliber machine gun, she had provided suppressive fire all day long. The Islamic fanatics she shot up would have been horrified to know that they had suffered at the hands of a woman—an "infidel" female.

Still, Hoenes was a person who was sensitive to the religion and culture of the men she was fighting. Among the many casualties lifted out of the palace that day were a number of Iraqis. Typically the corpsmen would remove or cut away the clothing of the injured; among other advantages, this also helped make their job easier. But in order to save the beaten enemy fighters the extreme humiliation of being exposed to a woman, Hoenes prevailed on the medicos to leave their clothing intact unless it absolutely precluded thorough treatment. Hoenes's kindness was something the Iraqis would never be aware of and was something she never had to give. It speaks volumes about the maturity of a young woman barely removed from high school.

Amanda Hoenes ultimately earned more Strike/Flight Air Medals than any other Marine—pilot or crewman—in HMM-268.

Major Mark "Butts" Butler and his wingman, Captain Tyler "Hefty" Bardo, Mover 01 flight, had just finished a high-cover escort for a group of helicopters flying low overhead Baghdad when they were directed to contact Aaron Locher. Locher had been awake since the day before but was still running the air fight at the palace. "The FAC came up on the radio," Butler remembered, "and said that they were trying to hit a tower—they had been taking RPG and machine-gun fire from it all day."

The tower that Locher wanted hit was actually one of the minarets that made up a corner of the Abu Hanifah Mosque. There, Iraqi fighters tenaciously carried on their fight. He was excited when the two Harriers checked in, but knew that both he and they would have to be quick and good to accomplish what needed doing. "Between them both they had just one LGB and two Maverick missiles. And not much fuel."

The Iraqis in and around the mosque had been sniping at the Marines almost since the beginning of the fight, and Locher wanted them dead. "All day we had been taking fire from the tower. I wanted the Harriers to level that thing." He passed the tower's coordinates to Butler along with a short brief. His expeditious control of the two ships was savvy and reflected his experience as a Marine aviator on his second combat tour as an FAC.

"After I passed the grid coordinates of the mosque tower to the lead Harrier," Locher recalled, "I asked him to tell me what he saw through his FLIR."

"A tall round building," Butler replied.

Butler had the correct target, but it still took several more exchanges over the radio to convince him of this. "I was looking at the biggest tower I could see," he explained, "but I still thought that I had the wrong one because it was the minaret of the mosque." His confusion was understandable. Religious centers and other cultural features were lawful to strike only on very rare occasions. This was one of them. The minaret was being used by enemy combatants to launch attacks and so now met the criteria that made it a valid target.

"Do you have time for a practice run?" Locher asked; he was concerned because there were so many friendly troops in close proximity. "We've got to get this right."

Butler was willing. With Bardo on his wing he swung around and set up for an attack on the tower.

"It was flawless," remembered Locher. "I told him to set back up and make the run for real this time—and that I wanted him to give me a thirty- and ten-second time-to-impact call over the radio."

Butler set up for his run. Bardo was still in formation. Locher checked that the jets were pointed away from friendly troops and toward the target.

"Wings level," the Harrier pilot transmitted, indicating that he was in his dive, had the target in sight, and was prepared to drop his bomb.

"You're cleared hot," Locher replied.

"One away." Butler let the bomb fall. "Thirty seconds." The Harrier started a climb back to altitude and a turn away from the target.

"Ten seconds . . ."

There was a puff of dust on the ground below the tall structure. Nothing more.

"That bomb hit exactly at the base of the tower," Locher recounted. "Unfortunately it was a dud."

All of their work had been for naught. Still, the FAC wasted no time: "I had them set up for another run with their Maverick, and told them to aim for the bottom of the top third of the tower."

"We reset so that Hefty could shoot one of the laser Mavericks he was carrying," Butler recounted. "I was starting to get nervous—we were attracting some AAA now and getting low on fuel as well." The two Harriers dived on the tower as Locher and his team watched from the roof of the palace. Inside his aircraft Butler slewed the crosshairs of his Litening pod over the minaret. When the display indicated that the two Harriers were in range, he fired the laser and called over the radio to Bardo: "Target captured, laser's on."

In the cockpit of his aircraft Bardo watched his Maverick display for the indications that the weapon was locked on to the tower that Butler was marking with his laser. He heard Butler call "Wings level" over the radio and Locher's response: "Cleared hot." Still, there was no indication that the Maverick was ready to launch.

Butler flew the section of Harriers at the mosque until they were too close and he had to abort the run. He pulled his aircraft out of the dive and called out to Locher: "Mover 01's aborting." Bardo followed him out of the dive. "It was make-or-break time," Butler said. "We had time for one more quick pass if everything went perfectly." He knew he was taking a risk. "Flying at the same target, from the same direction, four times in a row was just asking for trouble," he remembered. "I could just see the Weapons and Tactics Instructors back home raising their eyebrows." Regardless, the instructors back home weren't being counted on just this instant to help their comrades under fire.

Butler brought the two jets around for one more attack. Again, he captured the tower in his FLIR display and fired the laser. At the same time he called out: "Wings level." Locher replied just as he had three times earlier: "Cleared hot." Bardo's missile finally locked on to the laser energy that Butler was bouncing off the mosque. He squeezed the trigger on the control stick and simultaneously made the call: "Rifle." The Maverick rocketed away from where it had been hung underneath his aircraft's left wing.

Butler remembered: "I kept thinking to myself, *Don't fuck this up . . . center the pipper . . . keep it slewed on the target.*" He did. The missile struck the minaret a third of the way from the top. Chunks of masonry rained down on the street.

"I never saw anything so pretty as when that missile came off and smashed exactly on target," Locher said. "The entire top of that tower turned into rubble. We didn't get shot at from there anymore."

Above him, Butler arced the two Harriers into a climbing turn to the southeast. They were out of fuel and headed back for the base.

Locher continued to control sections of fighters until well after nightfall. Finally he reached the point where he was so exhausted that he literally could stand up no longer. "Spanky" Lawler was awakened and sent to the roof to relieve him. Moments later Locher was curled up and fast asleep amid the sound of exploding bombs. He woke up only once, when a Laser Guided Bomb streaked overhead; the *clack-clack-clack* of the bomb's fins was the only distinctive noise in the din of the entire battle. He rolled back over and was quickly asleep again.

It was good to be a Marine FAC.

The battle at the Azimiyah Palace and Imam Abu Hanifah Mosque fought itself out by the next morning. Estimates of Iraqi and Fedayeen dead ran into the several hundreds. The Marines of First Battalion Fifth Marines sustained heavy casualties as well. The Purple Heart, awarded for injuries sustained in combat, went to ninety-eight men. Miraculously only one Marine was killed. This astonishing ratio of wounded to dead can be attributed in part to the immediate care that was administered by brave Navy Corpsmen and Marines on the battlefield, as well as their hasty evacuation by air.

38

Cobra Down

The battle for Baghdad never really happened. Perhaps it was the recognition that Saddam's government wouldn't survive, combined with greed and an overriding commitment to self-preservation, that sent his high-ranking officials across the borders or into hiding. It is certain that what played a huge part in convincing most of the military leadership to desert or stay in garrison was the realization that they were hopelessly outmatched. In the end the coalition could find no one with the authority to surrender the city, and so the Army and the Marine Corps were left to enforce law and order. In the closing days of Iraqi Freedom the coalition began the awkward transition from wartime operations toward security and stability efforts.

Nevertheless, one more task remained that called for powerful forces in the field. Tikrit, Saddam Hussein's hometown and traditional base of support, had to be taken and subdued. If the big fight hadn't happened in Baghdad, Tikrit was the only logical location that remained. In fact, there were reports that there were substantial forces in and around the city, and that Tikrit was indeed where the Iraqis intended to put up a last stand. The Marines were given the assignment to take down the city, and after hastily cobbling together a force to do it—Task Force Tripoli—they were on their way north on April 12 under the command of Brigadier General John Kelly.

They had been flying and fighting hard for more than three weeks. The Cobra crew from HMLA-169—callsign Fisty 37—had spent much of the previous several days tearing up targets north of Baghdad in preparation for Task Force Tripoli's assault on Tikrit. On April 14 the attack was well under way. Nevertheless, First Lieutenant Jeff Sykes and Major John Smith* had done most of their fighting well south of Tikrit on that day. Earlier they had helped shoot up half a dozen lethal but abandoned S-60 anti-aircraft guns. More and more as the campaign progressed they found that the Iraqis were less inclined to fight.

By the early afternoon they were working as a two-ship near Samarra. "Our FAC, 'Ugly,' came up on the radio," Sykes recalled, "and sent us out to investigate the area around Samarra airfield. There were reports that units from RCT-5 passing through that location had received fire from BRDMs or some other type of APCs."

Smith, the section leader, led the two gunships toward the enemy air base; they carefully probed the roads that led away from it for any sign of Iraqi activity. Although the main effort of the fighting was now well to the north, Tripoli's rapid charge was no different from any advance of the previous few weeks—it had passed by many enemy units. However, none of them seemed to be located in the desert around the airfield at Samarra. At the airfield itself, though, the picture was different.

"As we approached the perimeter of the base," Sykes recounted, "we were able to use our sensors to make out some enemy vehicles. The FAC immediately cleared us to engage using Type III CAS ROE." The two AH-1W crews made a series of passes back and forth, perpendicular to their axis of advance, as they crept closer to the

---

*Not his real name.

enemy positions. Sykes continued to examine the targets through the gunship's Telescopic Sight Unit as he tried to determine which one of them was most deserving of the first weapon they would send downrange. He remembered: "I realized after a good, close look that all of the vehicles had been hit already. There were burn marks on most of them while others were in pieces. There was nothing there that was worth wasting a missile on." Smith called off the attack. "At the same time, we called the FAC and let him know what was going on," said Sykes. "He went ahead and cleared us for armed reconnaissance of the airfield."

The two crews made tentative passes up and down one side of the field—wary of anti-aircraft ambushes. Seeing nothing threatening, they crossed to the other side and made a couple more orbits, still watchful for any threats. "We looked inside the hangars as best we could and saw nothing that was particularly noteworthy," Sykes remembered. "There were no people there at all, but what was remarkable was the large number of ammo caches that were scattered all over the place." These were U-shaped earthen berms that contained a collection of barrels, boxes, and slatted crates. Their exact contents were not immediately apparent, but it was likely that the boxes and crates held bombs and other aviation ammunition while the barrels probably contained fuel or lubricants of some sort.

They decided to destroy what they could. Smith swung the flight around to the southeast and set up for a cruise attack with the other aircraft offset about two hundred yards to the left and slightly behind. Making their run from five hundred feet of altitude at about eighty knots, the two Cobras let loose a total of three TOW missiles. Two of them lost their guidance and went "stupid"—rocketing off into the distance. The third hit one of the ammo caches. There were no secondary explosions. "We came off of that attack," Sykes said, "and set up for another quick run. We fired a Hellfire missile into one of the bigger caches in the center of the airfield." This missile hit its intended target and detonated, but like the earlier missile it failed to set off the contents inside.

The crews aboard the two helicopters weren't impressed with their own efforts to destroy the Iraqi weapons stores. "By this time we realized that the airfield was essentially abandoned—or at least no one there was committed to shooting us down," Sykes said. Accordingly, Smith split up the flight to execute attacks from a cloverleaf-like pattern. The aircraft would strike out singly from different directions at intervals that would keep them from passing over the target at the same time. As they came off the target they would egress on a heading that differed by ninety degrees or more from the original course. This pattern ensured that they would be as unpredictable as possible in the event that anyone was tracking them, as well as enabling them to keep an eye on each other.

"We used rockets and guns on these runs," Sykes recounted. "We started out from an altitude of about three or four hundred feet but the geometry worked out so that we had to fly too close to the targets to shoot over the edges of the berms." Smith adjusted their altitude by popping up to about seven hundred feet so that the resultant dive angle was steep enough to get their weapons over the earthen walls and hit what was inside the caches. From where he was sitting in the front cockpit—perched at the end of the aircraft's nose—Sykes had a first-rate view of the target and the effects of their weapons.

Those effects weren't much. "We sprayed the caches with 20-millimeter fire and a rocket or two on each pass," Sykes said. "None of us scored a direct hit with the rockets, but some of our 20-millimeter rounds were hitting inside the berms." Sykes kept his head down looking into the "bucket" of the TSU whenever Smith fired the cannon; the magnification that the device provided enabled him to help correct the other pilot's aim. Conversely, he was able to see the rocket hits better simply by looking forward through the windscreen.

Still, the two gunships had no significant effect on the material inside the berms; nothing caught fire or exploded. They continued their attacks. "We lined up for another run," explained Sykes, "and were set up perfectly to fire into two different caches—a near one and a far one." Smith fired a 2.75-inch rocket that went left of the near target, and he followed it up with 20-millimeter cannon fire that went long. Switching to the second target he again opened up with the cannon. "Through the TSU I could see the rounds hitting the near, left-hand corner of the berm," Sykes said, "and then they started walking across to the right."

The Cobra was three to four hundred yards from the berm when Smith started pulling it out of the dive and turning right, away from the target. Sykes pulled his face out of the TSU and blinked against the sun—his tinted visor was up so that he could better see through the sensor. He had a good view of the enemy cache through the left front quarter of the canopy.

It was at that instant that the Iraqi ammunition store went high order. There was a bright flash and then a hugely powerful concussive blast. It took only the tiniest fraction of a second for the shock wave to reach the helicopter.

Before either flier had time to react, hundreds of pieces of what used to be the canopy blasted straight into the cockpit with a deafening boom. The sudden rush of wind ripped at Sykes's lacerated face as, too late, he threw his left arm up for protection and tucked his head into his chest. Shards of metal and dirt and other debris swept over them with a hammering roar that made the aircraft shudder even as it fell.

Behind Sykes the instrument panel had shielded Smith from a portion of the blast. Yet he still struggled to control the aircraft—or rather, he struggled to set the aircraft up for the crash that was inevitable. The concussion of the explosion had robbed the engines of the airflow they needed to operate. They gasped at the lack of air with several sharp, banging compressor stalls and then started winding down; there was no way to get them restarted.

Sykes brushed at the shards from the canopy that were lodged in his eyelashes. "It was hard for me to see but I could tell that we were pitched over, nose low, in a right-hand turn." The Cobra plunged into a pitch-black cloud of smoke and only a second or two later emerged very close to the ground. Sykes got onto the controls with Smith as they both wrestled with the collective to set up for an autorotation. From the back he heard Smith shout "Skids level, skids level!" as they both tried to get the aircraft into a level attitude before it hit the ground.

At precisely the correct moment both aviators pulled up on the collective in time to soften the impact. Twelve seconds after the blast they smashed into the ground. Sykes felt his head slam into the TSU; his upper teeth buried themselves into his lower lip. "We had managed to get the aircraft more or less level when we hit, but we were still going about sixty knots when the skids made contact," he remembered. Nevertheless, the aircraft was sledding along upright until the right skid made contact with the edge of one of the bermed caches and collapsed. The Cobra tipped to the right, and the main rotor blades started disintegrating themselves as they chopped away at the ground. The aircraft continued to roll to the right and then abruptly rocked over onto its back as it continued to slide.

The nose of the aircraft dug into the ground as it scraped across the airfield upside down. Sykes—hanging wrong-way up in his harness with his eyes scrunched shut—was little more than a rag doll. "My head was just bouncing along over the ground; there was nothing I could do about it except hope that my helmet stayed on." Dirt and rocks filled his nose and mouth and ears. His arms and hands dragged across the dirt, only barely protected by his flying gear.

The impact with the ground combined with the torque from the rotor blades tearing into the earth broke loose the aircraft's transmission, which slammed three feet forward against the cockpit bulkhead, smashing Smith and pinning him into his seat. His back, neck, and shoulders were wrenched; like Sykes, his arms flailed and his hands were taking a beating.

At last the carcass that had been a Cobra juddered to a stop and Sykes opened his eyes. His hands automatically found their way to the straps that made up his harness and released the buckles that held him in the shell of the front cockpit. The six-inch drop to the ground forced a grunt from his battered body, but he rested there only an instant—even in his condition he knew that the biggest danger he faced was fire. He rolled out from under the aircraft and forced himself to his feet.

"I was disoriented," he understated. "I had rolled out of the aircraft on the wrong side, so it took me a moment to figure out where to go—you access the front and rear cockpits of the Cobra from different sides." Sykes finally got his bearings and stumbled back to the rear cockpit. There he knelt down to check on Smith.

"He was conscious but his weight against the straps and the transmission had him pinned in pretty good." This was particularly alarming as the dreadful sound of fuel splashing out of the wreck and onto the ground caught their immediate attention. Straightaway the two fliers secured the fuel pump and turned off power to the battery. The very real horror of burning alive while trapped in an aircraft is a nightmare that has terrified every pilot since the dawn of powered flight. Sykes and Smith were no exceptions.

While the two pilots struggled to get Smith free, the crew of the other Cobra roared overhead—checking to see if anything remained of their two squadron mates. Sykes gave them a weak wave. It took another few minutes before Smith crawled free of the wreckage. In the meantime the second Cobra had landed a couple of hundred yards away. Sykes and Smith headed toward the other aircraft and met the copilot, one of Sykes's good friends. "He looked at me like I was a ghost. I guess our little ride had been something of a roller coaster to watch. First we had been hit by the blast, then they saw us roll over into the smoke, and then we hit the ground and they saw us skidding along on our back . . . They'd thought we were dead about three times over!"

The two crews had an impromptu powwow right there on the airfield. Smith made the decision that he and Sykes would stay with the aircraft while the other crew coordinated their pickup. Technically the option existed for the two downed crewmen to ride out on the ammunition doors of the other aircraft, but this was a measure that Smith didn't feel was warranted under the circumstances. Already several sections of fixed-wing aircraft had arrived overhead to protect the crew and what remained of their aircraft, and it wouldn't be long before other more suitable helicopters would arrive to lift them out.

A few minutes later the crew of the other aircraft roared airborne, leaving Sykes and Smith behind with their M4 carbines for self-protection. Not seeing any real reason to wait alongside the wreck that had been their aircraft, they made their way over to one of the abandoned hangars to wait. "We sat there and talked for a while," remembered Sykes. "He was really concerned that we'd go into shock and he made sure that we drank plenty of water. We both started getting pretty stiff right away."

Sykes's face had been badly torn up when the blast had exploded the canopy; the subsequent head scraping he had endured after the crash had made the wounds worse. He had been lucky; although they bled badly, the lacerations were largely superficial. Nevertheless, the amount of blood that wept from the injuries had him convinced otherwise. "I kept reaching up and pulling great gobs of bloody mud off of my face," he recounted. "I was certain that I was horribly disfigured and kept asking Smith if my face was okay. He kept telling me that I was fine but I didn't believe him—I thought he was just trying to keep me calm. Finally I pulled my survival mirror out and checked for myself. It's funny the things you worry about in a situation like that."

The pair was still waiting quietly for their ride when they were shocked by a tremendous explosion from somewhere behind them. Ironically, one of the caches they had struck earlier with no effect had finally cooked off, with spectacular results. Chunks of shrapnel rained down on the freshly stunned aviators as they huddled against the hangar walls and waited to leave the seemingly cursed airfield.

Within an hour a pair of CH-46Es and a Huey arrived to extract Sykes and Smith. The next day their Cobra was declared a loss and blown up in place.

There was no coherent defense along the route from the Iraqi capital to Tikrit, and Task Force Tripoli was engaged only sporadically. As required, the combined arms of the Marine Corps were brought to bear, augmented by airpower from the sister services when it was available. Major Randy Nash, the FAC of Weapons Company, First Light Armored Reconnaissance Battalion, recalled how his unit came under small-arms and RPG fire just south of Tikrit. A deadly and overwhelming response was immediately forthcoming, but it was only part of a greater design that smashed down on anything that threatened the Marines as they closed on Saddam's birthplace:

> The battalion simultaneously directed CAS onto no less than four different sites, while taking fire from the Fedayeen to their direct front. South of the position, fixed-wing aircraft engaged enemy vehicles in a revetted complex. On the north side of town Air Force A-10s destroyed targets at the Al Sahra airfield. Just west of the city SA-2 and SA-3 missiles were discovered and demolished. To our direct front, Cobras shot up the enemy with rockets, 20-millimeter cannon, and Hellfire missiles. All the while surface fires from our artillery and mortars were integrated into the barrage. In just a few hours more than fifty sections of CAS aircraft were used in the vicinity of Tikrit alone. This orchestration of combined arms was beautiful music to those of us on the ground—a symphony of sweet violence conducted by a team of airborne and ground FACs, the likes of which we'd never seen before.

Like Baghdad, Tikrit rolled over—a leaderless city with no organized defense. The war against Saddam's regime was over.

Now, with the major engagements finished, the Marines snatched a few hours here and there to relax. Lieutenant Colonel Joe Strohman's FARP team set up for operations at Tikrit South, site of one of Saddam's private airports. The boundary fence also corralled his collection of gazelles. When one of the Marines came back from the perimeter with some freshly killed and dressed meat, the MWSG-37 commanding officer took the high and proper road and declared that shooting the gazelles was forbidden.

"My Marines would have never disobeyed the colonel, but when I found them spearing Saddam's gazelles from HMMWVs with bayonets lashed to tent poles I felt that they were not exactly adhering to the intent of his order," Strohman remembered. "But still, barbecued over a grill that someone had pulled off the front of their vehicle, that was some of the best meat I'd ever had."

By April 15, 3rd MAW aircrews were ordered to stop offensive operations. They were to engage targets only under the control of a FAC when Marines were under fire. Business dropped off nearly completely.

39

Realization

It was April 15, the day that major combat operations ceased. The Coalition controlled Iraq. Lieutenant Colonel Steve Heywood walked away from his Cobra to the wreckage of Ford's and Sammis's aircraft, a twisted, burned pile of scrap—unchanged since he'd been there more than a week earlier. He was tired. He had been shooting and killing for six straight days.

Heywood stopped next to the debris. Suddenly—almost violently—he was crushed by an overwhelming sense of loss and helplessness and fatigue. He dropped to his knees and took in great, shoulder-racking lungs full of air. Short, sharp, half-suppressed cries came, unbidden, from his throat.

His own reaction stunned him, but with it came a newfound realization. The grief was not just for the dead men and their families. It was also for him, for his own family, for the men he flew with who still were alive, and for their worried families.

Everyone knew it intuitively—but few came by the knowledge from experience. During the past month he had. War was not fun. It was not a game. It was not movies. It was not the History Channel. It was not books. War was dead friends and dead fathers and dead sons. Sometimes it was dead mothers and sisters and daughters. War was fearful and ugly.

He had come back to the wreck for a wedding band. The ring of one of the dead pilots hadn't been found with the personal effects or remains that had been sent home. The wife had asked if an effort could be made to recover it. Looking at the crushed mess that had been one of his aircraft, he knew that it was hopeless. Still, he stood up and looked into what was left of the cockpit. He pulled at black, sharp, and fire-fused pieces of metal. He sifted and dug in the dirt underneath the fuselage, and walked around the entire wreck, one, two, three, and more times.

After a while Heywood walked back to his Cobra where the copilot was waiting. He didn't have the ring. Rather he had a deeper understanding of war and loss and despair.

Afterword

===

As was mentioned in the introduction, the fighting in Iraq continues as this book goes to press. In fact, many, many more Marines have died in Iraq subsequent to the end of Saddam Hussein's government than perished during the fighting that toppled him. Most of these deaths have not been the result of direct engagements with insurgents but, instead, have been caused by IEDs (Improvised Explosive Devices) or other sorts of ambush-style bombings. Where Marines have encountered guerrillas in face-to-face combat, the Islamists have been utterly crushed. Still, the enemy is not stupid; indeed he realizes that he can't hope to win a conventional war and instead has resorted to remote control, or random homicidal killing and terrorization, as his only means of influencing what happens in Iraq. This type of fighting—if it can be called that—is radically different from what the Marine Corps was designed to combat. It is frustrating for the Marines to suffer casualties at the hands of an enemy who fights in disguise or from hiding places that allow him to detonate bombs by remote control. But it is the age-old nature of the ugliness that is guerrilla warfare, and it must be defeated in order for peace to prevail.

Marine aviation elements are in Iraq today supporting their ground brothers just as they always have. Nevertheless, the Air Combat Element's part is not as prominent as it was during the push to

Baghdad. Combating insurgents neighborhood by neighborhood is the gritty and very dangerous work of the infantryman. The role of Marine fliers in this sort of fighting is still important, but it is diminished when compared with the engagements of March and April 2003.

None of this should detract from what was done and learned during Operation Iraqi Freedom. The successes were spectacular in a war that was unlike anything seen before. In the space of three weeks, the Marine Corps fought across a hostile landscape while traversing an expanse equivalent to the distance from the Mexican border to San Francisco. That it did so with so many moving parts and so few miscues was all the more remarkable. Brigadier General Terry Robling remarked: "I'm still amazed that after all was said and done, everything worked. All the training we had done, all the planning we had done, all the equipment that was procured and deployed—it all came together just like it was supposed to. Particularly across the various service boundaries, the level of cooperation was outstanding. Sure, there were problems, and certainly not everything worked perfectly, but all in all the work and vision of a generation of Marines was validated."

Those aspects that did not perform as well as desired will receive greater scrutiny. The difficulty in maintaining good communications is one of the chief considerations. As good as it was, and as tirelessly as the communications Marines worked, the hard boundaries of physics often conspired against them. Maintaining line-of-sight links was impossible when the rapid advance took units over the horizon. The witchcraft that is High Frequency radio is always bewildering, and improvements will come only slowly given how many factors can influence this means of communicating. Satellites hold great promise, but this scheme of maintaining contact is expensive and hardly fail-safe. The best method for mitigating the vagaries inherent in the command, control, and communications arena is to train Marines who have the capacity, the will, and the intelligence to make on-the-spot decisions in the thick of combat. Fortunately these are traits and characteristics that the Marines have always strived to imbue in their warfighters.

Imagery intelligence was improved over what was available during Desert Storm, but it is still lacking. The F/A-18D-mounted ATARS system provided valuable imagery, but most of the time the Marines doing the fighting saw little of it. Additionally, UAV imagery helped to influence the fight on the ground, and there were even infantry units with small, hand-launched systems. This was an improvement over years past, but it still failed to meet all the warfighter's needs. Rather, it was only the continuation of what promises to be a UAV-enabled revolution in information gathering and dissemination. The Marine Corps is pursuing these possibilities with vigor.

One of the most important lessons the Marine Corps learned, and is still learning, is that equipment can be operated only so hard. Regardless of what magic the maintenance Marines work, eventually material just physically wears out. Right now the service is in a crisis as its aircraft are simply running out of life. Whether or not they will be replaced in time to maintain an inventory—one that is already substantially less that what it was only a dozen years ago—remains to be seen. It is quite likely, though, that in an environment where more interests are competing for fewer resources, Marine Corps aviation will not receive the aircraft it needs. A failure of this sort will endanger not just the infantryman but also the nation's interests.

In the meantime, the Marine Corps will continue to do what it has always done: It will accomplish the mission. Hopefully the time will never come when a lack of material or equipment cannot be overcome by intelligence, imagination, and courage. I never want to see that day.

Acknowledgments

═══════

My mom, my dad, my dead dog, the neighbor kid who plays his stereo too loud, blah, blah, blah . . . This is the part you the reader normally skip, because there's nothing or no one in here that you really care about. I used to do the same until I wrote my first couple of books and came to understand how many people make a difference in whether a book ends up being worthwhile or not. So I'm going to point them out. First, of course (*of course* because she'd stop feeding me if I said otherwise), is my wife, Monica. Normally, writers relate here how they neglected their spouses during the writing, and trash piled up and lawns went unmowed. Yeah, all of that, but during the time I wrote this manuscript my wife has seldom been more pleasant or happy. I strongly believe that it's because I haven't had the time or energy to paw after her as I've done for most of the past twenty-some years. She's much more rested and is eager for me to continue writing.

I asked my brilliant older daughter, Kristen, to edit the initial manuscript, and she happily agreed to do so—for cash. The little money-grubber did a nice job, and the publisher got a better-looking book because of her fine work. My younger daughter, Katherine, the mean one, had no interest at all in what I was doing. She only asked that somewhere in the book I include the phrase: "Katherine Stout's rockin' party with her wicked-cool parents." I told her no.

You know how there's someone in your life that has done something nice for you, and you're never quite sure that you can ever thank them enough? Eric Hammel — one of the best aviation writers and historians ever — gave me a good start by teaching me to write several years ago. He continues to mentor me and give me great advice. Either he's a really, really nice guy or he wants something. Keep him distracted and buy lots of his books.

It's time to get more serious. No one in this book had to cooperate with me, but nearly everyone I approached was happy to do so, and was very enthusiastic about the project. This wasn't necessarily easy, as most of them are still on active duty and busy training for war. For some of them it was also an emotional task. Death isn't an easy subject, and you don't often read about the nuts and bolts of it in an aviation chronicle. Normally our heroes disappear in a blaze of glory and then we flip to the next page. Lieutenant Colonel Steve Heywood shared a very difficult experience with us that put the reality into that glory, and this book is better because of it.

Dozens of folks provided source material and insight into what went on in the sky above Iraq during March and April 2003. The obvious ones are those whose names you've already read. Among those who went well above and beyond what is readily apparent are Major Randy Nash and Colonel Robert Milstead. They both provided insight and material that gave the book a fidelity it wouldn't otherwise have had. Brigadier General Terry Robling gave the book a continuous thread and insight from the upper echelons of command; I consider it an honor that he took time from his very busy schedule to work with me in recording what went on within 3rd MAW during this time.

Okay, next is the list that you always see. These are the gentlemen who provided help of varying sorts, but if I took time and space to note their contributions in detail I'd run out of writing room. They are: Corporal Micah Snead; Captains Llonie Cobb, Kyle Moore, John Havener, Adam Musoff, Derek Abbey; Majors Louis Gundlach, Michael Rodriguez, Ken Woodard, Scott Cooper; Lieutenant Colonels Robert Lloynd, Darrell Thacker, Karl Brandt, Mike

Kennedy, Pete Woodmansee, Anton Nerad, Robert Claypool, Chris Lamson, Freddie Blish; and Colonel Juan Ayala. I know I've forgotten just as many people—please forgive me.

You know how the writers talk about their agents and the awesome job they did? Well, I never had one before now, but I can tell you that I won't leave home without one in the future. Mr. E. J. McCarthy looked me up, talked me into doing the right sort of book, guided me through the proposal process, handled the publisher, the contract, and the money, and then dealt with all the little details in between. Sort of like a personal assistant for writers. He deserves twice what I'm paying him (but won't get it). Thank you, E. J.

And thank you to Random House and my editor, Ron Doering. They recognized the importance of this work and—with the fine editing of Crystal Velasquez—have produced the top-notch book you're holding this minute. I hope to have many more happy book-publishing experiences with them.

Finally, thank you to all the men and women of all the armed forces. When you're in the service and you hear thanks like this, it often seems like so much patronizing blather. But having been in uniform, and now being out, I want to reassure you that no matter where you are and what you're doing, there are millions and millions of American citizens who are thanking God every day that you're out there doing it. God bless and keep you.

Glossary of Terms

===

AAA:	Anti-Aircraft Artillery
AAV:	Assault Amphibian Vehicle
ACE:	Air Combat Element
ANGLICO:	Air Naval Gunfire Liaison Company
AO:	Area of Operations; Air Officer
AOR:	Area of Responsibility
APC:	Armored Personnel Carrier
API:	Armor Piercing Incendiary
APU:	Auxiliary Power Unit
AR:	Aerial Refueling; Armed Reconnaissance
ASE:	Acceptable Steering Error; Aircraft Survivability Equipment
ASP:	Ammunition Supply Point
ATACMS:	Army Tactical Missile System
ATARS:	Advanced Tactical Airborne Reconnaissance System
ATF:	Amphibious Task Force
ATO:	Air Tasking Order
AWACS:	Airborne Warning and Control System
BBC:	British Broadcasting Corporation
BDA:	Battle Damage Assessment
BHA:	Bomb Hit Assessment

bingo:	minimum fuel
BMO:	Black Moving Object (slang)
BMP:	A Soviet-designed armored personnel carrier
BRC:	Base Recovery Course
BRDM:	A Soviet-designed armored personnel carrier
CAAT:	Combined Anti-Armor Team
CACO:	Casualty Assistance Calls Officer
CAS:	Close Air Support
CASEVAC:	Casualty Evacuation
CDE:	Collateral Damage Estimate
CENTCOM:	Central Command
CFACC:	Coalition Forces Air Component Commander
CFIT:	Controlled Flight Into Terrain
CFLCC:	Coalition Forces Land Component Commander
CIA:	Central Intelligence Agency
CO:	Commanding Officer
CP:	Command Post; Contact Point
CRAF:	Civil Reserve Air Fleet
CSSC:	Combat Service Support Companies
CSSD:	Combat Service Support Detachment
CSSE:	Combat Service Support Element
DASC/DASC(A):	Direct Air Support Center (Airborne)
DMPI:	Desired Mean Point of Impact
DPICM:	Dual Purpose Improved Conventional Munition
ECMO:	Electronic Countermeasures Officer
EO/IR:	Electro Optical/Infra Red
EPWs:	Enemy Prisoners of War
FAC/FAC(A):	Forward Air Controller (Airborne)
FARP:	Forward Arming and Refueling Point
FLIC:	Flight Line Intelligence Center
FLIR:	Forward Looking Infra Red
FO:	Forward Observer
FSC:	Fire Support Center
FSCC:	Fire Support Coordination Center
FSCM:	Fire Support Coordination Measures

FSSG:	Field Service Support Group
FST:	Fire Support Team
GCE:	Ground Combat Element
GPS:	Global Positioning System
HARM:	High Speed Anti-Radiation Missile
HDC:	Helicopter Direction Center
HEMTTs:	Heavy Expanded Mobility Tactical Trucks
HMLA:	Helicopter Marine Light Attack
HMMWV:	High Mobility Multi-Wheeled Vehicle
HUD:	Heads Up Display
IEDs:	Improvised Explosive Devices
IFF:	Identification Friend or Foe
I MEF:	First Marine Expeditionary Force
IP:	Initial Point
IR:	Infra Red
IZLID:	Infrared Zoom Laser Illuminator Designator
JDAM:	Joint Direct Attack Munition
JFACC:	Joint Forces Air Component Commander
KI:	Killbox Interdiction
KIA:	Killed in Action
LAR:	Light Armored Reconnaissance
LGB:	Laser Guided Bomb
LHD:	Landing Helicopter Dock
LOD:	Line of Departure
LPD:	Landing Platform Dock
LSO:	Landing Signals Officer
LZ:	Landing Zone
MAG:	Marine Air Group
MAGTF:	Marine Air Ground Task Force
MANPAD:	Man Portable Air Defense
MAW:	Marine Air Wing
MAWTS:	Marine Aviation Weapons and Tactics Squadron
MBT:	Main Battle Tank
MEDEVAC:	Medical Evacuation
MEU:	Marine Expeditionary Unit

MEZ:	Missile Engagement Zone
MISREP:	Mission Report
MOPP:	Mission Oriented Protection Posture
MPS:	Maritime Prepositioning Ships
MSR:	Main Surface Route
MTLB:	Mashina Transportnaya Legkaya Boyevaya (Russian transport vehicle for combat)
MWSG:	Marine Wing Support Group
MWSS:	Marine Wing Support Squadron
NBC:	Nuclear Biological Chemical
NCO:	Noncommissioned Officer
NIPR:	Non-secure Internet Protocol Router
NTS:	Night Targeting System
NVD:	Night Vision Device
NVG:	Night-Vision Goggles
OIF:	Operation Iraqi Freedom
ONW:	Operation Northern Watch
OP:	Observation Posts
OSW:	Operation Southern Watch
PGM:	Precision Guided Munition
POW:	Prisoner of War
PSAB:	Prince Sultan Air Base
rack:	sleeping/bed
RAF:	Royal Air Force
RATO:	Rocket Assisted Takeoff
RCT:	Regimental Combat Team
ROE:	Rules of Engagement
RPG:	Rocket Propelled Grenade
SAM:	Surface to Air Missile
SAW:	Squad Automatic Weapon
SCUD:	Soviet designed surface-to-surface missile
SEAD:	Suppression of Enemy Air Defenses
SEAL:	Sea Air Land Special Forces
SIPR:	Secret Internet Protocol Router
SITREP:	Situation Report

STU:	Secure Telephone Unit
TAA:	Tactical Assembly Area
TBS:	The Basic School
TACC:	Tactical Air Command Center
TAD:	Tactical Air Direction
TAOC:	Tactical Air Operations Center
TOT:	Time on Target
TOW:	Tube-Launched Optically Tracked Wire-Guided Missile
TSTs:	Time Sensitive Targets
TSU:	Telescopic Sight Unit
UAV:	Unmanned Aerial Vehicle
UHF:	Ultra High Frequency
USAF:	United States Air Force
WP:	White Phosphorous
WSO:	Weapons Systems Officer
WTI:	Weapons and Tactics Instructor
XO:	Executive Officer

Bibliography

"Government: Marine Fights for Life as Relatives Fight On." March 29, 2003. http://www.infoarizona.com.

"Jessica Lynch." Nationmaster.com. http://www.nationmaster.com/encyclopedia/Jessica-Lynch.

"Mystery Hovers Around Sergeant Left Behind." *Detroit Free Press*. http://www.freep.com/news/portraitsofwar/gossmeyer.htm.

"No FARP Too Far!: Operation Iraqi Freedom." Marine Wing Support Group 37.

Chapman, Susan. "The War Before the War." *Air Force Magazine* 87, no. 2 (February 2004). http://www.afa.org/magazine/Feb2004/0204war.html.

Crawley, James W. "Officials Confirm Dropping Firebombs on Iraqi Troops." *San Diego Union-Tribune*, August 5, 2003.

Descheneaux, Major "Triple A" Ray. "4 Days at Joe Foss Field." *Marine Air Transporter*, June 2003: 1, 8–11. http://www.mcata.com.

Garamone, Jim. "Thunderbolt Over Baghdad: 'Pilot-Dude' Down in the Countryside." *DefenseLINK News*, July 16, 2003. http://www.globalsecurity.org/wmd/Library/news/iraq/2003/07/iraq-030716-afps04.htm.

Grant, Rebecca. "Marine Air in the Mainstream." *Air Force Magazine*, June 2004: 60–64.

Groen, Michael S., Lt. Col. *Operation Iraqi Freedom: No Better Friend, No Worse Enemy.* First Marine Division, 2004.

Guzman, Richard. "Marine Deployed from Local Base Injured in Ambush Grenade Attack." Desertsun.com, March 27, 2003. http://www.thedesertsun.com/news/stories/war/1048770932.shtml.

LaForte, Nathan K., Sgt. "Unmanned Planes: Eyes in the Sky." *Flight Jacket* 6, no. 4 (January 30, 2004).

Moreno, Sylvia. "Injured Marines Get Wish: Citizenship. President, First Lady Witness 'Amazing Moment' of Oath Taking." Washingtonpost.com, April 12, 2003.

Moseley, Michael T., Lt. Gen., USAF. "Operation IRAQI FREEDOM—By the Numbers: Assessment and Analysis Division." April 30, 2003.

Murray, Williamson, and Maj. Gen. Robert H. Scales Jr. *The Iraq War: A Military History.* Cambridge, MA: The Belknap Press of Harvard University Press, 2003.

Purdum, Todd S. *A Time of Our Choosing: America's War in Iraq.* New York: Times Books, 2003.

Roberts, L. R., Lt. Col., and Maj. J. P. Farnam, USMC. "Airborne Region Supported: Marines' Advances in Iraq." *Proceedings: U.S. Naval Institute*, June 2004: 40–43.

Rousseau, Caryn. "Navy Medic in Iraq Is Killed in Action." MyrtleBeachOnline.com, March 27, 2003. http://www.myrtlebeachonline.com/mld/myrtlebeachonline/news/5498379.htm.

West, Bing, and Maj. Gen. Ray L. Smith, USMC (Ret.). *The March Up: Taking Baghdad with the 1st Marine Division.* New York: Bantam Books, 2003.

About the Author

===

Jay A. Stout is a retired Marine fighter pilot whose twenty-year career included thirty-seven missions in Operation Desert Storm. He is the co-author of *The First Hellcat Ace* and the author of *Hornets Over Kuwait, Fortress Ploesti: The Campaign to Destroy Hitler's Oil*, and articles for journals and newspapers nationwide. He currently works in the aviation industry for a major defense contractor.

About the Type

This book was set in Electra, a typeface designed for Linotype by W. A. Dwiggins, the renowned type designer (1880–1956). Electra is a fluid typeface, avoiding the contrasts of thick and thin strokes that are prevalent in most modern typefaces.